The Bitter Sea Book 5

IN DEFENCE OF THE EI

'O words are lightly spoken,'
Said Pearse to Connolly,
'Maybe a breath of politic words
Has withered our Rose Tree;
Or maybe but a wind that blows
Across the bitter sea.'

W. B. Yeats

IN DEFENCE OF THE EMPIRE
Roman Gwynedd
398–1301

David Leedham

PENRHYN BOOKS

Published in 2010 by
Penrhyn Books,
83 Five Ashes Road,
Westminster Park,
Chester CH4 7QS

email: info@penrhynbooks.com
www.penrhynbooks.com

A catalogue record for this
book is available from the
British Library.

ISBN: 978-0-9565884-5-6

Book and Cover Design:
FL@33, Agathe Jacquillat
and Tomi Vollauschek,
www.flat33.com

Printed in United Kingdom

In memory of the years at
John Bright Grammar School,
Llandudno, North Wales,
T. I. Davies, T. Charles Jones,
L. W. C. Brookes, and all the
friends I made there.

CONTENTS

ACKNOWLEDGEMENTS

I should like to thank the following for kindly granting permission to quote from copyright material. Without this the book would have been vastly the poorer.

Oxford University Press for permission to use Bertram Colgrave and R. A. B. Mynors, eds. and transl., *Bede's Ecclesiastical History of the English People*, Oxford, 1969.

Penguin Books Ltd UK for permission to quote from Geoffrey of Monmouth, *The History of the Kings of Britain*, Lewis Thorpe, ed. and transl., Penguin Classics, 1966, translation copyright © Lewis Thorpe, 1966, and for the use of *Virgil, The Aeneid. A New Prose Translation*, David West, Penguin Books, 1990, introduction and translation copyright © David West, 1990.

Phillimore & Co. Ltd., for permission to quote from Michael Winterbottom, ed. and transl., *Gildas. The Ruin of Britain and Other Works*, London and Chichester, 1978.

I am also indebted to I. Ll. FOSTER, and G. DANIEL, eds., *Prehistoric and Early Wales*, London, 1965, for the translation of Taliesin, *Trawsganu Cynan Garwyn*, In Praise of Cynan Garwyn,
Carl Lofmarck for *A History of the Red Dragon*, Llanrwst, 1995,
Maurice Platnauer for *Claudian with an English Translation*, 2 vols., London, 1922,
and to the Rev. A. W. Wade-Evans, ed. and transl., for extensive quotation from *Nennius's History of the Britons together with The Annals of the Britons and The Court Pedigrees of Hywel the Good and also The Story of the Loss of Britain*, London, 1938.

Every effort has been made to trace copyright holders. The author apologizes for any errors or omissions in the above list and would be grateful to be notified of any such lapses.

PREFACE

This book, like its predecessors on Emperor Magnus Maximus and Vortigern, is based on what surely has to be one of the most crucial facts about Roman Britain. This is that it faced an Ireland that was not a land apart, but instead was the focus for much of the military thinking in the province and later the diocese right up to the end of formal control and beyond.

The approach adopted is also underpinned by the incontrovertible fact that for this, the earliest period of British history, the evidence is so slight that *everything we say about it* will be provisional, having the character of a construct or model or, more accurately, a series of constructs and models. Therefore, we *can* liberate ourselves from the straitjacket imposed by current approaches to early history, which are based on the false certainty that minute and painstaking research in all sorts of remote areas concerning texts or physical remains will one day add up to something called history. A general readership still wants, still needs, its history, and now.

In other words, History in its fullest sense is more, a lot more, than just analysis and process, and in abandoning even the attempt to recover the story even the analysis itself can be shown to be deficient. Too often the supposed demands of modern scholarship have ruled out speculation: speculation that is, in fact, our *only* route to an understanding of what did probably happen in these last years of Roman Britain and in the first years of a Britain standing on its own. Linguists, archaeologists, and others have considerably advanced our knowledge about the minutiae of the past but, paradoxically, in the process we have been deprived of any overall view. What follows is an attempt to give a narrative history of the early years of Britain and Wales. As such it represents another small plea for the continued importance and utility of storytelling as part of the effort to understand a history which belongs to all of us and not just to a few specialists.

Inevitably, the subject touches on a nationalism, which is still fiercely strong in a Wales beginning to emerge from centuries of control by its more-powerful neighbour, England. Those sensitive on this subject have, I believe, little to fear in what follows. This story is an extraordinary one, involving a people who had to fight for survival from the very start. Gwynedd emerged out of a welter of foreign invasion, economic collapse, internecine strife, plague, and climate change experienced to a degree unimaginable in its earlier history as part of the empire. Certainly, some parts of the story do have uncomfortable resonances with developments in our own day. Here we will find attacks on immigrants, moves towards what we would describe today as ethnic cleansing, and a violence that is, unfortunately, seemingly part and parcel of the process we call nation building. But if people behaved with appalling cruelty, they also suffered with amazing perseverance and dignity. And throughout this extraordinary history, the eagle and the dragon cast their long shadows: the shadows of the Roman empire which had given Gwynedd, as other states in Wales, its birth, and for which its people fought against the barbarians until 1283. When they finally succumbed, in Gwynedd at least, they did so under what was, in effect, a colossal and single-minded effort not only to complete the Norman conquest, but also to restore the Roman province of Britain in a western Europe itself groping to recover the idea of a unity that had been Rome's great and lasting gift.

As in the earlier books, my thanks have to go to academics, including philologists and archaeologists, without whose work the story could not even have been attempted. I have to particularly mention Professor Steve Rigby of Manchester University, Professor Roger Scruton, and Lord Robert Skidelsky, who have been extremely generous with their time even though they are in no way associated with the end result. Also Professor Mike Baillie of Queen's University Belfast, Professor Antony Carr of Bangor, Dr Sydney Elliott of Belfast, Dr Dan McCarthy of the University of Dublin,

Professor Donnchadh Ó Corráin of University College
Cork, and Robert Warren, formerly of the Royal
Observatory, Greenwich, gave more help than they could
ever have realized. Professor Mary Beard and Professor
Kathleen Coleman offered excellent advice on publishing
issues. In Chester, and over many years, the librarian
Mr Angus Madders and his staff have provided
invaluable assistance.

Carol Fellingham Webb did a magnificent job of
copy editing and rescuing the text from the eccentricities
with which it was littered. Tomi Vollauschek and Agathe
Jacquillat of FL@33 beautifully designed the book,
creating its website and advertisments, all to a standard
I could barely have dreamt of.

Debts of a more personal nature remain. Two names
in particular stand out. Howard Lockley, whose
knowledge of the Welsh language, deep interest in Welsh
history, and time spent reading through the manuscript,
all saved me from making terrible blunders. The
mistakes which remain are all my responsibility. Dr Mark
Stowell-Smith inspired me to persevere, and without
that encouragement it is unlikely that this book would
ever have seen the light of day.

Caer/Chester

ABBREVIATIONS AND CONVENTIONS

AC   *Annales Cambriae*

AClon   *The Annals of Clonmacnoise*

AFM   *The Annals of the Kingdom of Ireland by the Four Masters*

AI   *The Annals of Inisfallen*

ASC   *The Anglo-Saxon Chronicle*

AT   *The Annals of Tigernach*

AU   *The Annals of Ulster*

LG   *Lebor Gabála Erenn*; The Book of the Taking of Ireland

[ ]   All square brackets throughout enclose additions by the author.

( )   All round brackets throughout are part of whatever is being quoted, found either as part of the original text, or containing an interpolation by the editor of that text.

d.   died

NN   No name

ND   No date

c.   Approximately. As nearly all dates for this very early period in the history of the British Isles are approximate and open to all sorts of challenges, the temptation to preface every date with this shorthand for the Latin *circa* has been resisted.

Quotations   I have taken the somewhat unusual step of splitting up quotations from the sources into sections that make particular points. I hope in this way it will be easier to see the relevance of the extract to the subject under discussion. Very often the original runs as a continuous text, and the choice of where to split into paragraphs is merely that of the modern editor. I hope the reader will find this practice helpful.

TABLE 1
Kings over Meath:
Revised Dates and those given in AFM

	Name	Suggested Historical Dates	AFM Dates
1	LUGAID REÓDERG	46–71	–
2	CONCHOBAR ABRAT-RUAD	71	–
3	CRIMTHANN NIA NAR	71–87	7BC–AD9
4	CAIRBRE CATCHENN	87–92	AD9–14
5	FERADACH FECHTNACH	92–112	14–36
6	FIATACH FINN	112–114	36–39
7	FIACHA FINNFOLAD	114–121	39–56
8	ELIM	121–124	56–76
9	TUATHAL TECHTMAR	124–154	76–106
10	MÁL	154–159	106–110
11	FEDELMID RECHTMAR	159–167	110–119
12	CATHAÍR MÁR	167–170	119–122
13	CONN CÉTCHATHACH	170–190	122–157
14	EOCHAID of LEINSTER	183–190	–
15	CONAIRE	190–197	157–165
16	ART ÓENFER	197–217	165–195
17	LUGAID MACCON	217–224	195–225
18	FERGUS DUBDÉTACH	224–225	225–226
19	CORMAC ULFHOTA	225–267	226–266
20	EOCHU GUNNAT	267–268	266–267
21	CAIRBRE LIFECHAIR	268–285	267–284
22	FOTHADH CAIRPTHECH	285–286	284–285
23	FOTHADH AIRGDECH	285–286	284–285
24	FIACHA SROBTINE	286–304	285–322
25	? DAIRE DRECHLETHAN	304–310	Three Collas
26	? FECHO	310–325	–
27	MUIREDACH TÍRECH	325–355	326–356
28	CÁELBAD	355–356	356–357
29	EOCHU MUGMEDÓN	359–389	357–365
30	BRION	389–412	–
31	FIACHRA	412–422	–
32	NATH Í	422–445	405–428
33	NIALL NOÍGIALLACH	445–452	379–405
34	LÓEGAIRE	452–462	428–458
35	CONALL CRIMTHAINNE	462–480	–

TABLE 2
Likely Roman Interventions in Ireland

	Year	Protégé	Governor of Britain	Emperor/s	Description and Outcome for Rome
1	78–81	–	Gnaeus Julius Agricola	Vespasian Titus Domitian	Reconnaissance work of the Irish Sea fleet
2	92	Feradach son of Crimthann	NN	Domitian	Indirect support Success
3	124	Tuathal son of Fiacha	Aulus Platorius Nepos	Hadrian	Indirect support Success
4	175	Eoghan of Munster	Quintus Antistius Adventus	Marcus Aurelius	[I] Direct intervention Defeat for troops fighting in the battle of Moylena near Tullamore
5	217	Lugaid Maccon son of Eoghan	NN	211-17 Geta and Caracalla 217 Macrinus	[II] Direct intervention Victory for troops in the battle of Mucruma, Co. Galway, but the legate Benignus is killed
6	259	Cormac son of Art	NN	Gallienus	Indirect support
7	429	Niall and son Lóegaire	Vortigern	Valentinian III	Indirect support
8	432	Conall son of Lugaid	Vortigern	Valentinian III	Indirect support

TABLE 3

Rulers of Gwynedd: Counts, Kings, and Princes, c.398–1283

	Name	Epiphet		Reign
1	Paternus son of Tacitus	*Peisrudd*	Red Robe	c.398–410
2	Eternus successor to Paternus			c.410–428
3	NN successor to Eternus	*Cunedda*	The Good King	c.428–450
4	Anianus – Einiawn/Einion – son of Cunedda or NN	*Einiawn*	The Anvil	c.450–485
5	Eugenius/Owain, possibly son of Anianus but probably from Meirionydd	*Danwyn*	White Tooth	c.485–490
6	Cadwallon brother of Owain	*Lawhir*	Longhanded	c.490–517
7	Maelgwn son of Cadwallon	*Hir* *Gwynedd*	The Tall Of Gwynedd	c.517–545
8	Einion ab [i.e. son of, or ŵyr, grandson of] Owain Danwyn i.e. son of Cynlas of Rhos			c.545–566
9	Rhun ap Maelgwn			c.566–580
10	Beli ab Einion			c.580–597
11	Iago ap Beli			c.597–616
12	Cadfan ab Iago			616–625
13	Cadwallon ap Cadfan			625–635
14	Cadafael ap Cynfedw			635–656
15	Cadwaladr ap Cadwallon			656–664
16	Idwal ap Cadwaladr	*Iwrch*	The Roebuck	664–712
17	Rhodri ab Idwal	*Molwynog*	Bald and Grey	c.712–754
18	Caradog ap Meirchion			754–798
19	Cynan ap Rhodri	*Tindaethwy*	Of Dindaethwy	798–816

	Name	Epiphet		Reign
20	Hywel ap Rhodri			816–825
21	Merfyn grandson or son-in-law of Cynan	Frych	The Freckled	825–844
22	Rhodri ap Merfyn	Mawr	The Great	844–878
23	Anarawd ap Rhodri			878–916
24	Idwal ab Anarawd	Foel	The Bald	916–942
25	[i] Idwal and Iago ab Idwal Foel	Fychan	The Lesser	942
26	Hywel ap Cadell ap Rhodri	Dda	The Good	942–950
27	Rhodri ap Hywel Dda			950–951
25	[ii] Idwal and Iago ab Idwal Foel			951–985
28	Hywel ab Ieuaf ab Idwal			980–985
29	Cadwallon ab Ieuaf			985–986
30	Maredudd ab Owain ap Hywel			986–987
31	Cynan ap Hywel			987–1003
32	Aeddan ap Blegywryd			c.1004–1018
33	Llywelyn ap Seisyll			c.1018–1023
34	Iago ab Idwal ap Meurig ab Idwal Foel			1023–1039
35	Gruffudd ap Llywelyn ap Seisyll			1039–1063
36	Bleddyn ap Cynfyn – half-brother of Gruffudd			1063–1075
37	Trahaearn ap Caradog			1075–1081
38	[i] Gruffudd ap Cynan ab Iago			1081
	Interregnum	Lordship of Robert of Rhuddlan		1081–1093
		Lordship of Earl Hugh of Chester		1093–1094
38	[ii] Gruffudd ap Cynan			1094–1137
39	Owain ap Gruffudd	Gwynedd Fawr	Of Gwynedd The Great	1137–1170
40	Hywel ab Owain			1170
41	[i] Rhodri ab Owain			1170–1174

	Name	Epiphet		Reign
42	Dafydd ab Owain			1174–1175
41	[ii] Rhodri ab Owain			1175–1193
43	Gruffudd ab Cynan ab Owain			1193–1200
44	Llywelyn ab Iorwerth ab Owain	*Fawr*	The Great	1200–1240
45	Dafydd ap Llywelyn			1240–1246
46	Owain and Llywelyn ap Gruffudd ap Llywelyn			1246–1255
47	Llywelyn ap Gruffudd	*Y Llyw Olaf*	The Last Leader	1255–1282
48	Dafydd ap Gruffudd			1282–1283

Note

Fifty-one known separate periods of rule by Welsh princes.

TABLE 4

Known Appeals from Britain for Extra Military Assistance and the Relief Expeditions Sent, 43–410

Arrivals of new governors might or might not have been accompanied by forces large enough to be considered relief expeditions. Only those known to have resulted in an increase in the size of the British garrison are included. Some inclusions are open to argument. Also, many smaller troop movements into and out of Britain would have occurred.

	Date of Expedition	Problem	Expedition	Troops Involved
1	48	Activity of Caratacus The Roman front line now bordering the highland zone	Ostorius Scapula, 2nd governor, to implement Welsh campaigns	?
2	57	Problems continuing in south Wales	Quintus Veranius, 4th governor, to lead new forward push cont. by S. Paulinus	?
3	71		Quintus Petillius Cerialis, 9th governor, to begin policy of all-out conquest	Legion II Adiutrix leaves 86
4	122	Need to stabilize frontier at chosen Solway–Tyne line	EMPEROR HADRIAN to confirm frontier policy	Legion VI Victrix
5	131	Trouble in northern Britain aided by Irish	Sextus Julius Severus arriving as the new governor	1,000 legionaries each from Spain's VII and Germany's VII and XXII legions

	Date of Expedition	Problem	Expedition	Troops Involved
6	155	An extensive and threatening rising in Brigantia from 152	Gnaeus Julius Verus, new governor	Reinforcements from Germany for the now three British legions
7	197	After 191–3 civil war and the 196 rebellion of governor Albinus taking massive forces to the Continent, Pictish and Irish raiding brings Britain to crisis point	Virius Lupus, new governor	This starts the gradual return of the legions. The raiders are bought off until troop levels are sufficient when the war resumes, c.205
8	207–11	"	CARACALLA JOINT EMPEROR	Begins reinforcement of British garrison
	208–11	"	EMPEROR SEVERUS with son Geta. 211 EMPERORS CARACALLA and GETA	Troops and an immense sum of money
9	?285	Increased Saxon attacks on the British coast from c.225	Carausius: in 286 prefect/admiral of the British fleet	A naval expedition in British waters against Saxon pirates

	Date of Expedition	Problem	Expedition	Troops Involved
10	296–7	286–93 Usurpation of Carausius and from 293 of Allectus in Britain and northern Gaul	Western CAESAR CONSTANTIUS CHLORUS invades but in the event Aesclepiodotus prefect of Gaul and Britain lands to do the work – Constantius arrives later in calm weather	An invasion force therefore probably the biggest single entry of troops since 43
11	305-306	Renewed trouble in northern Britain	EMPEROR CONSTANTIUS I with son Constantine CONSTANTINE EMPEROR 306	?
12	307	Still outstanding problems to be dealt with	CONSTANTINE as CAESAR	?
	311	–	CONSTANTINE acting as EMPEROR	? Probably to take troops out rather than reinforce
13	314	–	Western EMPEROR CONSTANTINE I	? Probably to return troops taken out in 311
14	343	More trouble with the Picts – the Maeatae	Western EMPEROR CONSTANS I crossing early in the year for a short campaign	A small imperial escort of 100 men but also probably the *comes* Gratian with a detachment of the western field army

	Date of Expedition	Problem	Expedition	Troops Involved
15	353	350 usurpation of Magnentius in Gaul involves Britain where the unknown Carausius II and Genseris emerge as rulers	*Comes* Paulus *Catena*, Paul the Chain, arrives to restore legitimacy and weed out malcontents including Magnentius's men	?
16	Jan. 360	359–60 Picts and Irish return to the offensive	*Comes* Lupicinus	Four units of lightly armed elite troops, but withdrawn c.Feb.
17	367 to early 370	364–7 Picts, Irish, and Saxons active, leading to near collapse of Roman government	*Comes* Theodosius following two fact-finding expeditions of Severus and Jovinus. Valentinian abandoned the idea of personal intervention because of illness. The last major constructive imperial intervention in Britain's affairs	More than 1,000 troops of the western field army including élite units
18	?382	Picts and Irish return to the offensive	*Comes* Magnus Maximus returns to Britain for third time heading a relief force	Probably some of the force taken to the Continent in 383 in Maximus's usurpation

	Date of Expedition	Problem	Expedition	Troops Involved
19	c.384–5	Picts and Irish again attacking	Acting western EMPEROR MAGNUS MAXIMUS with *comes* Gracianus	A section of the western field army
20	396–401	395–6 Attacks by Picts and Irish increase, forcing the government of the semi-detached Britain still under supporters of the late Magnus Maximus to appeal to Milan	? Victorinus a new vicar to head Britain's civilian administration – leader of army units unknown	Accompanied by a relief expedition – size unknown. Its work done it prepares to leave in 398
21	398–401	Renewed attacks by Picts and Irish lead to another appeal for the 396 force to stay and for more aid	Personnel unknown – the last imperial relief expedition to be sent to Britain	? but combined with the 396 force it wins a massive victory over the Picts in the battle of the Forest
	–	410 Britain suffers from damaging raids by Saxon pirates, evicts the administration of the current usurper Constantine III, and appeals to Honorius in Ravenna	No expedition – Honorius's government tells Britain there are no troops available and that it must look to its own defence	

Date of Expedition	Problem	Expedition	Troops Involved
–	426 Britain's last appeal to the continental empire particularly to the master of soldiers in Gaul, Aëtius	No expedition	But the church sends Germanus in c.429, bishop Palladius to the Picts in 431, and bishop Secundinus to the Irish in 443

Notes

The twenty periods between expeditions average out at seventeen and a half years each, hardly altered if the last two appeals had resulted in intervention instead of refusals.

The three longest periods during which such interventions were unnecessary are
i   the seventy-eight years following the appalling devastation wreaked by Severus and Caracalla, 208–11,
ii   the fifty-one years after Cerialis, the ninth governor, began the policy of all-out conquest, and
iii   the forty-two years following the suppression of the 152 Brigantian Rising beginning in 155.

TABLE 5
Emperors and Caesars in Britain

#	Role	Name	Year	Role	Name	Year
1	Sole Emperor/s	HADRIAN	122			
2	"	CARACALLA	207–11			
3	"	SEVERUS	208–11			
4	"	GETA and CARACALLA	211			
				Western caesar	CONSTANTIUS CHLORUS	296–7
5	Western emperor	CONSTANTIUS I	305–6			
6	"	CONSTANTINE I	306			
				"	CONSTANTINE	307
7	"	CONSTANTINE I	311			
8	"	CONSTANTINE I	314			
9	"	CONSTANS I	343			
10	Western usurper	MAGNUS MAXIMUS	383			
11	Acting western emperor	FLAVIUS MAGNUS MAXIMUS	385			

Note

Eight emperors made eleven visits; two caesars each visited once.

TABLE 6

Leinster's Traditional History

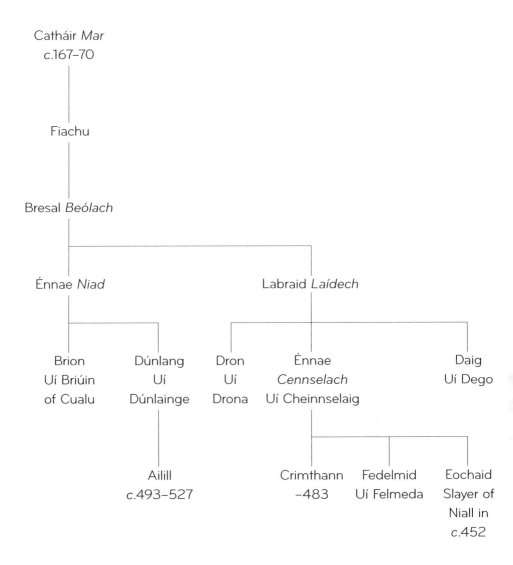

Source

Based on Mac Niocaill, 1972, p. 20.

Maelgwn the great king [c.517–45]
was reigning among the Britons, that
is in the region of Gwynedd, because
his grandfather's great grandfather,
that is, Paternus, had come previously
from the northern part, that is from
the region which is called the plain
of the Gododdin ...
And Cunedda, Paternus's grandson,
with his sons ... drove out with
immense slaughter the Irish from
those regions, who never returned
again to inhabit them.

Nennius, *Historia Brittonum*, Ch. 62.

CHAPTER ONE

FIGHTING YOUR ENEMIES FOR YOU
Relief Expeditions to Roman Britain, 388–398

THE COST OF HOLDING BRITAIN

There may have been many an occasion when those in
government in Rome wondered whether holding Britain
was worth the cost and the effort. Yes, of course, there
was its mineral wealth. Perhaps even more important
were the strategic reasons that prompted Rome to invade
the island in the first place. But having failed to subdue
the whole island, by the late fourth century those reasons
looked less convincing. If Roman arms were not on
the British side of the Channel, disaffection in Gaul
would no doubt again receive support and direct help
from the independent British states. But the move into
Britain had exposed yet another threat, this time from
the island lying to the west. Agricola's solution to the
problem in the first century, that Rome should conquer
Ireland also, had been rejected. At the time the decision
was understandable, but an opportunity had been lost,
and as the years passed it was no longer an option. The
result was that Britain was constantly under attack from
a combination of Pictish and Irish forces and the drain
on the exchequer was considerable. Worse, such a
volatile situation encouraged those from within Roman
ranks who believed that they did have the answer to
the problem. The island became almost a breeding
ground for claimants to the throne and rebellion. Was
Britain really worth holding when problems facing the
continental empire were growing almost daily?

BRITAIN'S SEMI-DETACHED STATUS, 388–396

Between 388 and 396, the period following the fall of
Magnus Maximus, Britain had been 'semi-detached' from
the Roman empire. Maximus had set out from Britain in

383 as a usurper, and it was only with the greatest reluctance that Theodosius I in the east and Valentinian II in the west accepted him as co-emperor. Overreaching himself, in 387 Maximus invaded Valentinian's Italian territory. The following year Theodosius marched against him leading the whole might of the east, and Maximus fell. Just less than a hundred years before, in 296 the western *caesar* Constantius *Chlorus* had recovered Britain from the ten-year grip of the usurpers Carausius and Allectus. The cost of re-establishing legitimate government at that date had been colossal, involving what in effect was a second invasion of Britain. The Channel was an enormous obstacle. In 388, another invasion of Britain was well beyond what the western empire could afford, so it was probably a matter of hard calculation in Milan and Constantinople that, left to their own devices, the authorities in Britain would come back to the imperial fold of their own accord. The times were too dangerous and threatening for Britain to be able to stand alone for long.

Britain's independent stance in the years after 388 was encouraged, if not directed, by the presence in the island of members of Maximus's family, including his widowed empress. Even if much of the traditional material concerning this, probably British, Helen or Helena is rejected, it is still the case that the majority, if not the whole, of the political and military establishment of the diocese in these years would have been made up of people appointed directly by Maximus or his government. For these, it was now a matter of using the security and independence given by Britain's island position to negotiate favourable terms and honourable reinstatement. If these were initially refused, matters were complicated further when Eugenius and Arbogast took Gaul into another rebellion in 392. However, the appearance of this new Gallic empire would have created further opportunities for the British hierarchy to show its essential loyalty to Milan and Constantinople.

CONTINUING PICTISH/IRISH INFILTRATION

The Picts, in conjunction with their Irish allies, continued to attack. Western Britain saw Irish infiltration of a more peaceful sort and, with a weaker military presence following the 383 withdrawals, such immigration probably increased. This is particularly evident in southwest Wales, in *Demetia*, Dyfed. Here, before the death of Maximus, in about 385 Eochaid *Allmuir*, Eochaid Over-Sea, arrived. He was of a people in Munster in southern Ireland known as the Deisi. He, his family, and followers merged with the local population and eventually took their part in the defence of the area against other Irish immigrants or attackers. This peaceful immigration probably continued quite independently of any moves by raiding kings, but it might well have brought such intervention in its wake. It looks as though Crimthann of southern Munster was one such king, interfering in Britain in order to continue his control over those like Eochaid who thought they had escaped him.

BRITAIN'S RECORD OF RELIEF EXPEDITIONS

In the history of the Roman province of Britain and then what became the diocese made up of a group of provinces, the number of relief expeditions that had to be called for is extraordinary. The three legions based there, itself an unusual arrangement matched only in Palestine, had to be constantly helped out by temporary reinforcements coming from the Continent. These expeditions were often led by military figures of considerable note arriving to give a new direction to affairs. It is not always easy to separate out these moves from the more normal operations of military and civilian government and many smaller troop movements must have occurred. Arrivals of new governors might or might not be accompanied by forces large enough to be considered relief expeditions. Nevertheless, it is possible to use the written records to isolate these extraordinary, emergency interventions.

Britain was invaded in 43 and under direct Roman control until 410 when the diocese was told there were no troops to spare for relief expeditions and it would have to fend for itself. The implication of this communication was that this would be the situation for the foreseeable future. In this period of 367 years, at least twenty-one major relief expeditions were sent to Britain. The interval between these arrivals averages out at seventeen and a half years. The three longest periods when such intervention was considered unnecessary, spans of seventy-eight, fifty-one, and forty-two years, which we might interpret as periods of peace, reveal in quite a dramatic fashion the shocking and awful effects of Roman military intervention. The longest period of seventy-eight years followed the appalling devastation inflicted in the far north of the island during the intervention of Emperor Septimius Severus and, already joint *augustus*, his son Caracalla, between 208 and 211. The second followed a change in policy with regard to Britain which ushered in the work of the ninth governor, Quintus Petillius Cerialis, and the start of the process of all-out conquest. The third period, following the suppression of the 152 Brigantian rising, started in 155 under a new governor, Gnaeus Julius Verus. Eight emperors made eleven visits to Britain leading such expeditions and two *caesars* each visited once.[1]

395/6: BRITAIN IS FORCED BACK INTO THE IMPERIAL FOLD

British and Irish affairs were inseparably linked. Maximus had been brought to power by his resistance to Irish and Pictish attacks. It was a recurrence of such onslaughts, up to and including the year 395, which forced Britain to appeal to Milan for aid, and in 395 this involved once more accepting direct imperial control. Milan had been

[1]_ See Tables 4 and 5.

Septimius Severus,
emperor 193–211.
(Photo: Jean-François
Peiré. Courtesy of
Musée Saint-Raymond/
Musée des Antiques
de Toulouse)

The continuing power
of Rome. The
*Amphitheatrum
Flavium*, the Colosseum,
begun by Emperor
Vespasian in 72, and
opened in 80 by his
son Titus.

proved right: Britain did come running. If Maximus's family was still in Britain, the best its members could hope for now was some form of internal exile. The western government had acted promptly in response to the British pleas. The master of soldiers, Stilicho, the power behind the throne of the thirteen-year-old western emperor Honorius, sent a new vicar to the diocese, probably Victorinus, accompanied by a relief expedition which backed up this restoration of legitimacy. Whatever work was needed against the Irish and Picts was done and the necessary changes in the diocesan government implemented. Later, Victorinus was lauded in a poem for the extraordinary tact he showed during his work in Britain, so it is doubtful whether much force had to be used against internal disaffection.

By the end of 397, the relief expedition was preparing to evacuate. Stilicho's resources were stretched and, though still needed in Britain, these troops could not be allowed to stay indefinitely. Worse still for Britain, it may be that the departing units were to take with them yet more of the troops who had been serving in the diocese. 'The evacuation [of Britain] may already have begun.'[2] Though not conclusive, the *Notitia Dignitatum* lacks any reference to a *dux Britanniarum*. More and more responsibility for defence was falling to locally-recruited bodies, *feoderati*, in particular those under the friendly native dynasties in the north and west of the diocese. Behind such frontier zones, local councils, as well as the governing diocesan council, must have been becoming increasingly aware that Milan would be sending further aid only with the greatest reluctance and only in times of the direst emergency. Britain's recent history of rebellion and support for usurpers must have made everyone in government acutely aware that little else could be expected.

2_ Frere, 1967, p. 235.

Certainly, the problems faced by the governments of
Honorius in the west, 395–423, and Arcadius in the east,
395–408, grew no less. In 396, western *Illyricum*, Austria
and the former Yugoslavia, had been ceded to the west
to rationalize the defences. In the following year,
Stilicho managed to defeat Alaric and his Goths in an
expedition to the Balkans which clearly intruded into
the eastern empire. The victory was not followed up,
Alaric escaped, and the expedition simply ruptured
relations between east and west. In 397 Eutropius, who
was the power behind the eastern throne, declared
Stilicho *hostis publicus*, public enemy, and opened up
negotiations with Gildo, count of Africa, for the transfer
of his African territories to the eastern empire. Finally,
he legitimized Alaric's Balkan rule by creating him
magister militum per Illyricum, master of soldiers over
this area, thus winning his support as well.

Between 397 and 398, all this erupted into the revolt
of Gildo in north Africa and the withholding of the corn
supply to Rome which caused enormous problems. In
November 397, five thousand men were despatched from
Pisa to deal with the rebellion, surprisingly under Gildo's
brother Mascezel. The campaign resulted in Gildo's
defeat and death at *Tabraca* on 31 July 398. While the
invasion force was on its way, in February 398, Stilicho's
daughter Maria married the fourteen-year-old emperor
Honorius in Milan.

All this time, the Egyptian poet Claudian was
continuing his propaganda on behalf of Stilicho. In
Milan in April 398, he recited his *De Bello Gildonico*,
The War against Gildo, placing Gildo's revolt on a par
with those of Magnus Maximus and Eugenius. Only
Book I, dealing with the journey of the expedition, was
ready by this time, yet even in this there are signs that
Mascezel's rôle was being deliberately minimized. Stilicho
was unpopular amongst the strictly orthodox Catholic
party dominant at court because of his leniency towards
heretics and pagans such as Claudian. Rumour had it

that Stilicho's position was threatened. The finger of suspicion pointing at Mascezel, Stilicho struck. Sometime in the second half of 398, Mascezel was pushed off a bridge in Milan when he and Stilicho were crossing together. Stilicho's rôle was obvious. He is even alleged to have smiled as he watched his rival drown.

The kingdom of the south is restored to our empire, the sky of that other hemisphere is once more brought into subjection. East and West live in amity and concord beneath the sway of one rule. We have joined Europe again to Africa and unswerving singleness of purpose unites the brother emperors.[3]

BRITAIN: THE 397/8 INVASION

However, according to Gildas, in 397/8 the Picts and the Irish resumed their attacks on Britain, both coming by sea, the Picts sailing to avoid the Wall, the Irish, no doubt, landing to the south of it.

Which [wall, that is, the Antonine Wall] being made not so much of stones as of turves, did not profit the unreasoning [foolish] populace, destitute of a rule [?such as a *dux Britanniarum*].
    That [relief 'legion' of 396] returning home with great triumph and joy, the former enemies [the Irish and Picts] like Aubrons [a displaced Gaullish people who lived by plundering], wolves rabid with deepest hunger, leaping with parched jaws across the sheepfold, no shepherd being at hand, borne with wings of oars and arms of rowers and sails bulged with wind, break through the boundaries and slay everything, and what they meet with crop it like ripe corn, tread under foot and walk through.[4]

The original Latin, *domum ... repedante*, literally means 'departing ... for home', which could mean that the relief force of 396 was still in Britain whilst making

[3] Claudian, *The War against Gildo*, Book I, 398, Platnauer, 1922, Vol. 1, p. 99.

[4] Gildas, *De Excidio Britanniae*, The Loss or the Fall of Britain, Book 2, Chs. 15 and 16, Wade-Evans, 1938, p. 136 and note 3.

preparations to leave, or was actually in the process of leaving when the attacks began.[5] That it was given the title of legion is, at this date, of no particular military significance.

398 THE LAST RELIEF EXPEDITION TO BRITAIN

Possibly the British authorities hoped that another appeal to the Continent would lead, not just to the first force staying on, which during the emergency at least would have been almost inevitable, but to another force being sent to augment the permanent, if badly depleted, garrison.

A second time suppliant ambassadors are sent [no doubt. in the first instance, to the headquarters of Gaul's prefecture], with rent clothes, as is said, and heads covered with dust, imploring assistance from the Romans, even like timid fowls crouching under the most trusty wings of parents, that the fatherland [or *their wretched country*] might not be utterly destroyed and the name of Romans, which [now] sounded as mere talk to their ears or as a taunt to alien nations, might grow vile as a thing gnawed at.[6]

The continental officials who heard the news were 'moved as much as is possible for human nature by the story of such a tragedy'.

The differing translations of Gildas's flowery and complicated Latin seem to emphasize the plight he is trying to describe. In Bede, this Gildas passage appears as '[that] the name of a Roman province, long renowned amongst them, might not be obliterated and disgraced by the barbarity of foreigners'. In 1841 J. A. Giles rendered it as 'that the Roman name, which now was but an empty sound to fill the ear, might not become a reproach even to distant nations'. Dr Molly Miller in the 1970s translated it as '[that the] name of Romans, which among themselves rang in their ears at the words alone,

[5] Miller, 1976/8, p. 520 and note 2.

[6] Gildas, *De Excidio Britanniae*, Book 2, Ch. 17, Wade-Evans, 1938, p. 137. Giles, 1841, has *wretched country* instead of *fatherland*.

would be cheapened and nibbled away to the scorn of alien peoples'.[7] Miller believed that the appeal was not to continental officials, but instead to a *dux Britanniarum*, still somewhere in Britain at the head of a Roman field army, who was hard to move. But Gildas's words seem to point to an expedition, sent in response to this renewed appeal, not from another part of the diocese, but from the Continent.

By the autumn of 398, this second relief expedition was in Britain and campaigning.

They [in all probability the imperial authorities in Gaul], moved as much as is possible for human nature by the story of such a tragedy, first accelerating unexpected relays of horsemen on land, of sailors on sea, like flights of eagles,
then [they] plunge terrible points of swords in the necks of their enemies, and execute a slaughter on the same to be likened to the falling of leaves at [this] the fixed time, as if it were a mountain torrent ... [which] in one engulfment overwhelms obstructions set in the way.

So did the illustrious helpers very quickly put to flight the bands of the enemies, if any however had been able to escape across the seas, because across the seas they [had formerly] heaped up their annual plunder with no one resisting.[8]

The ninth-century Nennius collection has a garbled version of this in which the Britons are pitched against their Roman governors whilst still needing them to fight off the Picts and the Scots. Geoffrey of Monmouth certainly understood the account to mean that the relief force came from the Continent.

A legion which had played no part in the earlier disaster [that is, in the 395 attacks and in the 396–8 relief expedition] was immediately put under their [the British authorities'] command. Once this legion had been shipped across the ocean to the country, it met the enemy in hand-to-hand conflict. The Romans eventually

7_ Gildas: Giles, 1841, p. 14; Miller, 1976/8, p. 520; Bede: Colgrave and Mynors, 1969, p. 43.

8_ Gildas, *De Excidio Britanniae*, Book 2, Ch. 17, Wade-Evans, 1938, pp. 137–8.

slew a great number of the enemy and drove all who remained out of the territory.[9]

THE BATTLE OF THE FOREST

In the 1970s, Molly Miller suggested that Gildas's 'decorative prose' possibly disguised quite specific details of a battle fought in the autumn, *the fixed time* of *the falling of leaves* when a body of invaders were trapped in woodland.[10] Such a battle, *Cat Godeu*, the battle of the Forest, appears in both Welsh and Scottish tradition. The oldest corpus of the Welsh Triads links it with two very significant battles.

Three Futile Battles of the Island of Britain:
    One of them was the Battle of Goddeu [*Vn onaddunt a vu Gat Godeu*]: it was brought about by the cause of the bitch, together with the roebuck and the plover.
    The second was the Action of Ar(f)derydd, which was brought about by the cause of the lark's nest;
    And the third was the worst: that was Camlan, which was brought about because of a quarrel between Gwenhwyfar and Gwennhwy(f)ach.
    This is why those [battles] were called Futile: because they were brought about by such a barren cause as that.[11]

The battle of *Arfderydd*, Arthuret in Cumbria, was fought in 573 between branches of the northern British kingdom of Rheged, the dynasty of Coel. The lark's nest for which it was fought was possibly *Caerlaverock*, a harbour commanding the approach to the Solway Firth. The battle of *Camlan* was fought according to AC, the *Annales Cambriae*, at a date between about 512 and 537. Little is known about its immediate cause or where it took place, although from its name it was possibly in a 'crooked glen'. Its result, however, has often been seen as little short of catastrophic for the Romano-British struggle against Saxon encroachments. The period of

9_ Geoffrey of Monmouth, *The History of the Kings of Britain*, VI. 1, Thorpe, 1966, p. 144.

10_ Miller, 1976/8, p. 520.

11_ *Trioedd Ynys Prydein*, The Welsh Triads, Bromwich, 1961, p. 206, No. 84.

what might well have been largely united British action under three consecutive military leaders, Vortigern, Ambrosius, and Arthur, now ended with Arthur's defeat and death. Lowland Britain was at the mercy of the invaders. According to later legend, Mordred was Arthur's nephew who was living adulterously with Arthur's queen, Guinevere, *Gwenhwyfar* in the triad. Then, during Arthur's absence, he took 'the throne' and the scene was set for this battle in which Mordred supposedly brought Picts, Irish, and Saxons to his aid. There is more here than just legend and myth. We are looking at something far more concrete, and the fact that references to 'the cause of the bitch … the roebuck and the plover' are now beyond our understanding does not mean that they were not referring to matters of real political importance at the time.

Of course, the triad was stating an important historical truth, claiming that battles, and indeed wars, having the most disastrous consequences, can be caused by incidents or situations that were in themselves trivial. The great twentieth-century English historian A. J. P. Taylor was often keen to make the same point, especially concerning events as momentous and devastating in their consequences as the two world wars. It is in this sense that these battles were unnecessary or futile. Was the immediate cause of the battle of the Forest put down to a wood that was providing food for a starving and demoralized army, with the result that the men discovered scavenging in this way were easily surrounded and put to the sword? Whatever the causes, its linking with the triad's other battles underlines its significance.

The legendary Welsh poem *Cat Godeu* suggests something else which should not surprise us: that the encounter took place in the territory of the Novantae in southwest Scotland, a territory that would have been very much a meeting place of Irish invaders and northern tribes on the move into a Britain no longer able to defend itself adequately. It mentions *Caer Nefenhyr* which appears elsewhere only twice. In one of these references, it is found without the *caer* in a praise-poem addressed to Llywelyn the Great, where his ferocity was said to be like that of Nefenhyr. The word apparently derives from *Novantorix*, possibly a reference to the king of the Novantae. This family, ruling over Galloway, claimed its descent back to the emperor Maximus. The *Novantorum* peninsula was the Rhinns of Galloway from where Agricola looked over the water to Ireland and contemplated its conquest; the *Novantorum Promontorium* was the Mull of Galloway. Goddau was an actual region, almost certainly lying in the British kingdom best described as Greater Rheged but with its heartland centred on Carlisle and the coastlands of the Solway Firth and Morecambe Bay. In 588 Urien *Rheged*, ruler over this confederation, accompanied by his son Owain, defeated an attempt by the Anglians of Bernicia to retaliate for his retaking of Catterick in 581. The battle of *Argoed Llwyfain*, the battle of the Leven Forest, was celebrated in one of Taliesin's better-known poems. In this, Urien called up his troops so that 'Goddau and Rheged gathered in arms'.[12] *Goddau* meant shrubs or brushwood and it may be that the battle was fought in its area.[13] However, land in the wild remote parts of southwest Scotland would have been as heavily forested as other areas and this attempt at identification cannot be pushed too far.

In the autumn of 398, somewhere in Galloway, there took place one of those battles which gave the Roman army its reputation for being one of the most terrible killing machines in history.

12_ *Gwaith Argoed Llwyfain*, Conran, 1967, p. 73; Clancy, 1970, p. 30; and Jarman in Jarman and Rees Hughes, 1976, p. 60.

13_ A recent analysis of *Cat* or *Kat Godeu* is in Haycock, 2007, pp. 167–239.

I was in the Fort of Nefenhyr ...
soldiers were attacking.
A resurgence for the Britons ...
an unexpected (source of) hope –
the trees hewed down (the enemy)
by means of (their) powerful tendrils ...
   At the head of the line ...
It caused us no disaster
the blood of men up to our thighs ...

I myself am not sluggish
between the sea and the shore:
I caused a bloodbath
for nine hundred picked warriors.
My round shield is of ruby,
my shield-ring is of gold ...
   (Like) a magnificent jewel in a gold ornament
thus I am resplendent
and I am exhilarated
by the prophecy of Virgil.[14]

And what was Virgil's prophecy? In the first book of the *Aeneid*, Jupiter, 'the Father of Gods and Men', reassures his daughter Venus, the mother of Aeneas, about the fate awaiting the Trojan and his successors. He outlined the stages by which these war refugees would establish themselves in Italy up to the birth of the twins Romulus and Remus.

'Then Romulus shall receive the people, wearing with joy the tawny hide of the wolf which nursed him. The walls he builds will be the walls of Mars and he shall give his own name to his people, the Romans. On them I impose no limits of time or place. I have given them an empire that will know no end.'[15]

Later, when Aeneas as part of his search enters the Underworld, the task ahead of this people who would settle on the Tiber is expanded upon.

Your task, Roman, and do not forget it, will be to govern the peoples of the world in your empire. These [the operations of government] will be your arts – and to impose a settled pattern upon peace, to pardon the defeated and war down the proud.[16]

Well might the poet feel exhilarated, but the cost to Rome and to the peoples it conquered was tremendous as this battle demonstrates.

14_ *Kat Godeu*, transl. Haycock, ibid., pp. 176–86: the complete poem in Welsh and English, pp. 174–86.

15_ Virgil, *Aeneid*, Book 1, West, 1991, p. 12.

16_ Ibid., Book 6, p. 159.

REORGANIZATION PRIOR TO THE 398 WITHDRAWAL

Gildas in his largely imaginary reconstruction of these events, for that is what he may be giving us, continues by describing advice then given by the commanders of the relief force to the British authorities. However, it has been suggested that Gildas, far from making it up, is at this point using the words, or at least a paraphrase of the words, of the famous letter sent by the emperor Honorius to the cities of Britain in 410.[17] In this vitally important communication, Honorius's government informed the diocesan council made up of representatives from the cities of Britain, that its citizens were, in effect, independent of the empire. In other words, Britain for the foreseeable future had to be responsible for its own government and defence. Some reservations about whether the letter was really addressed to Britain can now be discounted.[18]

Gildas, whether he realized it or not, was therefore suggesting that such a decision was in fact several years in the making and that the relief expedition of 398, which did indeed turn out to be the last, was, *at the time it was sent*, already thought of as the last that Honorius's government could be expected to supply. In the following translation of Gildas, the lines which may well have been taken from the imperial letter are given in italics. When he refers to the 'Romans', as usual using the term misleadingly to distinguish these from the British, we have to read 'the Roman commanders'.

[17]_ Stevens, 1957, pp. 333–5.

[18]_ Some have claimed that the letter was directed to the cities in the province of *Bruttium* in southern Italy. Zosimus, however, who also notes it, seems clear that it was addressed to Britain.

The Romans therefore, [on this 398 expedition] giving notice to the fatherland [Britain] that in no wise could they be too frequently harassed by expeditions so laborious, and the Roman standards, such an army and so great, be wearied on land and sea on account of the unwarlike vagabond thieves [the Picts and the Irish],
but [are] *urging that [Britain] should rather by itself, after accustoming itself to arms and bravely*

fighting, defend with all its powers, land, property,
wives, children, and, what is greater than these, liberty
and life,
and that it should hold forth hands in no way armourless
to be bound in fetters by nations in no wise braver
than itself, unless it were rendered dissolute by idleness
and torpor
but [that the Britons should have their hands]
provided with shields, swords and spears and [be]
ready for striking ...[19]

   Gildas was correct in believing that this expedition represented something of a watershed in the history of the diocese. Unfortunately, he drags in an account of the building of Hadrian's Wall, which he felt fitted in with his view of the significance of these events. In fact, it is almost certain that some measures would have been taken on Hadrian's Wall at this time.

The Romans ... because also they thought this to be
of some advantages to the people to be left [that is,
the Britons], level out a wall not as the other [the
Antonine made of turves], at the public expense and
private, the wretched natives being joined with them
[in the enterprise], in their accustomed mode of
structure [that is, in stone], in a straight line from sea
to sea between fortresses, which had been erected
there perhaps from fear of enemies.[20]

   More accurately, Gildas surmised that the commanders on such an expedition would be concerned to ensure that the island diocese was in the best possible position to shift for itself when the time came.

They give bold counsel to the timorous people. They
leave patterns for the manufacture of arms.
   On the shore of the ocean [almost certainly the North
Sea coast, but the shores of the Irish Sea might also
be meant], also towards the south [on the Channel
coast], where their ships were wont to ride, because

19_ Gildas, *De Excidio
Britanniae*, Book 2, Ch. 18,
Wade-Evans, 1938,
pp. 138. It appears, more
succinctly, in Bede.

20_ Ibid.

45

thence too, wild barbaric beasts [the Saxons and the Irish] were feared, they erect towers at intervals overlooking the sea.[21]

Again it is likely that the number of lookout and signalling stations was increased now, but more probably Gildas is explaining how he thought the Saxon Shore defence system, dating like the Walls to years before this time, came into being. Nevertheless, Gildas's guesswork on the sort of thing that would have occurred around the year 398 may not be very far off the mark.

Nennius's ninth-century *History of the Britons*, continuing with the theme of deep antagonism between distinctly separate groups, Britons and Romans, gives Gildas's description a darker tone.

The Romans used to come [to Britain] to avenge the empire and to afford help, and when Britain had been spoiled of its gold and silver together with its bronze and every costly garment and honey [!], they were wont to return [home] with great triumph.[22]

This finds its way into the *Anglo-Saxon Chronicle* under the year 418.

In this year the Romans collected all the treasures which were in Britain, and hid some in the ground, so that no one could find them afterwards, and took some with them to Gaul.[23]

This *Anglo-Saxon Chronicle* date then led to speculation that a relief force under Constantius may have come to Britain as late as 417, an idea nowadays dismissed.

Typically, Geoffrey of Monmouth was able to elaborate further. He claimed that the Roman commanders delivered their warnings to the British at a meeting of all men of military age gathered in London. It was left to Guithelinus, supposedly archbishop of London, to press home the now altogether pithier message.

21_ Ibid.

22_ Nennius, *Historia Brittonum*, Ch. 30, Wade-Evans, 1938, p. 53.

23_ ASC 418, Whitelock et al., 1961, p. 9.

"The Romans are tired of all this perpetual travelling-about which they have to do in order to fight your enemies for you."

A glance at Table 4 listing relief expeditions to Britain between 43 and 410 will show just how near the mark Geoffrey was. In return for the Britons taking responsibility for their own defence, Rome would now forgo all tribute.[24]

THE BIBLE, VIRGIL, AND GILDAS

It seems clear that Gildas used two works to inspire him in the creation of his model or construct for the events of these years, particularly for the British appeals for assistance, and if not for this, at least for the wording of his descriptions.[25] The first is the Bible. Britain's pleas to the Roman authorities in Gaul and Milan could so easily be compared to the prayers of the Israelites after their exodus from Egypt, caught between the waters of the Red Sea and the forces of Pharaoh. This is seen most clearly in Britain's last appeal which, as we shall see, is probably to be dated to 426. 'The barbarians drive us to the sea, the sea drives us to the barbarians; between these two modes of death either we are killed or drowned.'[26] For Gildas, the chosen people of Britain were in the same plight as the chosen people of Israel and were just as foolish. The Jews blamed Moses for bringing them out of captivity and, seemingly lost in the desert, returned to their ancient gods.

But it was Virgil's *Aeneid* which provided even more exact models. This is the great foundation myth purporting to describe the origins of Rome. What is perhaps paradoxical in Gildas's use of this work is that the passages most suggesting the position of Britain in the last years of its formal control by Rome occur at the end of Virgil's work, where the scene is set for the *start* of Rome's history and the beginnings of its empire. It is obvious why Gildas found Virgil's work so resonant of

24_ Geoffrey of Monmouth, *The History of the Kings of Britain*, VI. 2, Thorpe, 1966, pp. 145-6.

25_ Higham, 1993, *passim*.

26_ Gildas, *De Excidio Britanniae*, Book 2, Ch. 20, Wade-Evans, 1938, p. 141, followed by Bede and Geoffrey of Monmouth.

Britain's situation. This is especially the case in the references to 'feeble birds' and 'the pitiless stranger'.

Most of the *Aeneid* is given over to Aeneas's attempts to establish his Trojans in Italy in the face of enormous resistance.

"Now take up your arms, O my poor countrymen, into whose hearts the pitiless stranger [Aeneas and his men] strikes the terror of war. You are like the feeble birds and he is attacking and plundering your shores."[27]

Suddenly, as these texts echo the plight of Britain at this time, one comes across lines that throw us back to what happened to Maximus's empress, whose life had taken the most dramatic turns. First, she had to cope with the death of Maximus in 383, and then, if she was still alive in 396, she must have been forced to relinquish any semblance of her former position when Britain had to appeal to Milan. Towards the end of the *Aeneid*, with the Latins in a losing battle against the Trojans, *Latium*'s Queen Armata is deranged with grief.

Her hand rent her purple robes, and she died a hideous death in the noose of a rope tied to a high beam.[28]

Certainly, Gildas's account of the 398 embassy seems to echo Tolumnius, "You are like the feeble birds", with his talk of ambassadors 'imploring assistance from the Romans, even like timid fowls crouching under the most trusty wings of the parents'. But need we necessarily assume that it was all an invention? As Professor Higham points out, historians are loath to abandon Gildas for, if they do so, they have precious little left. Gildas could even have heard of such embassies from the legates that had been sent. As always, the aim would have been to fill out the bare scraps of information and in Gildas's case to turn these into material for sermonizing.

27_ Virgil, *Aeneid*, Book 12, West, 1991, p. 310.

28_ Ibid., p. 321.

A major victory over the Picts and the Irish in the autumn of 398 would have given the military authorities one last opportunity to reorganize Britain's defences and make any necessary redeployments of the by now largely home-raised forces in the diocese. Possibly the battle of the Forest had been so overwhelming, or the treaties entered into after it, if any were made, seemingly so sound, that it was considered unlikely that there would be another Pictish invasion for a very long time. The Irish were a different matter, and the threat to the west coast was one that in all probability would remain constant. At this stage in Britain's Roman history, there was simply no chance of any army leaving Britain to deal with Ireland as the Picts had just been dealt with. There could be no question of reducing the size of local forces in the region of the Walls, although it is probable that there was yet another retreat to the Hadrian's Wall line by whatever troops had been operating beyond it. All this would have eased the pressure on manpower. Peace, and the redeployments it made possible, would have released key personnel for service in those places where the need was greater. One of this group was a man named Paternus son of Tacitus, his British name Padarn ap Tegid, of the northern Votadini, who was now transferred to north Wales with the rank of *comes*, count.

CHAPTER TWO

COMES LITORIS HIBERNIAE.
Paternus in North Wales, 398–410

THE NORTHERN VOTADINI, 368–599

It looks as though the rulers of the northern Votadini at the eastern end of the Antonine Wall had been granted the status and rôle of protector in order to patrol and pacify the Lothian plain, known later as the plain of the Votadini. These rulers eventually became kings of the Votadini or Gododdin. The person first indicated in the genealogies of the kingdom to have been elevated to this position at the time of the relief expedition of Count Theodosius around 368 was either Tacitus, his British name Tegid, or his father Iago. Paternus was the son of Tacitus and, with Paternus's removal to north Wales the genealogies focus on him as the founder of a line of rulers over the area that developed into the great north Wales kingdom of Gwynedd. In the king list for the Gododdin, if it can be called that, this means that the name of whoever succeeded Tacitus in the north is unknown, and this is the case for probably the next six protectors or kings. We have no name for a ruler of this small and little-documented kingdom until the period when Mynyddog *Mwynfawr*, Mynyddog the Wealthy, occupied the position in the period *c.*583–99. We know him because of his rôle in what was to be a last major push against the incoming Angles launched from his capital, Edinburgh. We only know of this and the resulting battle of *Catraeth*, Catterick, in which virtually the entire British army was wiped out, because of a famous poem on the venture, *The Gododdin*, by the British poet Aneirin.

PATERNUS

For a move to north Wales, holding a position that the history of his successors might indicate was one of considerable power, Paternus must have served his time in the army and risen to the highest rank. Supporting this is the fact that he is always referred to as Paternus of the Red Robe, indicating a military position of some distinction, and the area of his new appointment. Even after the *c.*398 battle of the Forest, Hadrian's Wall was still garrisoned because the southern Picts would always have to be watched. The only other area in which troops can be shown to have operated into the period when

Britain was acting alone was north Wales. Here, the perceived threat from Ireland and the importance of the copper and lead mines in the area meant that the army continued to operate and direct affairs.

DEVOLUTIONS OF POWER

In other areas, where there were no troops available, we see the elevation of local rulers, sometimes even mercenaries or recent settlers, to positions of power with responsibility for defence. Above all, they were charged with the upkeep and policing of the roads. Now that Rome had been forced on to the defensive, the road system on which its conquests had depended was becoming a major liability, enabling invaders, even just piratical groups, to move quickly to centres of population and wealth. Therefore, the roads had to be patrolled and, if necessary, defended. With this job went their maintenance, and responsibility for the staffing and upkeep of hotels and the provision of stables and horses on which the continuance of the imperial post service depended. What was at stake was the effective administration of the diocese. Devolution of powers and responsibilities had been resorted to from the earliest times, but it now became commonplace throughout the empire as the army, originally responsible for this work, was increasingly reduced. When forts were decommissioned local populations were used to fill the gap. Titles were given, areas of control delineated, and so in the British diocese we see these arrangements developing to the point when, as central control virtually ceased, we have the emergence of kingdoms that in this way inherited their power and title to rule from the empire.

In Wales, apart from the northern parts where the army still operated in an arc from Chester in the east to *Segontium*, Caernarfon, and Holyhead in the west, by 398 there were a whole series of these quasi-military commands using the local populations for this work: in some areas even immigrants were employed in this way. By 410 these authorities provided an impressive bulwark covering virtually the whole of Wales, parts of its coastline, and what we call the Welsh marches. Just inland of the Dee estuary and the north Wales coast were a bunch of Irish mercenaries, immigrants who had moved into the Clwyd Hills. Their responsibility was the road system as it left military control, probably in the Vale of Clwyd, and from there to Chester. To their south, another group, probably related to the northern appointees, guarded from Wroxeter into the centre of Wales. At a later date, another branch separated out from these to take particular responsibility for the roads north from Wroxeter to *Mediolanum*, Whitchurch, and Chester, and east to *Letocetum*, Wall near Lichfield. These three groups, if there were three, represent the beginnings of what came to be known as the northern, southern, and eastern *pagenses*, the country people: a command structure which grew into the later kingdom of Powys.

To their south, these Powys groups bordered those whose job it was to patrol and guard the Severn crossings and the routes into Wales which this great river provided. Its line of protectors was to produce the British military commander known by his epithet of *Vortigern*, the Great Leader, and he was the person most probably responsible for elevating this area into the province of *Gwrtheyrnion*. To the west of this was the later kingdom of Brycheiniog centred on Brecon. The genealogies seem to hint that this was the area in which some of the earliest appointments of the sort we are looking at had been made. These seemingly date to the time when the western usurper Magnentius withdrew troops from Britain in 351. They were made to guard the fort at Brecon Gaer and the road system of south Wales of which it was the pivot.

To the southwest of these areas were the coastal commands such as those in Glywysing, Glamorgan, which probably operated in both a military and maritime capacity. This would have been particularly the case with the commanders in southwest Wales, in *Demetia*, Dyfed. Here, protectors may have been able to trace their positions back to the time of the usurpation of Carausius and Allectus, 286–96, but would have received further confirmation of their positions from Count Theodosius and then Emperor Maximus. They would have patrolled the coastlands as well as the sea, probably as far as the Dyfi. In this way, these arrangements circled Wales for it was probably at the Dyfi, or further north at the tip of the Llŷn peninsula, that we once again enter the area of the north Wales military command.

BRITAIN'S MILITARY AND CIVILIAN GOVERNMENT

The north Wales command structure still operated as part of the regular army, and was headed by someone who in effect was *comes litoris Hiberniae*, a count of the Irish Shore. His responsibilities covering both land and sea forces may have included the Cumbrian Shore forts, Lancaster and Chester, in addition to the north Wales bases. To understand these military dispositions, it might be helpful to look briefly at how the British diocese developed. Britain was a single province of the empire from the start of its occupation in 43 up to the period 197–207. From then until 296, it was a two-province diocese with, in the north, *Britannia Inferior* or Lower Britain, and in the south *Britannia Superior*, Upper Britain, with Chester and Caerleon, two of the three legionary HQs, in the south. The third, *Eburacum*, York, was in *Britannia Inferior*.

After 296, when the western *caesar* Constantius *Chlorus* recovered Britain from the usurpation of Carausius and Allectus, Britain became a three- and then almost immediately a four-province diocese, partly as a result of the introduction of Diocletian's system of government. However, it was not until 314 that Constantine I completed these changes by separating the military and civilian commands of at least three of the four provinces, a step towards the creation of a mobile field army which was now the norm on the Continent. From then on we have *Britannia Secunda* in the north, its provincial civilian capital *Eburacum*, York, operating under a *praeses*, protector or president, with the military commander of the area, the *dux*, also based there. *Flavia Caesariensis*, from the Humber down to the Wash, including Norfolk and stretching across to the Dee and Mersey, though almost certainly not including Chester, had its civilian capital in Lincoln. *Maxima Caesariensis* lay southeast of this, extending round as far as Southampton Water. Its civilian capital was London. The military commander for both *Flavia* and *Maxima Caesariensis* was the count of the Saxon Shore. His coastal responsibilities may even have extended north into the territory of the *dux* as far as the walls. During the 367–70 expedition of Count Theodosius, *Britannia Secunda* was split with the creation of a new western civilian province, *Valentia*, based on Carlisle. It was the Irish threat which possibly complicated the necessary arrangements in the west. As a result, *Britannia Prima* kept unified military and civilian control exercised from Caerleon and Chester.

The details of this reorganization of both the civilian and military government of the diocese could not have been implemented overnight. It was probably not until the 380s and the involvement of the emperor Magnus Maximus that the two last military commands were created. The first was that of the *comes Britanniarum*, the count of the Britons, for south Wales and the southwestern peninsula, who operated out of Cirencester, the civilian capital of *Britannia Prima*. The other military command is entirely hypothetical. The relevant sections in the *Notitia Dignitatum*, the Register of Offices, which was a survey of the administrative structure of the late empire dating to between 408 and 423, and probably

CONNACHT
CRUACHAIN
ULSTER
THE ULAID
EMAIN
MACHA
DUMBARTON
Alcluit
LOUGH
LARNE
MUNSTER
BELFAST
LOUGH
TARA
THE ANTONINE WALL
UÍ
LIATHAIN
MEATH
RERIGONIUM
Stranraer
EDINBURGH
Dunedin
DÉSI
MUMAN
DUBLIN
BAY
LEINSTER
MAN
TRAPRAIN
LAW
THE COUNT OF
THE IRISH SHORE
HOLYHEAD
CARLISLE
SEGONTIUM
Caernarfon
CAERHUN
LANCASTER
HADRIAN'S WALL
RIBCHESTER
CARMARTHEN
CHESTER
CAERSWS
BRECON
GAER
WROXETER
YORK
THE DUKE
OF BRITAIN
KENCHESTER
CAERWENT
CARDIFF
CAERLEON
GLOUCESTER
CIRENCESTER
THE COUNT OF
THE SAXON SHORE
The Solent and
The Isle of Wight

55

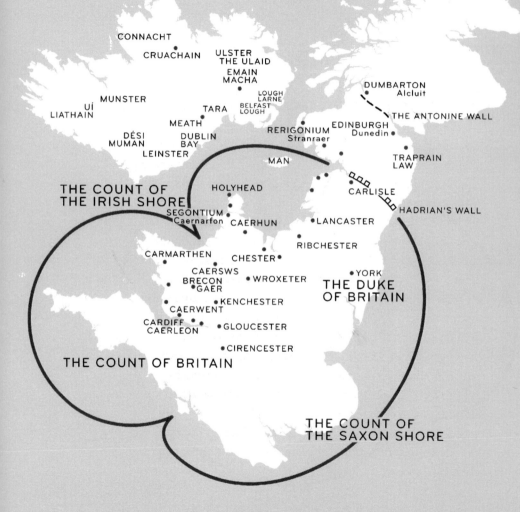

CONNACHT

CRUACHAIN

ULSTER
THE ULAID

EMAIN
MACHA

DUMBARTON
Alcluit

THE ANTONINE WALL

MUNSTER

UÍ
LIATHAIN

TARA

LOUGH
LARNE
BELFAST
LOUGH

MEATH

RERIGONIUM
Stranraer

EDINBURGH
Dunedin

DÉSI
MUMAN

DUBLIN
BAY

TRAPRAIN
LAW

LEINSTER

MAN

THE COUNT OF
THE IRISH SHORE

HOLYHEAD

CARLISLE

HADRIAN'S WALL

SEGONTIUM
Caernarfon

CAERHUN

LANCASTER

CARMARTHEN

CHESTER

RIBCHESTER

CAERSWS
BRECON
GAER

WROXETER

YORK

THE DUKE
OF BRITAIN

KENCHESTER

CAERWENT

CARDIFF
CAERLEON

GLOUCESTER

CIRENCESTER

THE COUNT OF BRITAIN

THE COUNT OF
THE SAXON SHORE

already out of date on its publication, gives us *Maxima Caesariensis, Valentia, Britannia Prima, Britannia Secunda,* and *Flavia Caesariensis* as the five provinces under the *vicarius Britanniarum* who headed the civilian administration. It then lists the places and units supposedly under the *comes litoris Saxonici* and the *dux Britanniarum.* But it is clear that headings are absent, and Chester and the Welsh forts are not even mentioned. This section is clearly missing.

COUNTS OF THE SAXON AND IRISH SHORES, 367

If, on the east coast, the count of the Saxon Shore was given responsibility for coastal defence from the Wall right round to the Solent at the time of Count Theodosius's expedition of 367–70, it is very probable that a western equivalent was given a similar commission extending from Stanwix at the western end of the Wall right down the western coast of Britain into the Channel and up to the limit of his eastern counterpart at Southampton Water. In other words, a post that could be described as *comes litoris Hiberniae* was created. When later, in the 380s, a new military command was established specifically for the southwest, a *comes Britanniarum*, this would leave the rest of the west coast, north of the Dyfi or Llŷn, under the original arrangement. A glance at the map might indicate that the geographical logic of the situation would suggest that this command was then linked to the operations of the *dux* and the *praeses* in York rather than remaining tied to the more southerly and inaccessible commands in Cirencester, although we have no evidence pointing in this direction.

To complete this history, we need go only eight years beyond the time of Paternus's appointment to the north Wales command. In 406, another usurper to emerge in Britain, Constantine III, took the bulk of the British garrison across the Channel, probably even calling for reinforcements in 407. The troops who remained in Britain operated, in fact had to operate, as part of a single diocesan field army, and so the separate military commands of *dux* and count of the Saxon Shore were abolished. The two exceptions to this were the army commands operating in north Wales and on Hadrian's Wall.

PATERNUS: *COMES LITORIS HIBERNIAE*

We can now return to Paternus. He was a high-ranking army officer from a distinguished family background: a family with Roman titles and the rôle of protector. He must have been someone who by this date had proved his ability and worth. This was the officer, known later as the man with the red robe, who was moved to the north Wales army command in 398. The history of military and civilian reorganization in Britain coupled with the history of his family, or at least of those *thought* to be his successors in north Wales, reinforces the idea that he was indeed being transferred to a post which, whether it had the name or not, was in effect that of the *comes litoris Hiberniae*. The post would always have had as its *raison d'être* the aim of maintaining cohesion and efficiency in the operation of whatever land and naval forces remained in the region in order to combat Irish piracy. Such a job may have been part of his responsibilities earlier when operating in the north in conjunction with the commanders of the relief expeditions of 396/7 and 398.

CUNEDDA: MIGRATIONS AND OBFUSCATIONS

It should be clear by now that what is being proposed involves considerable speculation. We are, in fact, moving into an area of real controversy and into a period of history considered so impenetrable that some would claim that there is little or nothing that can be said about it. This is how one scholar recently presented the issue:

Certainly by the early ninth century, the royal line of
Gwynedd saw itself as descended from a north
British hero, and owing its position to right of conquest.
Cunedda [grandson of Paternus] has attracted
scholarly debate, and there is no consensus of opinion
on his historicity.

The ancestry given to him in the pedigrees hints at a
Roman background (or at a belief in such a background
by the time the pedigrees were composed). He is said
to have been a grandson of Padarn *Peisrud* (of the
Red Robe), a name which may reflect Latin *Paternus*.
On the basis of this, it has been suggested that he
was the descendant of some Roman or sub-Roman
official, perhaps in the vicinity of Hadrian's Wall.

More elaborately, it has been suggested that his
migration to Gwynedd was part of a deliberate policy
imposed by a pan-British overlord, perhaps Maximus
or Vortigern, or even Coel Hen the Old King Cole of
the nursery rhyme.

More cautious historians have stressed the
retrospective nature of the pedigrees and its
susceptibility to manipulation by later dynastic need.
It would be unwise to place too much emphasis on
Cunedda's putative Roman ancestry or upon theories
associating him with some sub-Roman British empire ...
he may be no more than a dynastic fiction.[1]

Wendy Davies, now Emeritus Professor of History at
University College London, wrote in similar vein some
years earlier.

Welsh tradition as recorded in the early ninth century
in the *Historia Brittonum* [Nennius] remembered and
honoured ... the movement of North Britons – from
the eastern Lowlands of Scotland – led by Cunedda of
the Votadini.

A great king, Maelgwn, ruled among the Britons, that
is in the district of Guenedota [Gwynedd], because
his great great great grandfather, Cunedag, had come

1_ Maund, 2000, p. 28.

previously from the North with his sons, of whom the number was eight, from the district called Manau Guotodin, one hundred and forty six years before Maelgwn reigned, and expelled the Scots (that is the Irish) with immense slaughter from those districts; and they never returned again to inhabit them [Nennius, *Historia Brittonum*, Ch. 62].

Contemporary and later historians believed that Cunedda was the ancestor of the principal royal lines of north-west Wales and thereby attributed to him a significant part of the establishment of the post-Roman framework ... Influenced by the historical perspective of the ninth and tenth centuries, modern commentators have sought to give substance to the tradition by supposing some planned movement of the Votadini, at the direction either of the late Roman government or of some successor British government, in order to meet the Irish problem.

Irish immigration certainly does not appear to have been as dense in the North-West as it was in the South-West and close contacts between the Britons of north Britain and those of Wales are suggested by the preservation of northern traditions in a Welsh cultural milieu – much of the corpus of Old Welsh poetry mourns or celebrates the lost heroes of the North.

The movement, however, entirely lacks contemporary notice and its circumstances are quite beyond reconstruction. It *could* have happened, but we cannot be sure that it did and the nature of the record casts severe doubts on its historicity.[2]

As we have seen, dating and other evidence, as well as guesswork, indicate that it was Paternus rather than his descendant or successor Cunedda who was moved. Also, one cannot help but wonder how much early history we would have if we had to reject everything that *could* have happened but about which doubt exists.

What is striking about these two summaries of the situation is not so much the dismissal of the story, as the cautious way in which this is expressed. It was rather

2_ Davies, 1982, p. 89.

different in the first heady days of deconstruction based, as it largely was, on a narrow study of texts and their transmission: a work very much associated for this period with David Dumville. In June 1977 he produced his article *Sub-Roman Britain: history and legend.*

[One] main idea, in early Welsh scholarship, about sub-Roman Britain is closely connected to the story of Maximus. It seeks to explain and justify the creation of the kingdoms of north and west Wales. This is, of course, the story of Cunedda.

Cunedda is said by sources of the *ninth* century, and later, to have been ruler of the area known as Manaw of (the) Gododdin ... [and] is said to have come with eight of his nine sons, from the North to Wales from which he expelled the Irish who had settled there ...

A great deal of time and energy has been wasted in attempts to establish where within the period 350–450 this alleged movement – it has been called a migration – can be fitted ...

[Mrs Nora Chadwick in 1958] pointed out that this story represents a typical piece of Celtic antiquarian lore, an origin-legend, a genre especially well known to students of Irish literature and historiography. Its function is a political, as well as an antiquarian one ... After 826, also, it presented a welcome parallel no doubt much cultivated by the Second Dynasty of Gwynedd [that of Merfyn *Frych*, The Freckled, grandson of Cynan of Gwynedd, 798–816, who came to power in Gwynedd in 825 having spent his childhood in the Isle of Man], of an outside dynasty coming to power in Gwynedd. Finally, it explains too how the sub-kingdoms of greater Gwynedd came into existence, by making the head of each of the pedigrees – be these figures legendary or historical – one of Cunedda's sons.[3]

Dr Dumville noted how the 146 years preceding the accession of Maelgwn Gwynedd, at the time of Nennius thought to be in 534, given in that text as the time of this migration, brings us to none other than the year of

3_ Dumville, 1977, pp. 181–2.

Maximus's death, 388. He also highlighted the unlikely confusion in Nennius between *atavus*, the fifth ancestor, mentioned there, and the tenth-century pedigrees that show Cunedda to have been the third ancestor, that is, the great-grandfather, or *proavus*, of Maelgwn. Clearly, he claimed, the whole story is a fabrication.

What is clear and important is that the perfectly incredible modern constructs of migrations from Manaw to Gwynedd organized by Maximus or Stilicho, Aetius or Vortigern, or some other pan-British representative of Roman imperial power, must be firmly rejected.[4]

One point should be made immediately before returning to these problems later. Professor Dumville, as he now is, approached and approaches these issues above all with the concerns of palaeography, the study of ancient writings and inscriptions and their transmission, and of philology, the science of language, uppermost in his reasoning. But there are other equally valid ways of looking at this material. What one finds when these problems are placed in a wider historical context is that they can appear in a very different light. Professor A. T. Q. Stewart recently underlined the great problems that have arisen as the study of the past has fallen into the hands of such narrow and highly technical specialisms. He was writing about early Irish history, but early British history has suffered the same fate.

Few, if any, historians were then competent to follow the linguists into the labyrinthine recesses of their specialism. To a large degree the determination of certain questions came to depend on the nuance of language ...
While the contribution of the philologists has been considerable, their approach and working methods have been different from the historians or the archaeologists. Like the former, but to an even greater degree, they are restricted in their investigation of a remote past by the essentially literary nature of their evidence. However, Celtic scholars and historians worked for a long time in

4_ Ibid., p. 183.

isolation from each other [and the situation has still not radically changed], and when their efforts were compared it was found that they had been travelling on roads which did not converge.[5]

In 1968, Francis John Byrne, Professor of Early Irish History at University College Dublin since 1964, wrote an article entitled 'Ireland before the Norman Invasion' prior to the appearance in 1973 of his monumental *Irish Kings and High Kings.* There, Byrne noted the same problem and Professor Stewart, using Byrne's words, makes the same appeal.

Byrne then turned to the language problem, the chief reason why Celtic scholars and historians have worked in isolation from each other. 'Since the historians are not bold enough to challenge the pretensions of the philologists, early Irish history was relegated to the realm of philology', and given 'the curious forms of academic apartheid', the paths of the investigations were bound to diverge further.

From all this Byrne concluded that in 'the difficult terrain of Irish proto-history, the linguist, the archaeologist and the historian must advance cautiously, and as a team, to work out possible or plausible correlations of significant phenomena'. This is easier said than done, however, since no one can hope to master all the disciplines involved, 'all of which are growing in complexity and specialisation, and each of which has attracted a circle of satellite auxiliary sciences'.

Moreover, the individualistic temperament of Irish scholars does not help. Teamwork is even less congenial to them than to academics generally.[6]

Proto-history is very early history, virtually pre-history, where most of what we have concerning it dates from many centuries later. These, often our earliest extant records, would have been a mixture of oral traditions still current, and texts known then but now lost to us. They *could* have all been made up, but we cannot

5_ Stewart, 2001, p. 51.

6_ Ibid., pp. 52–3.

assume this, and such a view does seem to smack of an appallingly condescending attitude towards the past and our forebears. It is an attitude unfortunately far too common today.

The avowedly nationalist politician and historian Gwynfor Evans followed the old view concerning Cunedda. These events *did* occur and marked the birth of a Wales which would endure to the present day, a 'Wales [that] was a nation more than a thousand years before Great Britain came into existence'.[7]

The story of the liberation of the people of the land that would become Cymru (Wales) is an extraordinary one. It involved a Roman emperor who was born and bred in Celtic Galicia. Before he left the shores of Britain in A.D. 383 with a battle standard bearing a dragon at the head of his troops, after being proclaimed Roman emperor by his troops, Magnus Maximus transferred responsibility for the defence and government of Wales to leading families in the infrastructure created during the Roman occupation. These families became royal houses which ruled the canton-sized states ...

Irish colonists had been allowed to settle in Wales during the later years of the Roman occupation, particularly in the south and north west, but according to Nennius who wrote about A.D. 800 they came in great numbers after the departure of the Romans.

In consequence Brittonic-speaking Cunedda came with his eight sons from near Stirling in Scotland to expel them from the northern part of Wales. In this way a Celt from Scotland ensured that Wales would be a Welsh speaking, not an Irish speaking land. According to tradition Cunedda founded the royal line which would rule Gwynedd for seven [?nine] centuries.[8]

7_ Evans, 2000, p. 17.

8_ Ibid., pp. 13–14. Much of what Gwynfor Evans wrote on this very early period needs to be altered, and the development of which he was talking involves Paternus not Cunedda, thus giving a period closer to nine centuries for the history of which he was so rightly proud.

SIGNIFICANCE OF THE 398 BATTLE AS SEEN IN MILAN

There is nothing inherently implausible in Paternus, Padarn ap Tegid of the Votadini, finding himself being ordered south to take up a new and even more prestigious command in an area extending from Chester in the east to *Segontium* and Holyhead in the west and probably from the Wall down to the Dyfi. Despatches from Britain telling of the exploits of the 398 relief expedition in the Pictish war, and of the battle of the Forest which had brought it to a conclusion and made Paternus's move possible, could have easily reached Milan by early January 399. A little later, in the spring, Claudian recited Book I of *In Eutropium*, Against Eutropius: 'a savage, hysterical flood of invective more eloquent than anything since Juvenal'.[9] In this attack on the eastern empire's eunuch chamberlain, Claudian contrasted that eastern abomination with his own patron, Stilicho, and inevitably, therefore, with Stilicho's son-in-law, the emperor Honorius. Rome's goddess is seen as towering over the young emperor.

Examples near at hand testify to the extent of my power now thou art emperor.
   The Saxon is conquered and the seas safe; the Picts have been defeated and Britain is secure.
   I love to see at my feet the humbled Franks and broken Suebi, and I behold the Rhine mine own, Germanicus.[10]

In Book II, recited in September 399, we find a dramatic passage in which Britain is envisaged as one of the dioceses of the empire coming to Rome to urge its goddess in her temple on the Palatine to ensure that Stilicho was made consul.

Next spake Britain clothed in the skin of some Caledonian beast, her cheeks tattooed and an azure cloak, rivalling the swell of ocean, sweeping to her feet:

9_ Cameron, 1970, p. 127.

10_ Claudian, *Against Eutropius*, Book I, Platnauer, 1922, Vol. 1, p. 169. Germanicus is Honorius.

"Stilicho gave aid to me also when at the mercy of neighbouring tribes, what time the Scots roused all Hibernia against me and the sea foamed to the beat of hostile oars.

Thanks to his care I had no need to fear the Scottish arms or tremble at the Pict, or keep watch along all my coasts for the Saxon who would come whatever wind might blow."[11]

Book III of this work, in effect a separate poem and recited probably as late as March 400, contains the justly famous eulogy of Rome.

'Tis she alone who has received the conquered into her bosom and like a mother, not an empress, protected the human race with a common name, summoning those who she has defeated to share her citizenship and drawing together distant races with bonds of affection. To her rule of peace we owe it that the world is our home ...[12]

THE IRISH SEA PROBLEM

The movement to the west of Britain in 398 of someone who probably had considerable experience in the co-ordination of both land and sea forces was, in itself, of no great moment or account. As the number of experienced officers decreased, such transfers from one area to another must have been common. Defence needs on the west coast would have been acute at this time and, as has been noted already, it would have been well beyond the diocese's resources to move into Ireland to deal with the invaders at source. The Irish Sea was proving an enormous obstacle to peace, not least because, unlike the situation across the land frontier in northern Britain, it made the detection of coming raids extremely difficult. For some time this problem had been lessened by use of squadrons of scouting vessels, but one suspects that by this date, with the withdrawal of the bulk of the

11_ Claudian, *Against Eutropius*, Book II, recited in Milan, Platnauer, 1922, Vol. 2, p. 21.

12_ Claudian, *Against Eutropius*, Book III, Platnauer, 1922, pp. 53–5.

Rome. The temple
of Saturn.

Top: Rome. The arch
of Titus.

Bottom: Britain.
Segontium, part of the
west wall.

fleet to continental duties, the numbers of these would have been considerably reduced.

UNRAVELLING NENNIUS

If Paternus's rôle was one of *comes*, exercising the ultimate military authority in the north Wales region, then his authority overrode that of the individual garrison commanders and extended to whatever units of the British fleet were still operating in the Irish Sea – probably no more than a small flotilla of scouting vessels. Hence his later epithet, *peisrudd*, Of the Red Robe, or just Red Robe. As we have been told, the story of the foundation of the kingdom of Gwynedd is enshrined in a passage found in the ninth-century *History of the Britons*, the collection attributed to Nennius.

Mailcunus the great king was reigning among the Britons, that is in the region of Guenedota [Gwynedd] because his *atavus*, that is Cunedag with his sons, whose number was eight, had come previously from the northern part, that is from the region which is called Manau Guotodin, one hundred and forty six years before Mailcun reigned. And they drove out with immense slaughter the Scots from those regions who never returned again to inhabit them.[13]

The older view, and one still attacked, is based on taking this Nennius passage at face value, accepting that it was Cunedda, Paternus's grandson, who moved from the north to Wales, and that he came accompanied, not only by his eight sons, but also, given what he was supposed to have achieved in Wales, by a large section of the Votadini. Instead of a mere transfer from one command post to another, the picture conjured up and then gleefully attacked is one of wholesale migration. But as far back as the 1970s, an interesting suggestion was made which helps to unravel the development of the story and takes away some of its more unlikely aspects.

[13]_ Nennius, *Historia Brittonum*, Ch. 62, Wade-Evans, 1938.

Dr Molly Miller suggested that the text as we have it has been clumsily altered from the original, compressing what were in fact descriptions of *two* stages in the history.[14] Rather than correcting the text, a separating out of the two strands makes the account perfectly intelligible. The writer of the Nennius text was at this point talking of the kings of the Anglian Bernicians, in particular of the time when Ida became their king in *c.*547. On one reading of the evidence, Ida of Bernicia ruled *c.*547–59. The two parts of the account are indicated by numbering them and by the use of italics for the second.

1

i Mailcunus [Maelgwn] the great king [of Gwynedd c.517–45/9] was reigning among the Britons [in c.547 when Ida came to power], that is in the region of Guenedota [Gwynedd], because his *atavus* [his grandfather's great-grandfather Paternus],

2

i [deleting – *that is*] Cunedag [Cunedda] *with his sons, whose number was eight*

1

ii [Paternus, following on from 1 i] had come previously from the northern part, that is from the region which is called Manau Guotodin [Manau of Gododdin], one hundred and forty six years before Mailcun reigned [*or was reigning in c.547*].

2

ii and [deleting – *they* – Cunedda and his sons] *drove out with immense slaughter the Scots* [that is, the Irish] *from those regions, who never returned again to inhabit them.*[15]

This reworking of the passage is demanded because Maelgwn's *atavus*, that is, his grandfather's great-grandfather, was not, as the text states, Cunedda, who

[14] Miller, 1976/8, p. 529.

[15] Nennius, *Historia Brittonum*, Ch. 62, Wade-Evans, 1938, p. 80: the rearrangement, although not including the reference to 146 years possibly connected with Ida, in Miller, 1976/8, p. 529 and note 4.

was his *proavus* or great-grandfather, but Paternus, who was Cunedda's grandfather. Continuing the rearrangement of the text beyond what was originally suggested, the 'one hundred and forty six years before Mailcun reigned' could, in terms of the text itself, refer to the time Ida came to power in *c.*547 and so the text would be saying 'one hundred and forty-six years before Maelgwn reigned around the time Ida came to power in *c.*547'. This would mean that a year around 401 is intended, and even here there is some leeway because we cannot know what particular year the writer had in mind for Ida's accession.[16] Therefore, the text can be interpreted as pointing to 398–401 as the period of Paternus's move to north Wales.

Leaving aside all the explanatory detail, the passage thus re-ordered would seem to be saying something *very* different from what is nowadays usually attacked as being downright fanciful or, to use David Dumville's word, incredible.

Maelgwn the great king was reigning among the Britons, that is in the region of Gwynedd, because his grandfather's great-grandfather, that is, Paternus, had come previously from the northern part, that is from the region which is called the Plain of the Gododdin, one hundred and forty six years before Maelgwn reigned which was around the time Ida came to power in *c.*547; in other words, in the period 398–401.

And Cunedda, Paternus's grandson, with his sons, whose number was eight, drove out with immense slaughter the Scots, that is, the Irish, from those regions, who never returned again to inhabit them.

[16]_ Cf. Dumville, 1977, who noted that 146 years before the accession of Maelgwn *Gwynedd*, which at the time was thought to be in 534, brings us back to 388, the year Maximus was executed.

It might be helpful to set out the likely early part of the king list for Gwynedd starting with Paternus.

1	Paternus son of Tacitus Peisrudd Red Robe	c.398–410
2	Eternus possibly son of Paternus	c.410–428
3	NN son of Eternus Cunedda The Good King	c.428–450
4	Anianus/Einion or NN son of Cunedda Einiawn/Einion The Anvil	c.450–485
5	Eugenius/Owain supposedly son of Anianus/Einion Danwyn Whitetooth	c.485–490
6	Cadwallon brother of Eugenius/Owain Llawhir Longhanded or Generous	c.490–517
7	Maelgwn ap Cadwallon Hir The Tall and Gwynedd Of Gwynedd	c.517–545

If the dates for these commanders or early rulers are anywhere near correct, then it might be that when the leaders of the northern Votadini were chosen for elevation to positions within the hierarchy of Britain's imperial government, the original appointment was not of Paternus, but of his father Tegid or Tacitus, or even of *his* father, Iago. Paternus must have been in the army, and his move to north Wales may have had little to do with his family's work, though the fact that he came from such a distinguished background must have played a part in his rise through the ranks. More important would have been his record as a commander. Of course, given Paternus's position in north Wales, later writers saw him as the ancestor of the future kings of Gwynedd, and so genealogists gave them a prestigious pedigree which, in one case at least, traced the line back to Saint Anne, cousin of the Mother of God.

Carannog son of Ceredig son of Cunedda son of Edern son of Patern Pes Rudauc [Paternus of the Red Robe] son of Tacit son of Kein [in other versions son of Iago] son of Guorchen son of Doli son of Gurdol son of Domn son of Guordumn son of Amguoloid son of Amguerit son of Omnid son of Dobunn son of Britguenin son of Eugen son of Aballach son of Canalech son of Beli and Anna his mother whom they say was cousin to the Virgin Mary.[17]

CHAPTER THREE

HARDER THAN BONE TOWARDS THE ENEMY
Eternus and the Good King Cunedda, 410–450

GWYNEDD – THE INHERITANCE PROBLEM

It might well be that Paternus's position as *comes* made the eventual establishment of the Gwynedd dynasty much easier than would have been the case in other areas where devolvement of authority over more limited functions, such as highway patrol and maintenance, would have given far less power. It may also be that Gwynedd's later history as the most expansionist and dynamic of the states to emerge in western Britain following the end of direct Roman control owed much to this same exalted position of Paternus and his successors' awareness of these considerable origins.

If Paternus was the father of Eternus and the grandfather of Cunedda as the pedigrees claim, in other words, if there was this continuity, then it might be that his rôle was considered sufficiently important to leave him and his family to get on with the work of dealing with the Irish attacks at a time when many in the rest of the diocese were dragged into the turmoil surrounding the elevation of three more usurpers. On the face of it, this seems unlikely. For such a situation to have developed so quickly would imply

17_ *The Life of Carannog*, the second life, Wade-Evans, 1944, pp. 143 and 149.

that the military authorities in Britain were not only lax but also negligent during the years following his initial deployment.

Nevertheless, the years after 406 were extremely difficult ones for the diocese. There could, therefore, be a context for Paternus being in the position to hand on his title to his own son, assuming that Eternus had served his time in the army, which is more than probable. The usurpers who caused this crisis in Britain's affairs were Marcus, Gratian, and Constantine III. Like Maximus before him, Constantine, who was proclaimed in about February 407, took to the Continent a sizeable proportion of the already greatly reduced British garrison. For a brief period in 409, he was even accepted as co-emperor by Honorius, just as Maximus had been by Theodosius, but it was all over by 411. The year before, having ejected Constantine's administrators, the members of the diocesan council in Britain, consisting for the most part of representatives from the cities, were no doubt dumbfounded to be rewarded with the announcement that Britain was now on its own: in effect it was independent of the empire. Such events must have come near the end of Paternus's period or early in that of his successor, Eternus. At this point, and in an area as remote as north Wales, the control exercised by what remained of the military hierarchy may have been negligible. If so, provided this command continued to report successes against Irish attackers, it was probably sensible to let it get on with the job. Such isolation must have thrown these commanders closer to those they were entrusted to defend, and one might guess that intermarriage with the local aristocracy began to place a control initially sanctioned by the Roman diocese on a somewhat different and more local basis.

If Eternus, Paternus's successor, ruled from about 410 to 428, to be succeeded then by Cunedda, they were to live through yet more dramatic events for the diocese.[1] Increasing attacks on Britain by the Picts and their Irish allies led to appeals to Gaul, Ravenna, and Rome, and then to the army's move which culminated in Vortigern's dictatorship. Vortigern was the man's epithet; we do not know his name. It would seem that the failure of these appeals, coupled with the limited military resources available, enabled Vortigern to press home the gravity of the crisis facing Britain and in this way to take total control of the diocese in what was effectively an army coup. This was a return to the position in Britain between 43 and 197/207. It was only by taking what in effect were emergency powers that any revival in the diocese's fortunes could be hoped for. There would have been, had to have been, a massive recruitment drive to bring Britain's fighting force up to something that could at least contemplate the long struggle ahead. North Wales and the Hadrian's Wall line were more fortunate than the rest of the country, having garrison troops surviving from the days before Constantine III, but they also faced the greatest threat, and now for north Wales this threat was to become acute.

With rumours of further Pictish and Irish incursions, Vortigern, the Great Leader, commander-in chief and dictator, invited in a small force of Saxons as mercenaries to help in Britain's fight, and if necessary to repel their compatriots. There was nothing new in this. Saxon forces had probably been employed for centuries in this area known as the Saxon Shore. Indeed, it may be that part of the aim was to mobilize the resident Saxon population on the east coast under these mercenaries. What *was* new was a British government acting independently in this way. The problem for Vortigern was that by this date the employment of outsiders, barbarians, was universally seen as the root of the problems now bringing the western empire to its knees.

[1]_ Estimates and guesses as to the likely dates of such rulers during this period are extremely difficult. See for example, Miller, 1975/6, pp. 96–109, 1976/8, and *Pictish King Lists*, 1979.

Despite this, as tradition has it, Hengest and Horsa and their men now entered British history. More came in around 438. They operated to defend the east coast not only from other Saxons but also from seaborne Pictish attack. It looks as though they were also used to reinforce the garrisons on Hadrian's Wall.

THE THREATENED INVASION OF BRITAIN

Rumours now started to come in of an imminent Pictish invasion, this time on a massive scale and planned, as usual, in conjunction with Irish allies. As Dr John Morris pointed out in the 1970s, who are meant by Picts is open to question. Later Welsh tradition, seen in the Jesus College MS 20 pedigrees, called the Irish living in Powys *Gwyddyl Ffichti*, Irish Picts.[2] All the sources, both Roman, and British of a later date, link the *Scotti* and *Picti* together in these years. Certainly, we can discount the involvement of Saxons in the northeast region of Wales in *c.*429, even if some variants of the story refer to these. Almost certainly they would have been Irish. Memorial inscriptions show Irish settlers in the region of Clocaenog just to the southwest of the Clwyds in the period 470–97 and earlier, in the period from 383, in northern Powys. It seems clear that the main players in the events of 429 were the Picts and the Irish: allies who had been fighting alongside each other from the earliest days of Roman Britain.

The aim of the invaders, so it was being said, was to move into the Midland Gap between the Pennines and the Welsh hills, not just to take plunder, but to settle. If such a plan involving the control of the Midland Gap was successful, the rest of the lowland south and east would have been open to attack. This information must have been passed to London by the *praesides* of *Valentia* and *Britannia Secunda*, and the *comes* on the north Wales coast, the *comes litoris Hiberniae*. They in turn must have had this news from agents, spies, and traders who possibly observed unusual shipping activity.

2_ Jesus College MS 20, late fourteenth century but based on a pre-1200 source, Bartrum, 1966, p. 47, No. 23. Morris, 1973, p. 64, note.

Perhaps Vortigern was hearing other reports from the north Wales *comes* of worries concerning an Irish immigrant group already settled in north Wales, in the area of the Clwyd Hills just to the west of the former legionary base at Chester. Even here it has to be admitted that the idea that Benlli, the leader of this gang, was Irish hangs by mere threads. The only historian, ancient or modern, who emphatically insisted on this was Dr John Morris in his 1973 book *The Age of Arthur*. Benlli does not even appear in Gildas and in the other sources is never described as Irish. The story as we have it would, however, make a great deal more sense if the invaders who now arrived were attempting to link up with Benlli's army in the Clwyds.

It is probable that the group commanded or ruled by Benlli had been given authority back in the days of Magnus Maximus in the 380s to maintain, patrol, and, if necessary, defend the road system linking Holyhead and *Segontium*, Caernarfon, with Chester and the southeastern lowlands as it passed through the Clwyd Hills. Instead of guarding that area, Benlli had apparently been terrorizing the inhabitants. In the Nennius *Life of St Germanus* he is described as 'unjust and very tyrannical', 'the tyrant most vile'. The story had it that if his servants were not in the citadel before sunrise, they were killed: in other words, executed for being late for work. What happened next indicates that Benlli was suspected of being in contact with his Irish compatriots at home, and through these with the Picts. The *comes* who had responsibility for this area would have been weighing up the pros and cons of dealing with the problem, all the while passing on information to Vortigern and the high command in London. And it looks as though by this date the *comes* was Eternus's son nicknamed *Cunedda*, who may have wielded power in north Wales between about 428 and 450.

Perhaps a policy was being adopted of holding back in order to watch what was going on. In this way, preparations could be made so that once the invaders made their move they could be surprised and, with luck, annihilated. Waiting for the opportunity of a decisive encounter was a constant feature of army strategy. As Britain's armed forces were hopelessly overstretched, this tactic would have had much to recommend it. It is also possible that Vortigern was already beginning to envisage a plan involving the creation of two new provinces for the diocese which would run down the whole length of what we call the Welsh marches. The first, in the north, would include not only Chester but also the area of Benlli's activities in the Clwyd Hills. Certainly, Benlli would have to go. The province would also embrace Benlli's compatriots further south who, in contrast, had been operating well in their job of protecting the roads to the west of Wroxeter. Provided they proved their loyalty in this testing period, they could continue with their work.

CONSTRUCTS: FACT, OPINION, AND JUDGEMENT

We have so few pieces of evidence for the fourth and fifth centuries that this guesswork is inevitable *if*, that is, we still want to continue with the struggle to gain a glimpse of what possibly did happen. We constantly have to remind ourselves about the tentative nature of our conclusions, but we do have scraps of evidence and perhaps more bits and pieces than some realize. History *did* happen, and the attempt to recover it *is* worthwhile. Dr John Morris, of University College London, was convinced of this, even if his attempt to write about these years was derided in some quarters precisely for the reason given above.

He [the historian] has to sum up like a judge, and decide like a jury. He may not blankly refuse to decide, but he cannot proclaim certainty. He must give an informed opinion on what is probable and improbable, and return an open verdict when the balance of evidence suggests no probability. He may not insinuate like an advocate [today a philologist or an archaeologist], whose plea that evidence falls short of absolute proof covertly invites his hearers to disbelieve the evidence.[3]

THE GERMANUS PROBLEM

Our source for these *c.*429 events unfolding in north Wales is Constantius's *Vita Germani*, The Life of Saint Germanus: a source put together for a specific purpose and one to be treated with the greatest caution. It was the failure of the *c.*426 appeals to the military commander in Gaul, Aëtius, to the imperial government, and to the church, that had brought Vortigern to power in Britain. However, one somewhat delayed result was that in *c.*429, the Gaulish bishops Germanus and Lupus were in the country on a fact-finding expedition and, the *Vita* says, they accompanied the army to the front. Bede follows Constantius's account almost verbatim. The problem is that the *Life of St Germanus* is obsessed with trumpeting the saintliness of the man and exalting his rôle as the Catholic champion against Pelagianism, a heresy that was rife in Britain at the time and one possibly energizing many to confront the country's difficulties. So we are told that the Britons had 'besought the help of the holy bishops' and assembled an army. Constantius's *Vita Germani* was also concerned to diminish, if not totally wipe from the record, Vortigern's rôle. This was because Vortigern was a heretic, a Pelagian.

Pelagianism defied Augustine and the rest to reject much of the church's teaching about sin and humankind's inability to save itself other than through God's grace. Man, so these heretics proclaimed, was not born in original sin, and was in charge of his own destiny. He had to act and be judged by his actions. For many, this was a form of moral rearmament; for the church, it struck at the heart of Christian teaching. For Catholics, these ideas had to be confronted and

3_ Morris, 1973, Introduction, p. xv.

79

repudiated by whatever means. If this meant what we would call falsifying the record, such an approach was justified by a higher cause and by God himself. Vortigern was inevitably the object of attack because his position made him the leading representative of this anti-Catholic stance. As a result, he and perhaps others were erased from the description of this western campaign to be replaced, inevitably, by Germanus himself. Man was weak, God and his church infinitely stronger, as was now to be demonstrated. Some have accepted the possibility of Germanus's military rôle, although our scanty evidence for this bishop indicates a secular education followed by imperial administration in Gaul before he entered the religious life. He was eventually appointed bishop in his home town of Auxerre. Germanus and Lupus *may* have accompanied the Great Leader to north Wales. The restructuring of local government possibly already being planned by Vortigern, including the setting up of his son over this north Wales region, would probably have involved changes in church organization, but the rest is extremely suspicious.

In fact, the description of this campaign given in Constantius and followed by Bede looks to have been for the most part a fabrication, using little pieces of a history that must have happened to give it the appearance of truth, the impression that it was a factual record. The person in charge, who had the troops and who was *in situ* ready to act was not in fact Vortigern but Cunedda. We know that troops were stationed in Holyhead, Caernarfon, and probably in Caerhun on the river Conwy into the fifth century. We can also assume that the lookout signalling system that for centuries had been a key part of Britain's defences was also functioning, even if at some reduced efficiency. This extended from the Wall forts and their Cumbrian-shore outposts right round to Holyhead. When the ship force of Picts and Irish neared its destination, and they must have come by sea, it would have been spotted by these lookouts. Even Constantius's *Life of St Germanus* says 'their approach was observed by British scouts'.[4] Possibly news of its setting

4_ Bede, *Ecclesiastical History*, Book I, Ch. 20, Colgrave and Mynors, 1969, p. 63.

out from whatever the port of embarkation had already been passed to the north Wales command.

INVASION PART I: RECONNAISSANCE IN FORCE

Very quickly it would have been realized that this was *not* the rumoured invasion but, instead, something like a reconnaissance in force. All that we are told would fit this. It was most certainly *not* an invasion large enough to take over northwestern Britain. On his side, we know Vortigern was short of troops simply because Britain was short of troops. Before the ships appeared what was he to do? Gather an army, march to the northwest, and simply wait? But Cunedda was there and ready, and probably more than equal to the task. We need not, however, follow Germanus's biographer Constantius and dismiss any idea of Vortigern's involvement. We have seen that this interfering with the record was all to do with church politics and the battle against heresy. It was not just ignorance. From the Germanus story itself, the genealogical evidence, and the inscription on the Pillar of Eliseg that we will look at later, it seems clear that Vortigern must have been on hand at one stage or another to organize and inaugurate the new provincial arrangements and oversee the installation of his son as *praeses*.

THE HISTORICAL PRECEDENT

To call the fleet now approaching the northwest coast of Britain a reconnaissance force is to suggest something about its size. To repeat, this was not the mass incursion people had been talking and worrying about: this could not be compared to events in 376 when virtually the entire nation of the Visigoths crossed the Danube. Nevertheless, something like this *was* feared, and rumours to this effect were widespread. That single event in 376, more than any other, had changed the empire for ever, and the educated élite in Britain just as elsewhere would have been acutely aware of the fact.

THE FRONT LINE – THE *COMES LITORIS HIBERNIAE*

But was it simply for reconnaissance that the Picts were coming? Roman armies used this tactic repeatedly when exploring new territory. Later, Viking campaigns reveal a complete commitment to this method of penetrating areas they hoped to exploit, initially sending in smaller forces to assess the routes to be used, the likely targets, the most vulnerable parts, and the threats to be avoided. The Picts had been invading British territory since the start of the Roman conquest. By this date, their leaders would have been very familiar with the troop dispositions, garrisons, roads, and the most vulnerable parts in the British diocese. Against this is the consideration that probably few Pictish expeditions had reached this far south. If a wholesale immigration was being contemplated, much would certainly have to be ascertained before the move took place. On the other hand, if we are right in seeing direct involvement by Benlli and his army, big or small, in the Clwyds, then the Picts with their Irish allies would have had all the up-to-date information they required. From him they would have already been aware that any move into the Midland Gap would first have to confront the only major Roman military presence in the area. This was our no-name *Cunedda* and his field army. With him out of the way and his forces decimated, the task of settlement would be vastly more manageable. It looks then as though Cunedda and the military power he headed was the likely target of this incursion in 429.

The 376 Danube crossing teaches us something else about what the Picts and Irish intended. That move into the empire had been threatened for some time, but it was finally agreed to by the eastern emperor Valens apparently after it had already begun. The area the refugees had decided on was *Thracia*, Thrace, today Bulgaria. In Britain, and here we are talking of settlement on very much more limited scale than in Thrace, the hope would have been that once in, agreements could be reached with the government whereby they would be accepted as legal immigrants. After all, there could be benefits for the host community. Valens had been persuaded that he was being presented with a unique opportunity, not only to expand his army to a size where it would be wellnigh invincible, but also greatly to increase his wealth because of the fall in the number of troops needing to be hired. In Britain, immigration on the east coast into the area known as the Saxon Shore had no doubt proved the same. But first, the Picts and the Irish had to establish a presence, a bargaining counter that could not be ignored. And again, to do this they had to eliminate the man whose job it was to keep them out, namely Cunedda.

CATHOLIC PROPAGANDA

Placing developments in Britain in the context of these recent and, as some would now have seen them, cataclysmic events on the Continent, explains the sense of impending crisis. It also provides the context for Constantius's eagerness to seize on this as a way of demonstrating the power of the church and the importance of Germanus. The likelihood is that when messages reached Vortigern that the invading fleet was on its way, he gathered a small body of élite troops, almost certainly cavalry, and made a dash for the Dee and the forces led by Cunedda. He could easily have been on other business nearer to the area precisely in order to be able to move quickly.

In Constantius, however, the story is very different.

Fearing they were no match for their foes, they [the Britons] besought the help of the holy bishops [Germanus of Auxerre and Lupus of Troyes]. These came at once to fulfil their promise and inspired such confidence in the timid people that one would have thought that a large army had come to their support. Indeed, with such apostolic leaders, it was Christ Himself who fought in their camp.[5]

The implication, of course, as Constantius could have added, is that it was these Catholics and not just the Pelagian-inspired few thinking boldly and acting bravely who were about to have the victory. In other words, this extract is not only libellous, a flat contradiction of what probably occurred, it was also a direct anti-Pelagian statement.

We are told that it was Lent and that, instructed by the bishops' teaching, many flocked to receive the grace of baptism: another stab at the Pelagian stand, for grace bestowed by baptism is God-given and owes nothing to man's efforts.

Vast numbers of the army were baptized. A church of wattle was built in preparation for Easter Day and set up for the army in the field as though it were in a city. So, still soaked in the waters of baptism, the army set out. The people's faith was fervent and putting no trust in their arms, they expectantly awaited the help of God.[6]

Constantius, followed by Bede, might just as well have said, putting no trust in themselves, because by this point the anti-Pelagian attacks have become repetitive.

This Catholic propaganda is most obvious in the part of the story dealing with the destruction of Benlli's fortress. Here, the fundamental doctrine of the Trinity, which Constantius and the rest saw as the church's answer to the Pelagians, is spelled out. Germanus, rather than the Roman army, was supposedly responsible for bringing down fire from heaven on the iniquitous tyrant and his citadel, but on the day before this happened the bishop, having risen early to wait outside the gate of the fort, saw someone running towards him clearly late for work.

5_ Ibid.

6_ Ibid.

84

And his sweat was dripping from his crown to the soles
of his feet. He prostrated himself before them, and Saint
Germanus said, "Believest thou in the Holy Trinity?" and
he replied, "I believe." And he was baptized, and he
kissed him, and said to him, "Go in peace, this very hour
thou shalt die, and the angels of God await thee in the
air, that thou mayest accompany them to the God, whom
thou hast believed." And joyfully he entered into the
citadel and the prefect took him and bound him. And
being led before the tyrant, he was killed, because it was
a custom with the tyrant most vile, that, unless anyone
had arrived before sunrise for service in the citadel, he
was killed.[7]

After the Easter celebrations, the Germanus story tells
how the British army confronted the Irish and Picts, on
ground specially chosen by its commander, not Vortigern
or Cunedda, but Germanus. Here, the British, apparently
outnumbered, set their trap.

So when the Easter solemnities had been celebrated and
the greater part of the army, still fresh from the font, were
beginning to take up arms and prepare for war,
Germanus himself offered to be their leader. He [in
Nennius the 'unanimously chosen commander' against
people wrongly identified as Saxons] picked out the
most active, and, having explored the surrounding
country, he saw a valley surrounded by hills of moderate
height lying in the direction from which the enemy was
expected to approach. In this place, he stationed his
untried army and himself took command.[8]

Emphasis on the untried troops, hopelessly outnumbered,
made the victory to be ascribed to Germanus and the
Catholic church all the more miraculous.

[7]_ Nennius, *Historia
Brittonum*, Ch. 33,
Wade-Evans, 1938,
pp. 56–7.

[8]_ Bede, *Ecclesiastical
History*, Book 1, Ch. 20,
Colgrave and Mynors,
1969, p. 63.

In the eighteenth century, a local squire and antiquarian, Nehemiah Griffith of Rhual Hall, marked what he thought might be the site of the battle near Maes Garmon, the Field of Germanus, close to Mold in Flintshire, by erecting an obelisk. The place's name, Rhual, from *Rhuddallt*, in English, Red Hill, possibly suggested this as the likely spot, especially as it is in a field known as Maes Garmon and near a church dedicated to Germanus. However, the choice might owe more to the proximity of Rhual Hall, being a way of adding distinction to the estate. Modern writers have usually accepted that the site is more probably to be looked for a few miles away in the valley of the Dee near Llangollen. Dr John Morris found a Moel-y-Geraint near here, suggesting the name of a commander who fought under Germanus, described as Geraint or Gerontius, citing 'a late poem'.[9]

Against the Dee at Llangollen is not just the fact that the surrounding hills are somewhat more than of 'moderate height', but also the question as to what the Picts and Irish were doing marching up that river. Here, certainly, the British could have launched a surprise attack. The account does say that the victory was won without a blow, although this is another detail of the Constantius/Bede account that is almost impossible to believe. Such formulas were part of the stock-in-trade of Christian writers, particularly those attacking Pelagianism. But, if fighting did occur along this part of the Dee, by the time the British force had descended to the valley floor, the enemy could have easily escaped to regroup and fight on more favourable terrain another day.

Talk of moderately-sized hills and British troops lying in wait to deliver an ambush when the enemy was moving along a valley suggests two other possibilities, both related to the ultimate objective of the invaders. It seems almost certain that there is a direct link between the landing of this reconnaissance force in north Wales

9_ Morris, 1973, pp. 62–4.

and the expulsion shortly after of Benlli *Gawr*, the giant Benlli, the 'unjust and very tyrannical' king. This second part of the story, which takes place on Foel Fenlli, a prominent hill in the Clwyd range, is found in the ninth-century collection known as Nennius. It seems to be part of an elaborated version of the *Life of St Germanus*, and this account is clear that these events took place on Germanus's first visit to Britain, if indeed he ever made a second. Therefore, Germanus was supposedly at the Alleluia Victory *and* at Benlli's fall. We have some corroborative evidence for this in the story told on the Pillar of Eliseg and in the genealogies.

It can only be a guess, but one seemingly reasonable, that the Pictish–Irish force was expecting to link up with Benlli's army, either somewhere between Benlli's bastion on Foel Fenlli and the coast where it landed, or at the Clwyd hill-fort base itself. This reconnaissance force, perhaps better described as a group of commando units, was in all probability not very large. Constantius tries to disguise this by talk of the Britons on their own 'being no match for their foes', seeking 'the help of the holy bishops', the Picts being 'sure of victory as though they were attacking an unarmed foe'. However, when the 'fierce enemy forces' were defeated, suddenly a river which, if not the Dee, even allowing for differences over time, could hardly have been a raging torrent, was sufficient to drown most of them, so that the British force 'became inactive spectators of the victory freely offered to them'. The victory was, of course, 'heaven sent'; indeed, it was won 'without the shedding of blood'. We can readily believe that the invading soldiers, having endured a voyage from the Wall area to the north Wales coast, would have been exhausted and in need of rest and recuperation. Given their numbers, the plan would almost certainly have been to link up with Benlli's army. Only their combined strength could take on Cunedda's troops, and even then it was probably envisaged that some form of subterfuge would be needed.

If the invaders were pushing from the coast to Benlli's HQ then two landing places spring to mind. One would be at a point on the river Clwyd, from which they could have moved quickly up into the Clwyd range. If they were ambushed in this attempt, then the only valley with a river, as mentioned in the Germanus account, is that of the river Clwyd's tributary, the river Wheeler, which cuts through the Clwyd range along a route now used by the A541 Mold to St Asaph road. Although at the point where the river first cuts back into the hills one side rises to Moel y Parc's 398 metres, further up the valley hills that could be thought of as moderate in height, hardly an exact description, are evident. If it was somewhere in this region that these troops were ambushed, it would imply that Cunedda had based his army somewhere further east, possibly on the eastern side of the Clwyds, where extensive views over the Dee estuary would have helped ensure that there was no surprise move from this side. The problem is that the route then to Foel Fenlli, some considerable distance further south in the range, would have been long and complicated, using valleys probably far less accessible than they are today.

The other and more likely possibility is that the invaders sailed boldly into the Dee estuary as far as present-day Flint, Connah's Quay, or even Queensferry. The higher they sailed up the estuary, the shorter the route to the hill-fort, which would also be made easier by use of the road system. Such a move would underline the probability that this invasion force was using information given by Benlli and was now guided by his men. These would have known to the last detail the position in *Deva*, Chester, the former legionary HQ, no doubt being able to report that there were no longer any troops there, and that the place, despite its reputation, was finished. Better still, as the force responsible for the upkeep and safety of the road system in the area, Benlli's men would have known of any troop movements further west. If the ship force, tired and needing rest, could reach the main road which started at Chester, they would be on the most direct route to Benlli's base at the head of the Pen Barras Pass, a road that passed through present-day Buckley and aimed straight at this Clwyd defile. They could be there in hours rather than days. If at the last moment it was realized that Cunedda *was* on the move, this might or might not mean that their plans had been discovered. It would dictate speed, even a night's march, to find this main highway.

How then the Picts and Irish found themselves in a valley facing ambush requires further ingenuity on Cunedda's part but also on our part as we try to guess. It could be that as soon as they entered the Dee, signals were sent from lookout posts to various units of Cunedda's army indicating a rendezvous for these imperial forces at some little distance from the coast. It could well be that Cunedda and his commanders, acutely aware of how the road system now made so many areas vulnerable to attack, saw exactly the route that would be taken once a landing in the Dee estuary had taken place. Knowing this they could easily have placed some threatening presence, a unit big enough to deter further advance, but not so big as to change the enemy's plans, blocking the straightforward road route. Strategically placed, this could have forced the invaders and their guides to leave the road, possibly at a point near present-day Buckley, and descend to the valley of the river Alyn, a tributary of the Dee. Somewhere here, as this valley led towards present-day Mold, the ambush was sprung. Such a scenario should place the battle at a site just *south* of Mold, as opposed to the choice of the eighteenth-century Nehemiah Griffith who plumped for a point back from the river, northwest of this small town near his own residence at Rhual Hall. To proceed so far would have taken the invaders past the route leading up to the Pen Barras Pass and their object, Benlli's court and settlement.

But this is all guesswork. If the invading force had landed lower down the Dee in the vicinity of Flint, they could have used one or other of the many trackways up from the coast used by traders and those involved in the mineral mining that took place in this area throughout the Roman period. This then opens the possibility that they moved south from the estuary virtually following the line of modern roads. If they then moved west into the valley of the Alyn north of modern Mold, they would, indeed, have been near the spot picked by Nehemiah Griffith.

BATTLE: THE LACK OF DETAIL

How Cunedda's men defeated the Pictish–Irish army is something else we know nothing about. Constantius, and later Bede, probably knew nothing of Cunedda, of a count of the Irish Shore, let alone Vortigern's strategy for saving Britain from the barbarians. Constantius would hardly have been interested. He was writing, and we are looking at, a piece of Catholic propaganda, not a history. Constantius turned to his *Bible* and found in the account of the fall of Jericho in the *Book of Joshua* a sufficient description for what took place.

And it came to pass on the seventh day, [having marched round the city of Jericho mostly in silence, apart from the blowing of horns, once a day for six days] that they [the children of Israel] rose up early about the dawning of the [seventh] day, and compassed the city after the same manner seven times. And ... at the seventh time, when the priests blew with the trumpets, Joshua said unto the people, Shout; for the Lord hath given you the city ... So the people shouted when the priests blew with the trumpets: and it came to pass, when the people heard the sound of the trumpet, and the people shouted with a great shout, that the wall fell down flat, so that the people went up into the city, every man straight before him, and they took the city. And they utterly destroyed all that was in the city, both man and woman, young and old, and ox and sheep, and ass, with the edge of the sword.'[10]

Concentrating on the Alleluia shout, historians have only looked at the story of Joshua. However, there is another biblical story which was also used to create this

[10]_ *The Book of Joshua* 6:15–21.

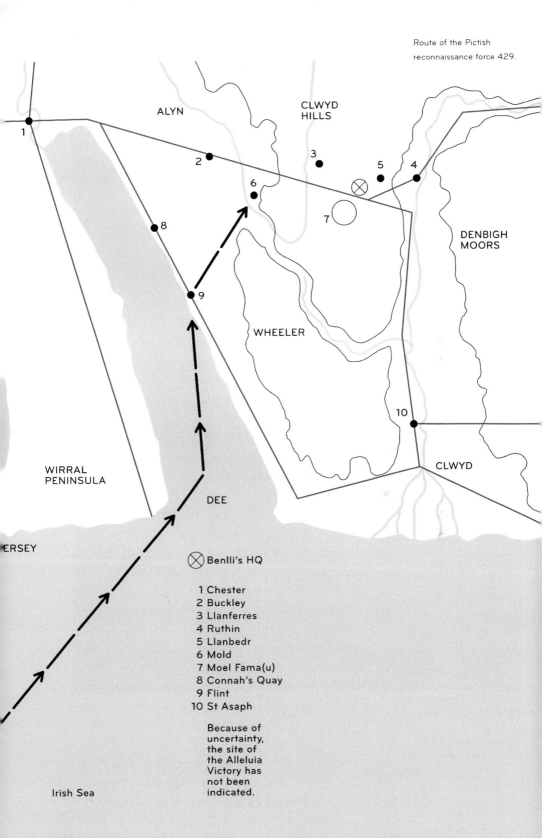

Route of the Pictish reconnaissance force 429.

CLWYD HILLS

ALYN

DENBIGH MOORS

WHEELER

WIRRAL PENINSULA

DEE

CLWYD

ERSEY

⊗ Benlli's HQ

1 Chester
2 Buckley
3 Llanferres
4 Ruthin
5 Llanbedr
6 Mold
7 Moel Fama(u)
8 Connah's Quay
9 Flint
10 St Asaph

Because of uncertainty, the site of the Alleluia Victory has not been indicated.

Irish Sea

And the three companies
blew the trumpets, and
brake the pitchers ... and
they cried, The sword of
the Lord and of Gideon –
Judges 7:20.
W. G. Simmonds, 'Gideon
the Deliverer', in Chalmers,
Muriel, J., *The Bible
Picture Book*, London, ND.

supposed record of events in north Wales. This is found in the *Book of Judges*, 7–8. Joshua was dead, but the children of Israel still had not secured the Promised Land. Midianites, Bedouin from the east, swept into the lands they had taken, reaching as far as Gaza. A man named Gideon was chosen by God to lead his people in opposing the invasion. After various heavenly signs, asked for by Gideon because resistance seemed hopeless, Gideon assembles a force. But God decides that it is too large, and needed to be pruned, 'lest Israel vaunt themselves against me, saying, Mine own hand hath saved me', a perfect anti-Pelagian stance. Gideon was told to send away all who were afraid. Twenty-two thousand promptly left, but ten thousand remained. They were told to drink at a stream. All those who knelt or used both hands to do this were dismissed. Only those who kept one hand on their swords, whilst bending down and using the other to lap up the water, a mere three hundred, were chosen. The Midianites were in a valley between the Hill of Moreh and the higher ground where Gideon's men prepared to attack. The story implies that the Israelites managed to surround the valley on three sides: a hundred men with Gideon, a hundred men at the head of the valley at its higher end, and the rest on its far side. The *Bible* can tell the rest.

And the Midianites and the Amalekites and all the children of the east lay along the valley like grasshoppers for multitude; and their camels were without number, as the sand by the sea side for multitude ...

And he [Gideon] divided the three hundred men into three companies, and he put a trumpet in every man's hand, with empty pitchers, and lamps within the pitchers. And he said ... When I blow with a trumpet, I and all that are with me, then blow ye the trumpets also on every side ...

So Gideon, and the hundred men that were with him, came unto the outside of the camp in the beginning of the middle watch; and they blew their trumpets, and brake the pitchers that were in their hands.

93

And the three companies blew the trumpets, and
brake the pitchers, and held the lamps in their left
hands, and the trumpets in their right hands to blow
withal: and they cried, The sword of the Lord and
of Gideon ...
and all the host ran, and cried, and fled [down to the
Jordan] ... And the men of Israel gathered themselves
together out of Naphtali, and out of Asher, and out
of Manasseh, and pursued after the Midianites.

We can now allow Constantius a hearing, if only
because it is his account which gave the battle its name.
But as a description of what happened, based as it is
on the stories of Joshua and Gideon and the fight to
conquer and retain the 'Promised Land', here Britain,
it can for the most part be ignored.

The fierce enemy forces approached, plainly visible
as they drew near the army which was lying in ambush.
Germanus who was bearing the standard, thereupon
ordered his men to repeat his call in one great shout;
as the enemy approached confidently believing that
their coming was unexpected, the bishops shouted
'Alleluia' three times. A universal shout of 'Alleluia'
followed, and the echoes from the surrounding hills
multiplied and increased the sound.
    The enemy forces were smitten with dread fearing
that not only the surrounding rocks but even the very
frame of heaven itself would fall upon them. They
were so filled with terror that they could not run fast
enough. They fled hither and thither, casting away
their weapons and glad even to escape naked from
the danger. Many of them rushed headlong back in
panic and were drowned in the river which they had
just crossed.
    The army, without striking a blow, saw themselves
avenged and became inactive spectators of the victory
freely offered to them. They gathered up the spoils lying
ready to hand and the devout soldiery rejoiced in this
heaven sent triumph. The bishops thus overcame the

enemy without the shedding of blood; they won a victory by faith and not by might.

So a widespread peace was restored to the island and foes visible [the Irish and the Picts] and invisible [the Pelagians] were overcome.[11]

Without striking a blow? We should remember that it was a Roman army, or at least an army trained in Roman ways, that defeated the Picts and Irish in this encounter, operating, no doubt, as Roman armies had for centuries. And this is what the *Book of Joshua* exactly describes: 'And they utterly destroyed all ... both man and woman, young and old, and ox and sheep, and ass, with the edge of the sword.' Had Vortigern arrived in time? Whether he had or not, we can be sure that the so-called Alleluia Victory was a Roman victory, and that it was Cunedda's victory.

THE MARCH ON FOEL FENLLI

Their blood lust roused, Cunedda's forces would have been determined and eager to see the job done. Now there would be plunder, booty to be shared, as well revenge to be exacted. Benlli had proved himself a traitor and Rome had always known how to deal with these. Perhaps in view of what happened next, we can allow that Vortigern, the supreme commander, was by now on the scene. No one would have been more concerned than he to eradicate pockets of disaffection such as had been exposed in the Clwyds. Benlli would have had only hours to live. That he was still in his fortress when the army arrived shows that Cunedda and Vortigern had acted fast. It is less than ten miles from the battle sites that have been suggested here and the probability is that the Roman army would have reached it the same day. This bastion on the conical hill named Foel Fenlli, either taking its name from this Irish ruler or giving its name to the otherwise unknown tyrant, now becomes the new focus of our story. It was a stronghold overlooking and

11_ Bede, *Ecclesiastical History*, Book I, Ch. 20, Colgrave and Mynors, 1969, pp. 63–5.

dominating *Bwlch Pen Barras*, the Pen Barras pass which, 1,000 feet above sea level, carried the Roman road from Ruthin in the Vale of the Clwyd to Chester in the east.

CREATION OF THE NEW PROVINCE – POWYS

Once more we are up against the poverty of our source, a piece of hagiography. Now, several stories from different periods have been conflated to produce more of the propaganda. Just as Molly Miller in 1976 showed how this had happened in the famous Chapter 62 account in Nennius dealing with Cunedda's supposed move from *Manaw Gododdin* and the expulsion of the Irish, so Graham Webster in 1975 suggested that the description of the events on Foel Fenlli comprises two quite separate stories. The first of these, from the evidence of the genealogies and our knowledge of events in Britain during these years, most probably occurred in the time of Magnus Maximus before his proclamation as emperor in 383. This involved the elevation of the leader of a group of Irish settlers in the Clwyds to a position of local control over the road system covering the Vale of Clwyd, the Clwyd range itself, and the approaches to the former HQ at Chester. The job would have involved the patrolling and upkeep of these highways, including the responsibility for the postal services operating out of the lowland southeast of the diocese *en route* to *Segontium* and Holyhead. The title granted the leader may have been as grandiose as that of prefect because the responsibilities were real and important.

In the Nennius extracts from the *Life of St Germanus*, almost certainly taken not from Constantius but from a later ninth-century version of the life by Heiric of Soissons, this earlier story is mixed up with the events which we can see involved Vortigern, Cunedda, and the destruction of Benlli. The account by Constantius, repeated by Bede, does not in fact mention the destruction of Benlli and is silent on Cadell and Britu or Bridw. All it does is to describe the Alleluia Victory.

It is the Nennius version of the *Vita* which completes the story though it has no mention of the Alleluia battle.

What happened on Foel Fenlli after the so-called Alleluia Victory is also hinted at in what was written on the pillar-cross of Eliseg, part of which still survives *in situ* near Llangollen in northeast Wales. Cyngen king of Powys erected this in *c.*826. Although the section of the pillar we still have once carried the inscription, it is now indecipherable to the point where nothing remains. As a result, we are dependent on a transcription from what was an already worn and damaged surface made by Edward Lluyd in 1696. With this transcript in hand, R. A. S. Macalister was able to report even as late as 1935 that he had still been able to make out most of what Lluyd reported.

In erecting the pillar, Cyngen, 808–56, was celebrating the recovery of land up to Offa's Dyke lost earlier by Powys, as well as commemorating his great-grandfather Eliseg, more correctly Elise, Eliset, or Elisedd, 739–62, who had fought a similar nine-year war against Aethelbald of Mercia. It was also a triumphant assertion of the dynasty's history and its imperial origins. The fact that it was sited near the Vale of Llangollen and close to Powys's border with Gwynedd is probably to be explained by what lies buried within the mound on which the cross was placed. In 1696, when Edward Lluyd examined it, the pillar had fallen, was in two pieces, and the cross at its top had disappeared. In 1779, part of the pillar was re-erected on its original pedestal. In the process, the tumulus was opened to reveal the bones of a 'very large' man. One possibility has to be that this is the burial place of Elise, king of Powys.

In the ninth century, Cyngen was proclaiming on his pillar that Powys had been founded in some arrangement or other made by the emperor Magnus Maximus. Two verses in the middle of the inscription, hardly visible even in 1696, apparently dealt with this beginning. One line of the first verse had either ET QUOD or PERTINEBANT ET APUD, meaning *and which* or *they extended to and in the presence of* and, after an obliterated phrase, another line had the word MONTEM, *the mountain*. The second verse came immediately before the entry concerning Vortigern and Britu.

+ ... ... MONARCHIAM ...
MAXIMUS ... BRITANNIAE
CONCENN PASCENT MAUN ANNAN ... .

+ ... ... the monarchy ...
Maximus ... of Britain
Cyngen, Pascent, Maun, Annan ...[12]

From the Nennius version of the *Life of St Germanus* it might be that the first story involves the appointment of someone named Cadell. This is probably to be dated to the time of Magnus Maximus, and Cadell was probably Irish like his apparent successor Benlli. His Welsh name Cadell might have stood as a convenient equivalent for the Irish Cathaíl, meaning literally strong in battle, or for Cathán, battler.[13] In the Nennius mix-up, this earlier Catel or Cadell becomes a member of the court of the 'iniquitous and tyrannical king, named Belinus' and was there when Germanus had arrived to remonstrate with him about his savage rule. Although ordered by his master Benlli to send Germanus and company packing, Cadell instead treated them with respect and kindness and had them stay the night with him. This is repaid by the bishop for, after being entertained to a meal from a calf killed specially for them, the next morning the calf is found whole and back with its mother. When, therefore, Germanus warned him that fire would destroy Benlli and his citadel, Cadell escaped with his nine sons and that night the stronghold was burnt along with all who were in it. Germanus then raised Cadell to the kingship of the area in Benlli's place.

If this first part of the story of Powys's origins dates to the time of Maximus, we can reconstruct the Nennius version as follows.

[12]_ Latin text and English translation, Bartrum, 1966, pp. 2–3. The text and translation given here are based on those but with additions suggested in Wade-Evans, 1938, pp. 33–4, and Macalister, 1935, pp. 330–3.

[13]_ Ó Corrain and Maguire, 1990, pp. 47–8.

Eliseg's or Cyngen's pillar
c.826.

View of the Pen Barras
pass from Benlli's HQ,
looking north to Moel
Fama and the Clwyd
range. To the left in the
distance the Vale of
Clwyd and the sea.

And he [Maximus or his agents in c.383, not Germanus in 429] blessed him [Cadell or Cathaíl] and added, and said, "There shall not be wanting a king of thy seed" – the same is Catell Durnluc, *Cadell Ddyrnllug* [from *teyrn*, prince, and *llwch*, dust, giving a 'prince raised from the dust', but even more probably from *dwrn*, hilt and *lluch* or *llug*, light or bright, giving 'of the gleaming hilt'] – "and thou thyself shalt be king from this day".

And so it happened, and there was fulfilled what was spoken by the prophet, saying "Raising the needy from the dust, and lifting up the poor from the dunghill, that he may sit with princes and occupy a throne of glory."

In accordance with the words of Maximus [Germanus in the text], from a servant he [Cadell or Cathaíl] became a king, and all his sons became kings, and from their seed the whole region of the Powysians [*omnis regio Povisorum*], is governed to this day.[14]

Of course this was not to be, other than in the sense that Cathaíl or Cadell could be accounted the first ruler of Powys or northern Powys. He seems to have been succeeded by a relative, later known as Benlli.

The second part of the history recorded on the pillar-cross concerns what happened *after* the so-called Alleluia Victory. Benlli was destroyed and all his people with him. Using the opportunity thus offered, Vortigern, who may by this point in the events of 428 or 429 have been present, placed his son Brutus or Bruttius, in British *Britu* or *Brydw*, over a new province extending down to mid-Wales. The main military rôle of this new command structure was to defend the flat land lying along the eastern side of the new province, extending from the Wirral between the Dee and the Mersey estuaries into the area known as the Midland Gap. This area was vitally important because it gave easy access from the sea to the flat, fertile and most settled parts of Roman Britain. Later, Brutus's province emerged as the mid-Wales kingdom of Powys.

This is outlined in the final part of the inscription on Eliseg's Pillar with its rather fine ending.

14_ Nennius, *Historia Brittonum*, Ch. 35, Wade-Evans, 1938, pp. 57–8, p. 57, note 2 and p. 58, note 1.

+ BRITU AUTEM FILIUS GUARTHI
GIRN QUEM BENEDIXIT GERMANUS QUEM
QUE PEPERIT EI SEVIRA FILIA MAXIMI
REGIS QUI OCCIDIT REGEM ROMANO RUM

+ CONMARC PINXIT HOC
CHIROGRAFIUM REGE SUO POSCENTE
CONCENN

+ BENEDICTIO DOMINI IN CON
CENN ET SUOS IN TOTA FAMILIA EIUS
ET IN TOTAM REGIONEM POUOIS
USQUE IN [?DIEM IUDICII AMEN]

+ Britu, moreover, the son of Vortigern,
whom Germanus blessed, and
whom Severa bore to him, the daughter of Maximus,
the king who killed the king of the Romans.

+ Conmarch/Cynfarch painted this
writing at the command of his king
Cyngen.

+ The blessing of the Lord upon Cyngen
and all members of his family
and upon all the land of Powys
until [?the day of judgement. Amen.]

The genealogies show that what was intended is the statement that after the earlier arrangements made by the emperor Maximus himself, Brutus or Britu was the area's first ruler, his inauguration being blessed by Germanus. Brutus was an appropriate name if the legend was already current that the first inhabitant of Britain was Brutus son of Aeneas. But Brutus was not only the son of Britain's ruler, the dictator Vortigern, he was also the grandson of an emperor, Magnus Maximus, 383–8, the son of that emperor's daughter. The blessing of the church was incidental.

The line on the pillar concerning Cyngen, Pascent, Maun, and Annan comes after lines barely decipherable in 1935 and presumably before a line completely missing. As for the identification of the Eliseg Pillar four, it could be that the Cyngen was Cyngen son of Millo *c.*470–94, who might conceivably have been the first to take the title of king. Now his namesake was erecting this pillar. Pascentius was the first *praeses* of the sister province of Gwrtheyrnion also established *c.*429. Could Maun be the Maucanu who was possibly Maximus's *c.*383 appointee over lands west of Wroxeter which, with Benlli's domain, became part of the province of Powys, the province of the *Pagenses*, established now by Vortigern? If these identifications are correct, than the last named, Annan, was almost certainly Annun, Anthun, or Antonius, son of Emperor Magnus Maximus. After 388 and the deaths of both Maximus and his eldest son, Victor, Britain was ruled in name at least by the emperor Antonius, even if it was really in the hands of Helena, Maximus's empress. In other words, the Eliseg four were all founding figures of the dynasty being celebrated by Cyngen ap Cadell when, in *c.*826, he erected his pillar-cross.

There are, however, more likely identifications. What the pillar seems to have been proclaiming was that the Powys line of rulers and kings stretched down through the ages, not only to Cyngen, the king of Powys who was erecting the cross, but also to Cyngen's eldest son, Pascent, the name a clear harking back to Pascentius, and to his grandchildren, Mawn and Annan, sons of his dead son Gruffydd.[15] Cyngen, therefore, was looking to the future as well as to the past.

[15] Gruffydd had been killed in 814, if not by the hands of his brother Elise, certainly at his instigation. Elise, not named on the pillar, was probably dead by 826.

The nature of the post now filled by Brutus indicates another aspect of the military coup that Vortigern had just effected in Britain. It looks as though these new arrangements in the west included the restoration of military power to the hitherto civilian rôle of *praesides*, the rulers of the provinces that made up Britain. These were now military posts filled by men who had seen army service. This would explain the emergence of not just one but two provinces down the marches of Wales. To the south of Brutus's lands, Vortigern further elevated the status of his own family by appointing another of his sons, Pascentius, as *praes* of the other new province extending down to Gloucester and the Severn. At its heart lay Vortigern's own family lands. Nothing else is known about this Pascentius who, as the *Historia Brittonum* put it, 'ruled in the two countries called Builth and Gwerthrynion [or Gwrtheyrnion, the land of the Great Leader] after his father's death'.[16] Brutus and Pascentius were both military men.

THE LOCAL CLERIC, GARMON

Yet another figure, apart from Vortigern and Cunedda, has been effectively wiped from the story. It would seem that Benlli was challenged by the church at some point prior to the final events of *c.*429, not by Germanus who had only just arrived in Britain, but by someone who was probably a cleric of note in north Wales, namely Garmon. It is obvious how his name suggested that of the more internationally famous Germanus of Auxerre. In the area between a line from *Segontium* to *Deva* and another across Wales from the Dovey are a whole series of churches dedicated to Garmon. In the northeasten part nearest the scene of these events we have Llanarmon-yn-Iâl, Llanarmon Dyffryn Ceiriog, Llanarmon Mynydd Mawr, as well as a whole series of Maes Garmons. Indeed, it may be that it was a local Garmon who blessed

16_ Nennius, *Historia Brittonum*, Ch. 48, Morris, 1980, p. 33.

Britu and not Germanus at all. Germanus may not even have been in north Wales or, if he was, he may have arrived too late to participate in events.

CYNHAFAL

Possibly it was just this doubt about Germanus's participation that led to another claim being made, although it now appears in nothing earlier than a sixteenth-century poem. This was that another churchman, Cynhafal, was responsible for Benlli's end. The claim comes on behalf of Llangynhafal, Cynhafal's church lying west of the Clwyds, in opposition to the Llanarmon-yn-Iâl, Garmon's church, on the east of the range. The poet was Gruffydd ab Ieuan ap Llywelyn Fychan, c.1485–1553, of Llanerch in Denbighshire. It is worth a mention because of the detail it gives about the tyrant's end that may or may not bear some relation to the truth or at least to a tradition about that truth. Cynhafal himself, however, can be discounted, the genealogies showing him to have been living in the sixth century in the time of Maelgwn *Gwynedd* or even later.

The substance of the poem is this. The bard [Gruffydd ab Ieuan] was suffering from acute pains in his leg, and he prays for relief to Cynhafal, whose merits, he says, possessed the peculiar property of removing rheumatic affections. The saint is reminded of his miracles in the flesh, how he tortured the "hoary giant", Benlli Gawr, till he became like a "frantic lion", filling his body with agony and wild fire, which drove him to seek relief in the cooling waters of the Alun [or Alyn]; and how that river refused to allay his agony, and became dry three times, and the giant's bones were burnt upon its banks at Hesp Alun (the Dried-up Alun). He then refers to the efficacy of the Saint's well in the removal of various bodily ailments by drinking its water and by bathing in it; and, lastly, implores him to cure his rheumatism, and finally to admit him to Paradise.[17]

17_ Baring-Gould and Fisher, 1907–13, Vol. II, 1908, p. 255: Cynhafal, pp. 254–5.

Hâf hesb, literally summer dry, is the name of the Alyn where for a time it disappears underground into the limestone rocks which are so much a feature of the area. Here, 'on the bank and corner of fierce Alun, all his [Benlli's] bones were burned'.[18]

THE DESTRUCTION OF THE PEN BARRAS PASS HQ

There is, of course, another version lurking somewhere behind all these accounts: this is the truth, now forever beyond our grasp. Certainly, if we take the people out of Nennius's version, what we are left with are events typical of the Romans at war especially when they were dealing with rebellion. For Benlli's followers, now including the best soldiers he could muster in preparation for the arrival of the Picts and the Irish, the approach of Cunedda's army instead of their expected allies must have caused panic. This would have meant abandoning a long spur commanding the complete length of the Roman road as it passed through the Pen Barras Pass lying to the north of the hill-fort. In all probability, this was where the main settlement and Benlli's *llys* or court with its stores and valuables were situated. An attempt would have been made to move the animals, horses, and cattle from this area, in medieval terms the outer bailey, into the fort above. In the lands around there would also have been a stream of people running and stumbling in their attempt to reach the safety of Benlli's fort before the advancing army cut them off. By the time Cunedda's men arrived, the area would have been wellnigh empty. Here was the soldiers' first taste of plunder, always eagerly anticipated and expected on such expeditions.

Surprised in his headquarters in this way, Benlli would now have been in the inner and highest part of his settlement, the Iron Age hill-fort at the very top of Foel Fenlli. Its defences of three ramparts, but with a double bank and ditch on the northwest and southwest sides and one rampart and ditch on the steepest south side, closely follow the contours of the oval-shaped hill. Even today,

18_ Gruffudd ab Ieuan, *Gweddi ar Gynhafal Rhag Gwaew Mewn Clun*, Morrice, 1910, p. 61, transl. Howard Lockley.

some of the banks made of earth and stones stand eight to ten feet high. At that date the entrance was on the west side. In time of emergency, as now, the area could be used for habitation, having a spring of water near its centre that was noticed by Camden in his 1600 edition of *Britannia*. Even the partial excavations of a limited area of the hill-fort in 1849 turned up evidence of occupation during the Roman period. The investigators discovered a 'rude pavement' for the entrance at the western approach, and found fragments of coarse and fine Roman pottery, iron, 'glass of a superior kind', a leaden ornament, and part of a brass or bronze ring.[19] Several hollows facing southwest on sloping ground within the defences indicate structures that possibly date to this period.[20]

Even Cunedda's troops, by this date mostly recruited in north Wales and therefore familiar with these forts, would have found what lay ahead awesomely impressive. Perhaps even Benlli believed he could hold out long enough for the besieging army to grow tired or rebellious at such a drawn-out campaign. We may have a hint of this in Benlli's response when told that Germanus and his party were outside seeking an audience: 'Even if they are here, and stay here till the end of the year, they shall never enter within my fortress!'[21]

There may have been some pathetic efforts to hide the contents of the treasury. In 1816 more than 1,500 Roman coins came to light on the inner northeastern rampart after a burning of heather. There was a further discovery of more than fifty coins in about 1847, on a 'sheep walk near the summit of the mountain'. Although these coins dated from the time of Constantine the Great only to that of his son Constantius II, from 306 to 361, they could easily have been part of hoards kept by Benlli. Dr John Morris believed that they were sufficient to show this to have been 'the residence of a powerful ruler'.[22]

The fort would have been encircled. Operations might have been postponed until the following day as the battle, the march up to the pass, and the necessary

19_ Davies, 1929, pp. 184–5.

20_ Ibid., pp. 183–4.

21_ Nennius, *Historia Brittonum*, Ch. 32, Morris, 1980, p. 27.

22_ Morris, 1973, p. 64.

reconnoitring to make sure they were not in any trap, if they did all take place on the same day, must have taken up the daylight hours. Next day would have seen scavenging over a wide area to bring together the wood necessary for the last act. With the fort surrounded there would have been no unnecessary rush and certainly no anxiety. Even the Germanus version has the bishop at the fortress two days before the place was destroyed 'after a moderate interval of the [second] night'. When all was assembled, that day or the next, operations would have begun with the sending in of combustibles to set the wooden buildings of the fortress on fire. Any person attempting to flee the conflagration would have been cut down. Perhaps Benlli was one of these.

Benlli Gawr became a frantic lion,
A spasm went into his body and wild fire.
There was a broken wound below,
It was the fire of a sermon.
To cool his burning, he went down on his knee[s]
To flee the Devil, to Alun's flood.[23]

A final storming of the gateway and it would have been over.

And after a moderate interval of the [second] night, fire fell from heaven and burnt up the citadel and all the men who were with the tyrant, and they have never appeared [or been seen again] to this day and the citadel has not been [re]built to this day.[24]

Certainly, Germanus's biographer wanted us to believe that the fire literally fell from heaven: to the fort's occupants it must have felt exactly as though this was happening.

[23]_ Gruffudd ab Ieuan, Gweddi ar Gynhafal Rhag Gwaew Mewn Clun, Morrice, 1910, p. 61, transl. Howard Lockley.

[24]_ Nennius, Historia Brittonum, Ch. 34, Wade-Evans, 1938, p. 57.

In the story of Benlli's fall and the start of the kingdom of Powys with the appointment now of Vortigern's son Brutus to administer the area, there is no mention of Cunedda, but neither, as we have seen, is there a mention of Vortigern. It is rather odd that we know Vortigern and Cunedda only by their epithets rather than by their real names. This is even stranger when we realize that the two epithets mean virtually the same thing: *Vortigern* is the Great Leader; *Cunedda* is the Good King. When we then turn to the famous description of Cunedda's work in north Wales given us in Nennius's *Historia Brittonum* it suddenly becomes clear. Is not what is said there *exactly* what we are told in the accounts of the Alleluia Victory and the fall of Benlli? Surely this passage is a summary of what had happened at the Alyn and on Foel Fenlli?

And they [Cunedda and his sons] drove out with immense slaughter the Scots [that is, the Irish] from those regions [of north Wales], who never returned again to inhabit them.[25]

In other words, Constantius's determination to place the Catholic church at the centre of these events has wiped *two* leading figures from the story, Vortigern *and* Cunedda. The almost certain fact is that this whole military campaign was the work of the local commander, nicknamed Cunedda, with Vortigern playing a secondary rôle as the architect of the political changes that were to follow. In all probability, the Catholic church played no part whatsoever.

We have a poem, *Marwnad Cunedda*, Elegy for Cunedda, from the *Book of Taliesin*. Taliesin was a sixth-century poet, but the date of this poem is much argued over. It represents something of a problem with its references to *northern* struggles against the Picts and/or the Saxons in which Cunedda was supposedly involved. This then is not a genuine contemporary lament for the dead king, and it most certainly cannot be used to

25_ Ibid., Ch. 62, p. 80: Paternus son of Tacitus c.398–410; Eternus c.410–29, and thirdly, N.N., the son of Eternus known as *Cunedda*, The Good King, c.428–50.

place Cunedda's work in the north of Britain. However, in the context of Cunedda's rôle as outlined here, the words are powerful.

Between the high place and the sea water
and the fresh [?stream] water,
because of Cuneddaf's ebbing away
shock is felt

...

It is the death of Cuneddaf that I lament,
that was lamented:
Lamented is the stout defender,
stout in co-operation,
invincible in joint battle-operation

...

harder than bone towards the enemy.[26]

CHAPTER FOUR

VENEDOTIA AND ITS *PRAESIDES*
The Emergence of Gwynedd, 450–490

ORDER AND LEGITIMACY

The situation in Britain during these years was nowhere near as anarchic as a superficial reading of Gildas might suggest. There was firm military control and at its head something approaching a dictatorship. Operating alongside the army, which must have been growing steadily in numbers and experience, were the provinces, and operating within these, and in some cases separating out to form separate provinces, were the various authorities committed to the more territorially limited task of controlling the road system. These early rulers of a Britain that was not yet *post*-Roman were in close contact with each other. Initially, no doubt, this was through the operations of the diocesan council, later through ties that were more personal. That certainly is what the Welsh Triads imply. For example, one triad

[26]_ *Marwnad Cunedda* or *Cunedaf*, Haycock, 2007, pp. 491–3: introduction, pp. 488–90, and notes, pp. 493–502. Cf. Koch and Carey, 1994/2000, pp. 292–3. Haycock believes the poem is late and its largely northern setting suggests Gwynedd's later identification with the northern seventh-century struggles. Rather than *Elegy for Cunedda*, it should perhaps be titled, *Cunedda Will Come Again*.

talks of Coel *Godebog*. *Godebog* means keen or resolute. However, it could also mean protector, the Roman *praeses*. It is possible that 'Coelestius', Coel *Hen*, the Aged, the Old King Cole of the nursery rhyme, who might be given dates *c.*410–43, was one of the *praesides*, presidents or protectors, ruling over the province of either *Valentia* from Carlisle or *Britannia Secunda* from York. He was certainly the founder of the later dynasty of Rheged. In the triad, Coel is the father-in-law of Eternus, *Edern*, 'son' of Paternus, and it suggests that Eternus inherited the title of protector, not from his father Paternus, but from Coel through his marriage to Coel's daughter Gwawl. This was one of the 'three times when the lordship of Gwynedd went by the Distaff', that is, the female line.

The second [instance] was Gwal daughter of (Coel) Godebog, mother of Cunedda Wledig and wife of Edyrn son of Padarn Peisrudd.[1]

The problem here is that this could simply be an attempt to deal with the unreconstructed account of Chapter 61 in Nennius, which leaves the impression, followed by generations of historians, that it was Cunedda who was given the title and that it was Cunedda, with his sons, who moved to north Wales.[2]

THE ROMAN CUNEDDA

'By what authority?' was a question that in Gwynedd would always have been met by a proud assertion of imperial origins, but over the years another question, also concerning origins, was making itself felt and creating new tensions. This involved a division between those who still clung resolutely to the last vestiges of Roman life and culture, and others who looked increasingly to the Irish Sea area and to the so-called Celtic world it represented, which was the one in which Gwynedd now had to function. It might be thought that this can be

[1] Bromwich, 1961, Appendix V, p. 257, No. 5.

[2] Miller, 1976/8, p. 529 and note 4.

seen in the simple matter of the first or Christian names chosen by the Gwynedd dynasty. After Tacitus, Paternus, and Eternus, it is often thought that it was Cunedda who was the first to have been given a British or Celtic name, but in all probability this is not the case. As we have seen, *Vortigern*, one of the first major characters to appear after the 410 letter of Honorius, is not a proper name but an epithet, meaning something like the Great Leader. As such, we do not know his actual name, in part because of the quite vicious attempt by the Christian church to wipe his existence and certainly any importance he may have had from the record. He was, after all, a heretic. Similarly, Cunedda is a nickname, meaning something like the Good King, from *cun-*, king, and *dag-*, good, giving originally *Cunedagos*, which became Cunedda. That his epithet is British causes no surprise. It then becomes more likely that, just as his father and grandfather proudly bore Roman names, Cunedda, whatever *his* Roman name was, would also have given imperial, Roman, names to his children.

VENEDOTIA: CUNEDDA THE FIRST *PRAESES*

As we have seen, how it is that a Roman *comes* such as Paternus was in the position to divide his lands and ultimately bequeath his authority to his sons is something of a problem. One possibility has to be that the hereditary nature of these posts only kicked in when central authority finally collapsed in the period between Ambrosius's rule and the end, at a diocesan level, of effective military resistance to the Saxons following the battle of *Camlan* sometime between 512 and 537. This would imply that the supposed father–son relationships so confidently asserted by the genealogists, placing *ap*, son of, between people appearing in what was in reality merely a king or succession list, have to be abandoned, at least in this early period and probably until the earliest years of the sixth century.

112

The other likelihood, which certainly fits the evidence we have, is that the hereditary nature of the post was the result of a formal grant. The most likely time for this would have been during the reorganization of local government and the establishment of the two new provinces of Powys and Gwrtheyrnion following the destruction of the Clwyd tyrant Benlli. In other words, it looks as though this new style of provincial government was extended to Cunedda's territory, replacing what here had been a purely military arrangement under the *comes litoris Hiberniae*. Gwynedd, then, was the *third* province created by Vortigern. Both military and civilian power would now have been vested in Cunedda as its first *praeses*, president, protector, or governor.

Venedotia, the name of the new province, has been the subject of some discussion. John Edward Lloyd noted that its first appearance, on an inscription, is in the genitive, that is *Venedotis*, meaning 'of Gwynedd'. He thought it presupposed a nominative such as *Venedas*.[3] It is now taken to be *Venedotia*. The word apparently derives from the same source as the Irish words *fine* or *féni*, a tribe or people, here meaning a group of these. There is a hint that the words implied that these were the true, the genuine, the original inhabitants. The source is the Indo-European root *uen* meaning strive, wish, even love. *Ueneda* means a war-band. In this land, only now emerging from what was a military command structure, it would refer to this province being a land of armies. It seems probable that Cunedda's choice of name deliberately underlined the military origins of his protectorship, and what would be its continuing struggle against both internal and external threats. We must also remember that this *Land of Hosts* was a land of many tribes. From the start, therefore, it must have been some sort of confederation. One important result of these developments was that Cunedda was now free to appoint his own successor, albeit subject to the agreement of the person or body exercising ultimate authority in the diocese. It therefore seems entirely appropriate that Cunedda is often regarded as the founder of his dynasty's

3_ Lloyd, 1912, p. 40.

fortunes, even if this fame in most people's eyes comes from fanciful ideas of a migration from the far north based on the jumbled passage in Nennius. We have to remember, however, that when Cunedda died, possibly in about the year 450, Gwynedd was still not an independent kingdom. It was just one province of the British diocese. Nevertheless, its geographical isolation meant that it was probably beginning to act like an independent entity.

CITIZENS AND MAGISTRATES OF GWYNEDD

If Cunedda died or was killed in c.450, to be followed by his son Anianus, 450–85, and then the person usually thought of as his grandson, Eugenius, 485–90, it is probably to the reign, as we by that date can almost certainly call it, of Eugenius's brother Cadwallon the Longhanded, 490–517, that we can ascribe the memorial to Cantiorix. This is the stone which gives us the earliest occurrence of the name Gwynedd. Today, the slab lies in the parish church of Penmachno, St Tudclud's, four miles south of Betws-y-Coed and the river Conwy, on Conwy's tributary the Machno. Its proud Roman claims are obvious.

CANTIORI HIC IACIT VENEDOTIS CIVE FUIT
(C)ONSOBRINO MA(G)LI MAGISTRATI (...)

CANTIORIX LIES HERE. HE WAS A CITIZEN OF
GWYNEDD AND A COUSIN OF MAGLOS THE
MAGISTRATE.

As Dr Molly Miller commented, the inscription reveals 'a civil fabric in good order by the 490s', and this was a Roman society as the Roman words *civis* and *magistratus* testify.[4] Hundreds of Latin-inscribed tombstones have survived from the fifth to the seventh centuries. One, again dating to around 500, has the name Carausius: the name of the prefect of the British fleet who took over the

4_ Miller, 1976/8, p. 12.

CANTIORIX HIC IACIT
VENEDOTIS CIVES FUIT
CONSOBRINOS
[and on the side]
MAGLI MAGISTRATI
Penmachno church,
Gwynedd. (Courtesy of
the Church in Wales)

Above: The remote valley
of the river Machno above
the village of Penmachno.
Even in this remote area of
Venedotia, the government
bequeathed by Rome was
still functioning in the fifth
and sixth centuries.

Right: Penmachno church.

116

diocese in 286 in a rebellion and usurpation that was only ended by a second invasion of Britain in 296 led by the western *caesar* Constantius *Chlorus*. That Carausius, a usurper, was held in sufficiently high regard all these years later for people to use his far from common name is remarkable. Possibly they were thinking back to this earlier period of independence when Britain had, like now, been forced to take desperate measures to defend itself. But then, as now, it was *Roman* Britain that was taking these steps.

THE SONS OF CUNEDDA

When we come to examine the names of Cunedda's sons and the territories associated with them, we find ourselves looking at an obvious example of the manipulation of what little was known at the time the pedigrees were compiled. This was done to make all these supposed sons the eponymous founders of areas of control that certainly at some point or other did fall under the domination of Gwynedd, and almost certainly between the times of Paternus and Maelgwn. In other words, the territories first came to mind, then sons were invented to appear as their founders. At least, this *may* have happened in *some* cases. Here we also encounter another example where doubts over the veracity of parts of the story have seemingly provided adequate justification for modern linguists and others to throw out the whole tale of Gwynedd's origins.

According to the famous Nennius passage, Cunedda had eight sons with him in north Wales, and the Harleian MS 3859 version of the same work, which is dated to between 830 and 988, agrees. The ninth son, so it is said, had been left in the north and died there. What is immediately noteworthy is the continued use of Roman names for a least some of the Good King's children. Romanus, giving us the British Rhufawn and then Rhufon, was the supposed founder of the line of Rhufoniog, the area lying immediately south of Rhos in Gwynedd's heartland. Donatus, it was claimed, did the same in Dunoding in southwest Gwynedd. Given that Maelgwn *Gwynedd*, *c.*517–45, is credited with annexing Meirionydd, the area south of Dunoding, control over Dunoding does not sound so unreasonable for the years previous to this. Aeternus or Eternus was the third son with a Roman name. His father apparently placed him over what later became Edeyrnion on the upper reaches of the Dee below Rhos, Rhufoniog, and with it, Dyffryn Clwyd.[5] The Welsh states, Gwynedd, Powys, Ceredigion, and so on, were divided into these *cantrefi*, cantrefs or hundreds, and these were later divided into smaller units known as *cymydau*, commotes, consisting usually of a number of townships. Donatus's territory Dunoding, for example, consisted of the two commotes of Eifionydd in southeastern Llŷn and Ardudwy which lay to its south.

Anianus, in British Einiawn or Einion, was the eldest son and the successor of his father Cunedda in Rhos. As such, he had direct rule over the cantrefs of Llŷn, Arfon and Arllechwedd on the mainland west of the Conwy, the three *cantrefi* in Anglesey, Aberffraw, Rhosyr or Rhosfair, and Cemais, as well as Rhos and Tegeingl to the east of the Conwy. But Anianus is never given this name and almost always appears as Einiawn. Immediately this strikes a jarring note. Is it likely that the eldest son of a family inordinately proud of its imperial origins and dependent on these for its claims to rule would not have had a Roman name? As in Cunedda's case, it seems that what we really have is his British epithet, the use of which has almost wiped away the original. In other words, Anianus, the eldest son of the Good King, could have been known, not only as *Gyrth*, the Harsh, which we know he was, but also in a play on his *praenomen* as *Einiawn*, the Anvil.

5_ In Welsh respectively Rhufon or Rhufawn, Old Welsh *Rumaun*; Dunod, Old Welsh *Dunaut*; and Edern, Old Welsh *Aetern* or *Etern*.

Ignoring for the moment Tybion, who supposedly died in the north, this leaves four other sons who did apparently have British names. With Ceretic or Ceredig, supposedly the founder of Ceredigion, the territory bordering the southern part of Cardigan Bay below the Meirionydd that was not annexed until the time of Maelgwn *Gwynedd*, we are almost certainly dealing with fiction. Other pedigree materials for Ceredigion which show attempts to link up rulers of this area with Cunedda are inevitably several names short. If Ceredig existed at all, he probably belongs, as Dr Molly Miller suggested, to the sixth century. He may have come from the region of the Severn following the collapse there of British rule after the battle of Dyrham in 577.[6] Ceredigion was not part of Gwynedd.

Two supposed sons named Abloyc/Afloeg and Osmael are interesting in the context of struggles in north Wales against Irish settlers from the time of Cunedda down to Cadwallon *Llawhir* c.490–517. They will be looked at below along with Docmail. Suffice it here to note that all three are credited with being the founders, not of main territorial blocks, *cantrefi*, but instead with comparatively small areas. Afloeg gives us *Afloegion*, known by its corrupt form Cafflogion, which became a commote on the south side of the Llŷn peninsula. With Docmail we supposedly have the ruler of Dogfeiling, later a commote in the cantref of Dyffryn Clwyd covering part of the Clwyd valley. It looks as though the pedigree compilers have simply filled the geographical gap between Rhos, Rhufoniog, and Tegeingl and Edeyrnion.

Tybion, even according to the Cunedda migration story, was not the founder of any Welsh cantref, but he was, supposedly, the father of Marianus, *Meirion*, the eponymous founder of Meirionydd. Tybion, we are told, died in *Manau Guotodin*, before the alleged emigration of Cunedda's family to north Wales. In all probability, the real Tybion had nothing to do with Cunedda and Paternus, at least not in a family sense,

6_ Miller, *Saints*, 1976/8, pp. 57–9.

but someone called Tybion was possibly the father of Meirion, grandfather of Cadwaladr and great-grandfather of the Gwrin who ruled Meirionydd during the early years of Maelgwn *Gwynedd*'s reign.[7] Adding Tybion to the sons, however, meant that one man, Cunedda, could shine forth as the founder of a dynasty and, with his sons, as ruler of an area that had an integrity stretching from the Dee in northeast Wales to the Teifi, the river forming the boundary between Ceredigion and Dyfed, in the southwest.

Here is their [that is, Cunedda's sons'] boundary from the river which is called Dyfrdwy, the Dee, to another river, Teify, and they held very many districts in the western part of Britain.[8]

In this way, the rest of Gwynedd's history down to 1283 had already been written. Here was a blueprint for the Greater Gwynedd that was to emerge, and one that gave it roots extending back to the time of Cunedda and, through him, to the Roman empire.

It might well be that *four* sons of the Good King did indeed take shares in their father's expanded area of control. If the reconstruction of the description of Maelgwn's ancestors in the ninth-century Nennius compilation is accepted, the one clearly showing *two* stages in the emergence of the Gwynedd dynasty, the first initiated by Paternus and the second involving Cunedda, then it is unnecessary to bother much with Harleian MS 3859's listing of Cunedda's sons. This says that Meirion, son of Cunedda's supposed first-born Tybion, was the brother who divided what was later the Greater Gwynedd between his siblings. Far more realistic is the belief that it was the father, Cunedda, who did this. As Meirion is the supposed ancestor of the rulers of Meirionydd, something we will look at, this seems to be an interpolation which relates to what happened later in Gwynedd's history.

[7]_ For the likely pedigree of Tybion's family, unconnected with Cunedda's until the time of Maelgwn, Miller, 1979, p. 111.

[8]_ Nennius, *Historia Brittonum*, Appendices, Wade-Evans, 1938, p. 113, No. 33. For the nine sons, see No. 32.

THE FOUNDERS OF GWYNEDD: CUNEDDA AND HIS FOUR SONS

Such considerations leave us with Cunedda's eldest son and successor Anianus, nicknamed *Einiawn*, the Anvil, and his brothers Romanus, Donatus, and Eternus.[9] Even this more limited family might be justification, along with the new recognition of Gwynedd's status as a province, for Cunedda, rather than Paternus, being regarded as the founder of what later came to be called 'the first dynasty of Gwynedd'.[10]

The existence of sons, even if only four rather than nine, raises the issue of inheritance, but this would have been less of a problem for the fifth-century participants in the story than it has been for modern commentators. In the last century, linguists working on the medieval Welsh laws seemed to have discovered a key to the interpretation of Welsh political history up to 1283, especially that concerning the division of land on the death of kings. The way in which this viewpoint gained such a hold might be compared with the more recent understanding of how pedigrees, genealogies, and king lists were often manipulated, and in many cases completely engineered, in order to serve a host of contemporary needs: political, religious, and social. This later theory has become almost an *idée fixe* among modern writers, with the result that babies are commonly thrown out with bath water. The earlier idea that Welsh rulers divided their territories among sons, just as landowners did their farms, skewed the vision of scholars as eminent as Professor John Edward Lloyd. It is Professor J. Beverley Smith, the biographer of Gwynedd's last great independent prince, Llywelyn ap Gruffudd, who has done more than anyone to unpick some of the tangle this former viewpoint created. The argument is his and so an extended quote is perhaps justified.

The need to ensure that the inheritance is conserved in its entirety from generation to generation may be

9_ Einion, Rhufon, Dunod, and Edern.

10_ This designation depends on an exaggerated view of Merfyn *Frych*'s stranger, foreigner, or intruder status when he came to the throne of Gwynedd in 825. He was, in fact, the grandson of Cynan of Tindaethwy who ruled Gwynedd 798–816, and the great-grandson of Rhodri ab Idwal, Rhodri *Molwynog*, Rhodri the Bald and Grey, who ruled c.711–54. Merfyn, it would seem, was brought up in Man.

counted among the abiding concerns of dynasties of the medieval West. A continuing attentiveness to the succession may be discerned in the kingdom of France and in its several principalities, and historical studies have recognized the care with which royal and noble lineages of many lands sought to ensure the integrity of the territory.

Welsh kingdoms have often been envisaged very differently, deemed to be inexorably subject upon the death of a king, in accordance with the dictates of Welsh law, to equal division between his sons. The Welsh lawbooks, of which several important texts derive from the thirteenth century, certainly deal in some detail with the manner in which an inheritance in land is divided. These expositions of partible inheritance are concerned, however, not with succession to kingdoms but with the practice which applied to the lands of free proprietors.

The lawyers' guidance on dynastic practice, the succession of kingdoms, is less explicit, but its indications are quite clear. The provision for the succession has two complementary features. In the lawyers' estimation there is but one heir to the throne, known in the Welsh texts as *edling* or *gwrthrychiad*, in the Latin texts as *heres* or successor. The single heir, who is accorded a place of particular honour at court, is raised from among the near kinsmen of the king who constitute the 'royal members' (*aelodau brenin, membra regis*). Designation is made by the ruling king, and the *edling* is the one 'to whom the king gives hope and expectation'.

The kingdom is bestowed in its entirety upon a single heir and, according to a further provision, each of the other 'royal members' was provided with an estate, so that thereafter his status was determined not by his membership of the royal kindred but in accordance with the status of the land bestowed upon him. An apanage was thereby created within the bounds of the kingdom to be vested in the heir to the throne, allowing each of his near kinsmen maintenance and honourable status

in a manner which in no way undermined the entirety
or the integrity of the kingdom.[11]

The pedigrees give separate king lists for Rhos,
Rhufoniog, Dogfeiling in Dyffryn Clwyd, and a Penllyn
which may or may not be referring to Edeyrnion, as well
as giving one for Gwynedd usually covering all these
areas.[12] Our information for this very early period of
Gwynedd's history is extremely meagre, yet despite this,
what Professor Beverley Smith says about inheritance
seems to be borne out right from the start.

GWYNEDD'S WESTERN MOVE

What does appear to change is the political centre of
gravity of the emerging kingdom, moving from a
heartland territory east of the river Conwy, when the
kings are referred to as kings of Rhos, to west of the
river in later years, that is, to Arllechwedd, Arfon, and
Môn, when eventually the kings were known as kings
of Aberffraw.

THE PROBLEMS OF DOWNSIZING: WROXETER

When Gwynedd's centre of gravity shifted westwards,
Chester apparently fell under the control of Powys, but
by then, the former legionary headquarters had been
abandoned by the military, if not by the church. The
end of Chester's Roman importance is interesting if,
inevitably, problematical. Comparison with what
happened later in *Viroconium*, Wroxeter further down
the Marches, highlights the problems Chester posed for
the likes of Vortigern and Cunedda. This is worth a
detour from our story.

It is difficult to ascertain who succeeded Brutus or
Britu as *praesides*, protectors, of Powys. Gaps in the main
pedigree between the Britu of the Pillar and Cyngen,
ruling *c.*470–500, *might* be made up with other names

11_ Smith, 1998, pp. 8–9
and notes.

12_ Bartrum, 1966, and
Wade-Evans, 1938.

provided in Harleian MS 3859: that is, Camuir and Millo. There may, of course, have been no direct connection between the rulers of what we later call Powys and its initial founders, Maximus and Vortigern.

Under Brutus, 'Camuir and Millo', Cyngen and Brochwel *Ysgythrog*, Long-in-the-Tooth, and then Cynan *Garwyn*, Cynan of the White Chariot, which probably brings us into the earliest years of the seventh century, Wroxeter's position was becoming increasingly untenable. Its great baths complex had fallen out of use by 380, and shortly thereafter stone was taken from the area to replace Wroxeter's earth defences. Possibly this was under Magnus Maximus and his administration, but it could have come earlier, in the days of his former boss Count Theodosius. The result was a circuit wall of stone some two miles in length, enclosing, at about two hundred acres, an area much larger than the original Wroxeter and one that was destined never to be fully occupied.

By Brochwel's reign it looks as if the town was becoming increasingly dilapidated. But there is still evidence of government control and direction. Possibly Brochwel was inspired and even forced to act because of the rise of Gwynedd. His daughter Sanan married Maelgwn Gwynedd. The result was a massive redevelopment programme in the period 530-80 evidenced in spectacular fashion by the building then constructed on the remains of the baths. The huge north wall of the basilica was demolished, and some of the rubble used to form the raft for a timber-framed residence of impressive proportions. With its verandah, central portico, even towers, this was no mere house but more of a headquarters, even palace. Constructed in timber, it was still thoroughly classical in both inspiration and style.[13] It could well be that we are looking at a new HQ for these governors, or rather kings, of the new Powys.

However, despite such extensive building operations, perhaps even as they proceeded during the reign of Cynan *Garwyn*, c.560–600, one fact must have been making itself felt. Two miles of wall enclosing two

13_ White and Barker, 2006.

Above: The south wall of the Wroxeter baths complex still standing to almost its full height.

Left: Detail. The wall would originally have been plastered and painted.

Column bases on the site
of the Wroxeter forum.

hundred acres required enormous reserves of manpower for its defence. Had pride and a determination to continue the boast about Powys's Roman origins blinded its rulers to the new political realities? And pride did come before a fall. Cynan's reign was followed by that of his brother Iago ap Brochwel. Accorded a two-year reign in *Vita Tysilio*, Iago was married to the delightfully named Haiarnwedd, literally Iron-Face. He died childless, but if the *Vita* is correct, Haiarnwedd failed in what was probably a scheme to prevent Cynan *Garwyn*'s son Selyf, possibly a minor, from inheriting. She was unable to get Tysilio, Iago's younger brother, the second abbot of Meifod, out of the religious life and into her bed. There may have been civil war. We are not told how Iron-Face died, but she was succeeded by Iago's nephew Selyf, Selim, or Solomon, who won the epithet *Sarffgadau*, Serpent of Battles. If he came to power in *c*.605, within no time we have Aethelfrith's invasion of north Wales in 616, the battle of Bangor Orchard, usually known as the battle of Chester, Selyf"s death, and the first period of Gwynedd's overlordship of Powys. Even an offshoot dynasty emerged in eastern Powys under Cyndrwyn the Stubborn, *c*.602–37, probably based on the old hill fort site of the Wrekin to the east of Wroxeter.

The carefully managed and inevitable move from Wroxeter was to two sites. The first, Shrewsbury, only five miles away, was on a hill in a bend of the Severn: a much more easily defended position. The fact that archaeologists have, up-to-date, found no evidence in the ground for this need not detain us as most of Shrewsbury remains unexcavated. The other was Berth, with nearby Baschurch, seven miles from Shrewsbury, probably mostly a civilian and religious centre relying for its protection on the nearby military site of Shrewsbury. Once this evacuation had been decided upon, there followed an unhurried dismantling of buildings and a removal of their contents, the material then being taken to the new bases.

However, these were not the only centres of power and government in Powys. Leaving aside northern

Powys, where possibly there were centres at Mold, Caergwrle, and Dinas Brân above Llangollen, there were a considerable number of other sites to the west of Wroxeter, in what already might have been thought of as southern Powys. Some of these would have been bases used from the fourth century, whilst others appeared later.

THE CHESTER PROBLEM

Chester was not Wroxeter. It was now for the most part an abandoned military site. Stuck out in the northeast corner of Wales, it must now have been something of a nuisance. Perhaps Vortigern, Cunedda, and Cunedda's successors, wished they had something akin to gunpowder to blow the place up. Its former military occupiers would already have taken anything of value, probably in the time of Constantine III. Paternus and his successors, as we will see, had their attention increasingly drawn westwards but would still have had to keep this area under surveillance. Chester's walls would have given protection for the north Wales field army when it was on the move but, for the rest of the time, the site would have been something of a white elephant. Invaders, pirates, robbers of every description would have been drawn as by a magnet to this former city of the legions, some of whose buildings, including its magnificent amphitheatre, were still standing. Enclosing a much smaller space than Wroxeter, nearly seventy acres compared with Wroxeter's two hundred, having a little over a mile of wall to defend compared with Wroxeter's two miles, Chester was still vulnerable as its population declined and its military personnel, no more than a locally recruited militia, also shrank. The obvious danger was that it could become a base for an enemy force, Pict or Irish, which intended to stay. There are signs that the entrances of the amphitheatre were blocked up, thus producing a mini-fortress in which some families might have been able to establish living spaces. Despite all this,

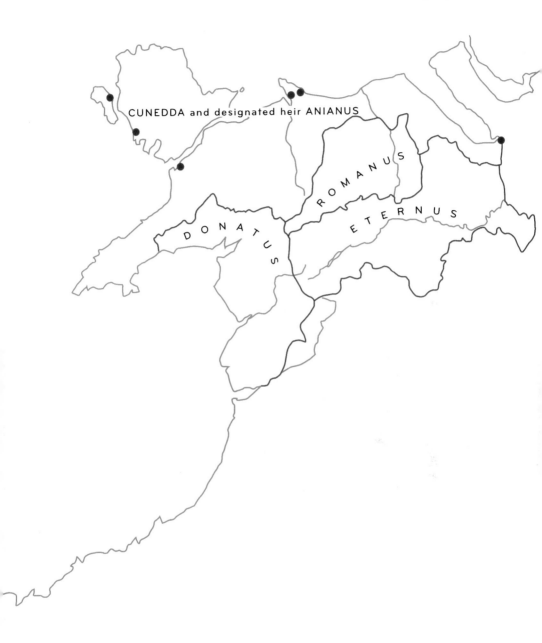

The Province of *Venedotia*,
Gwynedd, c.428–50.

CUNEDDA and designated heir ANIANUS

ROMANUS

ETERNUS

DONATUS

The north Powys
castle of Dinas Brân
above the Dee in the
vale of Llangollen.

it looks as though the church did decide to stay put, its centre, probably already a cathedral dedicated to Peter and Paul, possibly viewed as a missionary base. It was the site of a meeting of representatives of the British church with Augustine, archbishop of Canterbury, probably in 603 or 604.

Chester's occupants would have been of a very different class from those in Wroxeter and by this date must have been fewer in number. Graham Webster as long ago as 1951 questioned whether Chester's population would have stayed or whether they were more likely to have sought out safer sites. He suggested the hilltops of the Clwyds as one possibility.[14] But some people did stay on, and eventually the place became part of northern Powys. It may already have been absorbed by the time of the 603/4 church conference, and the possibility remains that it passed from the area administered by the *comes litoris Hiberniae* when that position was elevated to that of *praeses* in the *c.*429 reorganization.

GWYNEDD AFTER CUNEDDA

Talk of Cunedda's sons being the founders of parts of a Greater Gwynedd possibly disguises a more prosaic situation. Cunedda's designated heir and successor was his son Anianus, whose epithet, as we have seen, was *Einiawn*, The Anvil. He probably had direct rule over the coastal territories from the tip of Llŷn right across to the Dee estuary, including Anglesey. This would have included the courts of Rhos and even Degannwy, at the centre of the province's power, both on the Creuddyn peninsula known today for its seaside resort of Llandudno. To the south, his brother Donatus had as his appanage southern Llŷn and Ardudwy, pushing his authority as far south as the river Mawddach and the next, neighbouring and emerging state, Meirionydd. To the south of Anianus's territory east of the Conwy, Romanus had Rhufoniog and possibly Dyffryn Clwyd. Eternus had responsibility for the southeastern defences

14_ Webster, 1951, p. 39.

of Gwynedd made vulnerable by the valley of the Dee as it cut back into Wales from the east.

Anianus died, *or was killed*, possibly in a year near to 485. Nine years before this, to all intents and purposes the western empire came to an end. On 4 September 476, the western emperor Romulus Augustulus abdicated, and though the eastern emperor Zeno, 474–91, officially took control, with Odoacer at least theoretically his viceroy, in these areas that were once the heartland of the empire rule passed to the Germans. In north Wales, Eugenius, *Owain*, with his epithet *Dantguin* or *Danwyn*, White Tooth, succeeded. He is usually thought of as Anianus's eldest son because of the lazy scribal use of *ap* in what were really just king lists, and he is always referred to as being *of Rhos*. This designation implies direct rule over the same arc of territory along the northern coast that Anianus had controlled. Rhos was the cantref to the east of the Conwy river: the larger homeland included Rhos, Rhufoniog, Dyffryn Clwyd, and Tegeingl, the later counties of Denbighshire and Flintshire. To the British, this was *Gwynedd is Conwy*, Gwynedd below or to the east of the river Conwy. Again, this is exactly what one would expect if Paternus and his immediate successors had been appointed to control of a north Wales coastal area that in 398 included Chester.

If for a time the successors of Donatus, Romanus, and Eternus – that is, Eifion, possibly Brochwel, and Pebid *Penllyn* – came to succeed their fathers in their respective areas, the necessary territorial provision for Eugenius's brother, Cadwallon, later known as *Lawhir*, the Generous or the Long Handed, was made with the grant of *Môn*, Anglesey. With it, he inherited what might still have been considered the vitally important task of ridding the area of its last Irish immigrants.

CHAPTER FIVE

THE RIVER TIBER FOAMING WITH MUCH BLOOD

The Irish Threat Eliminated, 450–517

THE STRUGGLE AGAINST THE IRISH CONTINUES

The policy directed against the Irish can be seen as the logical continuation of Cunedda's work. It was a policy not just to defend Britain from Irish attack and invasion, but to clear the land of those who in previous times had moved in peacefully to settle and farm. It was part of a general backlash against *all* immigrants at a time when the diocese was feeling very insecure and unsure of its own identity. For a considerable period after 410, even beyond 476, Britain would have regarded itself as a self-governing part of the empire, responsible now for its own defence. Certainly, it would have thought of itself as very much an outlying bastion of civilization standing against the growing tide of barbarism. It is during this period that the word *barbarus*, barbarian, formerly meaning outsider, would have come to take on its full connotation of savagery, ignorance, and lack of civilization.

Nevertheless, Britain *was* on its own, whether we call this independence or not. It is unfortunately all too easy in the early years of the twenty-first century to imagine the growth of xenophobia directed against those now seen to have moved in unlawfully during the previous hundred-year period, only to herald, so it must have seemed, the imminent collapse of civilization and the predicament Britain now found itself in. The policy was hard-headed and calculating. For centuries, the diocese had endured the problem of settlers moving in peaceably and living happily alongside the resident population, only to see later generations of these immigrants stirred to action by fresh waves of invaders. This was spectacularly the case in Britain in the years before 367. Under Cunedda and those who followed him after *c.*450, the overriding needs of state security possibly made such a response inevitable.

> And they [Cunedda and his sons] drove out with immense slaughter the Scots [that is, the Irish] from those regions [of Gwynedd], who never returned again to inhabit them.[1]

We may have another indication that the work was systematic. In an admittedly rather late source, the thirteenth-century compilation the *Black Book of Carmarthen*, one of the *Stanzas of the Graves* says Anianus was killed. Interestingly, his death comes just before mention of another victim of these struggles, Beli, said there to be a son of Benlli *Gawr*, the Benlli killed by Cunedda.

> Every one who is not dilatory inquires -
> Whose is the mausoleum that is here?
> It is the grave of Einiawn, the son of Cunedda;
> It is a disgrace that he should have been slain in Britain.

CADWALLON'S IRISH WARS

Cadwallon, Cunedda's supposed grandson, who is credited with bringing this work to a successful conclusion, may have been called *Lawhir*, the Long Handed, not just in the usual sense of being generous, but also because of his determination to seek out all remaining pockets of potential trouble. We can probably dismiss the explanation of the fourteenth-century poet Iolo *Goch*, 1320–98, who came from Lleweni in the Vale of Clwyd, that Cadwallon's epithet was given because he could 'reach a stone from the ground to kill a crow without bending his back'![2] Cadwallon apparently ruled in *Môn*, Anglesey, from *c.*485, and then succeeded to the whole of Gwynedd after the death of his brother Eugenius in *c.*490. During this time, he is said to have finally broken any possibility of resistance from the

1_ Nennius, *Historia Brittonum*, Wade-Evans, 1938, p. 80.

2_ Baring-Gould and Fisher, 1907–13, Vol. II, 1908, p. 47, note 3.

134

Irish settlements. Although the triad containing the death notice of Anianus, Cunedda's son, is in an early fourteenth-century collection, Nennius's talk of this family's fight against the Irish shows that some version of the story might have been known at least as early as the ninth century.[3]

Cadwallon's victory appears in the triad *Three Fettered War-Bands of the Islands of Britain*.

The War-Band of Cadwallon Long-Arm,
who each one put the fetters of their horses
on their (own) feet, when fighting
with Serygei the Irishman
at the Irishman's Rocks in Môn.[4]

Dr Bromwich noted that the fetters in the above triad may have been some insignia or other, like warriors' torques. Earlier, Lloyd had suggested that the fetlocks, the parts of horses' legs where a tuft of hair grows behind the pastern joint just above the hoof, were tied in some way to their riders' feet, which 'made flight impossible, leaving victory and death as the sole alternatives'.[5]

Three supposed grandsons of Cunedda are mentioned as being involved in this battle against the Irishmen in a later, expanded, and doubtful version of the triad.

Kynyr or Kevyr (by another name) and Meilir and Yneigr, sons of Gwron ap Cunedda, who were all three
with Cadwallon Lawhir their cousin when he drove the Gwyddyl Ffichti from Môn.
And then they destroyed them (Gwyddyl Ffichti) completely, when Cadwallon Lawhir slew Seregri Wyddel [Serigi the Irishman] in Llan y Gwyddyl at Caer Gybi [Holyhead] in Môn.[6]

The Irishman's Rocks, *Cerryg y Gwyddyl*, is supposedly near Trefdraeth, just north of the Malltraeth Sands on Anglesey's southwestern coast.[7] An alternative identification, put forward as a result of the expansion of the triad, supported by Nicholas Owen, Thomas

[3] See the next chapter for another possibility concerning Anianus's death.

[4] *Trioedd Ynys Prydein*, Bromwich, 1961, p. 167, No. 62.

[5] Lloyd, 1912, Vol. I, p. 120; Bromwich, 1961, pp. 167–8.

[6] Bromwich, 1961, Appendix V, p. 257, No. 4. Also *Bonedd yr Arwyr*, 'The Descent of the Heroes', Bartrum, 1966, pp. 85–94.

[7] Lloyd, 1912, Vol. I, p. 120; Baring-Gould and Fisher, 1907–13, Vol. IV, 1913, p. 196.

Pennant, and Lewis Morris in the eighteenth century, turns *Cerryg y Gwyddyl* into *Llan* or *Capel y Gwyddyl*, also known as *Eglwys y Bedd*, the Church of the Grave, which apparently lay within the Roman fortress of Holyhead next to the parish church of St Cybi. Nicholas Owen thought that the ruins of this little building were removed in the mid-eighteenth century. In 1913, however, Baring-Gould and Fisher claimed that *Capel y Gwyddyl* was the building still standing today in the corner of the churchyard, although conceding that the chancel had been pulled down. In the version in *Bonedd yr Arwyr*, Descent of the Heroes, however, it appears as *Llam y Gwyddyl*, the Irishman's Leap, which is presumably nothing to do with a church.[8]

Writers on the subject are unclear whether the expansion of the triad is all the work of Iolo Morgannwg, 1746/7–1826, and just another piece of his usual elaboration.[9] Iolo, from Morgannwg, that is Glamorgan, in south Wales bears comparison with Geoffrey of Monmouth. Both had access to information now lost to us that would have been invaluable had they not been prone to highly imaginative elaborations and additions – some call them outright forgeries – making it almost impossible to tell the wheat from the chaff. However, the suggestion that Cadwallon did indeed build a church within the Roman fort, some time before his son Maelgwyn invited Cybi, a priest from Ireland, to be bishop there, is not so fantastic and fits the apparent reoccupation of sites in western Anglesey following defeat of the Irish settlers and their eviction.

It is possible that one of the places from which Cadwallon and his forces drove out or annihilated settlers of Irish descent was Bodedern in western Anglesey, just inland from the strait dividing it from Holy Island. In the process, it seems that the troops destroyed the cemetery, a place where up to a thousand people were buried. This, like the settlement itself, was apparently dedicated to *Ercagnos*, or in Irish *Ercán*. The name was on an inscribed stone in the centre of the burial area which, when excavated, was found

8_ Bartrum, 1966, p. 92, No. 29 (150).

9_ Baring-Gould and Fisher, 1907–13, Vol. IV, 1913, pp. 196–7; Vol. II, 1908, pp. 46–7; Pennant, 1784, Vol. II, Part 1, 1781, p. 287; Owen, 1775.

upended.[10] Yet again we have to remind ourselves that these British army officers were Roman officers, heirs to a frightening tradition and an army that was the terror of all who encountered it. In 210, the emperors Septimius Severus and his son Caracalla were campaigning in Britain.

When the inhabitants of the island again revolted, he [Severus] assembled his troops and ordered them to invade the territory of the rebels, and kill everyone they met.[11]

CADWALLON AND ELIAN: FROM POINT LYNAS TO ABERFFRAW

Cadwallon was supposedly a patron of the cleric Elian or Eilian, who is normally associated with the cantref of Rhos on the north Wales mainland.[12] In the northeast corner of Anglesey, however, there is a similar cluster of names testifying to the saint's influence. Again we find *Ffynnon Elian*, Elian's Well, *Bryn Eilian* and *Mynydd Eilian*, Elian's hill and Elian's mountain. Near Llanelian and just inland from Point Lynas, *Trwyn Eilian*, Eilian's headland, in 1908 at least, were to be seen the remains of buildings known locally as *Llys Caswallon*, Cadwallon's palace or court. Possibly using this as his base for operations against the Irish immigrant population in Anglesey, once the task was accomplished Cadwallon moved his court westwards, again contributing to the shift in Gwynedd's centre of gravity. It seems to be about this time that the Roman fort of Aberffraw was rebuilt and occupied. The place had never been much more than the equivalent of a marching camp and lookout post, only used in times of trouble. It had consisted of an earthen rampart fronted by a ditch backed by a road that skirted the perimeter. Its buildings must always have been of wood. By the time of Cadwallon's Anglesey rule, c.485–90, Aberffraw's ditch had silted up, and so at roughly this time a crudely-made rubble wall four

10_ Bromwich and Brinley Jones, 1978, pp. 352–3.

11_ Dio Cassius, *Roman History*, 76, 15, Mann, 1969, No. 148.

12_ Behind the modern seaside town of Colwyn Bay there are a church, hill, and well associated with Elian: Llanelian, Bryn Elian, and Ffynnon Elian.

feet wide was built as a new defence. The continued use of Aberffraw was secured.

By the twelfth century Aberffraw was one of the principal seats of the kings or, as they were then called, the princes of Gwynedd. Their other residences were at Abergwyngregyn, referred to locally as Aber, on the north coast of Arllechwedd, roughly opposite the Anglesey court site of Llanfaes and the Edwardian castle at Beaumaris, and Degannwy on the Creuddyn peninsula, only a few miles from the earlier and still-used site at Rhos. If Aberffraw was reoccupied now, it becomes even more likely that Holyhead's fort was recommissioned, possibly with the addition of a small church in one corner of the enclosure. This is possibly the *Llan* or *Capel y Gwyddyl*, also known as *Eglwys y Bedd*, noted above. By the time Cadwallon replaced his brother in the court of Rhos in *c*.490, northern Gwynedd, still the heartland of this emerging state, may have had Rhos, Degannwy, Aberffraw, with Llanelian, and Holyhead in Anglesey, as its capital sites. If Chester was still in Gwynedd and not already in Powys, it would have been increasingly eclipsed as attention focused more and more on the west.

OSMAEL, AFLOEG, AND DOCMAIL

We are now in a position to return to the choice of Osmael and Afloeg as names for two of Cunedda's invented sons. Osmael was said to be the founder or ruler of Osmeilion in Anglesey: he was *Ysfael* of *Maes Ysfeilion*, Osmael of the Plain of Osmael, which receives its first mention in the annals in the first years of the tenth century. After the Norse capital and kingdom of Dublin was taken by the combined armies of Brega and Leinster in 902, many 'leaving great numbers of their ships behind them, they [or at least some of the Norse] escaped half dead across the sea'.[13] On the other side of the sea, the result was recorded. 'Igmunt arrived in the island of Anglesey and took Maes Ysfeilion.'[14]

13_ AFM, O'Donovan, 1851, Vol. I, p. 557.

14_ AC, 902, Wade-Evans, 1938, p. 99. Also in the other Welsh annals.

Ingimund was only the first of a line of Norse and Danish invaders who would become familiar with this southeastern corner of Anglesey at the eastern entrance to the Menai Strait. It looks as though we are dealing with a territory smaller even than the commote of Dindaethwy in which it is found. The *maes*, field or plain, referred to in AC, is apparently the tiny valley of the river Lleiniog just north of Llanfaes and about two miles north of Beaumaris. The river empties on to a sand and stone beach sheltered, as is the strait itself, from bad weather coming from whatever quarter. In the period 1082–93, Earl Hugh of Chester, and more directly his commander Robert of Rhuddlan, moving into north Wales built a castle here on the northern side of the valley at Aber Lleiniog, still surviving as an impressive motte. Later Edward I was to build his magnificent castle at Beaumaris further south. Anyone wishing to control Anglesey saw this area as vitally important. In the context of the work of Cunedda, his son Anianus the Anvil, Eugenius of Rhos, and Cadwallon the Long Handed, struggling against the Irish, it could be that this was the original base for operations which eventually took their forces north to Point Lynas and then west across the island. If there really had been a son of Cunedda named Ysfael or Osmael involved in these operations, he would have finished up with more territory than this and, if he had been killed, there would probably have been some other notice. The name might have been that of a prominent citizen involved in these battles with his overlord. However, it might also have been a name carrying a deeper meaning.

Ysfael could have been a reference to the biblical Ishmael, not the son of Abraham but Ishmael son of Nethaniah of the old royal family of Judah. After the fall of Jerusalem to the Babylonians, with the burning of the temple and the demolition of the walls, its people, apart from the very poorest, were taken into exile. The new Babylonian governor was Gedaliah son of Ahikam, and he was encouraging those still in Judah to stay and serve their new masters. Because of this, Ishmael with ten

139

conspirators visited Gedaliah when he was in *Mizpah* north of Jerusalem. Dining together, Ishmael killed the governor and all others present on the grounds that they were nothing but puppets of the Babylonians.[15] Is this how the descendants of Cunedda saw their work, ridding north Wales of settlers who were merely puppets of the Irish Babylon and who might one day return as had nearly been the case at the time of the Alleluia Victory? It seems possible, even probable, that later genealogists saw the work of Cunedda and his descendants in exactly this light.

Afloeg was the person who supposedly gave his name to the little *cymwd*, commote, of Afloegion, known now in its corrupt form Cafflogion, in the south of Llŷn. The resort of Pwllheli lies on the centre point of its south-facing coast. The position again raises the possibility that this person, almost certainly not a son of Cunedda in any literal sense of that word, was involved in operations similar to those being carried out in Anglesey. We might even be looking at a faint echo of a situation common in Ireland where families having no links with the main ruling dynasties could be granted 'most favoured people status' in return for giving particular assistance to their overlords. The Múscraige in southern Ireland were accorded this position by later Eóganacht kings of Munster for their rôle in helping to establish the dynasty at the Rock of Cashel in *c.*431. Perhaps Afloeg and Ysfael were two such people, heads of families who might even have ruled as virtually independent lords because of their operations against the unwanted settlers. Docmail, or Dogfael, may be yet another example. The commote Dogfeiling named after him lies north to south in the higher stretches of the Vale of Clwyd. Immediately to its east in the Clwyd Hills lie the scenes of Cunedda's victories over the Picts, their Irish allies, and Benlli *Gawr*, Benlli the Giant.

15_ *The Book of Jeremiah*, 40–41.

According to the thirteenth-century *Stanzas of the Graves*, Benlli had a son named Beli. More importantly, it appears that Beli continued the fight, now a war of resistance, only to meet his death less than three miles northeast of Foel Fenlli on Ffrith Mountain. The next mountain to the north of Foel Fenlli in the Clwyds is Moel Fama or Famau which, at 554 metres or 1,820 feet, is the highest of the range. Protruding east is a round spur named *Ffrith* or Sheep Walk Mountain. On its eastern side, the small but fast flowing river Alyn runs to the north before a hairpin bend returns it south through the Vale of Mold. Just below the mountain is a ford across the river, still named as such on OS maps but now replaced by a small bridge. This could have been the place known as *Rhyd y Gyfarthfa*. *Cyfarthfa* meaning battle, this would make it the Battle Ford. There is, however, another ford only a little distance to the north near the modern bridge across *Nant Gain*, the Cain Brook, carrying its road into the village of Cilcain. To the west of the first of these fords and to the south of the second is a field still called *Maes-mawr*, the Big Meadow. If the story can be trusted, it looks as though Beli and his men had been surprised at one or the other of these fords in a fight that may have been like a more limited version of the Alleluia Victory. The encounters seemingly moved up on to the hill and there, in Maes-mawr, Beli was allegedly killed and buried.

This is the story as given us in the *Stanzas of the Graves* found in the *Black Book of Carmarthen*.

Whose is the grave in Maes Mawr?
Proud his hand on the blades [or his lance];
The grave of Beli, the son of Benlli Gawr.[16]

Commenting on this in his *Hanes Cymru*, The History of Wales, published in 1842, the Revd Thomas Price, noting that cairns were often used for burial and that

[16] Translated by Howard Lockley. On place-name evidence, see especially Owen and Morgan, 2008.

the *Stanzas of the Graves* gives more than two hundred examples of this, looks particularly at Beli's tomb.

But it is sad to relate the fate of this noted memorial, to which the stanza refers, and the destruction which came to it through the miserliness of the low-born serfling which is contained in the following story: *The Tall Stones of Maesmawr.*

There is a place on the mountain between Iâl and the Vale of Alun, above Rhyd y Gyfarthfa, which is called Maes Mawr, where there was a battle between Meilyr ab ... [*sic*] and Beli ab Benlli Gawr, where Beli was killed, and Meirion [? a mistake – Meilyr being intended or the reverse] put two stones standing at each end of the grave; these were there until within 40 years [that is, until c.1800]; then there came an atrocious man, one Edward ap Siôn ab Llywelyn from Iâl, who owned the portion of land which had been enclosed from the mountain in which were the grave and the above stones, and he raised the stones and placed them over the pipe of a lime kiln; and from too much heat and the weight, they immediately broke. And after they had broken he burned them in the kiln to lime, they which had been there many hundreds of years. And a bad end came to him who had despoiled the grave of the dead soldier, to whom sang the bard in the grave stanzas.

The missing name of Meilyr's father is another of those infuriating lacunae that complicate so many of these enquiries. If it could be filled with the name Dogfael, this might ease our path. But we are probably dealing here with the work of Iolo Morgannwg. In his probable expansion of the triad dealing with Serigi the Irishman, Iolo, if it is he, names the father of the Meilyr there mentioned as the almost certainly invented Gwron son of Cunedda. This fictitious name, probably an epithet meaning hero, appears in only two pedigrees, both seemingly Iolo's work. There, as in the expanded triad, we find the names of Gwron's sons, Cynir, an unusual Yneigeir, and Meilyr. If according to Iolo, Meilyr helped Cadwallon in Anglesey, this puts him in the right generation to complete Cunedda's work by defeating Beli. Beli seems to have existed, and the thirteenth-century *Black Book of Carmarthen* indicates his grave, but the rest we might have to ascribe to Iolo and should therefore hesitate.

THE CHURCH AGAINST PAGANISM

It is tempting to see other details of the story given us by the Revd Thomas Price as being supported by place-name evidence. There is a *Coed Cefn-goleu*, which might just mean Wood of the Hillside of Light, on the spur to the south of Ffrith Mountain, and a *Cae'r Odyn*, Kiln Field, just a little to the east. Other names might take us back, or at least remind us of the original story. At the start of the road up to the Pen Barras Pass and Benlli's stronghold, is a *Tafarn-y-Gelyn*, the enemies' tavern, although this is thought to be of much later derivation where the holly tavern changed into the enemy's tavern because of the turnpike gate erected here in the eighteenth century. Equally flimsy as evidence, between the Alyn and Ffrith Mountain we find two places with the name *Maes-y-Groes*, Field of the Cross, a very common name associated with cross-roads. To the south on a little tributary of the Alyn is *Rhŷd-yr-Eilun*, which could mean the Ford of the Idol.

All this gives us precious little to go on, but these names at least raise the question if Benlli and his followers were still for the most part pagan? This is certainly what the Germanus story about Benlli says. It might also be a reason why later the church was so concerned to have played a part in their downfall and eviction. Could it possibly be that to mark the restoration of legitimate Christian government crosses were erected in the neighbourhood and churches built either side of Foel Fenlli, at Llanbedr in the west and Llanferres in the east? We should remember the destruction of the settlement and cemetery at Bodedern in Anglesey under the protection of the pagan god Ercán whose stone was upended. Llanbedr, where the original church was abandoned for the site of the present building in 1862, is dedicated to *Pedr*, St Peter, and Llanferres to Britius or Berres, a fifth-century hermit. Was its first dedication to St Peter, making these two early dedications in north Wales to the prince of the apostles who held the keys of heaven and hell? Did Ruthin, already the site of a, by this date, long since abandoned Roman fort, take on a new lease of life as the seat and capital for the family of Dogfael which had played such an important rôle in these events? Its church is also dedicated to St Peter. And did the site of Llanbedr Hall, with possibly a settlement near the present Llanbedr Dyffryn Clwyd, both immediately below Foel Fenlli in the Vale of Clwyd, provide even more obvious reminders of the family's rise to power and the reason for this prominence?

ETHNIC CLEANSING?

These then were the first six rulers of Gwynedd: Paternus, Eternus, Eternus's successor nicknamed *Cunedda*, the Good King, his son Anianus nicknamed the Anvil, Eugenius White Tooth and Cadwallon the Long Handed, with some indication of at least three other families acting as allies and thereby reaching positions of importance. It is perhaps uncomfortable to look at this first period in the history of Gwynedd and realize this was a time, not just of bloodshed, for virtually all states that succeeded to the power and lands of the western Roman empire emerged in this way, but of what today we would call ethnic cleansing.

There really is no way and no need to shy away from this issue. Recently the fortieth anniversary of Enoch Powell's *Rivers of Blood* speech given on 20 April 1968 was marked on radio and television. Powell said he had been warned by a constituent, "In this country in 15 or

20 years' time the black man" for which in our context read Irishman and his former ally, the Pict, "will have the whip hand over the white man [the Roman or the native Briton]." This Wolverhampton MP knew his Virgil and so of course would the educated élite of Roman Britain. When Aeneas and his Trojans at last arrived in *Hesperia*, Italy, they came ashore at *Cumae*, Cuma, just twenty miles northwest of Naples in Campania and the site of Italy's oldest Greek colony. While his men explored and raided, Aeneas sought out the temple of Apollo, the god of prophecy, and residence of one of the earliest known Sibyls, women renowned for their prophetic powers. On a hill of the mountain range named Mount *Gaurus*, north of the promontory of *Misenum* where Rome was to have its western Mediterranean fleet base, Aeneas arrived at Apollo's shrine, a vast cavern with many shafts through which the Sybil spoke.

They had reached the threshold of the cavern when the virgin priestess cried: 'Now is the time to ask your destinies. It is the god. The god is here' ... her face was transfigured, her colour changed, her hair fell in disorder about her head and she stood there with heaving breast and her wild heart bursting in ecstasy. She seemed to grow in stature and speak as no mortal had ever spoken when the god came to her in his power and breathed upon her ...

She urged Aeneas to pray and he did so, pouring out the sufferings endured by his Trojans. He begged for mercy now that they had arrived in Italy, their new home, offering to build a temple of solid marble to Apollo. The Sibyl answered him.

'At long last you have done with the perils of the ocean, but worse things remain for you to bear on land ... I see wars, deadly wars, I see the Tiber foaming with torrents of blood ... You must not give way to these adversities but must face them all the more boldly wherever your fortune allows it ...'

With these words from her shrine the Sibyl of Cumae sang her fearful riddling prophecies, her voice booming in the cave as she wrapped the truth in darkness ...[17]

Powell took these lines and uttered his famous warning, one that the rulers of Gwynedd seemed to hear more than 1,500 years before.

I look ahead, I am filled with foreboding; like the Roman, I seem to see "the River Tiber foaming with much blood." ... Only resolute and urgent action will avert it even now. Whether there will be the public will to demand and obtain action, I do not know. All I know is that to see, and not to speak [and by implication, not to act], would be the great betrayal.

Of course, a similar thing had been going on in the east of the country with the Saxons, not, as is nowadays being realized, coming in the vast hordes implied by Gildas, but in sufficient numbers to cause mayhem once they had rebelled against their former paymasters. We are told specifically that before the rebellion there was growing resentment amongst the Britons at their presence and cost. The rebellion was apparently a reaction to this resentment. In the west, in Gwynedd, the British had taken early action to defend themselves from the threat of terrorism. And, just as today, it seems that any action towards that end was justified. Were the Good King, the Anvil, White Tooth, and the Long Handed being urged by their constituents, their subjects, to take the action Powell recommended, but with force more suited to the times? Was the air full of talk of no-go areas, of the Irish being reluctant to integrate, dangerous fragmentation, the state being pulled apart and undermined, and of immigrants bringing in ever more relatives? Had what today might be called racially-motivated attacks led to tension and then violence? Was all this going on, not just in Britain in 1968 or even 2008, but in western Britain after the c.429 Alleluia Victory and the fall of Benlli, and in the

17_ Virgil, *Aeneid*, Book 6, West, 1991, pp. 133–5.

146

east after the *c.*438 Saxon revolt? The Picts were defeated, the Irish expelled, but the Saxons after the battle of *Camlan* did indeed come to have the whip hand.

In Gwynedd the numbers of Irish were probably not that large, although the numbers in the Bodedern cemetery give pause for thought. In other words, we do not need archaeologists to tell us they haven't found evidence of large-scale Irish immigration. Such evidence, no matter how much digging, would be hard to find and, despite the numbers, the texts certainly imply a determined resistance on the part of the Irish who wanted to stay. As in the east with the Saxons, quite small numbers of displaced and disaffected immigrants would have been able to cause considerable dislocation. More importantly, we have to remember that their expulsion was the work of Roman troops operating against those who had shown themselves disloyal to the state.

LOYAL IMMIGRANTS

There are, however, pointers to the probability that the situation was not totally black and white. We can look at the situation in the Powys area further south. Here the Irish immigrants, probably appointed by Magnus Maximus in the 380s to patrol and maintain the roads to the west of Wroxeter, had seemingly been doing their job rather well. The memorial to Cunorix the king, found in Wroxeter itself and dated to about the 470s, would seem to be evidence of this.[18] Cunorix was very probably the leader of these road repairers and rural policemen, doing a job no one else wanted but one that was vitally important. They would have been rather a rough lot, not people to mix with more than was diplomatically necessary: indeed, it was probably this sort of patronizing attitude that had led to their northern relatives going into rebellion. The result here was that although Cunorix was sufficiently important to be honoured with a memorial, the stone had been used

[18] Wright and Jackson, 1968.

before, the inscription was not in straightforward Latin, and he was not buried in the Roman cemetery. Cunorix was not part of Wroxeter society.

If we move back to the north, we find a bilingual memorial in Irish ogam and Latin, dated to the 490s, which lay for centuries at a point just over three miles from Ruthin near Clocaenog. The description of its original position is remarkably like that given for the grave of Beli son of Benlli. One of only three stones found in north Wales with an Irish inscription, it has received considerable notice and is now in the National Museum of Wales. It commemorates SIMILINI TOVISACI, Prince Similinus, the word *tovisaci* being the same as the Irish *taoiseach* and Welsh *tywysog*. The name is also in Irish *ogam*, that is, it appears as lines cut into the two sides of the stone.

The questions now come thick and fast. What was a memorial to a member of the Irish immigrant community doing only three miles from the capital of Dogfeiling, the headquarters of someone who likely played an important rôle in the final elimination of the Irish followers of Benlli? Was he buried here in circumstances similar to Beli, but if killed in battle is it likely there would have been anyone around afterwards to inscribe a memorial? Could Beli's stones have been inscribed in the Irish manner? Do we necessarily have to believe that Beli *was* battling with the British? Two stones at either end of the grave apparently marked both burials. Surely these stones imply what we might expect: that the Irish immigrants were split in their allegiances, some taking the age-old anti-Roman stance whilst others were concerned to show their loyalty to their newly adopted home by siding with Gwynedd's rulers, even fighting for them against their compatriots?

With this Clocaenog stone having its southern Powys match in the memorial to Cunorix in Wroxeter dated to about 470, the genealogies then give further pause for thought. Any successor of Cunorix might be expected to have operated in the years between 470 and 490. The genealogies give us a Tithlyn or Tidlet *Prydyn*, the Pict, described as being of the *Gwyddyl Ffichti*, 'the Irish Picts' of Powys.[19] This designation probably arose because of the constant linkage in late Roman sources of *Scotti* and *Picti*. It may also in part have stemmed from the belief that these particular Irish came from northern Ireland, or from there but after a secondary migration from Scotland. Tithlyn or Tidlet is possibly an attempt to render the Irish *Tailech*, *Taillte*, or *Tuathal*, the latter meaning literally 'ruler of the people'. Where the pedigrees then show that the anti-Irish stance was not that deep seated or racially motivated, at least at government level where it was probably more a matter of statecraft at a time of emergency, is the marriage of Tithlyn's daughter Tubrawst or Prawst to none other than Anianus the Anvil of Gwynedd. This dating indication might allow Tithlyn to be the successor of Cunorix and might also indicate that the descendants of the original Irish appointees continued to hold power in this area of southern Powys under overlords who were the descendants of Brutus, or Britu.

IRISH INVASION – AILILL SON OF DÚNLANG

There are other pointers that would seem to confirm that these years of Cadwallon, *c.*490–517, were indeed years of emergency and that he was fighting against more than just the Irish settlers who had been in north Wales for generations. The sources are vague, but important. At a date soon after 493 when Eochu son of Cairpre became king of Ireland's north Leinster, Ailill son of Dúnlang took control, giving him a reign from some time after 493 up to possibly 527.

The aim of the Irish pedigree compilers was to show how Leinster's principal population groupings came into being, all descended from Catháir and his supposed grandson Bresal. Through Énnae son of Bresal, we have the Uí Briúin of Cualu, living south of the Liffey along the coast of Wicklow. These were said to be descended from Énnae's son Brión. More importantly, from Brión's

[19]_ Jesus College MS 20, late fourteenth century, based on a pre-1200 source, Bartrum, 1966, p. 47. Also *Bonedd yr Arwyr*, ibid., p. 91, and *Bonedd y Saint*, p. 64.

brother Dúnlang we have the Uí Dúnlainge – Ailill was Dúnlang's son – who in turn split into the Uí Fáeláin, Uí Failge, and Uí Muiredaig, all of north Leinster. For southern Leinster, its main group, the Uí Ceinnselaigh or Chennselaig, are descendants of Énnae or Enna *Cennselach*, the son of Labraid and grandson of Bresal. Another son of Labraid, Drón, was supposedly ancestor of the Uí Drona, and Drón's brother Daig that of the Uí Dego, both of mid-Leinster.

In an Irish *Life of Brigit*, 'the Mary of the Gael' and founder of the monastery at *Cell-dara*, Kildare, which was a double monastery for nuns and monks, the abbess confronted Ailill on behalf of her father for the return of a sword loaned earlier and also for one of his servants who wanted to become a monk.

'Why should I give that to thee?' saith the king.

'Excellent children will be given to thee,' saith Brigit, 'and kingship to thy sons, and heaven to thyself.'

Said the king, 'The kingdom of heaven, as I see it not, I ask it not. Kingship for my sons, moreover, I ask not, for I myself am still alive, and let each one work in his time [to achieve that goal]. Give me, however, length of life in my realm and victoriousness [sic] in battle over Conn's Half [the northern half of Ireland]; for there is warfare between us.'

'It shall be given,' saith Brigit. And this was fulfilled; for through Brigit's blessing thirty battles were broken before Ailill in Ireland and nine in Alba [Britain].[20]

Ailill's self-professed paganism is interesting in connection with observations above concerning Benlli as well as the cemetery at Bodedern in Anglesey, though Ailill had paid for the workers building the Kildare monastery.

[20]_ Stokes, 1890, pp. 193–4, Alba translated as Scotland.

Before underlining the perhaps obvious point of the last extract, another somewhat controversial possibility might be mentioned, even if there is no space here to argue a case. It could well be that the two founding figures of early Irish history, Niall of the Nine Hostages and Conall the Red, the first the founder of northern Ireland's Uí Néill, and the second the founder of the Eóganacht of southern Ireland, were in fact agents of the Roman-British state. It is more than probable that they had been sent back to Ireland by Vortigern in order to curb attacks from pirates and raiding kings and in the process to establish themselves as rulers who would follow a policy of alliance with Britain and hostility to its enemies. The Uí Néill from the time of Niall had the north of Ireland and Leinster in their sphere of operations and both areas had a long history of aggression against the Roman diocese to the east.

After Niall's death, when the annals become more reliable, the record of warfare between the Uí Néill and Leinster forces continues. A great slaughter of Leinster men is noted under 452. Niall was killed at sea that year by forces from southern Leinster. His son Lóegaire, now the leading Uí Néill representative, immediately returned to the attack, achieving another major victory in 453. Sufficiently strong in the face of Leinster, Connacht, and Ulaid hostility, and certainly the leading military power in the Meath area, Lóegaire marched to Tara in 454 and had himself inaugurated as king. If the theory being advanced here is correct, only certain rulers would have been singled out for this treatment by the Uí Néill; that is, those who had been foremost in the attacks on Britain which had brought Vortigern to power and had led to the fall of Benlli in north Wales.

We are told that Cunedda and his sons down to his grandson Cadwallon were successful in expelling the Irish 'who never again returned'. The statement is clearly something of a summary. The defeat of the reconnaissance force of Picts and Irish in 429 did seem to herald a lull in attacks, one used by Cunedda and his successors to weed out those thought to have been aiding the incomers. But there was apparently a return to direct intervention in north Wales by the north Leinster king Ailill so that not only were thirty battles broken before him in Ireland, probably most against the Uí Néill and their allies, nine were won in Britain. In other words Cadwallon, at least at one stage in his campaigns, was fighting not just against resident Irish who remained recalcitrant but also against Irish invaders. These, seemingly led by Ailill, may have been called in by Irish settlers determined not to leave.

Such an interpretation would also allow us to see Cadwallon and the Uí Néill, the descendants of Niall, taking *joint*, even *co-ordinated* action against Leinster forces. For the Uí Néill, this became a struggle for ultimate power over the best lands in Ireland, the plain of Meath, leading to a hostility that well outgrew any origins in a British–Irish alliance. Had Ailill begun his raiding in Britain before he became king, or did he start to involve himself in Gwynedd's affairs immediately he took control? Perhaps refugees were beginning to arrive in Ireland just as they had in the period when the Roman army was conquering Britain after 43. The Irish *Life of Brigit* has two blind men of the Britons coming to Brigit to be healed.[21] In possibly 494 the Uí Néill under Cairpre son of Niall again found themselves confronted by Leinster forces, but they defeated them at Teltown in Meath. There was no return to the fight until 499 when the Leinster men were again defeated by Cairpre, this time near Lough Slevin in Westmeath.[22] This then could have been the period, 495–500, when Ailill was active in north Wales and when Cadwallon was fighting hardest and winning his reputation.

[21]_ Ibid., p. 189.

[22]_ AU, 498; AFM, 492.

Above: Possible site of
Capel y Gwyddyl [Eglwys
y Bedd] built by Cadwallon
c.485–90, or when he
was ruler of Gwynedd
c.490–517.

Left: The fortress of
Holyhead and its garrison
would have played an
important rôle in the war
against Irish invasion.
(Courtesy of Roman Tours,
Chester and Caergwrle)

The great prize. Tara's Stone of Destiny. A pillar stone, it once marked the probable site of the inauguration of Tara's kings. Some time after 1798 it was moved to the next mound south to mark the graves of those killed in that year's rebellion.

Aerial view of Tara looking north. The original site of *Lia Fáil*, the Stone of Destiny, was the smallest clearly defined mound in the centre of the picture. It can be seen in its new position on the next earthwork to the south.

(Photos: © Dept. of Environment, Heritage and Local Government, Ireland)

In 501, possibly at the end of this trouble in Gwynedd, Cairpre invaded Leinster and defeated the Laigin, the Leinster men, at *Cenn Ailbe*, in south Kildare, Aillil's territory.[23] However, two years later in 503, Leinster forces defeated the Uí Néill at *Druim Lochmuidhe*, probably in County Louth.[24] This fightback reached what may have seemed to be a turning point in 507 when the Laigin not only defeated the Uí Néill, who were apparently invading, in the battle of *Ard Corann*, called the Field of Lightning in AFM, but also killed Lugaid, the son of Lóegaire and grandson of Niall.[25] In 510, another Leinster ruler, Failge *Berraide* of the Uí Failge, invaded Uí Néill lands and defeated the by now elderly Fiacha son of Niall at Frevin Hill, west of Lough Owel in Westmeath.[26]

450: THE FALL OF EMAIN AND THE 516 CONQUEST OF MEATH

The climax of this Uí Néill–Leinster struggle came in 516, possibly the year before Maelgwn succeeded his father Cadwallon as king of Gwynedd, with the battle of *Druim Derg* somewhere in Leinster.[27] This decisive defeat for Leinster arms was won by Niall's son Fiacha, not against Ailill, but against Failge *Berraide* of the Uí Failge. Earlier the Uí Néill had destroyed the Ulaid, the greatest opponents of Rome in Ireland and the main and constant allies of the Picts since the outset of the Roman takeover of Britain. The culmination of that struggle had been the fall of *Emain Macha*, the Ulaid's ceremonial and tribal capital, in about the year 450. The last king of the Ulaid inaugurated at the site, and the one killed in its defence, was reputedly Fergus *Fogae*, Fergus of the Spears. Now, in 516, after a struggle that had started in the last years of Niall, who died *c*.452, Meath was finally brought under Uí Néill rule. With it came control of the ceremonial site at Tara. Leinster rulers had resisted

23_ AU, 500; AFM, 494.

24_ AU, 502, AFM, 496, possibly repeated at 500.

25_ AU, 506, 507, with a later hand inserting a 'second' battle of *Ard Corann* under 510=511; AFM, 503; AI, 506; and Smyth, 1972, pp. 6–7.

26_ AU, 509; AFM, 501; AI, 508; and Mac Niocaill 1972, pp. 17–18.

27_ AU, 515; AFM, 507; AI, 513; AT; and Mac Niocaill, 1972, pp. 9–18.

attempts to take the ceremonial capital because the people of the area were Leinster people. Now it had fallen, and permanently so, into the hands of the southern Uí Néill, and from now on, whoever was overlord of the northern and southern Uí Néill confederation was known as the king of Tara.

The battle of Druim Dergaide [an unknown site in Meath] (won) by Fiacha son of Niall against Failge Berraide. Thence the plain of Mide was taken away from the Laigen, as Cend Faelad sang:

Vengeance in seven years' time
Was his heart's desire:
The battle at Druim Dergaide,
It was thereby Mag Mide [the Meath plain] was forfeited.[28]

The seven years wait for revenge followed the defeat of Fiacha by Leinster forces in 510. If the thesis propounded here is correct, *Druim Derg* was also a Roman victory. Roman Britain may have been changing into something different, but the victory still represented a defeat for those in Ireland who believed that they could take advantage of the difficulties faced by a Britain emerging out of more than three and a half centuries of imperial rule. Indeed, if the idea that the north Welsh and the Uí Néill were co-operating in their struggle against their Irish enemies is not out of the question, then we have to entertain at least the possibility that British forces could have fought in the battle alongside their Irish allies.

GWRIN OF MEIRIONYDD AND THE FIGHT AGAINST INVASION

One other piece of evidence, however tenuous, can be cited to support the idea that there was external intervention in Gwynedd's affairs from Ireland during

[28]_ AU, 516=517, Mac Airt and Mac Niocaill, 1983, p. 65. Also AI, AT, AClon, AFM. This reversed the defeat for Fiacha around seven years earlier by the same Failge *Berraide*. 'The end result was a line of Uí Néill kingdoms which stretched in a crude crescent from the east coast to Sligo Bay in the west and thence northwards to Inishowen' – Mac Niocaill, 1972, p. 10.

these years. We have seen that it is almost certain Tybion was not a son of Cunedda. Linking him to the Gwynedd family may have been to give added justification for the developments concerning Meirionydd that occurred in Maelgwn's reign.[29] This might make Tybion, if he existed, the father of Meirion, the grandfather of Cadwaladr, and the great-grandfather of Gwrin of Meirionydd. How and when this family gained control of the coastal area between the Mawddach and the Dyfi we are nowhere told. It seems likely that this came about through some appointment made between the move to north Wales of Paternus in *c.*398 and the reign of Cunedda, *c.*428–50. In this somewhat fragile sense, the rulers or administrators of this area could have owed their position to the Roman rulers of Gwynedd, which gives a certain justification for what Maelgwn did after he became king. If Gwrin was roughly contemporaneous with Cadwallon Long Hand when Cadwallon's son Maelgwn had Anglesey as his apanage, then Cadwaladr, Gwrin's father, was a contemporary of Eugenius, Meirion with Anianus the Anvil, and Tybion with Cunedda. As on so many other occasions, we are probably dealing with yet another piece of careless copying, when writers slapped *ap* between names in a king list, as much as with the deliberate manipulation of pedigrees for political ends. As for Gwrin's Roman name, could it have been something like Verinus?

We have wandered into Meirionydd's history for a purpose. The story about Gwrin is given by our somewhat untrustworthy friend Geoffrey of Monmouth. Though some of its details are clearly wrong, the essence of what it is saying may be true.

Gurguit Barbtruc [Gwrin Cutbeard], the son of Belinus [for which read Cadwaladr as the genealogies state] ... was a modest man and a wise one. In all his activities he imitated the deeds of his father, being himself a lover of peace and justice. When his neighbours rebelled against him, he took fresh courage from the example of his father, fought dreadful wars against them and

29_ Miller, *Saints*, 1979, pp. 101–12.

reduced them once more to the subjection which they owed him [as any Roman ruler would].

On a return voyage from exacting such obedience, ignoring the fanciful identification of that place as Denmark, he encountered a fleet clearly coming from Ireland, even if Geoffrey says it was from Spain. In itself this could be interpreted as indicating that for such a command or rule, Gwrin still found the sea the best and quickest way of exercising his control, something going back to the days of Paternus operating as a *comes litoris Hiberniae*.

On that occasion ... he came upon thirty ships full of men and women. Gurguit asked what they were doing there. Their leader whose name was Partholoim went up to Gurguit, did obeisance to him and asked him for his pardon and peace. Partholoim then described how he had been expelled ... and how he was now cruising in those waters in search of a land where he might settle ...

As Dr Molly Miller noted, Geoffrey would have read in Chapter 13 of the Nennius collection the story of how Ireland was first settled by Partholon with a thousand followers from Spain. In Nennius this comes immediately after a note of how the Picts occupied the Orkneys, which is where Geoffrey says Gwrin had sailed from on his voyage back from Denmark. Of course, we are looking here at a confused rendering of Ireland's foundation myth. In these stories, the first to arrive in Ireland was *Cessair*, the niece or grand-daughter of Noah, who, taking his warnings seriously, sailed to Ireland only to be washed away with her three male and fifty female companions by the predicted flood. Not until 311 years after the waters subsided did Partholon and his relatives land, coming from Greece rather than Spain. Others followed.

In Geoffrey's story, the implication is that Gwrin helped these ship-folk, sending them to an Ireland that, as in the foundation stories, was 'a completely uninhabited desert'. What the story seems to boil down to is the fact that Gwrin of Meirionydd intercepted an Irish fleet and forced it back to Ireland, and 'he ordered his representatives to go with them', making sure that they did go back. Perhaps he did not have the force necessary to fight the 'dreadful wars against them' for which, as a Roman, he was famous. Otherwise, one might have expected him to kill the lot and sink their ships. It is not much to go on but, in the context of everything else we have looked at, there *may* here be the outlines of a story that did happen.[30] If so, it also seems to underline the extent of the problem facing the rulers of Gwynedd before Maelgwn came to power.

THE FALL OF ROME, THE RISE OF KINGS, AND THE GROWTH OF STATES

The descendants of Paternus in Gwynedd might well have compared their own successes with events in the lowland southeast of Britain. Whilst taking pride in their own work they may have despaired of the evident decline and disintegration in the rest of Britain, regarding it, however, as something in which they themselves were no longer involved. Eternus, *c.*410–28, Cunedda, *c.*428–50, Anianus, *c.*450–85, and then Eugenius of Rhos, *c.*485–90, and his brother Cadwallon, were increasingly independent rulers *as of right*. We can now begin to talk, not just of military commanders and *praesides*, but of kings; not simply of commanders of men, but of hereditary rulers over territory.

Gildas may have railed against these developments like some latterday Welsh Calvinist minister, but they were almost inevitable. Possibly he was near the mark when he described these new men as a despicable lot. The kings of Gwynedd may have been able to look down with patrician disdain born of their aristocratic Roman origins upon the rest, but for others, unable to furnish such credentials, brute force and *de facto* control had to suffice.

30_ Ibid., pp. 105–7.

Kings were anointed not in God's name, but as being crueller than the rest; before long, they would be killed, with no enquiry into the truth, by those who had anointed them, and others still crueller chosen to replace them. Any king who seemed gentler or rather more inclined to the truth was regarded as the downfall of Britain: everyone directed their hatred and their weapons at him, with no respect ...

Britain has kings, but they are tyrants;
she has judges, but they are wicked.
They often plunder and terrorize – the innocent;
they defend and protect – the guilty and thieving;
they have many wives – whores and adulteresses;
they constantly swear – false oaths;
they make vows – but almost at once tell lies;
they wage wars – civil and unjust;
they chase thieves energetically all over the country –
but love and even reward the thieves who sit with
them at table;
they distribute alms profusely – but pile up an immense
mountain of crime for all to see;
they take their seats as judges – but rarely seek out
the rules of right judgement;
they despise the harmless and humble, but exalt to
the stars, so far as they can, their military companions,
bloody, proud and murderous men, adulterers and
enemies of God ...
they keep many prisoners in their jails, who are more
often loaded with chafing chains because of intrigue
than because they deserve punishment.
They hang around the altars swearing oaths – then
shortly afterwards scorn them as though they were
dirty stones.[31]

As we will see, the attack Gildas is developing was to be directed even more vociferously against one particular ruler of Gwynedd, namely Maelgwn.

Out of this confusion and horror emerged the kingdom of Gwynedd, which was to prove itself to be the most expansionist of the states comprising the area we call

[31]_ Gildas, *De Excidio Britanniae*, Book 2, Chs. 21 and 27, Winterbottom, 1978, pp. 24–5 and 29.

160

Wales. And when the Saxons came up against this highland mass and found it as difficult to conquer as the Romans had, they set up their lookout posts, dug their dykes, and named the people beyond the Welsh, *Wealas*, sing. *Wealh*, coming from the Old High German *Walh* or *Walah*, meaning, of course, Roman.

CHAPTER SIX

A DISGRACE HE SHOULD HAVE BEEN SLAIN
Dynastic Conflict in Gwynedd, 485–547

THE 485 COUP AGAINST ANIANUS

We should now be in a position to look at that pivotal figure of early Welsh history, Maelgwn son of Cadwallon, Maelgwn *Gwynedd*. On one estimate, Maelgwn could have been born in about 472 which would make him eighteen years old when we encounter the first obvious bout of dynastic conflict in the new kingdom of Gwynedd.

In *c.*490 he was responsible for the death of his uncle Eugenius. However, we may have been too precipitate in believing that Cunedda's eldest son and successor Anianus the Anvil, Maelgwn's supposed grandfather, had been killed in struggles against the Irish. The evidence is admittedly slight and late, coming in one of the *Stanzas of the Graves* in the thirteenth-century compilation known as the *Black Book of Carmarthen*, but it may be quite accidental that this notice comes just before another victim of these struggles, Beli son of Benlli *Gawr*.[1] The apparent disgust and outrage of the stanza possibly points to something underhand and unexpected in Anianus's end.

[1] We have seen that it may be wrong to assume that Beli was fighting *against* the British.

TABLE 7

The Gwynedd Dynasty – Traditional History
The First Dynastic Map
[a] Maelgwn = Marchell's and Gwrin's *brother-in-law* cf.
brother in Gildas: Clydno his nephew as in Gildas

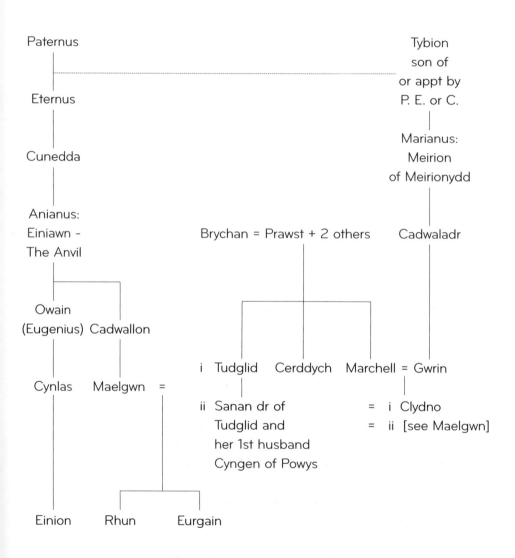

Paternus

Tybion
son of
or appt by
P. E. or C.

Eternus

Marianus:
Meirion
of Meirionydd

Cunedda

Anianus:
Einiawn –
The Anvil

Brychan = Prawst + 2 others

Cadwaladr

Owain
(Eugenius) Cadwallon

Cynlas Maelgwn =

i Tudglid Cerddych Marchell = Gwrin

ii Sanan dr of
Tudglid and
her 1st husband
Cyngen of Powys

= i Clydno
= ii [see Maelgwn]

Einion Rhun Eurgain

162

Every one who is not dilatory inquires –
Whose is the mausoleum that is here?
It is the grave of Einiawn [Anianus], the son of Cunedda;
It is a disgrace that he should have been slain in Britain.[2]

Could this refer to the first example of conflict in the
family of Paternus and Cunedda or, indeed, to a coup
which replaced the original family? If so, this might
implicate the Anvil's supposed sons, his successors
Eugenius, that is, Owain White Tooth of Rhos, and
Cadwallon. They did apparently succeed, but were they
necessarily his sons? Once again, we encounter the habit
of medieval scribes had of inserting *ap*, son of, between
names in what were no more than dimly-remembered
king lists.

EUGENIUS, CADWALLON AND MAELGWN

Possibly, though not certainly, indicating that he was
the eldest, Eugenius/Owain took the mainland coastal
belt with its courts at Rhos and Degannwy, whilst
Cadwallon ruled in *Môn*, Anglesey, succeeding to his
brother in *c*.490. So at least it appears. It was during
this time that Cadwallon began his campaign against
those communities of Irish settlers deemed too unreliable
in their support for Gwynedd's rulers.

If this scenario is somewhere near the truth, then a
precedent had been set and this was to be followed by
Maelgwn when he was only in his late teens, or at least
he was the person blamed. Maelgwn, Cadwallon's son,
hounded Eugenius, his father's brother, to an early
death, and as a result his father Cadwallon ascended the
throne in 490. Gildas in his later attack on Maelgwn
predicted God's judgement.

Didst not thou [Gildas is addressing the *dragon of the
island*, Maelgwn], in the very beginning of thy youth,
terribly oppress with sword, spear, and fire, the king thine
uncle [Eugenius/Owain, ruling Gwynedd *c*.485–90],

2_ Translated by Howard
Lockley.

163

together with his courageous bands of soldiers, whose countenances in battle were not unlike young lions?

Not regarding the words of the prophet, who says, "The blood-thirsty and deceitful men shall not live out half their days;" and even if the sequel of thy sins were not such as ensued, yet what retribution couldst thou expect for this offence only at the hands of the just Judge, who hath said by his prophet: "Woe be to thee who spoilest, and shalt not thou thyself be spoiled? and thou who killest, shalt not thyself be killed? and when thou shalt make an end of thy spoiling, then shalt thou thyself fall."[3]

Were Cadwallon and Maelgwn impatient with the progress of the campaign against the dissident Irish population or was it all for straightforward dynastic reasons? Gildas had Maelgwn in his sights as the supreme example of what his invective was directed against, the decline and fall of Roman Britain under its current rulers. In attacking Eugenius, Maelgwn might have been operating on his own with, at most, some encouragement from his father who may have turned a blind eye, but is that likely? Even Gildas's talk of sword, spear, and fire implies something akin to civil war. Maelgwn has come down to us as a strong, volatile character: clear-sighted, ambitious, determined, and in his youth something of a tearaway. But he may have inherited much of this from his father Cadwallon who, if what is suggested above is correct, had himself come to power as a result of bloodshed.

The king [Maelgwn] ... was easily moved from tranquillity of mind, and was known to be more prone to hurting than prompt to succour, conceding nothing to piety, nothing to sanctity, nothing to modesty ...[4]

We simply cannot know whether Maelgwn was a bad lot, even something of a juvenile delinquent, when he was young. All we know is that the churchman Gildas considered him a bad lot. It may be that Maelgwn

[3]_ Gildas, *De Excidio Britanniae*, Ch. 33, Giles, 1841, pp. 29–30.

[4]_ *Life of St Brynach*, Wade-Evans, 1944, p. 11.

finished his education at Llanilltud Fawr in south
Wales, the great monastic school where Gildas himself
was educated, but it is more likely that this association
came later. As long as Eugenius lived, his son Cynlas,
Cuneglasus as Gildas called him, would succeed in
eastern Gwynedd. His other children as given in the
genealogies look very suspicious, mere attempts to
give prominent churchmen a suitably aristocratic
background. Cynlas was possibly Eugenius's only son.
Was this the start of Maelgwn's involvement in his
father's plans? Get Eugenius out of the way, his son
would be too young to rule. This would make Eugenius's
brother Cadwallon the protector-regent, the Richard
duke of York of early Gwynedd. But this new scenario
creates difficulties. Even if Cynlas was born the year
Maelgwn, possibly with Cadwallon, brought about his
uncle's death, which would make sense, by the time
Cadwallon himself died in *c.*517, Cynlas the rightful
heir would have been twenty-seven years old and was
probably married. Possibly Cynlas was the strong one,
only waiting for Cadwallon to die before he attempted
to reunify Gwynedd. Maelgwn would have known
that if he were to stand any chance of power, he would
have to strike again when the time came.

CYNLAS/CUNEGLASUS

According to Gildas, after the death of his father
Eugenius, Cynlas's rule in Rhos was little short of
disastrous. The strong implication is that he was not that
bright, someone rather like the out-of-control sons of a
former ruler of Iraq.

Why have *you* [Cuneglasus/Cynlas] been rolling in the
filth of your past wickedness ever since your youth,
you bear, rider of many and driver of the chariot of the
Bear's Stronghold, despiser of God and oppressor of
his lot, Cuneglasus, in Latin 'red butcher' [*lanio fulve*]?
Why do you wage such a war against men and God? –

against men, that is our countrymen, with arms special to yourself, against God, with infinite sins.

Why, aside from countless other lapses, have you rejected your own wife and now, against the ban of the apostle, who says that adulterers cannot be citizens of the kingdom of heaven, do you cast your eyes, with all the reverence (or rather dullness) of your mind, on her villainous sister, although she has promised to God perpetually chaste widowhood, like, as the poet says, the supreme tenderness of the dwellers in heaven? Why do you provoke with continual injuries the groans and sighs of the holy men who are present in the flesh by your side; they are the teeth of an appalling lioness that will one day break your bones.[5]

Lloyd noted that of all the British rulers attacked by Gildas, only Cynlas is accused of oppressing the clergy, a 'despiser of God and oppressor of his lot'. All this was being observed by Cadwallon who ruled from Degannwy, only three miles to the west on the other side of the Creuddyn peninsula, the two strongholds actually within sight of each other. Could Cadwallon have represented the *appalling lioness*, that is, western Gwynedd, whose priests would one day see him deposed?

THE CREUDDYN PENINSULA – THE COURTS OF DEGANNWY AND RHOS

5_ Gildas, *De Excidio Britanniae*, Ch. 32, Winterbottom, 1978, pp. 31–2; cf. Giles, 1841, p. 29, who has *tawny butcher*, and Lloyd, 1912, Vol. I, p. 133, who notes that Cuneglassus's British name, *Cinglas*, was being held up to scorn and parodied in Latin as *Grey Butcher*.

The Creuddyn peninsula, on which these two capitals were situated, projects north into the Irish Sea. On its western side the river Conwy flows into the sea. Contrary to immediate appearances, a fortress on the limestone headland at the end of the peninsula now known as the Great Orme would have been able to do little or nothing for the defence of its hinterland. Seaborne invasion would simply move round and behind it. Instead, such incursions were guarded against by two great forts on the landward or southern end of the peninsula: at the Vardre on the west, and at Bryn Euryn on the east. During the

Roman period, both sites were used as lookout posts for they commanded extensive views over land and sea.

The western Vardre site at Degannwy, the fort of the Decantae, consists of two volcanic plugs surrounded by an extensive raised plateau. Its name is an anglicization of *faerdre*, originally *maerdref*, the mayor's township. The township and fortress of Degannwy extended from this, the highest part commanding what was actually the main estuary of the Conwy, to lower slopes extending eastwards up to Llanrhos church. It probably had its eastern bastion at what is today a densely-forested, conical-shaped hill known as Bryn Maelgwyn, a corrupt spelling. Bondmen would have worked the land and tended cattle, both here and further afield, working for the king and for their own subsistence. The mayor, who had immediate control of them, was just one member of the king's household. Degannwy looks westwards and is very much the bastion and gateway to what was then its territory of *Gwynedd uch Conwy*, Gwynedd abovethe Conwy, or western Gwynedd. The word *uch* hints at the Roman way of naming provinces, making it *Venedotia Superior* or Upper Gwynedd.

On the eastern side of the peninsula's base is Bryn Euryn, another conical-shaped hill with an extensive spur extending northeastwards to a point where the church of Llandrillo-yn-Rhos more directly overlooks the shore just above the small seaside resort of Rhos-on-Sea. This was the stronghold of Rhos and it was the capital of eastern Gwynedd: in Gildas *receptaculum arti*, the receptacle of the bear, perhaps better translated by Revd A. W. Wade-Evans as the lair of the bear. It looks as though it was precisely during this time of Cynlas's rule here that the area of the fort extending eastwards to the church came to be known as *Dineirth*, *din* being the fort and *arth* the bear, the Fort of the Bear.[6]

Between the two strongholds and almost linking them lies a ridge of highland cutting across the peninsula's wide base, extending east from the present-day Llandudno Junction. During the time we are dealing with, a branch of the Conwy left its main course here

[6] Wade-Evans, 1938, p. 108; Lloyd, 1912, Vol. I, p. 240.

and made its way eastwards along the south of this ridge to then swing northwards at its end, between it and Bryn Euryn/*Dineirth*, so emptying into the sea at Penrhyn Bay on the peninsula's eastern side. Even today, a tiny stream, the Ganol, flows along the same course. In effect, this turned the Creuddyn peninsula into an island and meant that *Dineirth*, enjoying a position exactly comparable to Degannwy, overlooked the eastern estuary of the Conwy. Just as Degannwy faced west, so *Dineirth* faced east and was the bastion of, and the gateway to, *Venedotia Inferior*, Lower Gwynedd, extending as far as the clearly visible Clwyd Hills and beyond to the estuary of the Dee. Between them, these two fortresses provided protection for the hinterland of Arllechwedd west of the Conwy and of Rhos to its east, otherwise vulnerable from landings on the Creuddyn peninsula and incursions up the river's estuaries.

CADWALLON'S INTENDED HEIR: MAELGWN

It is possible that Cadwallon decided that Gwynedd could not afford to be divided, but he was still the junior partner in an alliance dominated by Rhos. He may have envisaged the unification of northern Gwynedd to balance, even confront, the power of a growing Meirionydd. He may have been wavering, waiting to see how Cynlas would turn out. Another imponderable in all this is the power of the church. Eugenius's demise could be blamed on Cadwallon's headstrong, out-of-control son, but for Cadwallon now to eliminate Cynlas might have been a step too far. His first priority may have been to settle Maelgwn down, or at least give him something to keep him occupied. It appears that his apanage was his father's former battleground, Anglesey. So it was that Maelgwn gained the title accorded him by Gildas of *insularis draco*, Island Dragon. Marriage to produce heirs was also important. The genealogies give *three* names, though he was seemingly only married twice. One of the three he did eventually marry, which should leave us with

Gwynedd's Creuddyn
peninsula; the Great
Orme headland, the Sea
Marsh of the Very Royal
Place, and its courts.
(Photo: Courtesy of Conwy
County Borough Council)

Great Orme

Little Orme

The Sea Marsh
Of Rhionydd

THE COURT
OF RHOS

The Vardre

Bryn Euryn

THE COURT
OF DEGANNWY

R. Conwy

169

The volcanic plugs in
the court of Degannwy
overlooking the estuary
of the River Conwy.

Part of the area covered
by Degannwy's court.
The Conwy lies beyond
the look-out positions.

Right: *Venedotia Superior* seen, not from Degannwy, but from its eastern neighbour, *Dineirth*'s Bryn Euryn.

Below: *Venedotia Inferior* seen from Bryn Euryn in *Dineirth*. In the distance are the Clwyd hills beyond which lies the Dee.

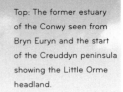

Top: The former estuary of the Conwy seen from Bryn Euryn and the start of the Creuddyn peninsula showing the Little Orme headland.

Below: Bryn Euryn, the stronghold of *Dineirth*, seen from part of the court site, now the Rhos-on-Sea Bowling Club.

Top: View of *Dineirth*,
Rhos, seen from
Degannwy's court. Bryn
Euryn is the highest point
to the right of centre.

Bottom: The same seen
from across the Ganol
stream which was formerly
one channel of the
river Conwy.

174

a choice from the other two for his first marriage. One is an unnamed daughter of Sawyl *Benisel*, king of the southern Pennines, brother of the Dunod king of Catterick killed in 595. The other is Gwallwen, daughter of Afallach the son of Brychan of Brycheiniog who possibly ruled in the period 465–500. Both might be just possible chronologically speaking. Whoever the bride, and we will soon encounter a much better candidate, we can be reasonably sure that it was what we would call an arranged marriage: one, we might conclude, that was entered into with little enthusiasm.

A GAY MAELGWN?

Accusations of homosexuality are only hinted at by Gildas but, unsurprisingly, are stated baldly by Geoffrey of Monmouth. For medieval churchmen, accusations of homosexuality were one of the ultimate insults that could be thrown. Unreliable at the best of times, by this point in his narrative Geoffrey has become a writer of fiction and romance. He has built up his picture of Arthur and is now dealing with Britain after Arthur, dragging in Maelgwn, *Malgo* from Gildas's *Maglocunus*, as somehow a successor of Vortipor the son of Vortigern.

Malgo came next. He was the most handsome of almost all the leaders of Britain and he strove hard to do away with those who ruled the people harshly [possibly a reference to Eugenius and Cynlas]. He was a man brave in battle, more generous than his predecessors [a reference to his gifts to churchmen] and greatly renowned for his courage. [Geoffrey later says that he fought bloodthirsty wars to subject six neighbouring islands.] Unfortunately he made himself hateful to God, for he was given to the vice of homosexuality.[7]

7_ Geoffrey of Monmouth, *The History of the Kings of Britain*, Thorpe, 1966, XI. 7, p. 263.

Leaving aside this attack, for, of course, that is what it was at the time, we come to the full enormity of the charge levelled against this young man. This is that he was responsible not only for the death of his uncle, Eugenius/Owain of Rhos, but also for the death of two others, his wife, that is his first wife, and his nephew. The nephew is described as 'your brother's son'.[8] As it stands, the Gildas text should mean that Maelgwn had a much older brother who is not named and appears nowhere else, certainly not in the pedigree material. For such an important family and with relatives like Cadwallon and Maelgwn, this seems very unlikely. It also means that this unknown's son was old enough to be married by the time Maelgwn killed him, for we are told Maelgwn went on to marry the widow of this nephew. The first and simplest way of resolving the problem would be to read this not as *brother*, but as *brother-in-law*.

We can then go ahead in Maelgwn's history and from what we find there say it is almost certain Cadwallon married his son Maelgwn to Tudglid the widow of Cyngen of Powys who may have ruled *c*.475–90.[9] The daughter of Brychan of *Garth Matrun*, the later Brycheiniog or Brecon, she had already had two children by Cyngen. These were Brochwel, later known as Brochwel of the Tusks or Long-in-the-Tooth, and a daughter Sanan. Probably considerably older than Maelgwn and past her best, Tudglid was seemingly foisted on the young heir to the throne as a pawn in Cadwallon's political game of building up alliances. If he was anticipating having to fight Cynlas *Goch*, Cynlas the Red, and even this butcher's brothers, if they existed, then his reasons may have been pressing. Gildas's description of Cynlas's behaviour might lend itself to this view. Cynlas might have been giving indications that he was building up to just such a challenge. In any event, Maelgwn had to be provided for, and the problem of providing heirs and alliances addressed. So Maelgwn was married.

[8] Gildas, *De Excidio Britanniae*, Ch. 35, Winterbottom, 1978, p. 34.

[9] Miller, *Saints*, 1979, pp. 101–12. Without reaching any conclusion, Dr Molly Miller hinted at the Meirionydd connection.

Possibly having rebelled once in attacking and killing his uncle Eugenius/Owain, it now looks as though Maelgwn decided to do it again, and with an equally dramatic gesture. He turned his back on his father and his wife and entered a monastery. Gildas himself tells us of the legal standing of such marriages when one of the partners entered a monastery: the marriage was automatically dissolved.

Your presumptive first marriage, [even] after your vow to be a monk had come to nothing, [because of that vow] was illegal – but at least it was [a marriage] to your own wife. You [later] spurned it [nevertheless], and sought another ...[10]

Of course, Maelgwn could have been moved by the enormity of his own actions in bringing about his uncle's death and have decided to devote his life to religion. Instead, it may be that Cadwallon was making it clear that when he deemed the time was right, he would hand over to the rightful heir, Cynlas, son of the dead Eugenius/Owain and so reunite Gwynedd. However, what we know of the later Maelgwn might make us pause. Entering a monastery would gain him a divorce, and freedom to plan.

So it was that Maelgwn gave up the friends of his misspent, noisy youth, entering a monastery to hear 'the sweet voices of the tuneful recruits of Christ … the melodious music of the church'. Later comments by Gildas, who seemingly believed Maelgwn had done this for the right reasons, indicate that the monastery chosen was Llanilltud Fawr, Llantwit Major in Glamorgan, founded by Illtud not many years before.

After your dream of rule by force had gone according to plan, were you not seized by the desire to return to the right road? Perhaps remorseful in the knowledge of your sins, you first pondered a great deal at that time, day and

[10]_ Gildas, *De Excidio Britanniae*, Ch. 35, Winterbottom, 1978, p. 34.

177

night, on the godly life and the Rule of the monks
[which, despite the increasing separation from the
continental Catholic church, would have been essentially
that of St Benedict]; then, publishing it to the knowledge
of the public breeze, you vowed to be a monk for ever,
with (as you said) no thought of going back on your
promise, before almighty God and in the sight of men
and angels [in this way divorcing himself from men, and
from his wife].
You seem to have broken through the vast nets that
normally entangle fat bulls of your kind in an instant. You
broke through the chains of all royal power, gold, silver,
and what is more than these, your own will. Where you
had been a raven, you became a dove ...[11]

Had he? Maelgwn was now doing his religious stint,
possibly with no real conviction, all the time nursing
an acute sense of disappointment and thinking of what
would follow.

It has been suggested that the virulence of Gildas's
attacks on Maelgwn may hide the simple fact that they
had both been pupils together under Illtud, and that in
this way Gildas was furious at having been taken in by
someone who may even have been a friend in these early
years. After all, Maelgwn was the son of a king; Gildas,
the most gifted and presumably most famous pupil of
the abbot.

MAELGWN THE RAVEN

Perhaps Maelgwn did have a genuine leaning towards the
scholarly and the academic as well as towards the cut and
thrust of politics and the outdoor pursuits of a prince.
If his sexuality was an issue, he would certainly not have
been the first person facing such a dilemma, or the last,
to finish up taking the religious path. Gildas does not say
how long he stayed in the monastery. If he had become
a fully professed monk then probably he would have
spent three years in this way. Did he leave as soon as

[11]_ Ibid., Ch. 34, p. 33.

news began to come in that his father was not well? The implication of what Gildas says is that this all happened when Maelgwn was still young. If he was married when he was twenty, he might have stuck marriage for a few years but was probably in the monastery by the time he was twenty-five. It then becomes a little difficult to imagine him as a monk right through until *c*.517 when Cadwallon died. He would have had to be ready with all his plans laid if he was to stop Cynlas taking Gwynedd and instead take it himself. Perhaps a long period of decline for Cadwallon would allow us to imagine Maelgwn leaving after around five years, arriving back in Gwynedd in *c*.502 when he was thirty. Pure guesswork, but this provides a construct enabling us to obtain a clearer picture of what may have been going on. And all this time Maelgwn may have been the raven Gildas accused him of being both before and after.

THE MEIRIONYDD PRIZE

There may have been another reason for Maelgwn leaving the monastery when he did. At some point news arrived that must have sent his mind racing. His former wife had two sisters, Cerddych and Marchell. Marchell was married to Gwrin *Farfdrwch*, Gwrin Cut Beard, king of Meirionydd. Possibly Gwrin, who because of Maelgwn's marriage to Tudglid was his brother-in-law, had been injured and was dying. Gwrin was a contemporary of Maelgwn's father, Cadwallon, and the story we have already encountered of Gwrin's redirection of an Irish fleet mirrors Cadwallon's own struggles against Irish settlers. Although the account only comes down to us from the storytelling pen of Geoffrey of Monmouth – Geoffrey is here dealing with a Britain *before* the Romans arrived – Gwrin, active against the Irish at sea as well as on land, may have become something of a rival, even threat, to the branches of the family ruling in north Wales.[12] Did Maelgwn see this as another obstacle he would have to confront?

12_ Miller, *Saints*, 1979, argued that some parts of the story may have been near the truth.

If we admit Geoffrey's account, it is possible to see Gwrin not only having a fleet, but using it to extend his power *across* the Irish Sea. At that period, what is called Meirionydd probably covered a much larger area than the later *cantref* of that name, possibly covering part of Ardudwy to the north and part of Ceredigion to the south. The homeland was for the most part mountainous, as Lloyd put it, 'a land of rocky confusion'.[13] History can furnish many examples where states have developed despite or indeed *because* of their inadequate resources, moving out to find new territory and other sources of power. In stark comparison, Brandenburg, later Brandenburg-Prussia, with its flat sandy wastes comes to mind because of its expansion in the eighteenth century. Perhaps that is what Meirionydd had been doing, developing its position and power, here through its naval might. Geoffrey's story seems to indicate that Gwrin had extended his lordship into Ireland, imposing this on at least some of those in Leinster who had begun to follow the example set by Ailill of the north Leinster Uí Dúnlainge in the period 495–500, returning to the age-old pattern of raiding into Britain. The text here has been changed to give the more likely alternative readings and names.

Gwrin ... was a modest man and a wise one ... a lover of peace and justice. When his neighbours rebelled against him, he ... fought dreadful wars against them and reduced them once more to the subjection which they owed him.

Among many other things it happened that a king of the Irish ... refused to pay ... [tribute] to Gwrin, saying that he owed him no allegiance. Gwrin bore this ill. He took a fleet to Ireland, fought the most frightful battles against the local inhabitants, killed the king and reduced the country [or at least this one small coastal area] to its former state of subservience.

On the same occasion, when Gwrin was returning home via [not the Orkney Islands but] the isles off Dyfed, namely Ramsey, Skomer and Skokholm, after his victory,

13_ Lloyd, 1912, Vol. I, p. 251.

he came upon thirty ships full of men and women.
Gwrin asked what they were doing there. Their leader ...
went up to Gwrin, did obeisance to him and asked his
pardon and peace ... He was cruising in those waters
in search of land where he might settle ...
When Gwrin learned that these men came from
Ireland ... [he rejected the request and] he ordered his
representatives to go back with them to the island ...[14]

The other potentially dangerous aspect of this activity
for northern Gwynedd was Gwrin's likely development of
what we might begin to call international relations with
powers on the other side of the Irish Sea. If the thesis
advanced earlier is correct, that Niall of the Nine
Hostages and Conall the Red were acting as agents of the
British state, sent into Ireland by Vortigern's government
to curb and if possible end attacks from Ulster, from
Leinster, and from the south coast of Ireland, then this
would be almost inevitable, a matter of building on
already close ties. As we have seen, Leinster kingdoms
were by this date locked into almost continuous warfare
with the sons of Niall, the emerging Uí Néill. The Uí
Néill finally wrested control of the Meath plain from
Leinster in 516. If Gwrin was involved in Leinster, he
could well have been co-operating with Fiacha, Niall's
son, the victor in this battle of *Druim Derg*. As Fiacha is
the last son of Niall to be noted, this co-operation would
also have been with Niall's grandsons. In other words,
northern Gwynedd was beginning to lose the initiative
and the pre-eminence it had once exercised to Gwrin
ruling over a Meirionydd we might even call *Venedotia
Maritima*, Maritime Gwynedd. And this was happening
when Gwynedd was still coming to terms with the
consequences of a dynastic coup which had seen the fall
of Cunedda's son Anianus.

If this is near the truth, then Gwrin was simply
continuing in the rôle originally exercised by Paternus,
that of *comes litoris Hiberniae*, a count of the Irish Shore.
It is more than likely that Paternus's command extended
from the Cumbrian coastal forts right down to the Dyfi,

14_ Based on Geoffrey of
Monmouth, *The History
of the Kings of Britain*,
Thorpe, 1966, III. 11 and 12,
pp. 100–1.

a zone that included Meirionydd. Gwrin, and here he may have had Maelgwn as a rival, was possibly setting his sights on recovering control of this area, at least as far as the Dee.

THE MEIRIONYDD TYBION

All this leaves us with the question as to how in the first place the southern area of Gwynedd, later known as Meirionydd, became detached from its northern parts. Here we come to the first of two far-reaching reappraisals of Gwynedd's early history. The pedigrees give Gwrin as the son of Cadwaladr son of Meirion, and therefore as the great-grandson of Tybion. We have seen how this person, if he existed, cannot have been a son of Cunedda, and how he is separated out from Cunedda's other supposed sons by being described as the one who stayed in the north at the time of the imaginary migration to Gwynedd. Gwrin possibly belongs to the generation of the brothers Eugenius and Cadwallon, Cadwaladr his father to that of Anianus, Meirion to that of Cunedda, making Tybion of the same generation as Eternus 'son of' Paternus. Did Paternus find that the responsibilities for coastal defence over such a vast area were too much for one command? Before his death, he was probably already treating his responsibilities as including the right to pass on power and divide areas and responsibilities as he thought necessary, especially as central government had its hands full elsewhere. Did Paternus pass on the main charge to his son, that is to his successor Eternus, whilst splitting off the south, even possibly including the coast as far north as the end of the Llŷn peninsula, giving this to Tybion? Tybion *could* have been a son of Paternus, but he was more probably a Paternus appointee. Strategically, such a split in responsibilities would make sense. Of course, Tybion may have lived later and been appointed by the Cunedda whom the pedigrees state was his father.

Geoffrey gives details about Gwrin of Meirionydd's wife *Marcia*, Marchell, even if he made her the wife, not of *Gurguit*, Gwrin, but of *Guithelin* his son.

His wife was a noblewoman called Marcia, who was skilled in the arts. Among the many extraordinary things she used her natural talent to invent was a law she devised which was called the *Lex Martiana* by the Britons. King Alfred [871–99] translated this along with the other laws; in his Saxon tongue he called it [wrongly] the Mercian Law.
When Guithelin [for which read *Gurguit*, Gwrin] died, the government of the kingdom remained in the hands of this Queen and her son, who was called Sisillius [in the pedigrees Clydno]. Sisillius was then only seven years old and his youth prevented him from taking the kingship into his own hands.
For this reason his mother, who was extremely intelligent and most practical, ruled over the entire island [for which read Meirionydd].
When Marcia closed her eyes for the last time Sisillius [Clydno] was crowned king and began to govern.[15]

For the benefit of the story as it seems to be emerging, instead of seven for Clydno's years, one might substitute seventeen; in other words old enough for marriage to be considered and young enough for Marchell to be still in control and to make the choice herself. Unfortunately, on dating grounds, this will not fit the later evidence we may have for this family. Marchell might have arranged the marriage, but Clydno was a man in *c.*517 when he was apparently murdered and was old enough to have had a son named Gwyddno who succeeded him.

Maelgwn of Gwynedd was married by his father Cadwallon to Tudglid, widow of Cyngen of Powys; Clydno of Meirionydd was married to Sanan, Tudglid's daughter. Maelgwn and Clydno were related. Then Marchell and Gwrin died at about the same time.

15_ Ibid., III. 13 and 14, p. 101.

Maelgwn might well have seen that if he was to take advantage of this opportunity, he would have to act quickly. He came out of his monastic retirement, or he was already out, and began to work overtime on the dynastic issues facing him.

GWYNEDD'S TRADITIONAL HISTORY UP TO ANIANUS'S DEATH

Perhaps it is at this point that we should take a step back and reconsider the evidence. It seems as though the appointment of Paternus can be dated to 398. He was followed, so we are told in the pedigrees, by Eternus, and then *Cunedda*, the unnamed successor, who probably operated in Gwynedd at the time of Vortigern. Cunedda saw his command changed from being an essentially military one, the *comes litoris Hiberniae* post to which Paternus was moved, into a territorial presidency over a new province, *Venedotia*, Gwynedd, created or named at the same time as the two other provinces coming into being then, those of Powys and Gwrtheyrnion. Cunedda was followed by his son Anianus, who is more usually known by his epithet *Einiawn/Einion*, the Anvil.

In the thirteenth-century compilation the *Black Book of Carmarthen*, one of the *Stanzas of the Graves* says Anianus was killed, and 'It is a disgrace that he should have been slain in Britain.' In the previous chapter, this was placed in the context of the ongoing struggles against the Irish. But if the Anvil had been killed in that conflict, would it really have been described as a *disgrace*? Surely, it would have been seen as a far more glorious affair, fighting the enemies of Britain: enemies who had been wreaking havoc on the west coast of Britain since the start of the Roman occupation. What would have been a disgrace would have been the death of this man, and one involved in such a struggle, at the hands not of the Irish, but of his own side, the Britons themselves.

This is our first reappraisal, which means we have to abandon the traditional history and produce our *second* dynastic map for Gwynedd. We know who succeeded Anianus: two brothers, Eugenius, better known as Owain White Tooth of Rhos, and Cadwallon. It has been assumed that Eugenius was the eldest because of the fact that he is constantly referred to as *of Rhos*, Gwynedd's capital at the time, and Cadwallon is best known for his exploits in Anglesey against the Irish. In other words, Anglesey must have been his apanage, until a date near 490 when he inherited. Maelgwn was then given Anglesey as *his* apanage. However, it can only be an assumption that makes these the sons of the man they killed, namely Anianus. We simply cannot trust that lazy *ap* appearing between names in a king list. What if Owain and Cadwallon were more distantly related or had no blood relationship with the Anvil at all? This gives us the second dynastic map.

TABLE 8

Gwynedd And The Meirionydd Usurpation

The Second Dynastic Map

[b] Maelgwn brother of Gwrin of Meirionydd

Meirionydd's line usurping the throne of Gwynedd in c.485 with the murder
of Anianus = Gwynedd's Second Dynasty

Maelgwn = Gwrin's brother as in Gildas and Marchell's brother-in-law
              Clydno his nephew as in Gildas. Sanan his step-daughter
                and 2nd wife

Gwynedd's First Dynasty

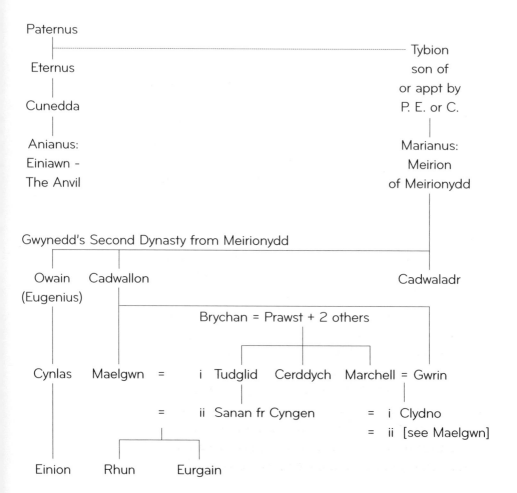

Coming to power in this violent way, it is perhaps unsurprising if the brothers disagreed as to who should rule and where. Eugenius/Owain may have been the eldest and so claimed Rhos and eastern Gwynedd; Cadwallon had the rival court in Degannwy and took western Gwynedd. He had a son. His name was Maelgwn: young, headstrong, and impetuous. But there was another son, Maelgwn's *older* brother. This is what Gildas says. Very possibly there is no need to convert the person Gildas names as a brother into a brother-in-law as suggested earlier. As Maelgwn's older brother and Cadwallon's eldest son, he would need to be provided for and so, possibly, this Gwrin was granted what we call Meirionydd or rather *Gwynedd Maritima*, the coastal belt from the tip of the Llŷn peninsula down to the Dyfi and beyond.

Ailill of north Leinster had possibly returned to raiding into Britain in response to appeals for help from refugees escaping the purges being conducted by Cunedda's successors. Events in Ireland indicate a likely period for this overseas adventuring as 495–500. We are told that Ailill won nine battles in Britain. If Cadwallon had a capable son, Gwrin, placing him over the lands south of Llŷn makes sense. The problem always comes in knowing what happened to territories granted as apanages in one generation and how far the descendants of the original appointees were able to keep control or whether they became merely landholders of personal territory with rule passing to whomever the ultimate lord decided upon. Cunedda may have granted the coastal areas of southern Llŷn and Cardigan Bay down to the Dyfi to his son Donatus, becoming the founder of Dunoding, which is Ardudwy and Eifionydd, and he, in turn, in the generation of Eugenius and Cadwallon passed this on to his son Eifion, or at least the cantref of Eifionydd. But now, it would seem, Gwrin, the eldest son of Cadwallon, was intruded to rule over the southern part, Ardudwy and Meirionydd down to the Dyfi and even further south. If the command was essentially military and naval, these particular responsibilities may have extended round to the end of the Llŷn. The story of the redirection of the Irish fleet and the hints of control over parts of the Irish coast imply that he became a figure of note.

'THE MEIRIONYDD THREE': CADWALADR, OWAIN, AND CADWALLON

The problem comes in trying to reconcile what the ninth-century genealogists say with Gildas's version. Looking at our second construct, is it really likely that the genealogists did not know that Gwrin was Maelgwn's elder brother mentioned in Gildas or that his father was Cadwallon? And so, based on the genealogies, a *third* dynastic map emerges which makes the Meirionydd usurpation one carried out by three brothers. These were Owain, who until this point has been called Eugenius, Maelgwn's father Cadwallon, and the brother of both Owain and Cadwallon named Cadwaladr. When these three usurpers from Meirionydd divided the spoils, Cadwaladr kept the homeland we call Meirionydd.

TABLE 9
Gwynedd And The Meirionydd Usurpation
The Third Dynastic Map
[c] Maelgwn cousin and *brother-in-law* to Gwrin

Meirionydd's line usurping the throne of Gwynedd in *c*.485 with the murder of Anianus = Gwynedd's Second Dynasty

Cadwallon, Owain, and Cadwaladr brothers
Maelgwn = Marchell's and Gwrin's *brother-in-law*
                    [cf. brother in Gildas]
                    and cousin to Gwrin
                    Clydno his nephew as in Gildas

Gwynedd's First Dynasty

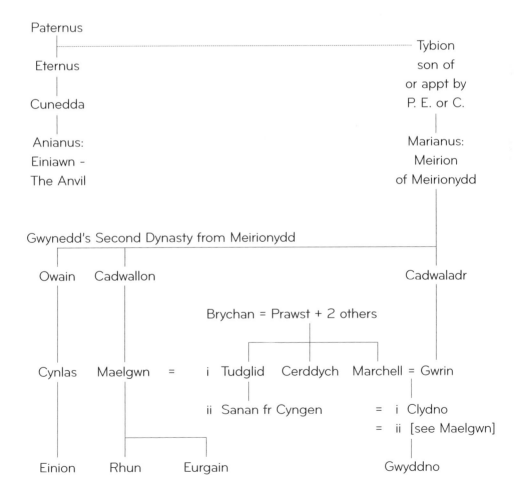

Paternus
Eternus
Cunedda
Anianus:
Einiawn -
The Anvil

Tybion
son of
or appt by
P. E. or C.

Marianus:
Meirion
of Meirionydd

Gwynedd's Second Dynasty from Meirionydd

Owain   Cadwallon   Cadwaladr

Brychan = Prawst + 2 others

Cynlas   Maelgwn   =   i Tudglid   Cerddych   Marchell = Gwrin

ii Sanan fr Cyngen   =   i Clydno
                                 =   ii [see Maelgwn]

Einion   Rhun   Eurgain   Gwyddno

Meirionydd was sufficiently powerful to be imposing its will on eastern Ireland. It had a fleet. It was seemingly determined to overcome its geographical limitations by pursuing a policy of expansion. In inheriting the rôle originally envisaged for Paternus when he was appointed to north Wales in *c*.398, it could claim to be the real power house or heart of this province of *Venedotia*. But increasingly it was being drawn into the Irish Sea world. It was developing a web of international relations with people who knew little of Roman control and whose outlook was quite different. It is noteworthy that two of the brothers' names are Welsh owing nothing to a Latin past. Perhaps this in itself is evidence of this more 'Celtic' orientation. In other words, this is possibly the point in these pages to drop the Roman name Eugenius in favour of Owain, his Welsh name which derives from it and which looks to have been his from the start.

This new dynastic map receives further confirmation in the genealogies because these all state that Cadwaladr was Gwrin's father. In this situation, Gildas could still describe Gwrin as Maelgwn's brother, or more specifically *brother-in-law* because of Tudglid's marriage to Maelgwn and her sister Marchell's marriage to Gwrin. Here, Gwrin and Maelgwn were also cousins – 'your father's brother's son' – as Gildas states. There is much to recommend this dynastic map as the correct one, giving the most convincing context for Maelgwn's actions at the start of his career. It is surely significant that another great founder or re-creator of Gwynedd's fortunes after the first devastating onslaught by the Normans, namely Gruffydd ap Cynan, 1081 and 1094–1137, named his three sons Cadwaladr, Owain, and Cadwallon.[16] Owain, of course, is better known as Owain *Gwynedd* or Owain the Great, 1137–70.

16_ I am grateful to Howard Lockley for drawing this to my attention.

We can, however, go one small step further in our redrawing of Gwynedd's dynastic map enabling *all* Gildas's conditions to be met. In this, our *fourth* and last dynastic construct, we have three brothers in the line of Meirionydd, Owain, Cadwallon, and the eldest, Cadwaladr. Cadwaladr's marriage results in Gwrin's birth. For some reason, his wife was then rejected or took herself off and married Cadwaladr's brother Cadwallon, and so Maelgwn was born in *c.*472. This makes Gwrin and Maelgwn brothers, to be exact half-brothers, and Clydno Maelgwn's nephew. Gwrin was the brother whose widow Maelgwn married and whose son, Clydno, he had murdered, which is exactly what Gildas says.[17]

At last, we may have the most convincing scenario for the early history of Gwynedd. After defeating and killing Anianus the Anvil, for the first time the victorious brothers, Cadwaladr, Owain, and Cadwallon, split what had briefly been a unified Gwynedd. We can possibly forget about apanages for the moment. Owain took eastern Gwynedd, *Gwynedd is Conwy*, ruling from Rhos/*Dineirth*, Cadwallon took western Gwynedd, *Gwynedd uch Conwy*, ruling from Degannwy just across the Creuddyn peninsula from Rhos, whilst Cadwaladr kept their original homeland, namely *Gwynedd Maritima*, Meirionydd, probably including Ardudwy to the north and part of what became Ceredigion to the south. These were the earliest days of this arrangement. It was for their sons to see how this division would develop in the years following.

[17]_ Bartrum, ND, Table 2, *Meirionydd*, and Bartrum, 1966, p. 49, No. 41 and p. 108, No. 23.

TABLE 10

Gwynedd And The Meirionydd Usurpation

The Fourth/Final Dynastic Map

[d] *Maelgwn Gwrin's brother: literally half-brother*

Meirionydd's line usurping the throne of Gwynedd in c.485 with the murder
of Anianus = Gwynedd's Second Dynasty

Cadwallon, Owain, and Cadwaladr brothers: X married in turn to i Cadwaladr
ii Cadwallon

Maelgwn = Gwrin's brother as in Gildas - half brother and Marchell's
    brother-in-law

Clydno his nephew as in Gildas - Sanan his step-daughter
    and 2nd wife

Gwynedd's First Dynasty

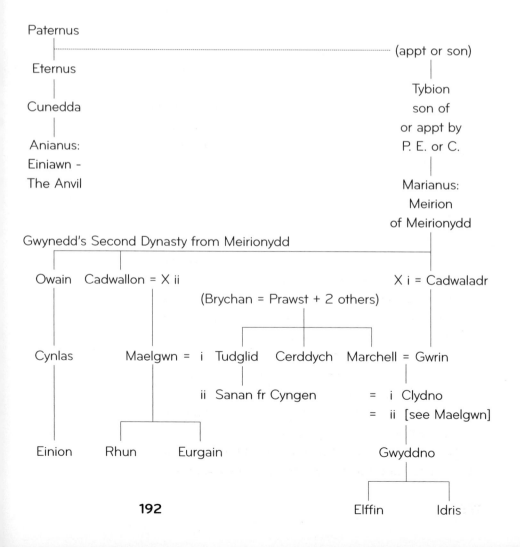

Paternus

Eternus

Cunedda

Anianus:
Einiawn -
The Anvil

(appt or son)

Tybion
son of
or appt by
P. E. or C.

Marianus:
Meirion
of Meirionydd

Gwynedd's Second Dynasty from Meirionydd

Owain   Cadwallon = X ii   X i = Cadwaladr

(Brychan = Prawst + 2 others)

Cynlas   Maelgwn = i Tudglid   Cerddych   Marchell = Gwrin

            ii Sanan fr Cyngen   = i Clydno
                                                   = ii [see Maelgwn]

Einion   Rhun   Eurgain   Gwyddno

192

Elffin   Idris

THE SECOND DYNASTY'S CONFEDERATION

In the next generation, therefore, we find Maelgwn son
of Cadwallon facing Cynlas son of Owain, and possibly
the most powerful partner, Gwrin son of Cadwaladr,
whom we nowadays limit unnecessarily by calling him
Gwrin of Meirionydd. The most interesting aspect now
is that, far from there being a Gwynedd under Maelgwn
attempting to restore Gwynedd's fortunes in the face
of an over-mighty Meirionydd under Gwrin, Maelgwn
himself was of this family. And this family could trace its
ancestry back to whoever appointed Tybion or Meirion,
whether it was Paternus, Eternus, or Cunedda, and, of
course, Tybion or Meirion *could* have been son of any
of these. Whatever the situation, it looks as if it was not
Cadwallon and then Maelgwn, but Cadwallon's brother
Cadwaladr and then Gwrin in Meirionydd who
represented the senior branch of the dynasty. From the
start, therefore, Maelgwn might have entertained the
plan – indeed it might have been one originating with
his father, Cadwallon – to reunify the different territories
into which the original Gwynedd had been split, and to
bring back to northern Gwynedd the supremacy it had
enjoyed in the time of Paternus.

MAELGWN'S DESIGNS ON MEIRIONYDD

At last, we can return to the story. Gwrin had died or
been killed. His only son, Clydno, was married to Sanan
of Powys. Possibly Marchell had been the power behind
the throne but she was dying. Maelgwn saw his chance.
Gildas says he had no lack of warnings, 'for you have
had as your teacher the refined master of almost all
Britain', that is, Illtud, founder and abbot of Llantwit
Major in Glamorgan. Nevertheless, Maelgwn left his
monastery, possibly arriving back in Gwynedd by sea
having stopped in Meirionydd *en route*. He established
contact with Clydno and with Clydno's bride, Sanan,
who, if Tudglid could still be regarded as his wife, was

Maelgwn's step-daughter. Maelgwn won her over: indeed, according to Gildas, Sanan fell for this good-looking youth, and worse, fed him with 'suggestions' on how he could be completely rid of the obstacles to ascendancy over Meirionydd. With this, and the inheritance of the territories west of the Conwy from his father, he would be in a position of overwhelming superiority to deal with the one remaining threat to his power, Cynlas, in Rhos.

What would be the joy of the church our mother if the enemy of all mankind [the Devil] had not somehow stolen you, to her grief, from her very bosom! If you had stayed on the good path, how generous a tinder of hope in heaven would blaze up in the hearts of men despaired of! How great and how glorious would be the prizes that awaited your soul from the kingdom of Christ on the day of judgement ... [Gildas continues in this vein for some time].

In fact your conversion to good fruit brought as much joy and sweetness in heaven and earth then as your wicked return (like some sick hound) to your disgusting vomit has brought grief and weeping now ...

Your excited ears hear not the praises of God from the sweet voices of the tuneful recruits of Christ, not the melodious music of the church, but the empty praises of yourself from the mouths of criminals who grate on the hearing like raving hucksters – mouths stuffed with lies and liable to bedew bystanders with their foaming phlegm ...

Your presumptive first marriage, [even] after your vow to be a monk had come to nothing, [because of that vow] was illegal – but at least it was [a marriage] to your own wife. You [later] spurned it, and sought another, not with some widow, but with the beloved wife of a living man [Clydno son of Gwrin of Meirionydd], no stranger either, but your brother's son [your brother-in-law's son, your nephew].

So that hard neck of yours, already laden with many burdens of sin, is bent from the lowest depths to still lower; for to crown your sacrilege, you ventured on two murders, the killing of this man [Clydno] and of your wife, after you had enjoyed her for some little time.[18]

CRUEL NECESSITIES

We really do have to be careful with Gildas. He was not pretending to be a historian. He was a preacher, a churchman, someone who clearly regarded himself as a latter-day prophet predicting the terrible calamity to come if Britain's rulers continued in their sinful ways. The *Old Testament* was full of such preachers, particularly Isaiah, Jeremiah, Ezekiel, and Daniel, so Gildas did not want for models. At times his fervour reaches what we might call hysteria, certainly a frenzy, to be compared to the *hŵyl*, the fervour of the Welsh Nonconformist preachers down to the twentieth century. This is important here because, clearly, Gildas was being carried away by his denunciation of Maelgwn and so we have to ask ourselves whether we really have to take his every word literally.

Clydno was seemingly eliminated, though more, it would appear, through the machinations of Sanan than of Maelgwn directly, but why should Maelgwn murder Tudglid, his first wife? Gildas has already reminded us that in entering the monastery, the marriage was automatically dissolved. Have we misunderstood him? When someone abandoned the monastic life, was a previous marriage once again valid? If this was the case, then Maelgwn would have needed to rid himself of Tudglid if his plans for Greater Gwynedd were to succeed. Alternatively, is Gildas speaking figuratively when he says he *murdered* his wife, meaning rather that he murdered *their marriage*? The 'killing of this man and of your wife' comes as a rhetorical flourish after his previous more sober assessment of Maelgwn's actions.

Churchmen of the evangelical stamp are rarely the best judges of political necessity, least of all if the necessities are cruel: the dilemma facing Oliver Cromwell comes to mind. If the scenario set out here is correct, Maelgwn

18_ Gildas, *De Excidio Britanniae*, Chs. 34–5, Winterbottom, 1978, pp. 33–4.

195

was faced with the messy consequences of the usurpation carried out by his father, Cadwallon, and his uncles Owain and Cadwaladr. The resulting division of the inheritance of Paternus and Cunedda had created the out-of-control monster in Rhos, that is Owain's son Cynlas, and Gwrin's and now Clydno's massive power in the south based on Meirionydd: a power which might soon swallow up northern Gwynedd and Maelgwn with it unless he acted. Nevertheless, it was a power game. Gwrin's claims to pre-eminence in Gwynedd were as legitimate as Maelgwn's, *unless*, and this is the conclusion we could reach, unless Cadwallon had been the eldest of the three brothers, and had been the one largely responsible for the death of Anianus in 490. If this was the situation, then Maelgwn was fighting for his rights and for legitimacy.

Sanan really does deserve Gildas's contempt for, if one reading of Gildas is correct, she was complicit in the murders of both her mother Tudglid, and her husband Clydno. Even if only responsible for Clydno's disappearance, she might seem a bad lot. Yet even here it is possible to envisage situations which excuse. With Sanan herself probably the victim of an arranged marriage, was Clydno something like Cynlas in Rhos? Of course, we will never know, but we must not blindly follow where Gildas would lead. For Maelgwn, marriage to Sanan the queen would greatly improve his own claim to succeed his nephew Clydno.

Next you married the woman with whose collusion and encouragement you lately entered on such masses of sin. The wedding was public, and, as the lying tongues of your parasites cry (but from their lips only, not from the depths of their hearts), legitimate: for she was a widow. But I call it most scandalous.[19]

19_ Ibid.

Maelgwn was now ruler of Gwynedd west of the Conwy.
All that was necessary was to persuade the leading men
of Meirionydd that he was indeed the rightful successor
of his nephew, married as he now was to the state's queen
or queen mother. Clydno's son Gwyddno might well
have been completely inexperienced, in his teens or even
younger. The story of some contest on the sands of the
Dyfi estuary, which Maelgwn won through ingenuity
verging on trickery, is a fantastic onomastic tale, trying
to explain the name *Traeth Maelgwn*, Maelgwn's Sands,
in the Dyfi estuary. Today, these are thought to be
those lying behind the spit extending out from the south
or Ceredigion side of the river's mouth opposite Aberdyfi
in Meirionydd.

After the taking of the crown of London and its
sceptre from the nation of the Welsh, and their
expulsion from England [Lloegr], they [the Welsh]
instituted competitions to see who would be the chief
king among them.
And the place where they held them was on Traeth
Maelgwn at Aber Dyfi, and there came the men
of Gwynedd and the men of Powys and the men
of Deheubarth and Rhunwg [Dyfed] and Morgannwg
[Glywysing and Gwent] and Seisyllwg [Ceredigion
and Ystrad Tywi].
And there Maeldaf the Elder son of Unhwch Unarchen,
lord of Moel Esgidion [a foothill of Cadair Idris] in
Meirionydd, placed a chair made of waxed wings under
Maelgwn; and when the tide came no-one could stay
there except Maelgwn himself because of the chair.
And because of that he [Maelgwn] himself became
the chief king, and Aberffraw his chief court, and the
earl of Mathrafal [the leading court of Powys] and the
earl of Dinefwr [the leading court of Deheubarth]
and the earl of Caerleon [the leading court of
Glamorgan] under him; and his word was over their
word, and the law was his; and he did not have to

keep their law [Iolo then glossing what might have been his own work to read: 'and ... his word being declared similar to theirs and his law supreme; and to be implicitly obeyed by those other chieftains']; And because of Maeldaf the Elder, Pennard [Iolo intending Pennarth in Arfon, or Clynnog Fawr, not the commote of Pennardd in Ceredigion] got the privilege[s] and he [Maeldaf] had the oldest chancellorship [? of this new expanded realm].[20]

If there is anything that might be salvaged from this for our purposes, it may be that Maelgwn proved to the leading landholders in Meirionydd that he was the most competent to be their king. Perhaps he did sail over the Dyfi estuary for a meeting on the Meirionydd shore. Maelgwn was never in a position to establish lordship over other areas in Wales, but the implication is that Gwynedd not only included Meirionydd but extended south into today's Ceredigion.

TUDGLID'S ATTEMPTED REVENGE – CYNLAS

All that remained was to deal with Cynlas. It appears that Maelgwn took over in Degannwy in about 517 after the death of his father, Cadwallon. However, tradition makes Maelgwn the donor to a cleric named Trillo of land at the other court on Bryn Euryn's spur where today his church stands.[21] Having inherited western and southern Gwynedd, Degannwy with its church now called Llanrhos, it looks as though Maelgwn established some lordship over Degannwy's twin capital, Bryn Euryn, *Dineirth*, the Lair of the Bear. Maelgwn was seemingly sufficiently powerful to intrude his own nominee Trillo to become bishop and possibly abbot of this other royal foundation which was later known as Llandrillo, the church or enclosure of Trillo.

What happened to Cynlas? He may have stayed on, reconciled to his subordinate position. We here come back to the charge that Maelgwn killed his first wife,

20_ Owen, 1841, Vol. II, pp. 48–50. The Welsh text is in Bromwich, 1961, pp. 439–40: the above translation by Howard Lockley. Also, Williams, 1848, p. 461. In this, Maeldaf had already been described as one of the three chief bards of Maelgwn, and Iolo describes him as 'the son of Unhwch Unarchen, a chief of Pennard *in Arvon*' replacing the text's 'lords of Moel Esgidion in Meirionydd'. Iolo also alters the last sentence as follows: 'It was through the instrumentality of Maeldav the elder that Penardd acquired its municipal privileges.' In all probability, Iolo was giving different versions of his own work.

21_ On the shore below the church is the 11 x 7 ft cell, 8 ft in height, built over a well. It is ascribed to St Trillo – Baring-Gould and Fisher, 1907–13, Vol. IV, 1913, pp. 263 and 264, and Tucker, 1953, pp. 30–9.

Tudglid. If Maelgwn did this, what follows might indicate that he acted because of something approaching treason. Tudglid was, after all, the mother of his second wife, Sanan. Gildas's denunciation of Cynlas provides the clue.

Why, aside from countless other lapses, have you [Cynlas] rejected your own wife and now, against the ban of the apostle, who says that adulterers cannot be citizens of the kingdom of heaven, do you cast your eyes, with all the reverence (or rather dullness) of your mind, on her villainous sister [in Giles, *detestable sister*, in Morris, *pestilential sister*] although she has promised to God perpetually chaste widowhood, like ... the dwellers in heaven?[22]

For what is suggested below, Gildas would have had to have written Chapter 32 which concerns Cynlas some time earlier than Chapters 33 to 36 which deal with Maelgwn. This is because in Chapter 35 Gildas says, if that is what he *is* saying, that Maelgwn had murdered his first wife. To have written this he would have had to have forgotten to update his comments on Cynlas. But this is not so unlikely. At several points, Gildas indicates that he wrote in spurts with gaps in between. The possibility seems to be that the three daughters of Brychan of Brycheiniog were determined women: in the case of Tudglid and her daughter Sanan this determination to be at the pinnacle of power might well have been all-consuming. We could ask, how many pestilential, villainous sisters were there operating in the topmost ranks of northern Welsh kingdoms at this time?

Tudglid, daughter of a king, Brychan of Brycheiniog, and already widow of another, Cyngen of Powys, suddenly, for it may have been like this, found herself abandoned when her husband, the hothead Maelgwn, entered a monastery. We might suspect that she knew he had done this precisely in order to ditch her. She could have bowed out of public life and entered religion, but this was the daughter of a king, the widow of another,

22_ Gildas, *De Excidio Britanniae*, Ch. 32, Winterbottom, 1978, p. 32.

and the wife of the king of Anglesey who was heir-presumptive to at least Gwynedd west of the Conwy. She would not have taken kindly to being treated in this way. It looks then as though she decided to repay Maelgwn with a dose of his own medicine. Gwrin's son Clydno had been eliminated. The other obstacle to complete mastery of Greater Gwynedd was Maelgwn's cousin Cynlas in Rhos. Typically, Cynlas had already kicked out his first wife: as Gildas says, 'you rejected your own wife'. Could this have been Cerddych, sister of the Marchell who was married to Gwrin of Meirionydd and of the Tudglid who had now been deserted by Maelgwn? This would make Tudglid the *villainous, detestable, pestilential* sister, whom Gildas thought should now be content with 'chaste widowhood like … the dwellers in heaven'. No doubt Tudglid would have laughed at this. Was she negotiating with Cynlas in Rhos with a view to marriage if he managed to oust Maelgwn and himself assert supremacy over Gwynedd? It would, after all, have been the perfect revenge. Is this why Maelgwn had to come out of the monastery to take power and deal with her machinations? Whether or not he took it through the courts or took justice into his own hands, for Gildas he became the murderer, not only of Clydno after Gwrin's death, but also of Tudglid. Cerddych, Tudglid's sister, had already entered religion, being provided for at Towyn on the coast of Meirionydd where she may have been the founder of the later *clas* church, literally a cloister church, coming to be served not by nuns but by a community of monks or canons under an abbot.[23] Perhaps Tudglid had already sought refuge here with her sister.

And what became of Cynlas? If not blinded and castrated, he may have been pensioned off, politely deposed, and allowed to live his life in some form of internal exile. Such might be the inference to be drawn from the commemoration of his name in the vill of Cynlas in Penllyn in the parish of Llanfor, Merionethshire.[24] But this is rather flimsy evidence. At the start of his attack on Cynlas, Gildas asks him,

23_ Bartrum, 1966, pp. 15, 18, 43, 81, and 84.

24_ Lloyd, 1912, Vol. I, p. 133, note 39. There was a Cunedda's Hill in the region of Cydweli and there are legends associating him with the area, ibid., p. 118.

'Why have you been rolling in the filth of your past wickedness … ?' possibly indicating that in his enforced retirement he behaved no better, though the wickedness he goes on to attack was 'since your youth'.

However, there is one more possible scenario for the way in which power was exercised in Gwynedd at this time: one underlined by Gildas's references to Cynlas, possibly at different times in his life. When Maelgwn established himself over Gwynedd to the west of the Conwy, adding this to his newly acquired Meirionydd and so beginning to recreate the territorial integrity of the area originally bequeathed to Paternus's care in c.398, he was still not in a position to complete this by ousting Cynlas. Owain, Cynlas's father, may have been the eldest of the three usurping brothers who killed Anianus in c.485, and he may have been the brother who had at least a theoretical lordship over his brothers Cadwallon and Cadwaladr. Cadwaladr and his son Gwrin still seem to have gone their own way, creating the most powerful part of the Gwynedd confederation. After Maelgwn had successfully challenged this by having Clydno murdered and marrying his wife, he may have found it a step too far to evict Cynlas, particularly if he had got rid of Tudglid. Possibly, with control increasingly in his hands, Maelgwn became *de facto* overlord. He had a more than sufficient power base. Hence, he is known as Maelgwn *Gwynedd*. But this Greater Gwynedd was still, in effect, a confederation.

CHAPTER SEVEN

CITIZENS OF GWYNEDD
State and Church under Maelgwn, 517–545

STATE AND CHURCH – A RULER'S NEED FOR SUPPORT

One key aspect of Maelgwn's reign was his relationship with the by now powerful Christian church. It has been claimed that Maelgwn's kingdom was the most Romanized of the Welsh states. In support of this, apart from the later monument to Cadfan, king of Gwynedd 616–25, which describes him as 'the most learned and renowned of all kings', learned, that is, in the classical Roman fashion, a stone from the very heart of Gwynedd, from Penmachno in Nant Conwy, is rightly cited.

CANTIORIX LIES HERE. HE WAS A CITIZEN OF GWYNEDD [AND] COUSIN OF MAGLOS THE MAGISTRATE.[1]

The use of the terms citizen and magistrate at a time, the fifth or early sixth century, when the infrastructure normally supporting such rôles must have been disappearing, is very significant. They indicate that the political and religious centres such as Degannwy and Rhos/*Dineirth* were vastly more important in the kingdom's life than we presently realize. Alongside these, churches and monasteries would have been becoming major centres of culture and learning: storehouses for the classical manuscripts that still existed. Gildas was inordinately proud of his own classical background and education.

Maelgwn was the son of Cadwallon who more than any other was credited with fighting the Irish settlers in north Wales. These had apparently linked up with a new wave of invaders coming in the wake of Illan of north Leinster. They may very well have represented a real threat to the state's existence. Increasingly, it was the

1_ Nash-Williams, 1950, pp. 92–3, Pl. VIII and Fig. 81.

Irish Sea world, this British Mediterranean, which came
to be the centre of Gwynedd's concerns and focus.
Following in the footsteps of his father Cadwallon and
also in those of his elder brother Gwrin, Maelgwn was
the king who, in his domestic and religious policies,
seemingly turned more and more to this world, to the
political and cultural area of the Irish Sea, and this
despite Gwynedd's Roman origins and outlook. Initially,
this was almost certainly because of strategic concerns.
Later, however, finding himself attacked by the church
he still needed for support but which still looked to Gaul
and Rome, it might have been inevitable that he should
turn to a branch less obsessed with this orientation, and
which, in its comparative isolation, was developing on
more eccentric lines. He had, after all, been educated
in a monastery grounded in this more insular tradition.

Added to his criminal political behaviour was the
charge of homosexuality. Gildas talks of Maelgwn
wallowing in the ink of his crimes, 'like a man drunk
on wine pressed from the vine of the Sodomites', and
after his return from monastic life, how 'your limbs
are presented to sin and the devil as instruments of
wickedness'. As we have seen, in the Middle Ages
monastic chroniclers were tempted to fling this
accusation at anyone considered as sinning against the
church, and Geoffrey of Monmouth may have had
no real justification for labouring the point. Nevertheless,
Maelgwn must have been aware that, in certain quarters
at least, he was regarded as something approaching
the Anti-Christ. Possibly it was this that motivated him
to cultivate people, sections, and factions: any whom
he could see needed his support and who in return
would support him.

What of you, dragon of the island, you who have
removed many of these tyrants from their country and
even their life? You are last in my list, but first in evil,
mightier than many both in power and malice, more
profuse in giving, more extravagant in sin, strong in arms
but stronger still in what destroys a soul, Maglocunus.

Why wallow like a fool in the ancient ink of your crimes, like a man drunk on wine pressed from the vine of the Sodomites? Why choose to attach to your royal neck such inescapable masses of sin, like high mountains? The King of kings has made you higher than almost all the generals of Britain, in your kingdom as in your physique: why do you not show yourself to him better than the others in character, instead of worse?[2]

Gildas then goes on to cover the political history we have looked at, 'crimes that have been published on the wind far and wide'.

Constantly in this diatribe, Gildas tells Maelgwn that he has never lacked warnings about his behaviour.

You may hear this with deaf ears, spurning the prophets, despising Christ, regarding me, worthless as I am, as of no importance; though it is with sincere piety of mind that I obey the pronouncements of the prophet: 'I shall surely fill my courage with the spirit and virtue of the Lord, to announce to the house of Jacob its sins, and its crimes to the house of Israel' ...

In fact, no wise man is in doubt how much more serious are the sins of today than those of earlier days. As the apostle says, 'anyone breaking the law dies, on the evidence of two or three witnesses present: how much greater, do you think, is the punishment deserved by one who has trampled on the Son of God?'[3]

MAELGWN'S BISHOPS

BIVATIGIRNUS

[2] Gildas, *De Excidio Britanniae*, Ch. 33, Winterbottom, 1978, p. 32.

[3] Ibid., Chs. 36 and 37, pp. 35–6.

We know of one bishop in Gwynedd who may have functioned at the time of Maelgwn, a married man of Gaulish origin, perhaps from the Audecavi on the Loire. These details are probably sufficient to see him as a member of the Letavian or Roman party in Gwynedd. Bivatigirnus's wife had a memorial in

Anglesey at Llantrisant, a little more than nine miles northeast of Aberffraw, and this gives us what little we know of the man.

... IVA (? ...INA), A MOST HOLY WOMAN, LIES HERE, WHO WAS THE VERY LOVING WIFE OF BIVATIG(IRNUS), SERVANT OF GOD, BISHOP (?PRIEST), AND DISCIPLE OF PAULINUS, BY RACE A ... DOCIAN, AND AN EXAMPLE TO ALL HIS FELLOW CITIZENS AND RELATIVES BOTH IN CHARACTER (AND) IN RULE OF LIFE, (AS ALSO) OF WISDOM (WHICH IS BETTER) THAN GOLD AND GEMS (OR GOLD FROM STONES).[4]

The stone has been dated to the middle or later part of the sixth century.

SANCTINUS

We have the name of another bishop who may have ruled under Maelgwn. Bishop Sanctinus apparently died on or near the Creuddyn peninsula, site of the courts of Rhos and Degannwy, and a memorial stone was set up, probably marking his grave, with the inscription SANCTINUS SACER(DOS LIES HERE) IN P(EACE), *sacerdos* meaning bishop.[5] The stone was found in 1731 'in the highway by Tyddyn Holland, between Bodafon and Rhiw Leding, in Creuddyn, near Conwy, on a grit stone of about a yard long'.[6] It was near a cottage named *Holant* on a spur of *Creigiau Rhiwledyn*, the Cliffs of Rhiwledyn, in other words, on an extension of the Little Orme headland. This spot is only 1¼ miles as the crow flies from the court at Rhos and just less than 3¼ from the court at Degannwy. A church or monastic community with a cemetery must have been sited here: the stone's eighteenth-century discoverer referred to the remains of ancient buildings in the vicinity. Though important churches were usually built near the centres of secular power and often on what were formerly

4_ Nash-Williams, 1950, p. 63, No. 33 and p. 64, Fig. 36.

5_ Ibid., p. 86, No. 83, Pl. VIII and Fig. 68. It was originally thought that this was the grave of the Sannan who founded a church at what is now Llansannan – Lloyd, 1912, p. 150. See Morris, 1896, p. 138, and 1897.

6_ Morris, 1896, p. 138.

Roman military sites next to main highways, others were in more secluded spots. Generally, it became a sensible arrangement for bishops to be part of monastic communities. What set a bishop aside from his fellow monks were the powers conferred on him at consecration, but the abbot was the absolute head of all the monastery's affairs. Such a monastic system had its roots in the early years of the church, especially in the Middle East, but it was Martin, bishop of Tours, the one-time friend and adviser of the western emperor Magnus Maximus in the 380s, who set the fashion.

KENTIGERN/ASAPH

Maelgwn became almost a stock figure in the *Lives* of bishops and monastic founders. Always written many years after these clerics had died, the consistent aim of these texts was to emphasize the sanctity of the person in question, and in such a laudable task, imaginations were allowed free rein. Almost certainly taking the lead from Gildas's attacks, the established pattern for stories about Maelgwn involved some event or other in which Maelgwn behaved badly, only to be confronted by the saint who was then able to extract a grant from the outwitted king, usually land to build a church. In this way, Maelgwn could be allowed his rôle as patron of the church, which he almost certainly was, without it becoming too obvious that these churchmen were accepting help from such a sinner.

Possibly the best example comes in the *Life of Kentigern*, founder of the church of Glasgow. Jocelyn of Furness wrote this *Vita* for his namesake Jocelyn who was bishop of Glasgow between 1175 and 1199. It relates how Kentigern travelled south to Wales to see Bishop David, a story which is now almost universally rejected.[7] Rather than Kentigern himself, it was probably his cult that arrived in north Wales in the period 872–8. Setting this aside, and sidestepping further confusion between Llancarfan, founded by Cadoc in Glamorgan, and the

[7] Jackson, 1958; Anderson, 1990, Vol. 1, pp. 132–4; Bowen, 1969, pp. 83–91; and Miller, *Saints*, 1979, pp. 114–15, 82, and 84.

church of St Asaph in north Wales, the story of
Kentigern suddenly shifts from south to north Wales,
making its king, *Catguollaun* or *Cathwallain*, the
490–517 Cadwallon *Lawhir* of Gwynedd rather than,
as is implied, a south Wales ruler.

King Cathwallain, who reigned in that country ... knowing
him to be a holy and righteous man ... after hearing him,
did much which concerned the good of his own soul ...
"My land is in thy sight: wheresoever it suiteth thee, and
seemeth good in thy sight, there construct the habitation
of thy dwelling place; there build thy monastery ..."

A wild pig or boar revealed to Kentigern the place
where he was to build his church, and the monks began
to build.

Some cleared and levelled the situation; others began
to lay the foundation of the ground thus levelled; some
cutting down trees, others carrying them, and others
fitting them together, commenced, as the father had
measured and marked out for them, to build a church
and its offices of polished wood, after the fashion of
the Britons, seeing that they could not yet build of stone,
nor were so wont to do.
    While they were hard at work, and the building was
increasing on their hands, there came a heathen
prince, Melconde Galganu by name [*Melcon*, a Norman
corruption of Old Welsh *Mailcun*, Maelgwn, and
Galganu possibly a corruption of *Deganui*, Degannwy]
with his soldiers, and along with them a great multitude
of people.
    The man, fierce and ignorant of God, in the indignation
of his wrath demanded who they were, and whence they
came, and how they had dared to do all this on his
land. The saint, humbly replying to the interrogation,
answered that they were Christians from the northern
part of Britannia, that they had come thither to serve
the living and true God. He asserted that he had begun
the mansion there by the permission, nay through the

kindness of King Cathwalain [Cadwallon, Maelgwn's father], his master, in whose possession he believed the place to be.

But he, furious and raging, ordered them all to be expelled from the place, and that whatever had been built should be pulled down and scattered; and so he began to return to his own home.

Therefore the man departed, breathing threatenings against the servants of Christ, and behold the hand of the Lord in chastisement touched him, and he was smitten with a sudden blindness ...

Wherefore inwardly enlightened and induced by penitence, he caused himself to be carried by his people to the man of God and began most devoutly to entreat, that by his prayers he would dispel the darkness, and wash him in the font of salvation.

Verily the saint ... laid his healing hand on the blinded man in the name of the Lord, and signing him with the cross of salvation, turned his night into day, and again after the darkness poured into him the hoped-for and eagerly-desired light ...[8]

Afterwards, so we are told, Maelgwn became a devoted fellow worker with Kentigern. Maelgwn is also blinded prior to a grant of land to Mechyll, the founder of Llanfechell in Anglesey.[9] A south Wales example of the same thing, where Maelgwn in a rage is prevented from carrying out his designs, is found in the *Life of St Cadog*.[10]

Although there is hardly a word of truth in the account of St Asaph's founding, something that given its provenance should give pause for thought, it might underline the likelihood that it was Cadwallon, Maelgwn's father, who was the instigator of this policy of ecclesiastical patronage. This is exactly what one would expect for one of three brothers who had usurped power in north Wales through the murder of its king.

Jocelyn's *Vita* says that one of the disciples who flocked to Kentigern's church was a boy named Asaph who from earliest years had performed miracles. He supposedly

8_ Jocelinus, *The Life of S. Kentigern*, Chs. 13–14, Forbes, 1874, pp. 159–242.

9_ Miller, *Saints*, 1979, p. 114.

10_ *Life of St Cadog*, Wade-Evans, 1944, p. 137.

succeeded Kentigern when the bishop returned to the north at a date that, were it to have happened, would have been about 550. Asaph was in all probability the actual founder or at least the monastery's first abbot, and to this day the cathedral there is named after him.

One probable aspect of this story we are not told about, and which still waits to be proved, is the likelihood that the chosen site was a Roman fort, guarding the river crossing below which carried the Roman road from *Segontium*, through *Canovium* on the Conwy, to the former legionary HQ at Chester. Another Roman dimension of the St Asaph story is the statement that it was a pig, 'entirely white', which indicated the site of the future monastery. The model for this comes from Virgil's *Aeneid*.[11] In this, Tiber, a river-god, assured Aeneas that his struggles to establish himself in Italy had not been in vain.

This is the home that is decreed for you, this is the home decreed for the gods of your household. Do not give it up. Do not be intimidated by the threat of war. All the angry passions of the gods are now spent. But come now, so that you may not think what you are seeing is an empty dream, I tell you that you will find a great sow with a litter of thirty piglets lying beneath ilex trees on a shore. There she will lie all white on the ground and the young around her udders will be white.[12]

DANIEL
The Early Years: Bangor on Dee and Chester

When looking at the foundation of Bangor on the Menai Strait, the seat of another of Gwynedd's bishops, we have even less to go on than in other areas. When *Deiniol*, Daniel, moved there, apparently to be its bishop, he did so from another Bangor, Bangor on Dee. Just less than a hundred years later monks from Bangor on Dee were to play a prominent part in the so-called battle of Chester, fought to resist an invasion of north Wales by Aethelfrith,

11_ On the rôle of pigs in the lives of Irish saints and the derivation from Virgil, Dr Karen Jankulak, 'Swine as Portents of Ecclesiastical Foundations', 11th International Congress of Celtic Studies, Cork, July 1999; see also Jankulak, 2003.

12_ Virgil, *Aeneid*, Book 8, the key text in which Tiber, the god of the river, reassures Aeneas, West, 1991, p. 190.

king of Northumbria. The event is of special significance because it brought the English to the Dee and the Mersey, in effect confining the British to Wales and cutting the land route to the northern kingdoms, just as earlier the Saxon push to the Severn had separated Wales from Cornwall and Devon. But the story is important for us as it illustrates the power and importance of this other Bangor on the Dee. Because Gwynedd's army had not arrived in time, monks turned out *en masse* to pray for Aethelfrith's defeat by the more limited forces of Powys.

Most of them were from the monastery of Bangor, where there was said to be so great a number of monks that, when it was divided into seven parts with superiors [abbots or priors] over each, no division had less than 300 men, all of whom were accustomed to live by the labour of their hands.

Of these, 'twelve hundred men were slain who had come to pray and only fifty escaped by flight'.[13]

The importance of this first Bangor, the one on the Dee, is too often overlooked. Was Daniel its abbot with a bishop living under him in the same community? Why is it that, despite Bangor on Dee's importance, we never hear of a bishop of that place? The answer is probably simple. There was one there, or more accurately, one came to be based there after its foundation. This person was probably someone who was originally, and in name still was, bishop of Chester.

The emergence of the diocesan system in Britain owes much to the personal involvement of Constantine I and his son Constans I, as well as to the split between Nicene and Arian Christians. The 325 Council of *Nicaea* defined God as being three in one and one in three, Father, Son, and Holy Ghost, emphasizing that Christ is 'of one substance with the Father'. This was an outright rejection of Arius, a Libyan priest in Alexandria, *c.*250–336, who saw the danger of Christianity developing into a religion where two gods would be worshipped, God the Father

13_ Bede, *Ecclesiastical History*, Book 2, Ch. 2, Colgrave and Mynors, 1969, p. 141

and God the Son. He rejected this growing orthodoxy of consubstantiality, in effect rejecting the divinity of Jesus. After *Nicaea*, he was condemned and all Arian books were to be burned.

Constantine increasingly came to accept that the Supreme God *was* the one preached by Jesus. Above all, he saw the Christian church providing the new cohesive power the empire needed and, importantly, he saw how it could encourage acceptance of his own divine right to rule. Christianity was by this date probably the largest single religion in the empire. Now churches appeared in towns and, by the end of the fourth century, almost every major city had its bishop. But Constantine was not a baptized Christian, nor was Christianity the formal religion of the empire.

When Constantine visited Britain in 314, he would almost certainly have visited the four provincial capitals of London, Cirencester, Lincoln, and York. As defence was still a vitally important issue, Caerleon and Chester would also have featured in the itinerary. The emperor would have encouraged the church to organize and control. When he left for the Continent, he took with him Restitutus, bishop of London, Adelphius, bishop of Lincoln, and, taking his name from the place, Eborius, bishop of York. Either no bishopric had been established in the west, which is unlikely, or there may have been vacancies at the time. Cirencester, Caerleon, and Chester could all have been possible bishoprics. The two priests accompanying the bishops to the Council of Arles *may* have been bishops-elect awaiting consecration. No bishops from Britain were among the three hundred bishops attending the great Council of *Nicaea* in 325, possibly because there was no emperor on hand to force their attendance.

But Constantine was a man of ruthless ambition, suspicious of everyone, including churchmen. In 326, he had his eldest son Crispus suffocated to death, and drove his wife Fausta to suicide. By 335, the Arians were winning him over to their side and so, at another church council, Arius was reinstated and restored to favour, whilst Athanasius, author of the Nicene Creed, was condemned and exiled. Constantine was baptized on his death-bed in 337, but by an Arian bishop.

In 343, Constans I, son of Constantine and western emperor, was in Britain for a brief visit. He left, probably taking the British bishops with him, to attend the church council of *Serdica* or *Sardica*, Sofia, held at *Philippolis*, Plovdiv. This had been called to grapple with the continuing Nicene–Arian split.[14] Julius, bishop of Rome 337–52, had at last brought the Roman see into the struggle, condemning the Arians, but Constantius II, the eastern emperor, was deeply committed to the Arian cause. Constans, 'depraved, dissipated and avaricious', was the champion of the Nicene Creed. At the council there were disruptions, excommunications, and vicious disputes, so the struggles dragged on.

It is not much to go on, but, with what few other pointers we possess, all this might indicate that certainly before 410 Chester *was* the seat of a bishop. However, as the site became more and more untenable because undefendable, possibly the title remained but the man lived elsewhere in a smaller, more secure place. This could have been to its south in Overton on Dee, a stronghold of northern Powys. When Daniel founded the monastery at Bangor on Dee right next door, if such a bishop of Chester still operated, and with the emergence of the new province of Powys after 429 this seems likely, he would have almost certainly taken up residence in this new prestigious monastery. Such a move might have had to wait upon a vacancy for the title, for the move from an urban-based episcopate, if Overton could be considered such at the time, to one based in a monastery was one some would have fought against strongly.

Events after the battle of Chester in 616 seem to confirm the existence of a bishop here. The battle was apparently in two parts. In the first, Aethelfrith defeated the Welsh army mainly drawn from Powys in the battle of Bangor Orchard, but was then forced to retreat with the late arrival of Cadfan, king of Gwynedd, and his

14_ According to some, British bishops were at *Philippolis*, but there is no note of this in the major study of the council – see Hess, 1958.

army. The battle of Chester proper, fought lower down the Dee nearer the city, was probably a matter of encounters between Cadfan's army and the retreating English. Geoffrey of Monmouth tells us that after seeing off this English threat, there was a gathering of Welsh princes in Chester. The buildings and enclosed spaces still made it a useful meeting place.

Only thirteen years before, representatives of the British church had met Augustine here for a second encounter. This was AC's 'The Synod of the City of the Legion', but Bede's is the only account.

When this [the plan to have a more representative meeting of the British church and to see Augustine again] had been decided upon, it is related that seven British bishops and many learned men came, chiefly from their most famous monastery which the English call *Bancornaburg* (Bangor Iscoed) [Bangor below the Trees or Bangor on Dee]. At that time it is said to have been ruled over by Abbot Dinoot.[15]

In fact, the British clerics were guided by a local hermit who advised that if Augustine stood up to greet them they would know he was a man of God and should follow him. If he remained seated, his own pride would condemn him. Of course, Augustine remained seated. Bede gives Augustine's warning to the British about the consequences of their actions, war from their enemies instead of peace from their friends. The slaughter of the monks from Bangor, Bede tells us, was fulfilment of this prophecy and just punishment for such heretics.[16] Abbot Dinoot/Dunod might himself have been the bishop, for the rôles were often combined. As time passed the position would have less and less connection to the fortress-city that was originally its seat and so the title referring to Chester would have been less frequently used.

When the British princes met in Chester in 616, Cadfan was already king of Gwynedd. Now he was faced with a Powys that had just seen its king killed in battle. This was Cadfan's brother-in-law, Selyf ap Cynan,

15_ Bede, *Ecclesiastical History*, Book 2, Ch. 2, Colgrave and Mynors, 1969, p. 137–9.

16_ Ibid., pp. 141–3.

Selyf *Serffgadau*, Selyf Serpent of Battles. Selyf was succeeded by his brothers, first Brochwel and then Elfoddw, but from 616 they probably accepted the lordship of Cadfan who was married to their sister Tandreg. This was a lordship that lasted until the 670s and for Gwynedd it represented a considerable extension of its power and influence. However, eastern Powys had split from the main line and it looks as though the appropriately named Cyndrwyn the Stubborn, *c*.602–57, and Cynddylan of Pengwern, *c*.637–57, remained aloof from this arrangement.

All the princes of the Britons [the usual Geoffrey exaggeration] then assembled in the city of Chester and agreed unanimously that they should make Cadvan their King and that under his command they should cross the Humber in pursuit of Ethelfrid [something that did happen, but not until 634].
    Once Cadvan had been crowned King of the realm, these princes [returned home, prepared, and eventually] gathered from all sides and crossed the Humber ...[17]

A coronation in Chester implies the presence of at least one bishop if not more. Local tradition, almost certainly taking its lead from the above reference in Geoffrey, says that Cadfan's successor, Cadwallon, 'the proud, haughty king' of the *Life of St Beuno*, was also crowned in Chester.[18] In Cadfan's case, it is more than likely that such a ceremony did take place in Chester.
    Unquestionably, the concept of overlordship was beginning to develop into the sophisticated and complicated system we see in the Middle Ages. These early events in Chester remind us of Edgar king of Wessex and his Whit Sunday imperial coronation in Bath on 11 May 973: a ceremony that was in addition to his earlier coronation when he came to the throne in 959. An even closer link to these events comes with Edgar's visit to Chester, probably in July of the same year, almost certainly arriving by sea. Here, Edgar received the homage of six kings, including Iago ab Idwal, joint-king

[17]_ Geoffrey of Monmouth, *The History of the Kings of Britain*, XII, I, Thorpe, 1966, p. 267.

[18]_ *Beuno Sant*, Wade-Evans, 1930, p. 319.

of Gwynedd with his brother, 951–85, and two earls, thereby acknowledging the simple fact that Edgar was the most powerful of the group. This act of Irish Sea solidarity had another symbolic enactment when the same rulers rowed Edgar down river to Chester from his residence in Aldford and back again. On the same visit he was supposed to have made a grant to the church of SS Peter and Paul within the walls, almost certainly the original seat of this fortress-city's bishop. When the city was refortified by the Mercians after 907, this church, which later became the Norman abbey of St Werburgh, would have achieved a new importance.[19] Perhaps, therefore, the 616 event *was* Cadfan's imperial coronation: an acclamation of the one who had saved the day after Powys's defeat.

Daniel is elected bishop of Bangor in Arfon

From his position as abbot of Bangor on Dee, Daniel moved to Gwynedd and the church on the Menai Strait. Here, it appears he remodelled what was already a monastery. In other words, he arrived as its new bishop and abbot, and if this is the case, this would have to have been with the agreement and support of Maelgwn. Gwynedd had been functioning as a political entity for virtually 120 years by the start of Maelgwn's reign, but we have no hard evidence that Bangor was already the seat of a bishop. Perhaps this was a development of these years of Maelgwn's rule. For what it is worth, Daniel's *Vita* of 1602 'from an ancient MS' tells us there *was* already a bishop here. This *Vita* is really just an order of service in honour of the saint: one consisting of nine lessons and psalms with prayers.

Lesson iv. In course of time, the Cathedral Church of Bangor becoming vacant through the death of its Bishop ... it was revealed from heaven that they should send without delay into Pembroke [for which read Bangor on Dee] ...

[19]_ Its remains are probably lying beneath the small chapel between the choir and the north transept of the present cathedral.

215

Lesson v. They at once sent messengers ... he, being incredibly astonished, says, "How can this be, that you claim me as Bishop-elect, since I have hardly the elements of learning nor any knowledge of letters?" ... And he, being overcome by their insistence, and wishing to obey the Divine call, left all he had and followed them ...

When Daniel arose from his first prayer in the Menai church, 'he was so endowed with all ecclesiastical knowledge that no one in Britain seemed then like him in knowledge and letters'. The *Life* says he was then promoted through all the lesser and greater orders, such as those of deacon and priest, and was eventually consecrated bishop.[20] If this did happen, it would mean that whilst in Bangor on Dee, Daniel had been its abbot, not its bishop.

We have absolutely no information about his time on the Menai Strait. The name of this Gwynedd monastery, *Bangor Fawr yn Arfon*, Great Bangor in Arfon, the *cantref* that faces *Môn*, Anglesey, might imply that Daniel expanded it on lines similar to his former establishment on the Dee. Perhaps when Daniel left Bangor, his brother Cynwyl also moved, as tradition claims he did, going south to visit David in Pembrokeshire and establish his own community at *Cynwyl Gaio* on the river Annell, though there are dedications to him elsewhere.[21] Deiniol the Younger, the son of Daniel who became abbot of Bangor in Gwynedd in succession to his father, is almost certainly a doublet of Daniel himself. As a separate figure, his existence owes much to Iolo's eighteenth-century industry.

THE ONENESS OF CHURCH AND STATE: SECULAR AND RELIGIOUS SITES

We too readily regard these monasteries purely as religious sites, places set apart from secular sites like Degannwy and Rhos. As we have seen, these capitals

20_ Baring-Gould and Fisher, 1907–13, Vol. IV, 1913, pp. 387–92 at p. 391.

21_ Ibid., Vol. II, 1908, pp. 275–6.

covered considerable areas and had one or more churches within whatever they had as enclosures, certainly ditches, possibly even walls. When we then find Maelgwn particularly associated with Llanrhos church to the east of Degannwy and almost certainly within its walls, and with Llandrillo to the east of the Bryn Euryn site, again within the Rhos stronghold, we have to remember the concern of most rulers to establish their own mausoleums. The patronage and care for these churches would further emphasize their importance. Priests serving them would have assisted the king in his rule and would have conferred the blessing of the church on the reign's key events, culminating in the funeral and burial of the king. If they were not monasteries, these churches would have been what were later called minster churches, served by a group of priests like later cathedral chapters, and having their own community of labourers. On such prestigious sites, is it conceivable that the priest heading the community would have been of a lesser status than a bishop? Today, the idea of bishops of the little churches of Llanrhos and Llandrillo may strike us as strange, but they would have existed. Sanctinus could have been one of these. The site of his memorial may have been a church now lost to us, by the eighteenth-century 'a vast many ruins about this place'.

If we still too often think of religious and secular sites as being somehow separate, instead of often being part of single governing and administrative centres, we also make too much of the supposed differences between the continental church of the later Roman empire and the so-called Celtic church of a semi-detached, some would claim wholly detached, Britain under its newly emerging rulers. Monastic institutions under abbots, where the bishop was merely one of the community, parallel the control of episcopal seats, cathedrals, by chapters. Later, such sites like those of Llanrhos and Llandrillo would have gradually lost their importance as Gwynedd's kings came to prefer residence in the more westerly courts of Aberffraw and Abergwyngregyn. Bishops would no longer have operated from the eastern churches, and their jobs here would have increasingly fallen to senior priests. Later on still, the medieval church *made* its bishops move their seats to the most populous cities in their dioceses.

MAELGWN'S BISHOPRICS

Geography would have also played its part in the establishment of bishops. If they were to perform their rôles effectively and not end up in dispute with other bishops, no doubt growing attention was paid to the territory in which they were expected to function. In this way, the job of bishop, which under the monastic arrangements had become more one of function, once again became territorial.

... it is related that seven British bishops and many learned men came, chiefly from their most famous monastery which the English call *Bancornaburg* (Bangor Iscoed) [Bangor on Dee]. At that time [c.603] it is said to have been ruled over by Abbot Dinoot.[22]

Bede implies that this was a meeting of the *whole* British church, planned because the first meeting at Aust on the Severn was too unrepresentative to come to a decision over Augustine's demands. It strikes one that, with only seven bishops present, this hardly sounds that sort of meeting. Possibly Bede had misunderstood and that this gathering in Chester in *c.*603 was instead one for representatives from the church in the northern part of Wales, Aust having been for the southern bishops. The 'many learned men' were the theologians, implying that Bangor on Dee was by this date the leading theological seminary or university in north Wales. In the light of what we have seen, the bishops would therefore have been those based in St Asaph, Llandrillo, Llanrhos, Bangor in Arfon, and Aberffraw. The other two bishops would have come from Powys, and one of these would have been the bishop of Bangor on Dee/Chester, who in

22_ Bede, *Ecclesiastical History*, Book 2, Ch. 2, Colgrave and Mynors, 1969, pp. 137–9.

Llandrillo church today.
A church here was once
part of the *Dineirth* court
complex, and at that time
a cathedral or minster.

220

effect hosted the gathering in his titular seat. If all of them, except for the bishop of Chester, came from Gwynedd, then the other man could have come from somewhere in Llŷn or more likely from *Segontium*. The site of *Segontium*, or Merfyn's Town as it came to be called because of a particular association with Merfyn *Frych* of Gwynedd, 825–44, would always have been important, both because of what it represented in terms of its Roman past and because of its eminently usable stone structures.

POST-ROMAN OR ROMAN?

Time was passing, and there is no doubt now that this *was* becoming a post-Roman society. Coinage had fallen out of use and the economy was essentially agricultural. Farming and stockbreeding were now the main occupations and the only real source of wealth. Anything of value or sophistication had to be imported. The once extensive pottery industry in Roman Britain appears to have collapsed so that even low-grade stuff had to be brought in. At the lower levels in society, wood and leather, the products of agriculture rather than of industry, had to serve. Quarries were no longer worked, so, as supplies of stonework from Roman sites were used up or were found to be too far away, buildings became smaller. Excavation at Degannwy, though concentrated at the Roman lookout high point of the much more extensive complex, shows that the little building that was taking place was crude and clumsy. It was mere dry-stone walling, far removed from anything erected in the Roman period.

Always, however, the problem is to avoid seeing this period through eyes that are looking back from later periods when these aspects of so-called Dark Age life were commonplace. There was much that was still essentially Roman. In the absence of coinage, revenue was in the form of tribute levied in corn, cattle, and other foodstuffs, but this was the situation that had

221

pertained throughout the Roman period to provide supplies for the army. So the *cais*, the revenue officer, still visited on circuits called *cylch* to collect the *annona*, the set tax.[23] The Penmachno stones in the heart of Gwynedd testify to the existence of the Roman law system with magistrates and a hierarchy of courts. The church was still a perfectly functioning part of imperial life. It helped to keep open the trade routes to Gaul and the Mediterranean because wine, essential for the main service that took place in every church in the land, was imported from southern Europe. With the wine came olive oil, still in large jars with thick handles at the top known as *amphorae*. A whole range of other pots show that Roman cooking methods persisted. The subject is endlessly written on and dissected, but the picture is clear enough. If there seems to be a sparsity of such evidence in sites such as Degannwy, this could well be because of the continuing Roman habits of cleanliness.

Churches, and more particularly the monasteries, housed the literature of Greece and Rome. When Cadfan who died in 625 was described as the most learned of kings, as Geoffrey Ashe noted years ago, this was 'learning not in the vernacular oral tradition of Celtic people, but in classical book-learning. Cadfan's descendants were claiming that he was educated in the Roman fashion.'[24] Was Virgil's *Aeneid* read in Degannwy, or Boethius's *Consolations of Philosophy*, written in 523, in Aberffraw?

MAELGWN: PELAGIANISM AND ARIANISM

Maelgwn, by the standards of his day, was extremely powerful, as Gildas put it 'exceeding many in power'. However, if the scenario put forward here is correct, his father had come to power in Gwynedd only though usurpation and the death of Anianus, and Maelgwn had the position he now enjoyed in Degannwy only through murdering his nephew Clydno of Meirionydd and by

23_ Morris, 1973, pp. 220–2.

24_ Ashe in Ashe et al., 1968, p. 89.

establishing a lordship over Cynlas in the court of Rhos. It would be interesting to know how far Maelgwn was himself influenced by the Pelagianism that had gained such a hold on Britain in the mid-fifth century. Germanus, despite the very best efforts of his biographer, had *not* been able to stamp it out. Neither had Arianism been defeated. To those brought up as pagans, a Christian term of contempt for those still managing to follow the traditional observances of the empire, Arianism allowed an accommodation with Christianity, placing Jesus as a religious teacher rather than God on earth. God could then be seen more as Apollo the Sun God once was, and as Constantine himself saw him, as the ultimate deity.

Maelgwn's reign saw more Nicene–Arian clashes, the result rather of Catholic intolerance than of Arian intransigence. Theodoric, the Gothic king of Italy 493–526, was an Arian, as were the majority of his people. However, with the encouragement of the eastern church, the eastern emperor Justin I, 518–27, was moving against the heresy, in this way infuriating Theodoric who, unsurprisingly, had practised a policy of religious toleration. With some considerable reservations on his part, Pope John I, 523–6, was sent on a delegation to Constantinople to demand an end to the persecution. In other words, a Catholic was being forced to speak up for Arians. However, the mission turned into something of a personal triumph for John and for Roman claims to supremacy. Not surprisingly, he failed to obtain an agreement to allow those forcibly converted to Catholicism to return to their Arian beliefs. On his return, he was detained in Ravenna by a furious Theodoric, and there he died. Stories of his imprisonment, and therefore of him, in effect, being put to death, reached Wales and Ireland and appear in the Irish annals.[25] As for Pelagianism, this was still common particularly in Gaul and had to be condemned by John's successor, Felix IV, 526–30. Following John and Felix, Maelgwn saw a further five popes come and go – Pope Vigilius, 537–55, was on the throne when he died – and

25_ AU, 524.

223

even then the nature of Christ's divinity was still being argued over. During his reign, three Roman emperors ruled in Constantinople, Anastasius, 491–518, Justin I, 518–27, and Justinian I, 527–65.

FOREIGN POLICY AND ECCLESIASTICAL OPPOSITION

Determined to rule, possibly inspired by the backwash of Pelagianism, and acutely aware of how rulers come and go, Maelgwn needed to buttress his position. One way in which those in power do this is through the workings of their foreign policy. Clydno's father, Gwrin, had apparently reached a position of dominance in the Gwynedd confederation by his power at sea *and* through his relations with rulers in Ireland. We have seen how the Gwynedd campaigns against Irish settlers deemed untrustworthy, and against incursions on their behalf by Ailill of north Leinster, probably in the period 490 to 500, and then against those who imitated him, were probably conducted *in concert* with the Uí Néill in Ireland. Further back still, it could be that Niall himself, ancestor of this great family in the north of Ireland, was essentially an agent of Vortigern's post-Roman British government, operating first against the Ulaid in the north of Ireland and then against the Leinster kingdoms, the two areas historically most opposed to Roman Britain. Maelgwn *had* to gain some international recognition for his position as king, not least to strengthen his credibility amongst his citizen-subjects. He had to continue to protect the now Greater Gwynedd from incursions from Leinster, and ensure that Cynlas of Rhos and the relatives of Clydno in Meirionydd had no opportunity to make use of Irish help. Behind all this was the need to protect trade, particularly with Gaul and the Mediterranean, on which Gwynedd's and therefore Maelgwn's wealth, position, and culture depended. The most obvious way in which Maelgwn could achieve all this was to cement, or at least, if he had not been involved in this area of politics before, to establish relationships with the current Uí Néill rulers in Ireland.

The first of the Uí Néill over-kings of note in Maelgwn's reign was Muirchertach *mac Erca*. Muirchertach, who despite his name was actually the son of Muiredach, was a great-grandson of Niall. After the battle of *Druim Derg* in 516, when the Uí Néill finally wrested the plain of Meath from Leinster, no clash between the two is recorded until after 520. Following what was possibly a period of internal dispute, Muirchertach, who had been over-king of the northern Uí Néill since *c*.482 when he must have been in his late teens, managed to defeat the southern Uí Néill king, Ardgal son of Conall of west Meath, in the battle of *Détnae* in 520.[26] Ardgal was a grandson of Niall. Rather than this being a struggle for some pre-existing lordship over the whole Uí Néill confederation north and south as suggested by Morris, it looks as though it was this defeat for the southern Ardgal which established this kingship. In other words, Muirchertach was the first over-king of the whole Uí Néill confederation comprising both the northern and southern branches of the dynasty descended from Niall.

It is worth noting that, despite emerging ideas in Britain and Ireland of a high-kingship over both the areas, there were differences. Kingship in Ireland, exercised either at a provincial level, as was coming to be the case in Leinster, Munster, or Connacht, or within the Uí Néill confederation, was always a matter of personal ties. As the Middle Ages developed, moves towards a high-kingship over Ireland never reached the point where the apparatus we would associate with government cut across the powers exercised by lesser kings. Had Ireland been a part of the formal empire as was the case for Britain, the situation might have been different.

Muirchertach, coming to power through family conflict similar to that which had brought Maelgwn to the top in Gwynedd, must also have been casting around for allies and external support. It is not too fanciful to imagine messages of congratulation going out from Gwynedd,

[26] AU, 519=520, repeated under 522=523; AFM, 513 and 504.

first when the Uí Néill finally took Meath from Leinster in 516, and then when Muirchertach became over-king of the entire Uí Néill confederation in 520. Indeed, both sides having co-operated against Leinster aggressors since the time of Niall, such contacts would almost certainly have taken place. This means embassies, entertainment, and gifts.

One could well imagine Maelgwn, tired of attacks on how he had risen to power and his operations as king, taking a perverse delight in antagonizing those who seemingly rejected him. Many of these were probably churchmen. If Gildas is to be believed, Maelgwn increasingly surrounded himself with the trappings of an Irish king and, in his attack on this, Gildas gives us the earliest reference to bards in early medieval Wales and to the praise-poems which made them famous.

... for now [having left your life as a monk] thou dost not listen to the praises of God sweetly sounded forth by the pleasant voices of Christ's soldiers [his fellow monks], nor the instruments of ecclesiastical melody, but thine own praises (which are nothing) rung out, after the fashion of the giddy rout of Bacchus, by the mouths of thy villanous followers, accompanied with lies and malice, to the utter destruction of the neighbours.[27]

But these praise-poems were simply taking the panegyrics of the later Roman empire, so much a part of the formal recording of political life, on to new levels of artistic achievement by the introduction of rhyme and the accompaniment of music.

The Irish *Life of Brigit*, talking of her visit to the court of Cashel, has an early mention of the harps which were becoming part of this whole process of praising the ruler. After the third king of Cashel, Óengus mac Nad-Froích who died in 490, we simply have a list of names with no dating evidence. Eochaid mac Óengus was the forth ruler. He was the founder of the Eóganacht of Glennamain and was succeeded in Cashel by his brother Feidlimid, founder of the Eóganacht of Cashel. We are

27_ Gildas, *De Excidio Britanniae*, Ch. 34, Giles, 1841, p. 31.

here into the reign of Maelgwn. Visiting the court to ask pardon for a prisoner, Brigit found that the king was away. If this actually happened, this king could have been Eochaid. Seeing harps hanging on the walls she asked to be entertained with music, but was told that the harpers were also absent. One of those present jokingly told his friends to take the harps and play, so that Brigit could bless their hands and give them the ability to entertain her. Ignoring the sarcasm, Brigit did as she was asked, and to their amazement, they found that they could play. On his return, the king was so impressed by the story that he released the prisoner.[28]

Brigit, the Prophetess of Christ, Queen of the South, Mary of the Gael, and patroness of the people of Leinster, died, possibly on Thursday, 1 February 524, on the eve of the feast of the Purification of the Virgin Mary 'in the 70th year of her age'.[29] Probably of more interest to Maelgwn was the death, apparently in the following year, of Cairell, over-king of eastern Ulster, Ulidia, when the over-kingship of Ulidia passed to the Dál nAraide Eochaid son of Conlae ruling until 553. This pattern of alternating rule between the Dál Fiatach and the Dál nAraide was then repeated down the years.

Maelgwn may have had a reason to celebrate when in 527 news arrived of the death of Ailill, the Leinster king who seems to have raided into Greater Gwynedd between c.495 and 500.[30] It is not possible to tell how far Leinster's moves towards a provincial kingship had developed by this date. The few names that we have were undoubtedly its leading kings, but how far their power extended beyond their family lands is unknown. Certainly Ailill was one such potential king over the whole area we later call a province, but now he was dead and it is possible that his son Cormac was a minor still, or because of this possibly unexpected elevation to kingship had not had time to build up a network of allegiances similar to that of his father. We are not told that Muirchertach made the first move, but it looks as though some of the Uí Néill now took advantage of the situation. Having swooped into north Leinster, they

28_ McGrath, 1979, p. 224.

29_ AU, 523=524, Mac Airt and Mac Niocaill, 1983, p. 67; AI, 524, Mac Airt, 1977, p. 69; and AFM, 525, O'Donovan, 1851, Vol. I, pp. 171–3, giving 1 February.

30_ AU, 526=527; AFM, 506 and 526.

proceeded to devastate the land. Ailill had been the son of Dúnlang son of Énnae son of Bresal. His uncle Bríon son of Énnae was the founder of the Uí Brúin of Cualu, living south of the Liffey along the coast of Wicklow, where we also find the Uí Garrchon, regarded later, if not already, as one of the outside or unfree peoples of Leinster having no claim on any wider power amongst the Laigin. We therefore probably have here the core of Ailill's power in Leinster, in effect exercising lordship over territory which took him to the sea at Wicklow. This haven, where the Vartry river enters the Irish Sea, is only fifty-two miles from the tip of Llŷn and seventy-five miles from landfall in Caernarfon Bay. This was the territory now under attack from the Uí Néill.

In desperation, the Laigin of these territories hastily gathered an army. Was the story of Brigit's supposed blessing to Ailill of 'victoriousness in battle over Conn's Half', that is the north of Ireland, over the Uí Néill, remembered, or was this added to the story of what now happened? Unfortunately, we here encounter confusion, either between two rulers, Ailill and Illann, who were brothers, or merely one over names so that they were, in fact, the same person. According to the *Life of Brigit* Ailill's body was taken from its resting place in the monastery at Kildare, placed in a chariot, and accompanying this, the Leinster army marched to confront the invaders. In AFM this is now Illann.

The battle of Luachair [a rushy place, impossible to locate in a Leinster full of such names] (was fought) by Cucorb [Cormac] against the Uí Néill, of which was said:
The fierce battle of Luachair, overhead, Brigit saw, no vain vision;
The bloody battle of Fionnabhair [Fennor near Kildare] was noble, about the body of Illann after his death.[31]

The next year, the man himself arrived. Muirchertach entered Leinster and inflicted two defeats on the Laigin, the first at Kineagh in north Kildare and the second at Assey, a ford over the Boyne in Meath. This second

31_ AFM, 506, O'Donovan, 1851, Vol. I, p. 165. The extract from the second Latin *Life of Brigit* – pp. 164–5, note b. In the Irish *Life of Brigit*, Stokes, 1890, p. 195, it has 'The Leinstermen carried his [Ailill's] body to the battle, and their foes were at once routed before them.'

victory may have been against the Leinster peoples in Meath who were still refusing to bow to the Uí Néill, or it was fought because the Laigin had actually invaded Uí Néill territory.[32]

AU has a confused entry for 533, which is largely in a second hand. The reliable part seems to be the original entry about a battle of *Éblenn*, which may or may not have been in Leinster. The second hand then has a battle of *Mag Ailbe* in northeast Carlow and a battle of *Almuin*, the Hill of Allen in Kildare, implying operations in Leinster. A battle in Connacht also features, and then there is a repeat note of the 528 events.[33] But by this date we are moving into a period when other matters entirely began to make themselves felt.

Of course, we have absolutely no evidence for any involvement by Gwynedd in these events. Nevertheless, Uí Néill victories increased Gwynedd's and therefore Maelgwn's security. What had happened to Gwrin's fleet? Were naval forces now operating not only out of the Dyfi and the Mawddach, but also out of the Seiont and the Conwy? Were the activities of the *classis Britannica* still remembered? Were there now units comparable to the swift and light *pictae* used by the Romans to give warning of any untoward naval activity on or near the Irish coast? We simply do not know, but Gwynedd was a Roman state still and would not have totally abandoned the behaviour and approach of previous centuries.

This increasing Irish focus of Maelgwn's reign was opening up a split between a church still looking to Rome and the past, and parts of it, based in the Irish Sea area, making necessary changes in organization, and with it outlook, that these uncertain times seemed to demand. As Maelgwn's reign unfolded, this new religious world was to come to an astonishing prominence through events, and the threat of events, which together can only be described as catastrophic.

32_ AI, AU, AFM. Also Mac Niocaill, 1972, p. 18.

33_ AU, 532=533.

CHAPTER EIGHT

CURSES SHALL COME UPON THEE
Warnings of the End: Challenge and Response, 534–545

DEATH OF THE UÍ NÉILL OVER-KING MUIRCHERTACH

In 534, news would have reached Maelgwn *Gwynedd* that Muirchertach, northern Uí Néill over-king of the Uí Néill confederation for the past fourteen years, was dead. The original entry in AU is short and intriguing.

The drowning of Muirchertach Mac Erca in a vat full of wine on the hilltop of Cleitech above Bóinn.[1]

Although the story may have been elaborated and expanded later, its essentials are simple enough. Muirchertach, bewitched by another woman, who was transformed by later tradition into a fairy, had apparently abandoned his wife, or at least was enjoying an extramarital affair. A Meath cleric, Cairnech, remonstrated with the king about the scandal so that he gave in, ended the liaison, and returned to his vows. The relationship with his mistress had been complicated by the fact that she had lost her father and other members of her family in the battle of Assey in Meath in 528 when Muirchertach defeated Leinster forces. Now furious, the spurned lover took her revenge, and when Muirchertach was staying in a house at *Cleitech*, Cletty, near Stackallen Bridge, on the south bank of the Boyne, she burned the place down about his ears. Stories said that the king had tried to escape by throwing himself into a vat of wine. It is clear the annalists did not know the woman's name and so, in AFM at least, which for the death gives the suspicious night of 1 November, the great spirit-feast of *Samhain*, she was called *Sin*, pronounced Sheen, which means storm. In a verse supposedly hers she says, 'I am Taetan, the woman who killed the chief

1_ AU, 534, Mac Airt and Mac Niocaill, 1983, p. 71. Also in AT, AClon, and AFM.

of Niall; Gannadhaigh is my name, in every place and road.' O'Donovan explained that *Sin* meant storm, *Taetan*, fire, and *Gemadaigh*, wintry. In other versions of the story, she is also called *Gaeth*, wind, *Garbh*, rough, *Ochsad*, a groan, and *Iactadh*, lamentation.[2]

MUIRCHERTACH AND THE THIRD-CENTURY CORMAC

There is here a remarkable coincidence for those prepared to accept that, during the period of Roman rule over Britain, rulers in Ireland of the line of Feradach son of Crimthann and Tuathal son of Fiacha acted as friends and allies of the Roman people and of the Roman authorities in Britain. The idea is worth a digression. After a brief flirtation with Munster rulers, particularly Lugaid *Maccon* in the early third century, the Roman authorities in Britain shifted their support back to the original line in the person of Cormac mac Airt, *c.*225–67. In 258, it appears that Cormac was in Britain for seven months being courted by its officials, unless of course the traditional tale is accepted that he was away with the fairies. If Cormac did return to Ireland full of pride, then he was to experience a considerable shock. Arriving home, Cormac found his main claim to be treated as an important ruler by Britain, his control over the hostile Ulaid, had been shattered, and his lordship rejected. Now this had to be fought for again, even though Cormac was probably well into his sixties.

In *c.*266, the year before his death, Cormac lost an eye in a fracas. Blinding was considered one of those taboos that automatically excluded anyone from exercising kingship. This was not peculiar to this age or to Ireland. As a result, Cormac withdrew to *Achaill*, on the Hill of Skreen, just three miles to the east of Tara, 'for it was not lawful for a king with a blemish to sleep in Tara'.[3] In the following year, 267, Cormac moved north to the Boyne, possibly a story designed to bring him near to the great Neolithic burial mound of *Brug na Bóinne*, Newgrange,

[2] AFM, 526=533, 527=534, O'Donovan, 1851, Vol. I, pp. 173–7, and p. 175, note j.

[3] *The Expulsion of the Deisi*, Meyer, 1901, p. 107. Also Ó Cathasaigh, 1977, p. 69, and Byrne, 1987, p. 55.

where, according to the speculations of later historians and story tellers who *may* have been correct, all kings of Tara of the line of Cormac were buried. Here, *Cleitech* near Stackallen Bridge, on the south bank of the Boyne, the place where Muirchertach of the Uí Néill was burned to death, Cormac was received by Spelán the Hospitaller, at his *ráith* or dwelling. There, a bone from a salmon accidentally got into bread which Cormac ate. The bone stuck in his chest and he died.

Another strand in the story makes Maelchenn/ Máelchend, described in AClon as 'the Priest of the Golden Calfe', responsible for the fish-bone death in Spelán's homestead. Cormac mac Airt had apparently become contemptuous of the religious outlook of Ireland because he now believed in one god. He *could* have become a Christian, but this period saw many new influences on religious thought and Christianity was only one of many beliefs in the 'growing drift into monotheism'.[4] Instead, it seems that Cormac had become a devotee of Mithras. Mithraism was one of the first mystery cults from the east to gain a hold in Britain. It had its origins in Persia with *Zoroaster*, Zarathustra, in the sixth century BC. It taught that *Ormazd*, lord of goodness, creator of humankind, and god of light, is continuously at war with *Ahriman*, the god of darkness. The religion emerged in the west as Mithraism, with its god Mithras. As the god of light, his cult easily absorbed similar beliefs centred on the sun like that of *Sol Invictus*, the Unconquerable Sun, to be then equated with the Greek god of the sun, Helios, who had already become identified with Apollo. Mithras was born from a rock that fell out of the solid vault of the skies. A standing image of the rock, *petra genetrix*, was worshipped in the cult's temples. Mithras then slew the sacred or mystic bull, cutting its throat to reanimate creation with its blood.[5]

Admittedly there is much here that is crude, but the pagan intelligentsia drawn to the faith made it respectable and gave it a philosophical basis that included much previous thinking. A 'modern' aspect of the faith was the belief that an intimate relationship could be

4_ Lane Fox, 1988, p. 575.

5_ Turcan, 1996, pp. 195–247.

established between believers and their god. Mithras, the creator god, demanded high standards of conduct, probity, and courage, and in return offered an afterlife.[6] Entrants into the religion, which was confined to men, had to pass through seven grades of initiation involving both physical and psychological tests. The cult's secrets were jealously guarded to the point where it adopted what has been called 'masonic secrecy'.[7] Particularly popular among army commanders and officers, the strongest adherents of Mithraism, and those heading the business community, its appeal was clearly to the governing class. London had its temple or *mithraeum* at Walbrook, which has been dated to around 240.[8]

The worship of Mithras in these temples was vividly impressive, and made more so by the mysteriousness of the *mithraea* themselves, the coloured robes of the participants, the masks worn by those playing key rôles, and the flickering light of torches. We find evidence of *mithraea* on the Wall, at Castlesteads, Carlisle, Newcastle, and Wallsend, beyond in High Rochester, and to the south in York, Chester, and Caerleon, and in the smaller Welsh forts like *Segontium*. In Chester and *Segontium*, the *mithraea* lay outside the fortress walls. Cormac mac Airt would almost certainly have encountered Mithraism in Britain. There must have been something immediately attractive in a religion that had as its fount the slaying of a mystic bull. It is an intriguing thought that an Irish king might have become a devotee of Mithras in such a place as Chester: that an 'illustrious father' of the brotherhood initiated him, and by the ceremonial *iunctio dextrarum*, the handclasp, received him as an 'initiate of cattle rustling'.[9] If so, then Cormac returned to Ireland, not just as an initiate, but with the Mithraic grade of Father, bearing the twin symbols of his office, the libation or communion cup and the wand of command, later considered Ireland's greatest treasures. More than anything else, these would have been the supreme signs of the Irish king's commitment, not just to a personal belief system, but to all the best values espoused by Roman society.[10]

6_ Richmond, 1963, p. 209.

7_ Salway, 1984, p. 711.

8_ Ibid., p. 712.

9_ Forbes, 1970, p. 155, note 93.

10_ Turcan, 1996, p. 237.

On his return, he would have had to face devotees of Ireland's traditional gods, who found themselves betrayed by their king's apostasy. When Cormac died in 267, half-blind, incapacitated, choking on a salmon bone, it was possibly not surprising that many said it was the work of the druid Máelchend, for 'Cormac had turned against the Druids on account of his adoration of God in preference to them.'[11] In the *Birth Tale of Cormac Mac Art*, Cormac instructs his followers that he is not to be buried in *Brug na Bóinne*, Newgrange, 'because it was not one and the same god that he and they [who] were sepulchred therein adored; but he prescribed his burial in Rosnaree, with his face set eastwards to the rising of the sun'.[12] They ignored him.

MUIRCHERTACH AND HIS SUCCESSORS: FRIENDS AND ALLIES OF THE BRITISH PEOPLE

So it seems, Muirchertach *Mac Erca*, following the same policy of alliance with the British state Cormac had pursued – albeit now with only one part of it, namely Gwynedd – was murdered in the same place, at *Cleitech* above the Boyne, and in an event 267 years after Cormac's 267 death, if, that is, Cormac did die in 267. If we can believe the storyteller's claim that his mistress was herself of the Laigin of Meath, then this murder probably did have a political dimension. Indeed, one wonders whether the annalists and storytellers were far more aware of what now we are only stumbling towards. That is, were they acutely conscious of this British dimension that somehow has been suppressed? And was this erasure effected after the Norman invasion seemed to be repeating the humiliation of domination by another power? By 534, Muirchertach and the Uí Néill would have been wedded to a policy that served their own interests rather than anyone else's, but it was still a policy having origins deep in the Roman past. It was also a policy that coincided with Gwynedd's domestic and foreign policy under Cadwallon and

11_ AFM, O'Donovan, 1851, Vol. I, p. 117: the death notice of Cormac under 266.

12_ *The Birth of Cormac Mac Art*, O'Grady, 1892, Vol. 2, p. 289: Ó Cathasaigh, 1977, pp. 71–2.

then Maelgwn: one that owed its origins to that same past.

Muirchertach's successor as over-king of the Uí Néill was Tuathal *Maelgarb*, Tuathal Bony Scalp, who was really something of an intruder. He was the grandson of Cairpre son of Niall. This line, the Cenél Cairpri, had lordship over territory that lay to the southwest of the northern Uí Néill, and northwest of the southern, in what is roughly south County Leitrim. What we are looking at are the earliest days of Uí Néill politics that would eventually lead to the alternation of the high-kingship between the northern and southern Uí Néill. Here, the Cenél Cairpri were making their bid to take on this rôle, lying as they did between the two, though possibly best considered as part the southern group. Although Tuathal succeeded, he was destined to be the only one of the Cenél Cairpri to become over-king of the Uí Néill confederation.

As we have seen, in 520 Tuathal's predecessor, the northern Uí Néill Muirchertach, had for the first time established a lordship over the Uí Néill confederation, north and south, by defeating and presumably killing the west Meath southern Uí Néill king Ardgal son of Conall Cremthainne, Conall of Cremthann, a grandson of Niall, in the battle of *Détnae* somewhere in north Meath adjoining County Cavan.[13] In order to take power, Tuathal had to brush aside the claims of Ardgal's nephew and heir, Diarmait mac Cerball, the southern Uí Néill contender for the post of over-king, which may have involved Tuathal having to battle with and defeat east Meath forces from Brega, at *Logher* in Meath.[14] Although Tuathal held the position of over-king for more than ten years, Diarmait was seemingly waiting his chance.

We have to remind ourselves that this was all family business. Ardgal, Fergus the father of Diarmait, Cormac the father of Tuathal, and Muiredach the father of Muirchertach, were all cousins and grandsons of Niall. Again, lacking information, we can imagine the same embassies, messages of congratulation, and presents

13_ AU, 519=520, repeated under 522=523: AFM, 513 and 504.

14_ AU, AI, AFM: Mac Niocaill, 1972, p.18.

making their way from Gwynedd to Ireland, but from then on we have precious little to go on, or so it might at first seem.

GROWING CLIMATIC PROBLEMS

There were now crop failures. They resulted in the Irish famines of 536 and 539.[15] As they were due to bad weather, Wales must have been similarly affected. In the 1970s, A. P. Smyth noted that up to the solar eclipse of 512, records of natural phenomena in AU are taken from foreign sources. From c.536, however, this type of entry becomes more frequent in these annals. They show a far greater variety and for the first time record local phenomena. The simple yet ominous entry 'Failure of bread' in AU for 536 begins the sequence.[16] The *Anglo-Saxon Chronicle* records an eclipse of the sun from daybreak until 9a.m. on what, appropriately enough in view of what happened, was 16 February 538, Shrove Tuesday in the Catholic church. On Wednesday, 20 June 540, it records that there was another eclipse 'and stars were visible for nearly half an hour after nine o'clock in the morning'.[17]

However, something altogether more alarming was happening than our impoverished and clearly incomplete record hints. Foreign sources imply a build-up from 530.

On 9th April, large shooting stars followed one another northwestward; trails which never ceased appearing, numbered in thousands, [were] seen from China.[18]

Always regarded as an omen, in 531 a great meteor shower was seen in Europe, and on 28 August 532 in China and Korea a similar event was recorded when stars were seen to fall like rain.[19] The *Chronicle of Theophanes the Confessor*, monk and abbot in the eastern empire, c.758–817, has a note of what seems to be the same event.[20] Part of the codex or manuscript volume of Valentinus, giving details and lists concerning the

15_ AU 535=536, 538=539; AI 537, which has *Perditio panis* and then the name *Coluimb*, showing that the annalist has omitted something from his text – Mac Airt, 1977, p. 69 and note i.

16_ Smyth, 1972, pp. 10–11.

17_ ASC, 538, 540, Whitelock et al., 1961, p. 12.

18_ Hetherington, 1996, quoting Zhuang Tian-shan, *Chinese Astronomy*, 1, 1977, pp. 197–220.

19_ Ibid.

20_ Ibid.

empire up to 354, contains an additional part, known as the *Fasti Vindobonenses*, the Vienna Annals, *c.*576, covering the period 390–573/5. Here there is a note of an eclipse of the sun from the third to the fourth hour on 29 April 534, almost exactly six months before Muirchertach was murdered.[21]

THE YEAR-LONG ECLIPSE, 536/7

It was in 536 that mere signs and portents became a terrifying fact of life that could no longer be ignored.

There was a grave portent that year [536, apparently from 1 September]. Indeed for the entire year the sun sent forth his rays without his usual brilliance, like the moon ... From this it happened that neither war not famine nor any manner of deadly evil ceased to beleaguer mankind. That was the tenth year of Justinian's reign [527–65].[22]

That was recorded by Procopius, one of the greatest of the late Greek historians, who lived through the first half of the sixth century, the period with which we are dealing. From the Middle East, details of this event spell out how awful things became:

the sun suffered an eclipse, which lasted a whole year and two months, so that very little of his light was seen; men said that something had clung to the sun, from which it would never be able to disentangle itself.[23]

John Lydus, John the Lydian, an eastern administrator, writing on antiquarian matters in his retirement in the mid-sixth century, also recorded this 'eclipse'. It comes in his *De Ostentis*, On Signs, an important work in the history of astrology, which was then still treated as a science.

21_ Newton, 1972, p. 455.

22_ Procopius, *De Bello Vandalico*, The Vandalic War, Book II, Ch. 14, Newton, 1972, p. 458; Baillie, 2000, p. 85.

23_ Gregory Bar Hebraeus Abu al-Faraj, 1226–86: Supplement to his *Historia Compendiosa Dynastiarum*.

The sun became dim ... for nearly the whole year ... so that the fruits were killed at an unseasonable time.[24]

Another contemporary, Flavius Magnus Aurelius Cassiodorus Senator, c.485–558, was *magister officiorum* under the Gothic king of Italy, Theodoric, his successor Athalric, and then Witigis. He was then promoted praetorian prefect for Italy, the leading administrative post of the Ostrogoth government, and in 537 or 538 he left for Constantinople. His *Variae Epistolae* of 537 could hardly be more contemporary with the events described.

The sun ... seems to have lost its wonted light, and appears of a bluish colour. We marvel to see no shadows of our bodies at noon, to feel the mighty vigour of the sun's heat wasted into feebleness, and the phenomena which accompany an eclipse prolonged through almost a whole year. We have had ... a summer without heat ... the crops have been chilled by north winds ... the rain is denied ...[25]

Michael the Syrian, c.1126–99, Orthodox patriarch of Antioch and the East, included these reports when he compiled his *Chronicle* written in Syriac or Aramaic, which is possibly the largest surviving medieval chronicle. He places this under 536.

The sun became dark and its darkness lasted for eighteen months. Each day it shone for about four hours, and still this light was only a feeble shadow. Everyone declared that the sun would never recover its full light. The fruits did not ripen and the wine tasted like sour grapes.[26]

In the 1980s, it was thought that all this was the result of a major volcanic event in Greenland causing great clouds of debris to obscure the sun. However, the evidence of dendrochronology, the study of tree-rings, which record the events during the life of trees, shows that there was something even more catastrophic in

[24]_ Baillie, 2000, p. 85.

[25]_ Ibid., pp. 85–6.

[26]_ Ibid., p. 85.

238

process, caused, so it is now argued, by cometary bombardment reaching its climax, as recorded in Ireland, in 540/1. Professor Mike Baillie of Belfast has challenged some conventional interpretations. He contends that the greatest earthquake in Byzantine history, that in *Antioch*, Antakya, Turkey, then in Syria and the town associated with the missionary Paul, which is conventionally dated to 526 occurred instead in 536. There were following quakes in *Soloi Pompeiopolis*, now in Turkey, 538/9, and then, another in *Antioch* in 539/40.[27]

Even more interesting for what happened in Ireland and Wales in these last eleven years of Maelgwn's reign, assuming that he died in 547, is Professor Baillie's disentangling of statements in the Syriac *Chronicle of Zachariah of Mitylene*, or rather in the pseudo-Zachariah additions. Speaking of events allegedly in 556, this part of the compilation almost certainly refers to people who had lived through the period 536–45.

In addition to all the evil and fearful things described above and recorded below [as Professor Baillie notes, *mostly lost!*], the earthquakes and famines and wars in divers places ... there has also been fulfilled against this last generation [including those living through the period 536–45] the curse of Moses in Deuteronomy when he admonished the people who had just come out of Egypt ...[28]

THE BIBLICAL EXPLANATION

Many in the sixth century came to believe that the curse put into the mouth of Moses in the *Book of Deuteronomy* gave God's reason for what the people of western Europe were experiencing. Today, however, it is becoming evident that what was happening in these years 536–41 had happened many centuries before, so that the biblical description may contain a memory of such events. A short extract could not possibly give the full impact of this terrible curse.

27_ Ibid., pp. 232–4.

28_ Ibid., p. 235.

But it shall come to pass, if thou wilt not hearken unto
the voice of the Lord thy God, to observe to do all
his commandments and his statutes which I command
thee this day; that all these curses shall come upon
thee, and overtake thee.
Cursed shalt thou be in the city, and cursed shalt thou
be in the field.
Cursed shall be thy basket and thy store.
Cursed shall be the fruit of thy body, and the fruit of
thy land, the increase of thy kine, and the flocks of thy
sheep.
Cursed shalt thou be when thou comest in, and cursed
shalt thou be when thou goest out.
The Lord shall send upon thee cursing, vexation, and
rebuke, in all that thou settest thine hand unto for to
do, until thou be destroyed, and until thou perish quickly;
because of the wickedness of thy doings, whereby thou
hast forsaken me.
The Lord shall make the pestilence cleave unto thee,
until he have consumed thee from off the land, whither
thou goest to possess it.
The Lord shall smite thee with a consumption, and with
a fever, and with an inflammation, and with an extreme
burning, and with the sword, and with blasting, and with
mildew; and they shall pursue thee until thou perish.
And thy heaven that is over thy head shall be brass, and
the earth that is under thee shall be iron.
The Lord shall make the rain of thy land powder and
dust: from heaven shall it come down upon thee, until
thou be destroyed ...
And thy carcase shall be meat unto all fowls of the air,
and unto the beasts of the earth, and no man shall fray
[scare] them away.
The Lord will smite thee with the botch of Egypt, and
with the scab, and with the itch, whereof thou canst not
be healed.
The Lord shall smite thee with madness, and blindness,
and astonishment of heart ...
   [And later generations and those who come from a
far land will see] that the whole land thereof is brimstone,

240

and salt, and burning, that it is not sown, nor beareth, nor any grass groweth herein. Like the overthrow of Sodom and Gomorrah, Admah, and Zeboim, which the Lord overthrew in his anger, and in his wrath:

Even all nations shall say, Wherefore hath the Lord done thus unto this land? What meaneth the heat of his great anger?

Then men shall say, Because they have forsaken the covenant of the Lord God of their fathers, which he made with them when he brought them forth out of the land of Egypt ...[29]

Professor Dorothea Weltecke of the University of Konstanz in Germany, who has recently worked on Michael the Syrian's *Chronicle*, reminds us not only how earthquakes, droughts, and famines shaped people's lives, but also how these natural events were regarded as signs leaving little doubt about how they were to be interpreted. Through them, God Himself was trying to reason with sinful humankind. Neither is the *Old Testament* alone in giving such warnings. One of the fundamental tenets of Christianity was the belief that Jesus would return in glory to judge the world and that this Second Coming would be accompanied by the most awful signs. The biblical texts are legion so *Matthew* must suffice. Here, Jesus had prophesied that the temple would be thrown down. The disciples asked him when this would be and 'what shall be the sign of thy coming, and of the end of the world?'

And Jesus answered ... For as the lightning cometh out of the east, and shineth even unto the west; so shall also the coming of the Son of man be. For wheresoever the carcase is, there will the eagles be gathered together.

Immediately after the tribulation of those days shall the sun be darkened, and the moon shall not give her light, and the stars shall fall from heaven, and the powers of the heavens shall be shaken:

And then shall appear the sign of the Son of man in heaven: and then shall the tribes of the earth mourn, and

29_ *Deuteronomy* 28:15–24 and 26–8, and 29:23–5.

241

they shall see the Son of man coming in the clouds of heaven with power and great glory ... *when ye shall see all these things, know that it is near, even at the doors ... Watch therefore: for ye know not what hour the Lord doth come.*[30]

Suddenly a whole era, however short lived, begins to make sense: events fall into place. From the first indications in the annals that something was going wrong, sparse as the record is, up to the major events recorded above and verified by the tree-ring record, churchmen in Wales and Ireland would have been reading the signs. All the indications given by Jesus himself were there. The preaching, ever more urgent, to our ears even hysterical, panic ridden, warned of the judgement to come. Wasn't it this that led to the great surge in monastic foundations both in Wales and in Ireland? Is this why Daniel was regarded as such a key figure in the rush to establish and expand monasteries in Powys and Gwynedd? Wickerwork and wooden posts would suffice, not because there wasn't stone, not because there weren't the skilled masons any longer or the slave labour in the quarries, but because there simply wasn't the time to build in stone, time to waste on such matters, because the Judge was almost at the gate.

DANIEL PREPARES FOR THE END

Deiniol, Daniel, was almost certainly the founder of Bangor on Dee in Powys. His flimsy *Life* is late – seventeenth century – and the genealogies for him mere nonsense, trying as they do to link him with a heroic, British, post-Roman past in northern Britain. Some stories associate him with Pembroke and St David, from where his *Vita* brings him to Bangor. On dating grounds, an education in Cadog's monastery at Llancarfan is not so unlikely and throws up interesting possibilities.

Brychan, king of the small, inland, south Wales kingdom of Garth Matrun on the upper reaches of the

[30]_ *Matthew 24:4–42,* the italics mine.

242

Usk, was quite some figure. His descent could probably be traced back to the earliest appointments in Britain of people drawn from local populations who were given particular responsibilities for the defence and upkeep of the road system as it radiated out from Brecon Gaer. But it was because of his own partnerships, his fecundity, and the systematic way he married his very many children into the other leading houses of Wales, that he is rightly regarded as the founder of his dynasty which continued into the first years of the tenth century.

We have already encountered three formidable daughters of this Brychan. Tudglid married Maelgwn on the death of her first husband, Cyngen of Powys, unless of course she had been divorced. Marchell was married to Gwrin of Meirionydd, whose son Maelgwn murdered, and Cerddych may have been married to Cynlas of Rhos before he jettisoned her and she entered religion. Another daughter, Gwladus, the modern Gladys, was married to Gwynllyw, king of Glywysing, the kingdom in the hinterland behind the Roman fort of *Tamium*, Cardiff, and these were the parents of Cadfael, better known as Cadog. This boy, brought up by an Irish hermit named Meuthi, went on to be the founder of a monastery in Nant Carfan, Llancarfan, which became one of the great teaching establishments in Wales, like Illtud's Llantwit Major. It had offshoots in the south rivalling the foundations of Padarn in mid-Wales and Garmon in north Wales.

Daniel, educated in Cadog's Llancarfan, was the ideal churchman to establish relations with Maelgwn *Gwynedd*. Maelgwn was uncle to Cadog through his first marriage to Tudglid, and was his cousin through his current marriage to Tudglid's daughter Sanan. His patronage, therefore, could be expected, and as we have seen, Maelgwn might have been something of an easy touch given his desire to put things right with a church he knew he had offended. However, Cadog was not only cousin to Maelgwn. Through his aunt Tudglid, sister of his mother Gladys, he was cousin to Brochwel *Ysgythrog*, Brochwel of the Tusks or Long-in-the-Tooth, ruling

Powys from the 490s till *c*.550. It is only an assumption that Bangor in Powys on the river Dee was an offshoot of the Bangor on the Menai Straits. If anything, it was the other way round, but this is to anticipate. Daniel's *Vita* says he succeeded at Bangor on Menai, not that he was its founder.[31]

It would seem that Daniel was first granted land in Powys, where, at his new foundation at Bangor on Dee, he gave orders for the construction of an enclosure of wattles surmounting a bank and fronted by a ditch. He was here imitating the layout and construction of Roman marching camps. The Bangor site, as the crow flies, is approximately fifteen miles upstream from Chester, although anyone sailing or being rowed from there would find the journey very much longer as the river meanders in countless tight curves which over the centuries have created many oxbow lakes. The river would have frequently changed course, but today the site possibly chosen by Daniel indicates that one of the bigger bends in the river was being used. Ditches would have completed nature's defensive work as well as acting as drains, because Bangor lay on the edge of the river's flat flood plain.

Its name Bangor, here Bangor on Dee, was originally thought to come from *côr*, a circle or congregation, in modern Welsh still a choir, or *cordd*, an obsolete word meaning a family, with *ban*, lofty, high, superior, or supreme, which as a noun means a peak.[32] But *bangor* also means a wattle enclosure or fence.[33] We still have far too restricted a view of what these sites may have been like. Bangor's enclosure would have included a vastly larger area than that taken up by the modern church and village. It probably would have extended east on higher ground to Worthenbury, and south to a point where it probably abutted the great bastion of Powys known in the thirteenth century as Overton Madog.[34] This Powys capital, consisting of stronghold, settlement, and church, covered an area two and a quarter miles northwest to southeast which includes today's Overton and Little Overton. Like the newly-formed Bangor, it occupied a

31_ Lloyd, 1912, Vol. I, p. 130, note 22, who says the first claim that Maelgwn, and possibly by implication Daniel, founded Bangor is in the *History of the Kings of Britain* by John Ross, dated 1716.

32_ See, for example, Giles, 1841, pp. xxiv–vi, note.

33_ Lloyd, 1912, Vol. I, pp. 192–3, note to Ch. VI.

34_ In 1160, Powys split between northern Powys, *Powys Fadog*, and southern Powys, *Powys Wenwynwyn*. Overton Madog is particularly associated with Madog ap Gruffudd of northern Powys ruling 1197–1236, even though he operated under Gwynedd's lordship.

crook of the Dee which it overlooked from impressive cliffs. The monastic enclosure now appearing next to it was hardly smaller in area. Church and state operating in this manner ensured that the monastic enclosure of Bangor on Dee became a great centre of monasticism and learning. Today, the church of Worthenbury, once probably within the enclosure, is still dedicated to Daniel. To the west across the Dee lies Marchwiel, its church also dedicated to the monastic founder. The name possibly lends weight to the idea that this was the place where wickerwork and monasticism met. *March* is horse, strictly stallion, and *gwiail* is wicker. The name could mean [the place of the] big withes, the word *march* serving here as 'big', as *cow* is used in *cow-parsley*. Alternatively, it could have meant [the place of the] withe or wicker horses.[35]

We also need to remind ourselves just how impressive enclosures and buildings made of posts and wickerwork could be. In Ireland in 1171, King Henry II had a palace or banqueting hall erected outside Dublin to entertain Irish chiefs at his Christmas feast. It was made of posts and wattle, with wickerwork of peeled osiers 'in the Irish fashion'. Here, 'they greatly admired the sumptuous and plentiful fare of the English table and the most elegant service by the royal domestics' in this 'great hall'.[36] When it came to monastic enclosures, wattle would have been but poor protection against anyone bent on attacking the place. Ditches, banks, and palisades were more the necessary adjuncts of such high-status sites, clearly marking territory and, in this case, delineating consecrated ground from that outside. They were also useful for deterring undesirables, stopping cattle from roaming, and for keeping other animals out.

In the context of the appalling climatic events at this time, the gloom and doom of what were coming to be interpreted as signs of the impending Second Coming, what Daniel did on the Dee, and afterwards possibly on the Menai, takes on a new, frightening significance. These places were, indeed, built in imitation of Roman marching camps, but they shared with them one

35_ I am grateful to Howard Lockley for pointing out these derivations.

36_ Giraldus Cambrensis, *Expugnatio Hibernica, The Conquest of Ireland*, Ch. 33, Scott and Martin, 1978, p. 97.

particular feature. None of them was intended to be permanent. Neither the Roman army nor Christ's army were stopping. They were camps *en route* to a clearly-defined destination. Perhaps Daniel remodelled the Arfon church along these lines, making it his new Bangor on the Menai. When the initial panic or fervour had subsided, later monasteries were sometimes known as Bangor, a good example being the one in northern Ireland on Belfast Lough, but by then the original meaning was perhaps being conveniently forgotten.

MONASTERIES: MAKING READY AND WAITING

Now the rush was on to establish monasteries, the assured gateways to heaven. In Ireland, although there are problems over identification, it seems that someone named Mac Creiche founded a monastery at *Inis-cealtra*, *Inishcaltra*, the island of the burial ground, now Holy Island in the Shannon's Lough Derg, surrendering it then to Colum mac Crimthainn. Said to be of the royal line of a Leinster house, Colum was buried at *Tír-dá-glas*, Terryglass, County Tipperary, and as a result is known as being of *Tír-dá-glas*. From here, Colum organized the founding of *Clúain-Ednech*, Clonenagh in Leinster's Leix.

At the head of Strangford Lough near Newtownards, Finnian moccu Fiatach founded the monastery of Movilla, the name coming from its Irish name *Magh-Bile*, the plain of the old or sacred tree. Colum *Cille*, Columba, was to study here under its founder. An even more famous school was to emerge at the new monastery of Clonard on the upper Boyne founded probably about this time by another Finnian, the more famous Finnian moccu Telduib. Its name *Clúain-Iráird* means no more than Erard's meadow. It became one of the most important monasteries of the Uí Néill, and the reputation of its school led to Finnian being viewed as the teacher of almost all the key religious figures in Ireland.

Thereafter the saints of Ireland came to Findian from every part to learn wisdom by him, so that there were three thousand saints along with him; and of them as the learned know, he chose the twelve high bishops of Ireland. And the learned and the writings declare that no one of those three thousand went from him without a crozier [the pastoral staff of a bishop or abbot], or a gospel [possibly indicating a monastic and monastic-school founder] or some well-known sign; and round those reliquaries they built their churches and monasteries afterwards.[37]

But this was years on. Initially, if the thesis being advanced here is correct, study and everything connected with the monastic life would have been concerned with the Last Things. This gives a certain emphasis to the following extract from Finnian's Irish *Life*, which though later than the Latin texts appears to reflect the original more fully and accurately.

And even as the angel promised to Paul that no one who should go into the clay of Rome should after Doom become an inhabitant of hell, even so the angel promised to Findian that no one over whom the mould of Ard Relic [the burial ground at Clonard] should go would be an inhabitant of hell after the Judgement.[38]

One story has Ciarán, the famous founder of the later monastery of *Clúain-moccu-Nóis*, Clonmacnois, coming to Finnian of Clonard to study. He brought with him a dun cow and a calf, which later followed him to his new foundation: 'Now the Dun's hide is in Clonmacnois and what soul soever separates from its body on that hide inhabits eternal life.'[39]

Was this in 536 or 539? The question might seem absurd, were it not for the annalistic references in these years to bread famines in Ireland. In the early, primitive Irish *Life of Ciarán*, there is a reference to 'a scarcity of corn and sustenance for that school [at Clonard] so that it was necessary for a good many of them in turn to

37_ The Irish *Life of Finnian of Clonard*, Stokes, 1890, p. 226.

38_ Ibid., p. 229. See also Kenney, 1968, pp. 374–6.

39_ The Irish *Life of Finnian of Clonmacnois*, Stokes, 1890, p. 268.

protect the sack of corn which was carried thence to the mill'. Ciarán prays for a sack of oats to become a sack of wheat. On this same occasion, he received a present, in effect a dowry from the family of a girl who had become fixated on this good-looking young monk but who had been fended off and agreed to become a nun instead. The dowry was 'three loaves of wheat with their proportion of bacon and of flesh and a vessel full of ale'. Embarrassed, Ciarán milled the lot to produce 'wheaten meal'. For healing someone, he was also granted the mill and all its land. He returned to the monastery, now with four sacks of wheat, and the community was fed, just as 'the mystical manna was found by the children of Israel' who were starving in the wilderness. He had fended off the unwelcome overtures by the miller's daughter with the admonition: 'Is it not this whereof thou shouldst take heed – the perishableness of the world, and Doomsday, and the pains of hell, in order to avoid them, and the rewards of heaven, in order to obtain them?'[40]

The emphasis on death and resurrection in the stories of these Irish clerics gave a pattern that was used in the description of any cleric's life in later periods. They became mere stock descriptions used time and time again by the storytellers. But the lives of these early 'saints', some of which are themselves of an early date, with their emphasis on famines and droughts, indicate a very different character. They speak of an agony experienced during a period of natural disasters in which the general perception was that the end of time and the Day of Judgement was fast approaching.

In the west of Ireland, Senán son of Gergenn founded a monastery on *Inis Cathaig*, Scattery Island, in the Shannon estuary, just off Kilrush. According to his Irish *Life*, Raphael the Archangel appeared to Senán, telling him he would show him where he would die. 'Behold the island there. Thy resurrection shall be therein, and the resurrection of a great host of saints along with thee. In the west of the world there is no more sacred island.' Having been set down in the place and expelled a monster, Senán and the angels consecrated the island,

40_ Ibid., pp. 268 and 269–70.

and Senán was given the promise we have heard before. 'God hath granted to thee,' saith the angel, 'that he over whom the mould of this island shall go, shall not be after judgement an inhabitant of hell.'[41] The *Life* talks of a year of great drought in which the community complained to Senán.[42] When Ciarán, the future abbot of Clonmacnois, and Brendan of the later Clonfert visited to ask Senán to be their spiritual director, their soul-friend, because he was an abbot and a bishop and they were just priests, 'there was no food to be seen in the convent when they arrived. So they were for the space of three days without food, both guests and community, and no food came from anyone.'[43]

THE CATASTROPHE OF 540-1

We are now near the years 540–1. For these dates, incontrovertible evidence from the analysis of tree rings in Ireland shows that something catastrophic did occur. It is not necessary to imagine a random asteroid or comet actually hitting the sea in the region of Ireland and Wales in 540. There is what is called the Taurid meteor stream, originating from a cosmic event thousands of years ago and blamed as the primary source of dust in the inner solar system. It has been calculated that the Earth passes through the core of this meteor stream every 2,500 years. We are passing through its outer edges at the moment. The last time we passed through its core was in the period 400–600 and before that in 2,200–2000BC. In the dust are asteroids, virtually small planets revolving round the sun mainly between the orbits of Mars and Jupiter, and meteors or comets, often huge, dirty snowballs of ice and rock which burn up as they enter Earth's atmosphere leaving a trail of light. When asteroids enter our inner solar system, the results can be catastrophic. Had one actually hit Earth, humankind itself would have been at risk of annihilation. Instead, the possibility seems to be that the events of 536–41 and particularly 540–1, were the result of the explosion of one or more of these bodies

41_ The Irish *Life of Senán*, Stokes, 1890, pp. 213–14: Kenney, 1968, p. 364.

42_ Ibid., p. 218.

43_ Ibid., p. 217.

in the upper atmosphere causing a dust veil that cut the power of the sun. As a result, winters were long with intense frosts and the summers miserable. Harvests were destroyed and famine stalked the land. Complicating matters for those grappling with a detailed understanding of what happened, it would seem that there was also an increase of volcanic activity.

PADARN'S ALARM

Those clerics and monks concentrating on the expected end were not to be disappointed. These were signs from God that the end *was* coming and *was* very near: further encouragement, therefore, to seek the salvation now promised. In Wales, even Padarn, who looks to have been on the conservative side in church politics, seems to have been drawn into this fervour concerning the Last Things. His *Vitae* are of little value, mixing him up with two other priests and bishops of the same name in France. Because of this, Padarn supposedly had his origins in Brittany, although this also may reflect his adherence to a growing Roman party in the British church. The ever-suspect Iolo manuscripts say he was instructed by Illtud, abbot of Llantwit Major. At some point arriving on the coast of Cardigan Bay near the later Aberystwyth, he founded his monastic settlement, which his biographer calls *Mauritana*, or *ecclesia maritima*. This is Llanbadarn Fawr. Of course, Padarn appears in a story involving Maelgwn who was said to be on his way to south Wales with an army, intent on its subjugation. The king tries to trick the cleric, but is found out and blinded until Padarn forgives him and a land grant follows. Later, Padarn sailed to Ireland, but apart from intervening between the armies of two kings bringing about peace, we are not told what he did there or whom he visited. If there *is* any truth in this, we might guess at a fact-finding mission to see how the Irish church was reacting to talk of the world coming to an end. If so we might expect contact to be made with one or other of

250

the great monastic founders there, Finnian of Clonard, Senán on Scattery Island in the Shannon, or less likely, with the other Finnian in the north at Movilla. Having returned, Padarn established other houses as offshoots of Llanbadarn Fawr, establishing thereby a *paruchia*, or family of churches, linked to the mother church. With those of Daniel and Garmon in the north, and Cadoc in the south, this formed one of the main foundation groupings in Wales. Llanbadarn Fawr became a famous monastic centre, its school a centre of scholarship.

THE BEGINNING OF THE END: FLEAS

We now have a credible account of one particular result of these catastrophic events caused by a dust veil spreading across the globe. It concerns insects and the plague that began in east Africa. This pestilence was carried by fleas living on the gerbil. The dust-laden atmosphere, so the theory goes, killed off the gerbil's predators with the result that this burrowing rodent moved out from its original homelands and in the process gave the fleas to mice, the rat-like *arvicanthus*, and then to the rodent *rattus*. The rats then carried their deadly cargo along the seaways of the Middle East.

It started from the Egyptians who dwell in Pelusium [an important town in Lower Egypt on the east side of the easternmost branch of the Nile Delta, two miles from the sea]. Then it divided and moved in one direction towards Alexandria and the rest of Egypt, and in the other direction it came to Palestine on the borders of Egypt; and from there it spread over the whole world, always moving forward ... [Arriving from Africa] this disease always took its start from the coast, and from there went up to the interior ... And it fell also upon the land of the Persians and visited all the other barbarians besides.[44]

44_ Procopius, *History of the* [Persian] *Wars*, Book 2, Chs. XX–XXIV, Dewing, 1914–28, Vol. I, 1914, pp. 451–73.

CONSTANTINOPLE, 542

In the middle of spring 542, the plague arrived in Constantinople like yet another bolt from the blue. The result was devastating. Some of those who were infected from the very first experienced delirium, but most were unaware of its onset. There was no change of colour, no heat, no inflammation, only 'a fever of … a languid sort'. It was in the next few days that a bubonic swelling emerged, in the glandular parts, usually the groin, hence its description as being below the abdomen, but it could be in the armpit. Sometimes it appeared beside the ears. Then people slipped either into a coma or into violent delirium, this last result being worse because often they could not be restrained. Many rushed into the sea. Suicide, intentional or not, was common. Many starved to death from lack of anyone to care for them. For those who avoided coma or delirium, the buboes became so infected that, in intense pain, death soon followed. Those who had black pustules or who vomited blood seemed to die almost immediately. Nothing worked as a prophylactic. It took whoever it wanted. Some who survived had apparently had strokes and could not talk properly. Even the emperor Justinian, 527–65, in 542 sixty years old, looked as though he might succumb, falling ill and, reportedly, having a swelling in the groin.

And when it came about that all the tombs which had existed previously were filled with the dead, then they dug up all the places about the city one after the other, laid the dead there, each one as he could, and departed; but later on those who were making these trenches, no longer able to keep up with the number of the dying, mounted the fortifications in Sycae [the suburb of Galata outside the main city on the opposite side of the natural-harbour inlet known as the Golden Horn] and tearing off the roofs threw the bodies there in complete disorder; and they piled them up just as each one happened to fall, and filled practically all the towers with corpses, and then covered them again with their roofs.

As a result of this an evil stench pervaded the city and distressed the inhabitants still more and especially when the wind blew fresh from that quarter ...
all the customary rites of burial were overlooked ... it was sufficient if one carried on his shoulders the body of one of the dead to the parts of the city which bordered on the sea and flung him down; and there the corpses would be thrown upon skiffs in a heap, to be conveyed wherever it might chance ...

And work of every description ceased, and all the trades were abandoned by the artisans, and all other work as well ... Indeed in a city which was simply abounding in all good things starvation almost absolute was running riot.[45]

Just as in Wales and Ireland, many who had lapsed into casual religious observance turned back to their faith with zeal, who 'being thoroughly terrified by the things which were happening, and supposing they would die immediately, did, as was natural, learn respectability for a season by sheer necessity'. Perhaps the most startling thing to the modern mind is to realize that, living and dying in this hell, the Christian church taught and people believed that these events were, to quote Procopius, following 'the wish of Him who brought the disease into the world'.[46]

As it raged, those observing it knew it was spreading. This information would have reached western Europe, including Maelgwn's Gwynedd and Tuathal's Meath.

During these times there was a pestilence, by which the whole human race came near to being annihilated ... it did not come in a part of the world nor upon certain men, nor did it confine itself to any season of the year ... but it embraced the entire world, and blighted the lives of all men ...[47]

[45] Procopius, *History of the* [Persian] *Wars*, Book 2, Ch. XXII, Dewing, 1914–28, Vol. I, 1914, pp. 467–7.

[46] Ibid., p. 459.

[47] Ibid., p. 451.

We have no direct indication as to how events, not just those of 542, but the whole accelerating set of climactic happenings since 536 with their terrible results, affected rulers like Maelgwn *Gwynedd*. As day succeeded day, it must have been possible to think that the end of the world and the Day of Judgement indicated by these dreadful occurrences might still be some way off. The religious always talked like this, but the world seemed to go on. News of continental political developments may have had a greater effect.

One of the greatest generals the Roman empire had produced, Flavius Belisarius, was now making an extraordinary impact. Having freed the eastern empire from the Persian threat in 531, in 534 he restored the north African provinces to the imperial rule of Justinian. Then, in 536, Belisarius led his troops on an invasion of Ostrogoth Italy, now under its king Witiges, and on 10 December he entered Rome.

From the materials which ... Procopius has collected, one may gather that Vitges abandoned Rome on the arrival of Belisarius in Italy, who at once marched upon the city.

The Romans readily opened their gates to him; a result mainly brought about by Silverius their bishop [pope 8 June 536–11 November 537, doing this in conjunction with the senate] ...

They accordingly surrendered their city to him without resistance: and thus Rome, after an interval of sixty years, again fell into Roman hands on the ninth day of the month [some sources say the tenth] ... called by the Latins December.[48]

The great Ostrogoth king, even emperor, Theodoric, 493–526, had previously managed to regularize his position by agreement with the east, ruling Italy, theoretically at least, as the emperor's deputy with the title of king. Now, the eastern empire was reasserting its control. But it was not to be so easy, or such a

[48]_ Evagrius Scholasticus, 536 – after 594, *A History of the Church from AD 431–594*, Book IV, Ch. XIX, [Walford] 1854, p. 402.

When ye shall see these things, know that the Son of Man is near, even at the doors.

Ostrogoth Ravenna
fell to Belisarius and a
Romans army in 540.
The palace, extreme right,
and its church.

blessing. Ravenna, western capital since the time of Honorius in 402, only became a genuine imperial centre under Theodoric, an extraordinary ruler who presided over a last flowering of Latin letters. The invasion of 536 ushered in, not only the Gothic Wars that lasted for twenty-five years and devastated Italy, but also Italy's 'Dark Ages': caused not by barbarians, but by the eastern empire. Rome was taken in 536, Ravenna fell by trickery in 540 along with Milan. The tide turning, in 541, whilst Belisarius was campaigning in Syria, the Ostrogoths managed to retake Rome and northern Italy. In 544 Belisarius was back to conquer again and his work was completed by the eunuch general Narses. Although from 568 the Lombards were to overrun Italy, Ravenna remained at the centre of what became a Byzantine or eastern imperial enclave, the Exarchate or Province of Ravenna, under a Byzantine *exarch*, overseer or protector. Just like Rome, it managed to continue as a virtually independent city-state surrounded by chaos.

NEWS FROM SOUTHERN BRITAIN

Could Maelgwn and his church advisers have seen imperial, Byzantine rule over Rome from 536 and again from 544 as some necessary precondition for the Second Coming? Events nearer home may have given further cause for thought. Gwynedd was almost certainly operating completely aloof from the south and east of Britain. Nevertheless, the government in southern Britain, representing as it did a tradition of central control dating back to imperial days, would have always represented a threat to the independence so proudly being asserted in Gwynedd. Even though Gwynedd's links were primarily with Gaul and with Ireland, it could never have completely isolated itself from affairs in lowland Britain. There, rule had passed from Vortigern to Ambrosius and lastly to that almost mythical figure Arthur, about whom we in fact know next to nothing save for a list of twelve battles and even these are now questioned. The last of these, fought sometime between 495 and 520, the battle of Mount Badon, was a victory for British forces over the Saxons, which, for a time at least, ended their constant encroachments and brought peace. These were the years of 'Arthur's peace' when we have to presume links would have been established with Owain, Cadwallon, and Cadwaladr in north Wales and after 517 with Maelgwn. But both British and Welsh rulers, if that distinction can be made, would have had their hands too full with their own affairs to be overly concerned about each other. Then, in the battle of *Camlan*, Arthur was decisively defeated and, as tradition has it, was forced to flee mortally wounded. It has even been suggested that the Isle of *Avalon* where he supposedly died was in fact Bardsey Island at the end of the Llŷn peninsula.

AC dates the battle of *Camlan* to 537, adding 'and there was a pestilence in Britain and in Ireland'. AU records the first failure of bread in Ireland in 536. In other words, AC associated the British defeat with an outbreak of what was almost certainly famine disease, the 'yellow pestilence', the *buidhe chonaill / buide conaill* in Ireland, *y fâd felen* in Wales, which, as we shall see, was to strike with far greater force in the period 547–9. The significance of *Camlan*, whenever or wherever it was fought, is only obvious with the benefit of hindsight. At the time, it could have registered as no more than yet another event in a long history of such encounters. Therefore, it may be that for Maelgwn the plague now decimating Europe after first surprising Constantinople in 542 would have caused greater concern.

THE SIXTH-CENTURY REFORMATION

It might be possible, therefore, to see the period from 542 to the year in which Maelgwn himself may have fallen in the pandemic, perhaps 547, as one in which many who had previously been hesitant about the doom being preached by increasingly hysterical clerics began seriously to consider their futures. Did Maelgwn in this gathering gloom begin to see the light? Had the austerities of the new wave of monastic founders impressed him? What did he now think of the church on which he had hitherto relied? Did even he begin to regard the Gwynedd church with its close links to Gaul and the Roman past as essentially corrupt? Gildas certainly thought so and devoted well over a third of the chapters in his book *The Loss of Britain* to the subject.

Britain hath priests, but they are unwise;
very many that minister, but many of them impudent;
clerks she hath, but certain of them are deceitful
raveners; pastors (as they are called) but rather wolves
prepared for the slaughter of souls (for they provide not
for the good of the common people, but covet rather
the gluttony of their own bellies), possessing the houses
of the church, but obtaining them for filthy lucre's sake;
instructing the laity, but showing withal most depraved
examples, vices and civil manners;
seldom sacrificing, and seldom with clean hearts,
standing at the altars;
not correcting the commonalty for their offences, while
they commit the same sins themselves;
despising the commandments of Christ, and being
careful with their whole hearts to fulfil their own lustful
desires ... detracting often, and seldom speaking truly;
hating verity as an open enemy, and favouring
falsehoods, as their most beloved brethren;
looking on the just, the poor and the impotent, with
stern countenances, as if they were detested serpents,
and reverencing the sinful rich men without any respect
of shame, as if they were heavenly angels ...
and after all these seeking rather ambitiously for
ecclesiastical dignities, than for the kingdom of heaven ...
singularly experienced in the deceitful shifts of worldly
affairs ... violently intruding themselves into the
preferments of the church, yea, rather buying the same
at a high rate ...

and ... after they have attained unto the seat of the priesthood or episcopal dignity (who neither have been installed or resident in the same) ... how can they ... be any way supposed meet ... to ascend unto any ecclesiastical degree ... without the foul offence of sacrilege ...[49]

Once again we encounter the temptation of modern writers to patronize the past. Firstly, the above passage indicates that we are now looking at a church that had survived the end of the empire in the west, to be, by this date, a complex, multi-faceted, and powerful structure, with all the attendant pitfalls that suggests. Secondly, it is clear that Gildas is talking of a church in Britain still for the most part organized along continental lines, in full communion and communication with the church in Gaul: in other words a church that was still essentially Roman. In Gaul, the church continued to be based in towns, and was increasingly being organized on a geographical basis into dioceses and archdioceses or provinces. This is seen in the 520s when measures were taken by the bishops of Tours, Angers, and Rennes, operating under Remigius or Remi, archbishop of Reims, Gaul's leading ecclesiastic who died in 532, to bring remote Brittany into the diocesan framework.[50] We have already encountered Bishop Sanctinus near the courts of Degannwy and Rhos. Bivatigirnus was another, possibly associated with Aberffraw. These seem to be Romans, members of the Letavian party, part of the older, Gaul-orientated, urban-based church that had hitherto dominated in the western empire. However, and particularly in Britain, circumstances were increasingly dictating the growth of a church based on monasteries.

Gildas was clearly writing *before* the cataclysmic events *c.*536–42 and their immediate aftermath. Had he been writing at that time we would certainly hear this reflected in what he wrote, and one suspects his attacks would have been even more urgent and extreme. Perhaps a useful construct, which may help us understand the stance Gildas was taking, is to be found in a modern

[49]_ Gildas, *De Excidio Britanniae*, Ch. 66, Giles, 1841, pp. 59–61.

[50]_ Miller, *Saints*, 1979, pp. 116–19: Kenney, 1968, pp. 183–4.

piece of research by Lacey Baldwin Smith which, at the time of its appearance, was a groundbreaking study. It dealt with bishops in the sixteenth-century Church of England during the Reformation.[51] What is extraordinary is that the accusations made by the sixteenth-century reformers are precisely those that were made by Gildas against his church. This is Hugh Latimer, martyred in Oxford under Queen Mary:

But now for the fault of unpreaching prelates, methink I could guess what might be said for excusing them. They are so troubled with lordly living, they be so placed in palaces, couched in courts, ruffling in their rents, dancing in their dominions, burdened with ambassages, pampering in their paunches, like a monk that maketh his jubilee; munching in their mangers, and moiling in their gay manors and mansions, and so troubled with loitering in their lordships that they cannot attend it. They are otherwise occupied, some in the King's matters, some are ambassadors, some are of the privy council, some furnish the court, some are lords of the parliament, some are presidents and controllers of mints.[52]

These, Latimer considered, were not the occupations of bishops, and Gildas would have agreed. He was saying exactly the same.

Many of these sixteenth-century bishops went to Cambridge University, which was then the centre of the 'new learning' of the Renaissance. Studies were long and hard and often split into theology on the one side, and law, both civil and canon or church law, on the other. When there was time for relaxation, many of these students met in the White Horse Tavern in the city, nicknamed *Little Germany*, the area that was the cradle of the Reformation, because of the excitement of the ideas and the events discussed there. Here came the later conservatives Gardiner and Heath, the future Protestant martyrs Nicholas Ridley and Thomas Bilney, and the Protestant theologian and translator of the *Bible*, Miles Coverdale. Here they *all* scoffed at superstitious nonsense

51_ Smith, 1953.

52_ Latimer, *Sermon on the Plough*, 1548, ibid.

and woeful ignorance. The divisions that were to open up between them, seen in the church in Gildas's day, developed as a result of the career choices which followed. The group studying divinity either retired to their monasteries or continued with their studies, becoming doctors of divinity and professors of theology. Cranmer, Latimer, and Ridley are three such. Those who had studied civil and canon law entered court or episcopal service. And so they separated both physically and mentally, eventually to confront each other, as Lacey Baldwin Smith put it, poles apart in temperament, experience, and wisdom. Of the eleven bishops who had graduated in canon law from Cambridge, Oxford, or even from universities on the Continent, not one can be called a reformer. In the discussions on the 1549 Prayer Book, Bonner was emphatic:

When anything is called into question, if ye dispute it, ye must see whether it be decent, lawful and expedient.

Gardiner, bishop of Winchester, 'in his velvets and satin, aloft upon his mule trapped with velvet, with golden stirrups and bridle, and with his gentlemen bare headed chained with gold, before and after him', had no worries about reporting what was being said of him:

Winchester now teacheth and writeth mixing the observance of the law with the grace of the gospel.

The reformers who remained in academic circles had no experience of and little interest in affairs of state, but for the conservatives, these were the fundamentals which allowed the proper exercise of religion. Gardiner, bishop of Winchester, Stokesley, bishop of London, Heath, bishop of Worcester and archbishop of York under Mary, and Bonner, bishop of London, the great conservative bishops of the sixteenth-century church, were bureaucrats who owed their career to the crown and were responsible for the country's security. So involved were they in court life, politics, and foreign affairs, that they had little time for their strictly episcopal or religious duties, farming these out to suffragens and others, thereby leaving themselves vulnerable to attack from the reformers. They were trained in diplomacy and thus in the art of compromise. They were not pious, but they were still sincere Catholics. Therefore, when the reformers, just like Gildas, started to throw their insults, Edmund Bonner of London being called a 'brockish boar of Babylon, a swill-ball, a blockhead, a belly-god' and Richard Sampson the 'double faced, epicureous, bite sheep of Coventry and Lichfield', there was bound to be a reaction.[53]

Did Maelgwn's bishops play a similar rôle to their sixteenth-century successors? This is where it becomes so easy to patronize the past, to imagine that things were so much simpler and easier in the sixth century than in the sixteenth or the twenty-first. Did Maelgwn's appointees act as his ambassadors not just to Ireland but to the Continent as well? In the sixth as in the sixteenth century, language difficulties alone demanded that these men be of advanced education, the sort only provided in the sixth century by the church. Certainly, they would have been the source of much of Maelgwn's information about events in the wider world.

[Finding promotion difficult at home, for many aspiring ecclesiastics, so Gildas claimed,] it doth not so much loath as delight them (after they have carefully sent their messengers beforehand) to cross the seas, and travel over most large countries [implyng what he hints at elsewhere, that Rome was one such destination], that so in the end, yea even with the sale of their whole substance, they may win and compass such a pomp, and such an incomparable glory [as ordination or consecration] ... And afterwards with great show and magnificent ostentation, or rather madness, returning back to their own native soil, they grow from stoutness to stateliness ... What do ye therefore ... expect from such belly beasts ... Shall your manners be amended by these ... Shall ye be illuminated with such eyes?[54]

[53] Ibid., *passim*.

[54] Gildas, *De Excidio Britanniae*, Ch. 67, Giles, 1841, p. 62.

Did study in law and diplomacy teach Maelgwn's bishops fundamental political principles, just as it undoubtedly had in the days of the empire, and as it does in any age? These, as Lacey Baldwin Smith put it, were the convictions that government is the result of power not of ideas and that change also involves the risk of social revolution. They came to these conclusions in the context of the German religious wars with all their terror and bloodshed. Maelgwn's bishops were operating in a world still reeling from the collapse of imperial power.

Gildas had already shown himself to be less than worldly wise in his attacks on Maelgwn's rise and the creation of what was in effect a Greater Gwynedd. Was Gildas committing a fundamental error, bent as he seems to have been on destroying the basis of church and political life in Gwynedd by attacking the traditional, Roman, Gaul-oriented church of his day, possibly represented by Sanctinus of Degannwy and Rhos?

On the reformers' side, the events of 534–43, the extraordinary cosmic events, appalling weather both summer and winter, crop failures, famine, disease or the threat of it, all pointed to the imminence of the Second Coming. God's priests and ministers had to make people realize the error of their ways before it was too late. Now there were signs that Maelgwn himself was moving into the reformers' camp. And if this *was* the result, Gildas, so closely associated with the Roman past and its church, yet so convinced of the evils of the time, must have found himself torn in two, attempting to straddle two worlds which he must have seen could not be held together. He might have been worried by the extremes to which the reformers of his day were prepared to carry matters, even whilst realizing the rightness of their stand. He was, however, more appalled by the laxity of the state–church operators. A history of reform in all areas of life, in all ages, shows that the greatest differences and the fiercest battles are fought, not between the reformers and those upholding the status quo, but between the reformers themselves, appalled that their stand is being compromised by colleagues who have simply got it wrong. Here we are at the logical outcome of those two stances represented so perfectly in the late fourth-century church by, on the one hand, Martin bishop of Tours, with his dishevelled hair and disreputable attire, and on the other by that prince-bishop of the church, a former governor no less, namely Ambrose bishop of Milan? Aren't we, in fact, looking at something that can only be called the sixth-century Reformation? With such far-reaching developments, Maelgwn's reign deserves a book to itself.

CYBI

If the above interpretation is anywhere near correct, then it was probably in the period *after* 543 that Maelgwn granted the church in Holyhead, possibly built by his father in the corner of the Roman fortress, along with the fortress itself, to Cybi, a cleric from Ireland. Dr Miller, in her 1979 pioneering study *The Saints of Gwynedd*, looked at the fragile record of Maelgwn's land grants as they have come down to us in a variety of sources, to conclude that the grant to Cybi was older than the others and provided the model for the rest.[55] In his *Vita*, Cybi had just arrived from Ireland.

And immediately a strong wind came on the sea, and his disciples feared greatly and saint Cybi prayed powerfully to God, by whose power God divided a rock into two parts, and the boat leapt up between the two rocks, and at last they landed on the island of Anglesey.[56]

This seems to be an explanation of how what today is called Puffin Island, *Ynys Lannog*, became separated from the mainland of Anglesey. Having sailed through the sound between the two, Cybi and his followers were in the sheltered waters of the Menai Strait where they landed.

King Maelgwn was hunting a goat when it gave him the slip and sought shelter in a cottage where Cybi was

55_ Miller, *Saints*, 1979, pp. 113–16.

56_ Life of St. Cybi, c.1200, Wade-Evans, 1944, pp. 245.

staying. This, in conformity with the above account, is described as being in Rhosyr in the southeast of the island. Cybi chose the opportunity to demand of the king as much land as the goat could encompass when chased by Maelgwn's hunting dog. The goat and dog were released and ran round the whole headland before returning. As a result, the land was given to the cleric. The writer possibly realized a mistake had been made, because Rhosyr in the southeast should have been Holyhead in the northwest where Maelgwn did make a grant to Cybi, and so he added a rather limp addition by way of correction.

And afterwards a conflict arose between king Maelgwn and saint Cybi, but he was not able to withstand the servant of God. And so he conveyed his fortress [at Holyhead coming now to be called *Caer*, the fortress of Cybi] to Almighty God and the holy Cybi as a perpetual offering of alms [the second version adding – *for the salvation of his soul* – but continuing as though it was the soul of Cybi that was intended, not that of Maelgwn!].[57]

Holyhead was a key strategic site, a ship-fortress probably begun in the period 286–93 when the former prefect of the *classis Britannica*, the British fleet, Carausius, was ruling Britain. This move by Maelgwn was quite remarkable, particularly when one remembers the recent history in Gwynedd under Cadwallon, Maelgwn's father, when the struggle against the recalcitrant Irish was at its height. Now this west coast fortress was given to Cybi and it was Maelgwn who made the grant. But if the end of the world was really nigh, what use would it be to anyone? The cleric could, at least, pray for the soul of his benefactor.

[57]_ Ibid., pp. 245–9.

Was Maelgwn now turning towards the west for inspiration, indeed, for his salvation? Dr Molly Miller thought this. Stories of numerous 'saints' or clerics *coming from Brittany* have fundamentally misunderstood what was originally intended by the use of the word 'Letavia', which does mean Brittany. There simply could not have been such an export of clerics from this northwest peninsula of Gaul at this time, and there was little or no reason for it later. The earliest source for the 'Letavian mission' is the *Vita Paterni* of *c*.1200, in which the leaders are named as Cadfan, Tydecho, and Padarn himself. The genealogies bring them into a family relationship as cousins. Cybi foundations are very much in evidence in Eifionydd, whilst to the east of this, running north to south, is a block of territory from Degannwy and Arllechwedd to the west of the Conwy, down through Ardudwy and so into Meirionydd, where church dedications are only to so-called Letavian saints. Dr Miller argued that the name Letavian is, in fact, a partisan term meaning, in effect, the Roman party in Gwynedd.[58] Her viewpoint was developed by bringing in Gildas's condemnation of Maelgwn including Maelgwn's imitation of Irish court life. This, as we have seen, is more likely to belong to an earlier period in Maelgwn's career when he was cultivating diplomatic and political ties with the Uí Néill. It may then have become a permanent feature of court life under Maelgwn.

What Dr Miller was not able to factor into her calculations was the recent work of dendrochronologists and climatologists concerning the cataclysmic events of 533–43. Even apart from all this, it may well be that in the last years of Maelgwn there was a growing split between those still looking back to a continental, Roman past and those increasingly looking forward to a new Irish Sea political and religious community. Indeed, it is likely that this tension had been simmering for years within church circles, only now, with the panic caused by predictions of the end, reaching really divisive

[58]_ Miller, *Saints*, 1979, esp. pp. 45–6 and 90–4.

proportions. For the reformers were convinced that the end of the world foretold in the *Bible* was now at hand.

It seems clear that there were similar tensions and then divisions in Ireland. The story of Finnian, bishop and abbot of Clonard, visiting Ruadan, abbot of Lothra, now Lorrha in north Tipperary near Loch Derg, would seem to underline this. Finnian had taught and trained Ruadan and now, not long before 549, he visited his former pupil accompanied by other abbots to urge him to come into conformity with them.[59] This possibly makes Ruadan a Letavian, forced now as a result of this pressure to conform to the reformers' creed.

A CONSERVATIVE COUNTER-REFORMATION?

The trade links with Gaul were still strong. Cloth, pottery, oil, and wine were all imported and with this the ecclesiastical link to the Gaulish church continued. For many this must have represented concrete evidence that Britain was still Roman, still part of the empire. The Letavian cause, and we should now be able to call it that, must have received much encouragement when news arrived that the eastern general Belisarius had reversed what had seemed like the tide of history. 'Rome, after an interval of sixty years, again fell into Roman hands.' In Gwynedd's Penmachno, a memorial stone that can be dated exactly to 540, the year in which the western capital Ravenna was taken back from the Ostrogoths, is eloquent testimony to the links with Gaul, the empire, and imperial institutions. Only the left portion of the pillar-stone survives so that the first line of the vertical inscription with three horizontal lines at the bottom is missing.

(THE STONE OF ...) SON OF AVITORIUS. (SET UP) IN THE TIME OF JUSTINUS THE CONSUL [540].[60]

[59]_ The Irish *Life of Ruadan*, Plummer, 1922, Vol. 2, pp. 311–12: The Irish *Life of Finnian of Clonard*, Stokes, 1890, p. 227.

[60]_ Nash-Williams, 1950, p. 93, Pl. VIII and Fig. 84.

Left: Mosaic showing Belisarius centre with, on the right, his emperor Justinian, 527–65. The basilica of San Vitale, Ravenna, Italy, consecrated 547/8 when the western capital was back in imperial hands. Its mosaic interior is one of the glories of Roman civilization.

Below: Over one thousand miles away from San Vitale, in the heart of *Venedotia*/Gwynedd, a stone was erected in memory of the son of Avitorius 'in the time of Justinus the Consul'. The year was 540. Penmachno church, north Wales. (Courtesy of the Church in Wales)

Gwynedd's Mediterranean.

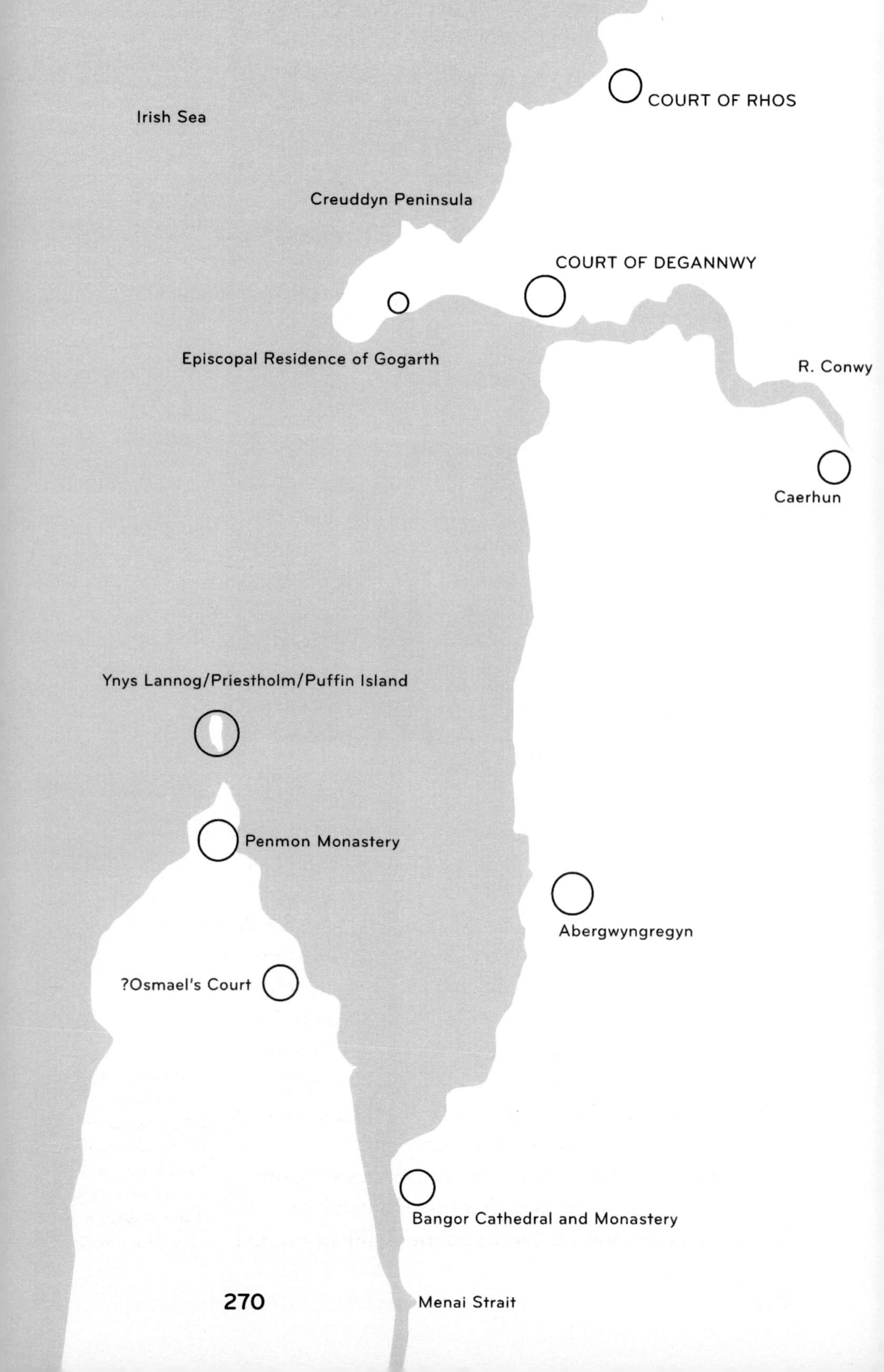

Irish Sea

COURT OF RHOS

Creuddyn Peninsula

COURT OF DEGANNWY

Episcopal Residence of Gogarth

R. Conwy

Caerhun

Ynys Lannog/Priestholm/Puffin Island

Penmon Monastery

Abergwyngregyn

?Osmael's Court

Bangor Cathedral and Monastery

270

Menai Strait

The consulships of 541, for Justinian and his subject Albinus Basilius, were the last to be noted on monuments in the west. Later, Justinian II, 685–95 and 705–11, merged the post of consul with that of emperor.

It may be true that someone named Tudno left the monastery of Bangor on Dee and moved on to the Creuddyn peninsula now that Maelgwn was at last turning west to the Irish church and its stricter discipline. Here, on what today, and possibly since Viking times, is called the Great Orme, though its old Welsh name was possibly *Cyngreawdr*, he built his church. Possibly he was accompanied by a tiny community. The cave *Ogof Llech*, the Cave of the Rock, is traditionally associated with the cleric, as usual thought to be a cell for solitary retreat. Further east along the coast at Rhos-on-Sea, did Bishop Trillo of *Dineirth*, not his foundation but a church from which he would have exerted influence at the heart of Maelgwn's Gwynedd, build his supposed cell or oratory on the shore below his church, and not so much for retreat but, instead, to protect an important spring, more vital than ever in times of climatic uncertainty?

If Padarn was one of the leading Letavians, with his principal church, Llanbadarn Fawr, on the Ceredigion Cardigan Bay coast, another leader of the movement, Cadfan, established his church further north at Towyn on the coast of Meirionydd. This was 'Cadfan's high church near the shore of the blue sea' in Llywelyn *Fardd*'s poem in honour of the saint.[61] It looks as though, as an offshoot of this, he founded a church, monastery, and school on Bardsey Island at the tip of the Llŷn peninsula which was visible across the northern part of Cardigan Bay. The eighteenth-century Iolo says the patron was Einion *Frenin*, Einion the King and, with no supporting evidence, that he was ruling in Llŷn. In fact, this would make sense if this is Einion, son of Cynlas of Rhos, Maelgwn's cousin. Llŷn could well have been his apanage in the complexity of the emerging Gwynedd confederation. It *might* have been a place of refuge for monks from Bangor on Dee after the 616 battle of Bangor Orchard, but the Northumbrians did retreat and

61_ Baring-Gould and Fisher, 1907–13, Vol. II, 1908, p. 5. Llywelyn *Fardd* lived c.1230–80. The king Cyngen, who is said to have received Cadfan at Towyn, is not in the genealogies.

the monastery on the Dee would have revived. Bardsey, partly because of its romantic position in the sea at the end of the Welsh world, has become overburdened with tradition. Baring-Gould and Fisher thought it could be called the Iona of Wales, but Iona was the burial place of kings. Certainly, probably because of its position more than anything else, it became a place of pilgrimage.

Owing to its sanctity and the danger often attending the voyage across, three pilgrimages thither were considered equal to a pilgrimage to Rome, ranking it as second to St David's in this respect.[62]

Perhaps it was for this reason rather than for any association with the Letavians that it was known as *Roma Britanniae* in the *Book of Llandaff.*

Another royal foundation was that on *Ynys Lannog*, from Viking days known as *Priestholm*, Priest's Island, and more latterly as Puffin Island, and opposite it, on the mainland of Anglesey, Penmon. This monastic community and school eventually came to rival Clynnog Fawr, a church in the Llŷn peninsula, as a centre of learning in Gwynedd. It is just possible, as tradition asserts, that Seiriol, its first abbot, *was* the brother of Cynlas of Rhos and that Cynlas's son Einion *Frenin* in Llŷn, Einion the King, was partly responsible along with Maelgwn himself for the foundation. Maelgwn could see *Ynys Lannog* from his court at Degannwy. The royal involvement may have been purely secular, but tradition does say that Seiriol was Penmon's abbot.[63]

Interestingly, when all these sites – Degannwy, Aber or Abergwyngregyn, Penmon, and *Ynys Lannog*, Bangor, monastery and cathedral, possibly a defensive site guarding the crossing of the Menai immediately below Bangor, and not forgetting the abbot/bishop of Bangor's residence on the Great Orme at Gogarth – are plotted on a map or, better still, if these places are viewed from the top of the Great Orme peninsula, it becomes clear that this was Gwynedd's inner sea: a Mediterranean at

62_ Ibid., also pp. 4–6; Miller, *Saints*, 1979, pp. 90–1 and 49.

63_ Baring-Gould and Fisher, 1907–13, Vol. IV, 1913, pp. 177–8; Williams, 1848, p. 526; Miller, *Saints*, 1979, pp. 14, 46–7, 77–9, and 106–9.

the centre of Gwynedd's heartland. It was dominated
by the Letavians because, however corrupt this church
looked to Gildas and to the reformers, it was a vital
arm of the state.

DAVID

At the other extreme of this growing religious divide is
David who, given his south Wales position, falls outside
our main area of concern. However, this was the cleric
who by his example and teaching achieved the leadership
of the reform party in Britain, his influence extending
over the Irish Sea through the work of Irish clerics who
had trained under him. It may be that it was about now,
c.547, that this supposed son of Sant, king of Ceredigion,
reached the site of his future monastery. This was in
vallis rosina, the valley of the swamp, or *vallis prospera*,
the favourable valley, the upper part of the valley of the
river Alun in what came to be called the Dewisland
peninsula in Dyfed or Pembroke. Had the inspiration,
in part at least, been given by Gwynedd? Like
Cadwallon, Maelgwn's father, earlier in Anglesey, here in
Pembroke David encountered Irish settlers under their
leader, Baia. Here, like Cadwallon, David proclaimed,
'It is we who stay: Baia must go!' But more importantly,
and more in keeping with the time that was waxing late,
and with the Judge waiting, Dewi Ddyfrwr, David the
Water Drinker, established an uncompromisingly
extreme monastic regime which was vegetarian and based
on hard physical work: the monks, literally yoked to the
plough, prayed in silence.

CHAPTER NINE

FROM THE SEA MARSH OF RHIONYDD

Plague – The End of Roman Gwynedd? 545–547

KINGS, OVER-KINGS, AND CONFEDERATIONS: IRELAND

In 547 or early 548, Ciarán the Carpenter sailed down the great highway of the Shannon. With him were eight companions. On the flood plain just south of Athlone, amidst meadows frequently inundated – wild fen country with few or no inhabitants – he decided to stop. Here he would build his monastery.[1] Some time during that winter, Ciarán gave shelter to the southern Uí Néill Diarmait mac Cerbaill. The northern Uí Néill Muirchertach had established a lordship over the Uí Néill north and south for the first time in 520 by killing the southern Uí Néill Ardgal son of Conall. Diarmait was Ardgal's nephew and heir, and as such he was the southern Uí Néill contender for the post of over-king in opposition to Tuathal *Maelgarb*, an intruder from the Cenél Cairpri who had ruled since 534.

Three years, then, and three months dwelt Ciarán in Inis Angin [Inchinneen or Hare Island in Lough Ree on the Shannon]; and after that [moving down river] he came to Ard Manntain beside the Shannon [but decided not to stay there] ...

After that he came to this place [Clonmacnois]. Ard Tiprat ('the Height of the Well') was its name at that time. 'Here then we will stay, for many souls will go to heaven hence, and there will be a visit from God [here] and from men coming for ever on [or to] this place.'

On the eighth of the calends of February [25 January] Ciarán set up in Cluain, on the tenth of the moon ... on a Saturday [Saturday, 25 January 548 according to the Roman calendar].

Now eight went with him ... Marvellous, then, was that monastery which was set up by Ciarán with his eight

1_ Kenney, 1968, pp. 376–9.

(companions) after they had come from the waves of the water ... Then Ciarán planted the first stake in Cluain [hinting at the same post and wicker structures associated with Daniel in Britain erected hastily in preparation for the Second Coming],
and Diarmait, son of Cerball, was along with him. Said Ciarán to Diarmait when setting the stake, 'Let, O warrior, thy hand be over my hand, and thou shalt be in sovranty over the men of Ireland.'[2]

The death of the over-king Tuathal appears in several sources including Ciarán's *Life* and AClon, the *Annals of Clonmacnois*. All indicate that it was in the remote fastnesses of the Shannon at Ciarán's Clonmacnois that Tuathal *Maelgarb*'s assassination was planned and organized. This is the account in the seventeenth-century language of one English translation of the *Annals of Clonmacnois*.

Twahal Moyle Garve began his raigne & raigned 11 years [AI's fourteen years is more correct] ... He caused Dermot mcKeruell to live in Exile & in Desert places because he Claimed to have Right to ye Crowen ...
King Twahal hauing proclaimed throughout the whole K. dom the banishment of Dermot mcKervel (as before is specified) with a great Reward to him yt would bring him his heart, the said Dermot for feare of his life lived in the deserts of Cluonvicknose (then called Ardtibra) ... meeting with the abbot St. Kieran ...

The saint's prophecy came true through the offices of Diarmait's foster-brother Mael *Mór* or Máel *Mórda*, whom AFM says had also been his tutor. Bearing some comparison with the English boarding school system, the Irish élite often sent their sons to be fostered by other prominent families for the greater part of their education and training, in this way creating new ties of friendship and alliance that would be useful in later life. Foster-brothers who had been brought up together were traditionally very close.

2_ The Irish *Life of Ciarán of Clonmacnois*, Stokes, 1890, pp. 275–6. Clonmacnois is on the east bank of the Shannon in a spot almost halfway between Dublin in the east and Galway in the west.

Mulmorry OHargedy, foster-brother of Dermott, seeing in what perplexity the nobleman [Diarmait] was in, besought him that hee might be pleased to lend him his black horse, & that hee would make his Repaire to Greally da Phill [*Greallach-Daphill* on the Liffey in County Kildare according to O'Donovan], where he hard K. Twahall to have a meeting with som of his nobles, & ther would present him a whelps hart on a speares head, instead of Dermots hart, and so by that means gett access to the K. whom he would kill out of hand & by the help & swiftness of the horse saue his one life whether they would or noe.

Dermott listing to the wordes of his foster-brother, was amongst two extremityes, loth to refuse him & far more loth to lend it him, fearing hee should miscarry & be killed, but between both he Granted him his Request,

Whereupon hee prepared himselfe & went as he was Resolved, mounted on the sd black horse, a hart besprinkled with blood on his speare, to the place where he hard the K. to bee; the K. & people seeing him come in that manner supposed it was Dermotts hart that was to be presented by the man that rode in post hast; the whole multitude gave him way to the K., & when he came within reach to the king as though to Tender him the hart, he gaue the K. such a deadly Bloe of his speare, that the K. Instantly fell dowen Dead in the midst of his people, whereupon the man was besett on all sides & at last taken & killed,
soe as speady news came to Dermot, who Incontinently went to Tarach [Tara], & there was crowned K. as St. Queran Prayed & Prophesied before.[3]

Despite Ciarán's blessing, Diarmait, who has come down to us in a host of traditional stories as one of the great kings of early Ireland, had quite a complicated relationship with the church, and this was not always amicable. However, this was almost the norm for any king of power and note.

To imagine Maelgwn eagerly gathering news on these Irish events and then postulate that this would influence

[3]_ AClon, 535, 547=548, Mageoghagan and Murphy, 1896, pp. 78–80. Also Llanerch, 1993. Aided Diarmata maic Cerr-béil, The Death of Dermot, in the Book of Sligo, O'Grady, 1892, Vol. 2, pp. 76–8, and AU, AI, and AFM.

his own thinking on the succession in Gwynedd would be to go too far. All rulers in the Irish Sea area would have followed these events with interest and all would have had food for thought in the news coming in. This is because the mid-sixth century was a period when kingship itself was developing and patterns were being laid down to be seized on in later generations as justifications for rule. Then, as now, lawyers would have seen their chance, and a whole series of writings on law and government began to make its appearance. The heart of this problem was who had the right to rule. As we have seen, in Britain in the earliest days, such questioning would have been met with proud assertions of imperial origins and mandates. To continue with the controversial view that Niall and Conall were agents of Britain's immediate post-Roman government, this would even have been the case in Ireland. But that was now long ago and kings, some undoubtedly having smashed their way to power as Gildas reported, would have been concerned to establish their position through rights of inheritance. The problem was that as families grew this was becoming increasingly complicated. Dr Mac Niocaill set this out clearly in his extraordinary book *Ireland before the Vikings*.[4]

The issue was who was eligible to rule. Was it to be someone from among the grandchildren of a founding figure and his sons? In Ireland, this, the smallest of the kinship groups, was known as the *gelfine*, the *fine* being the kin or kinship group. Or could you include the grandfather's brothers and their children, the *derbfine* group? Or was it permissible to go back another generation still, including all those descendants, the *iarfine*, or back to the great-great-great-grandfather, and include all his descendants, in the group known as the *indfine*? The theory came to be that outside this six-generation group, rights lapsed. In Ireland we have seen how the descendants of Niall separated into two geographical groupings, the northern and southern Uí Néill, the kingships of Ailech in the north and Uisnech in the south, and how an over-kingship of this whole

4_ Mac Niocaill, 1972, Ch. 3, pp. 42–69.

confederation appeared in 520. The Diarmait or Dermot who now took that over-kingship, the kingship of Tara, was within the *iarfine* group in descent from Niall, being Niall's great-grandson.

The division into northern and southern Uí Néill allowed power to be exercised over more manageable regions, with the over-kingship providing direction and cohesion to a group of rulers which could have easily fallen apart. What we then see is a developing alternation between the two parts of the confederation, though not necessarily reign by reign. The same is seen in the rise to the over-kingship of each of the parts, Ailech and Uisnech, between different lines descended from Niall. Within these areas other peoples *not* descended from Niall were considered ineligible to occupy positions of rule. As it developed, the system became flexible enough to allow those considered the most suitable candidates, perhaps because of their power or their contacts, to overrule the rights of others who on grounds of age or descent might have had a better claim. Nevertheless, it became increasingly common for sons to be specifically earmarked as designated heirs. In Ireland, this figure was known as the *tánaise*, in Wales in the later law texts *gwrthrychiad*, or in a Welshing of the Anglo-Saxon *aetheling* as *edling*. In Latin, it was *heres*, successor.

The same development of kingship in Ireland can be seen not only in the lands of the Uí Néill, the descendants of Niall, but also in all the other areas which grew into clearly defined geographical units known, as in imperial times, as provinces. Here we often find kingship alternating between population groupings viewed as descending from founding figures like Conall *Corc* in Munster, Eóchu *Mugmédon* in Connacht, and Bresal *Bélach* in Leinster.

Similar patterns emerged in Britain. For example, the dynamic kingdom of Rheged emerged out of appointments made originally in the late Roman period to defend Carlisle, the capital of the province of *Valentia*, and to protect the roads north to the Antonine Wall and the transport system in the areas extending out to the Rhinns of Galloway and to the south as far as Morecambe Bay. Its founding father was thought to be Coelestius, Coel, who could well have been the last regularly appointed *praeses*, president, of *Valentia* in the period *c*.410–40. At the time of Maelgwn, Rheged was what again we would have to call a confederation. By the fifth generation after Coel, the pre-eminent ruler was either Cyngar or Elidir *Llydanwyn*, Elidir the Stout and Handsome, with his brother Cynfarch, leader of his war-band the *Cynferchyn*. Ruling over the sub-kingdom of Elfed/Elmet in the region of Leeds was Gwallog. Over most of the Pennines, Pabo Pillar of Britain held sway with his brother Eliffer *Gosgorddfawr*, Eliffer of the Great Retinue, either of them being king of York. In other words, Greater Rheged was splitting between members of the family, but the dynasty was still under an over-king even if, at times, it is difficult to see exactly who this was. In the next generation the probable over-king was Gwenddoleu, with his war-band the *Coeling*, ruling over the Carlisle region. He was slain in the *c*.573 battle of *Arthuret* by his cousins Gwrgi and Peredur, joint kings of York. Seven years later in 580 they were themselves killed defending York against Adda of Bernicia when York probably fell under the control of Aelle of Deira.

Gwenddoleu the over-king was apparently succeeded by Urien *Rheged*, who in reaction to the loss of York led a counter-attack against the English in which he took Catterick. He then defeated the Bernician attempt to recover this in the battle of the Leven Forest in 588. But the struggle was unequal, so that when *c*.590–2 he made another push against the English with Rhydderch of Strathclyde, the venture collapsed and Urien was assassinated in the siege of Lindisfarne. Dunod, king of the northern Pennines, and after 581 Catterick, was killed in 595 defending his territories. His brother was the Sawyl *Benisel*, Samuel Lowhead or Flathead, king of the southern Pennines, whom we have rejected as Maelgwn's father-in-law through the marriage of his unnamed daughter to the Gwynedd king. Dunod's and Sawyl's cousin was Cynwyd of the *Cynwydion*, Cynwyd's war-band. Clearly the tasks facing these rulers were enormous, but it looks as though Greater Rheged, the Rheged confederation, acted as a unit to face it.

Three hundred swords of the Cynferchyn,
and three hundred shields of the Cynwydion,
and three hundred spears of the Coeling:
on what ever expedition they might go together,
they would never fail.[5]

Further north was the kingdom of Strathclyde. This had emerged out of the appointments made in the late Roman period to protect the western frontier zone of the Antonine Wall area and its road system. These were made among the Dumnonii where military and tribal leaders were elevated to the rank of protector and prefect for this rôle. Possibly starting with Clemens, *Cluim*, appointed by Count Theodosius and then confirmed by the emperor Magnus Maximus c.383, by the time we reach Maelgwn's period after c.520 it appears that Strathclyde was also developing along confederation lines. Gwyddno, son of Donald I, *Dyfnwal Hen*, of the Clyde was seemingly the over-king, but there were also Clydno, Cedig, Gwrwst *Briodor*, the Landholder, and Germanianus. Clydno was the father of Tudwal who was born c.510 and who was the father of Rhydderch, seemingly over-king in the period c.575–610. He was in communication with Colum *Cille* before June 597, and in 590–2 joined with Urien of Rheged in the push against the English that was to fail. Gwrwst the Landholder was the father of Elidir *Mwynfawr*, Elidir the Wealthy, whose epithet might indicate that in his

5_ *Bonedd Gwŷr y Gogledd*, The Lineage of the Men of the North, late thirteenth century, probably from a twelfth-century original, Bartrum, 1966, pp. 73 and p. 147, note.

generation, possibly *c*.540–75, he was the over-king.

Equally importantly for us, it might be thought, is the marriage Elidir supposedly made himself or which had been arranged for him by his father, Gwrwst. Two extremely doubtful sources, though they are probably one and the same, indicate that Maelgwn's daughter Eurgain was married to Elidir and that as a result of this, when Rhun, Maelgwn's son, was ruling over Gwynedd, possibly in the period 566–80, Elidir king of Rheged invaded by sea to assert his perceived right to rule and was killed in the attempt near Caernarfon. The story grows into one where Rhydderch, the over-king of Strathclyde, invaded to avenge this death, burning Arfon in the process, then withdrew. As a result, Rhun supposedly marched north to the Forth with a vast army. According to Dr John Morris, who accepted the tradition, this was in order to take revenge, to establish his own brother Bridei, another supposed son of Maelgwn, as king of the Picts, and to aid his brother fighting against the Irish of the Scottish kingdom of Dalriada.

For the moment, we can leave it that, in its present form, the story is extremely doubtful and that we are almost certainly looking at a classic case of where speculation on traditional material can lead us horribly astray. However, it is worth noting that we may, nevertheless, be here looking at a struggle for the over-kingship of Gwynedd, one which might have happened about the time of Clydno of Meirionydd's murder, or, more likely, one that was still to come after Maelgwn's death and even after the death of his successor.

GWYNEDD: MAELGWN AND HIS INTENDED HEIR, EINION

Although our evidence is extremely flimsy, it is probably helpful to imagine Gwynedd under Maelgwn sharing this same pattern of developing kingship; to think of it, in other words, as the Gwynedd confederation. If the scenario set out above for a usurpation in Gwynedd by

Meirionydd-based rulers, who may or may not have been related to Paternus, Eternus, and Cunedda, is plausible, the confederation idea looks to be inevitable. Greater Gwynedd, including Meirionydd, originally had three pre-eminent rulers – Cadwaladr of Meirionydd, Cadwallon over Anglesey and the area west of the Conwy, and Owain of Rhos ruling the lands east of the Conwy. In this arrangement, it would appear that Cadwaladr was the over-king. However, such neat geographical division could be a recipe for separatism. In the next generation, there was a scramble for the supreme position in which Maelgwn removed Clydno, who may have been attempting to claim the position of over-king previously held by his father. Maelgwn, the new over-king, then ruled from Degannwy. Cynlas son of Owain continued to hold Rhos. Rhun, during the rule of his father Maelgwn, probably had Anglesey as his apanage. This had been held before by Maelgwn in his youth under the rule of his father Cadwallon.

According to Iolo at least, Cynlas's son Einion was king of Llŷn. To create apanages outside the family's main area might have been one way of overcoming separatist tendencies, as well as, though we have to be careful about using such terminology, creating a sense of what we would call national unity. Operating under these rulers were a whole host of other relatives, firstly from the original dynasty of Paternus down to Anianus. In the second dynasty, there would have been yet more, most probably unknown to us or the later genealogists. What happened to Clydno's son, if that is who he was, namely Gwyddno? Almost certainly, for if later events are to be accommodated this has to be the case, Gwyddno was still an infant when his father was killed. The indications are that he was accommodated in Meirionydd itself. His son, or grandson, was later known as Idris *Garw*, the Rough or the Coarse, but this could have been *Gawr*, the Giant, even the Great, all of which might possibly imply a position of some power, and four generations later we find Ednyfed *Meirionydd*, Ednyfed of Meirionydd.[6]

6_ Bartrum, 1966, Nos. 18 and 41, pp. 11 and 49; Wade-Evans, 1938, No. 18, pp. 109–10.

Maelgwn may have had a keen sense of dynastic unity and the power which could be derived from this. He may have had an eye on developments within the Uí Néill dynasty in Ireland, not least because he had been in close contact with them and had been so impressed as to almost model his court along Irish lines. Gildas was probably misled as to his motives and, as a result, has been misleading us ever since. Of course, personal matters, now beyond recovery, may have intruded to encourage Maelgwn in his thinking. Whatever happened, it looks as though Maelgwn announced that his intended, designated heir was not Rhun, but Einion, Cynlas's son, currently ruling as king of Llŷn. It is extremely unlikely on dating grounds that this Einion was, as two genealogies imply, the *son* of Owain of Rhos. This would give him a rule when he was in his seventies and eighties. One pedigree, Jesus College MS 20, which is late fourteenth century but based on a pre-1200 source, inserts an *Ewein* between *Cenlas* and a *Meic*. Einion, therefore, looks to have been the son of Cynlas rather than Owain. If he had such a brutal father, as Gildas tells us he had, possibly the son was just the forceful character needed to keep the confederation together. Was Maelgwn even more far-sighted, hoping to see an alternation in Gwynedd between the descendants of the three usurping brothers, his own father Cadwallon, Owain, and even Cadwaladr? Or was it being confined to the successors of Owain and Cadwallon with Cadwaladr's Meirionydd successors permanently excluded?

Geoffrey of Monmouth gives us a story that may be very near the truth of what happened to the succession in Gwynedd following the death of Maelgwn. He talks of Cadwallon of Gwynedd, 625–35, who in *c.*632 was forced to flee to Ireland because of Edwin of Northumbria's invasion and brief victory over north Wales. Geoffrey then says that, despairing of ever being able to return, Cadwallon visited Solomon, king of the Britons in *Armorica*, Brittany. Here he related Britain's misfortune and, feeling slightly ashamed, told how it was the sins of the British that had brought this about. Here of course, Geoffrey is following Gildas, and both were churchmen. Then Cadwallon makes his appeal.

We had the same ancestor, you and I, and this encourages me to ask your help. For Malgo [Maelgwn], that mighty King of Britain who reigned fourth after Arthur, begat two sons, Ennianus [Einion] and the other Run.

Ennianus [king of Gwynedd c.549–66] begat Belin [king c.580–97], Belin begat Iago [king 597–616], Iago begat Cadvan [the saviour of Powys in the battle of Chester, king 616–25], and Cadvan was my father.

After his brother's death, Run [if we allow him rule in Gwynedd, c.566–80] was exiled by a Saxon invasion [or more probably an invasion launched by a descendant of Gwrin and Clydno of Meirionydd]. He came to this land and he gave his daughter to Duke Hoel, son of Hoel the Great who in Arthur's company conquered many countries. To him was born Alan, and from Alan came Hoel, your own father, who, while he lived, was no small terror to all Gaul.[7]

In other words, when the time came, Maelgwn was succeeded not by his son Rhun but by Cynlas's son Einion, and it was from the line of Owain of Rhos through Cynlas and Einion *Frenin*, Einion the King, that the line of Gwynedd's over-kings was then descended down to Cadwallon.

IRELAND AWAITS THE END

For many, however, such political considerations were becoming increasingly irrelevant. The time, predicted by some since *c.*536, *was* coming. In Clonmacnois, the monastery grew and attracted many. Here, Ciarán laid down a regime as punishing as that of David in Pembrokeshire. After all, this was preparation for the end of all things.

7_ Geoffrey of Monmouth, *The History of the Kings of Britain*, XII. 6, Thorpe, 1966, p. 274.

Since the coming of Christ into flesh, there never hath been born one whose charity and mercy were greater, whose labour and fasting and prayer were greater ... It is he that never put rich food or any intoxicating liquor into his body since he began to lead a devout life. It is he that never drank milk nor ale until a third of it was water. He never ate bread until a third of it was sand. He never slept until his side touched the bare mould. Under his head there was usually nought save a stone for a pillow. Against his skin there never came linen nor wool ...
A man enduring and steady in supporting sufferings and tribulations, like Job the sufferer.[8]

The same *Life* speaks of a cask full of wine from the land of the Franks being delivered to Clonmacnois that was not touched. More importantly, however, this evidence of trade with Gaul was, indeed, a portent of the end and in a way the monks could never have imagined.[9]

Finnian of Clonard probably produced a penitential, a book on monastic discipline and penance, and Gildas himself may have been in communication with Finnian on the subject.[10] Finnian's *Life* speaks of the same awful austerity.

Now, one day there [in Clonard] bishop Senach his pupil was gazing at him, and beheld his meagreness and his great wretchedness, so great that his ribs could be counted through his inner raiment. Moreover, Senach saw the worm[s] coming out of Findian's side ... from the cold girdle of iron which he wore around him as a penance for his body and which cut to his bone ...

Now this was his daily refection – a bit of barley-bread and a drink of water. On Sundays, however, and on holidays, a bit of wheaten bread and a piece of broiled salmon, and the full of a cup of clear mead or ale. He used to upbraid those whom he saw eating gluttonously, and weep and do penance for their sin. He used to sleep neither on down nor on [a] flock-bed, so that his side would come against the bare mould, and a stone for a bolster was under his head.[11]

8_ The Irish *Life of Ciarán of Clonmacnois*, Stokes, 1890, p. 278.

9_ Ibid., p. 276.

10_ Kenney, 1968, pp. 177, 191, 240, 236–7, and 244; Lloyd, 1912, pp. 142–3 and 156.

11_ The Irish *Life of Finnian of Clonard*, Stokes, 1890, pp. 228–9.

With his monastery established, on 1 May 549, the Feast of *Beltaine* and the start of summer, Ciarán went to the great Fair of *Uisnech* in Meath having been invited there by the Uí Néill over-king Diarmait. Ciarán was clearly intent on winning privileges for his monastery. Coming to meet him, Diarmait granted the land surrounding them to Clonmacnois, but then proceeded to burn a house that was on it belonging to an enemy along with all its inhabitants. Ciarán refused to forgive him and prophesied the king's own death. Despite this, Ciarán was at the fair for a fortnight, but the gathering was blighted by the drought which put the assembly's participants in peril of their lives. Ciarán performed a miracle and rain fell. It will be obvious that we are here following the *Life*.

On 1 August, the Feast of *Lugnasa*, the Festival of First Fruits, Ciarán was back in Meath, this time at the Fair of Teltown. What happened here appears in the annals and in the great collections of Irish history and tradition such as the *Book of Leinster* and the *Book of Sligo*.

Taillte's Convention is held by Dermot son of Cerbhall, S. Kieran the carpenter's son also, his confessor, being there beside him; the meeting's games are played, its races run.

There a certain woman accosts her husband and accuses him of intrigue with another woman. He persisted in denial of the fact, and the wife said: "I will accept his affidavit sworn under Kieran's hand." The husband accordingly swore under Kieran's hand that in the matter which his wife had laid to his charge he was guiltless; but it was a lie for him. Therefore upon his neck, just where the cleric's hand had lain, an ulcerous tumour took him ...

By Kieran ... [he] was conveyed to Clonmacnoise, there to be looked after for so long as God should appoint his life to be ... But the man died presently ...[12]

12_ *Abacuc's Perjury*, in the *Book of Leinster*, O'Grady, 1892, Vol. 2, p. 453, also pp. xix and 78; AT, 548, Stokes, 1993, p. 139; AFM, O'Donovan, 1851, Vol. I, p. 183; and Kenney, 1968, p. 381. In the above extract, the unnecessary embellishments concerning the man's decapitation and his seven-year stay in Clonmacnois have been omitted.

Here then we will stay, for many souls will go to heaven hence, and there will be a visit from God here.

Above and left: Ciarán's Clonmacnois on the Shannon.

Top and bottom: Senán's
monastery on Scattery
Island in the Shannon.

(Photos: © Dept. of
Environment, Heritage and
Local Government, Ireland)

In another story, a pious woman named Canair, from Bantry in County Cork, had become a hermit. One night, all the churches of Ireland appeared to her with a tower of fire above each reaching into heaven, but 'the greatest and straightest' went up from Senán's *Inis Cathaig*, his monastery on Scattery Island in the Shannon estuary. She went there in order to die so that her resurrection would be from that spot. Senán came to meet her and tried to persuade her to go elsewhere, saying that his monastery was not for women. Standing on a wave in the sea, Canair argued that Christ had come to save women no less than men, citing their rôle in the gospels and in the church. Senán relented. Canair was allowed ashore, given the sacrament, and died.

The plague had arrived in Ireland.

THE 545 PRECURSOR

In fact, the bubonic plague could well have arrived in Ireland and/or Wales in 545. This time scale, with the plague still affecting Constantinople into 543, seems more than plausible, although contemporaries noted the utter capriciousness with which the pestilence struck. Although he claimed that no part of the human race was unvisited by the disease, at least in the west, the Syrian Evagrius *Scholasticus*, a boy when the plague erupted, talks of this unpredictability and of his own narrow escape.

Some cities were so severely afflicted as to be altogether depopulated, though in other places the visitation was less violent. It neither commenced according to any fixed period, nor was the time of its cessation uniform; but it seized upon some places at the commencement of winter, others in the course of the spring, others during the summer, and in some cases when the autumn was advanced …

at the commencement of this calamity I was seized with what are termed buboes, while still a school-boy, and lost by its recurrence at different times several of my children, my wife, and many of my kin, as well of my domestic and country servants.[13]

There was an outbreak in southern Gaul in the time of Bishop Gall of Clermont-Ferrand, which can possibly be dated to 543.

In Saint Gall's time the plague raged in various parts of Gaul, causing great swellings in the groin. It was particularly bad in the province of Arles, and Saint Gall was anxious not only for himself but for his flock.[14]

An angel told Gall that he would have reason to fear in eight years' time, which was taken to mean that he would die then. He died in 551.

When we come to look at the records of pestilence and disease in Britain and Ireland, from what could be its first outbreak in Ireland in 545, it seems that for at least thirteen years before that and probably for much longer, the threat of pestilence, of epidemics, of sudden, unexpected, painful, and untimely death, had been hanging over these islands. But then in 545 disease struck with a vengeance. AU under 544=545 has 'The first mortality called *bléfed*, in which Mo-Bí Clá+rainech died.' The victim was Mobí, founder and abbot of the monastery of *Glais-noiden*, Glasnevin, near Dublin. According to the *Life of Colum Cille*, Mobí had been that cleric's last tutor and he sent him away because the plague was coming. The writer mixes up his pestilences because he called it *buide conaill* which was yellow fever or the 'Yellow Pestilence' of 556 and not the plague of 545.[15]

Estimates for plague mortality in past centuries differ widely. When the Black Death devastated Ireland in 1349, however, a figure of between 35 and 40 per cent of the population seems likely. Despite this, in 1949, W. P. MacArthur noted that AFM, for example, only named *one* death, that of Matthew son of Cathal O'Rourke.[16] He also suggested that the annalist's term

13_ Evagrius Scholasticus, *A History of the Church*, Rosen, 2007, p. 219.

14_ Gregory of Tours, *The History of the Franks*, Book IV, 5, Thorpe, 1974, p. 199.

15_ The Irish *Life of Colomb Cille*, Stokes, 1890, p. 174. In 546, Colum founded his monastery in *Daire-Calgaich*, Calgach's Oak-wood, i.e. Derry.

16_ MacArthur, 1949, p. 173; AFM, O'Donovan, 1851, Vol. III, p. 595.

bléfed, like the Norman French *botch* or boss, probably referred to the characteristic protuberance, the swelling that most usually appeared in the groin. It is from the Greek word for groin that we have the words bubo and bubonic.[17] The 545 outbreak may have lasted for more than a year and may or may not have been devastating. In AFM, the sense of the statement seems to be that this was the year when what it calls 'an extraordinary universal plague though the world, which swept away the noblest part of the human race' *first made its appearance in Ireland*. It names no victims. Also, A. P. Smyth noted that the 545 AU entry hardly looks to be a contemporary record, with its reference to this being the *first* mortality.

The *major* outbreak seems to have occurred in 549 when AU talks of 'a great mortality' and then lists its principal sufferers. AFM also gives a list, but at first glance it also seems to have its pestilences mixed up. It first mentions the deaths of Ciarán and Bishop Tigernach of Clones in County Monaghan, and then gives what it clearly understands to be a separate list of five important clerics who died this year, specifying dates for three of them. It actually repeats one, because the Colum son of Crimthainn, abbot of Terryglas, was in fact Colum of *Inis-Celtra*. Colum's successor on Church Island, Lough Derg, founded Terryglas and reburied Colum there.[18] It also has a rather clumsy ending which, in fact, indicates why the list has to be divided.

[These six died] Of the mortality which was called Cron-Chonaill, – and that was the first [appearance of the fever called] Buidhe-Chonaill, – these saints died [of this],
except [for] Ciarán and Tighearnach [who died of the plague].[19]

It then becomes clear that AFM has taken this from AU, which also repeats Colum's death, because the same division is made, the deaths of Ciarán and Tigernach being the first two entries with no cause given, and

17_ MacArthur, 1949, pp. 171–2.

18_ Kenney, 1968, pp. 384–6.

19_ AFM, 548=549, O'Donovan, 1851, Vol. I, pp. 187–9, at p. 189.

then, under the heading 'A great mortality', a list copied by AFM which adds Odran abbot of Terryglass.

We cannot be sure, but it appears that 545 *did* see a major outbreak of the plague in Ireland, and probably, therefore, in Wales. Hitting on such a scale, industry, agriculture, and transport would have all been disrupted, and this after climatic conditions that for years had been unfavourable, with cold summers and even worse winters resulting in poor harvests. It is estimated that 200,000 people or 40% of the population of Constantinople died, and we know that some of them died of starvation. But plague is *not* a famine disease, that is, it is not caused by famine, although, if weakened by lack of food, the chances of surviving the plague are drastically reduced. Without famine, it is estimated that one in three victims of plague, 'those with a combination of good fortune, strong underlying health, and an uncompromised immune system', could and did survive the infection. The emperor Justinian himself was one such.[20]

BUBONIC PLAGUE, FAMINE, AND THE YELLOW PESTILENCE

However, alongside plague and famine, with their heavy mortality, other diseases usually stalk, waiting their turn to take advantage of people's diminished strength and compromised immunity. The lack of vitamin C and the resulting scurvy can be lethally debilitating. Indeed, deaths in time of famine are more usually the result of infectious disease caused by micro-organisms rather than simply hunger. Even well-fed people, such as the kings in their strongholds on the Creuddyn peninsula in sixth-century Gwynedd, were at risk during famine if, as was likely, they were ignorant of the nature of the infection, transmission mechanisms, and the need to avoid contagion through greater hygiene and the provision of cleaner water.[21] Of course, we cannot rule out practices being adopted born of previous experience

[20]_ Rosen, 2007, pp. 213–14.

[21]_ Mokyr and Ó Gráda, 1999, pp. 1–32.

even if the reasons behind what was being done were not understood.

In the British Isles, the Great Mortality of 549 appears, therefore, to have been the result of a whole range of infectious diseases, the two most important being bubonic plague, now making itself felt again or striking now in different areas, *and* yellow fever or the 'yellow pestilence'. In Irish this latter was called the *chron chonaill* as in AFM, and it is also known as *buidhe chonaill*. In Welsh it was *y fâd felen*. The micro-organisms of this extremely virulent infectious disease, common in famine conditions, are spread by lice. Jaundice, the yellow discolouration of the skin and eyes, is often intense.[22]

THE VULNERABILITY OF MONASTERIES

We are looking at annals that were drawn up by monks and clerics and so, inevitably, the deaths that receive the greatest attention are those of abbots and bishops. Deaths of the laity, even if kings, appear far less frequently, and the lower orders do not feature at all, except for some general phrase which would include them also, such as 'a great mortality'. However, just as in the Ireland of 1843 where nearly two hundred doctors and medical students died, three times the pre-famine average, in 549 religious institutions were especially vulnerable. Having looked at the widespread perception that the Second Coming was imminent, the hasty gathering together of large communities of monks and nuns, and the awful austerities practised in some of these institutions, this should not surprise us. These were also the people most frequently in contact with the dying and deceased.[23]

So we come to the remarkably limited roll call of the dead, the names given us in the annals and the traditional *Lives* of saints. It might be easiest to set these out in lists as below, though there is no pretence that these are comprehensive.

22_ MacArthur, 1949, pp. 174–5.

23_ Mokyr and Ó Gráda, 1999, p. 22.

545: Deaths from the bubonic plague

? Canair the Pious, hermit, on Scattery Island.
? Conal son of Domangart, king of Dalriada in Kintyre
       and Ireland – 'as some say'.
  Mobí, abbot of Glasnevin, County Dublin,
      2 October.
? Iarlath, abbot of Tuam, County Galway.
? An oppressor of the innocents in the Liffey plain:
  'the fame of this sudden and dreadful vengeance
      was immediately spread … throughout many
      provinces of Ireland'.[24]

549: Deaths from the bubonic plague

  Tigernach, abbot of Clones, County Monaghan,
      4 April.
? Abacuc, discovered in the act of perjury at the
      Fair of Teltown, 1 August.
  Ciarán, aged thirty-three, abbot of Clonmacnois,
      County Offaly, 9 September.

549: Deaths from the 'yellow pestilence'

  Sinchell, abbot of Killeigh, County Offaly, 26 March.
  Mac Táil, abbot of Kilcullen, County Kildare, 11 June.
  Colum, abbot of Inis-Celtra, County Clare, becoming
      Colum of Terryglas, County Tipperary, because
      of his burial there.
  Odran, abbot of Latteragh, County Tipperary,
      2 October.
  Finnian, bishop and abbot of Clonard, 12 December.[25]

The Irish *Life of Finnian of Clonard*, not early but
still representing the traditions of Clonard through the
centuries, is clear as to the cause of Finnian's death:

'And as Paul died in Rome for the sake of the Christian
people, lest they should all perish in the pains and
punishments of hell, even so Findian died in Clonard for

[24] Adamnán, *Life of St. Columba*, Book 2, Ch. 25, Anderson and Anderson, 1961, p. 383.

[25] Smyth, 1972, pp. 111, 14, and 16, thought this the first historical contemporary note relating to ecclesiastics associated with Leinster, as opposed to notices culled from hagiography.

sake of the people of the Gael, that they might not all perish of the Yellow Plague.'[26]

549: Deaths from bubonic plague *or* yellow plague

? Senán, abbot of Scattery Island, visiting nuns
     nearby who were asking to bury one of his
     monks in their church.[27]
? Cybi, bishop in Anglesey, 8 November, 'to heaven –
     where is health without pain'.[28]

The confused and late legends surrounding someone called Curig the Blessed might at least indicate that he was a foreigner who landed in Wales at Aberystwyth. The likelihood is that he came from Ireland. He was reputedly the founder of Llangurig in the middle of Wales in Powys's Arwystli, roughly halfway between Aberystwyth and Knighton on the borders of Shropshire. Gerald of Wales, describing his tour through Wales in 1188, tells of the nearby church of St Germanus, that is, St Harmon's church in Gwrtheyrnion, Radnorshire, now in the modern county of Powys. From the sixth to the eleventh century, it was a monastery.

A staff which once belonged to Saint Curig, or so it is said, can be seen in the church of Saint Germanus in this same district of Gwrthrynion [Gwerthrynion or Gwrtheyrnion]. It is completely encased in gold and silver, and the top part has the rough shape of a cross. Its miraculous power has been proved in all manner of cases, but it is particularly efficacious in smoothing away and pressing the puss from glandular swellings and gross tumours which grow often on the human body. All those who suffer from such vexatious afflictions will be restored to health if they go to the staff in faith and offer an oblation of one penny.[29]

From here, at some date probably in the 530s, Curig, in the company of Tudwal and supposedly seventy-two monks, moved to Brittany, which was the usual route

26_ The Irish *Life of Finnian of Clonard*, Stokes, 1890, p. 229; Kenney, 1968, pp. 375–6.

27_ The Irish *Life of Senán*, Stokes, 1890, p. 221.

28_ *Life of St Cybi*, Version I, Ch. 20, Wade-Evans, 1944, p. 249.

29_ Gerald of Wales, *The Journey through Wales*, Book I, Ch. I, Thorpe, 1978, p. 78.

at this time rather than the reverse described in so many of these *Lives*. Here, he became known as Guervroc or Kirik, an identification made by Baring-Gould and Fisher, founding a monastery at Locquirec on the north coast of Brittany near Lanmeur. Then he became a hermit, and for a time joined Paul Aurelian at his monastery in *Occismor*, Saint-Pol-de-Leon, only about fifteen miles from Locquirec. Curig fell sick on a missionary journey, a risky venture in time of pestilence, and died on 17 February in a year that was probably before 550.[30]

In the *Book of Llandaff*, Teilo, who had been with David, supposedly founded the monastery and later cathedral of Llandaff. His *Life* in that book records the progress of the yellow plague or yellow fever across the land.

It was preceded by the appearance of a vaporous column sweeping over the land, one head in the clouds, and the other trailing along the ground. All who came within its course sickened to death, and the contagion spread, affecting beasts as well as men. No medicines were of any avail ... and physicians perished with the patients. The ravages of the plague were so terrible that the country was well-nigh depopulated.[31]

Instead of talk of miracles, the *Life* is remarkably honest. It speaks of panic and Teilo fleeing before the illness with his monks, bishops among them, as well as lay folk, escaping into Cornwall where for a time they were looked after by Geraint or Gerontius, who was ruler in south Cornwall into the 540s and possibly the 550s. From here, Teilo is said to have passed over into Brittany, returning some time later to refound Llandaff.[32] We are not told this, but Geraint too may have died in the pandemic, though there is an obvious danger in seeing anyone dying in the period after 545 as being a likely victim.

One possible sufferer was Vortipor of the Irish-Welsh kingdom of Demetia or Dyfed. In the genealogical information on these kings Emperor Maximus appears,

30_ Baring-Gould and Fisher, 1907–13, Vol. II, 1908, pp. 198–200.

31_ Ibid., Vol. IV, 1913, pp. 232–3, at p. 226.

32_ Ibid.

and before him names seemingly indicating Roman titles going back to the time of Carausius. These were the people charged with the care and defence of the road system. The compiler of the pedigree seems concerned to take his list back to a time well before Magnus Maximus, but only as far as the early fourth century. During Count Theodosius's relief expedition after 367 a second group may have been appointed to pay particular attention to the points of entry provided by the great finger of the sea known as Milford Haven. Then, in about 385, an Irish family under Eochaid, later known as *Allmuir*, or Over-Sea, moved from Munster in southern Ireland to settle in the region of the Prescelly Mountains, on the northwest coast of Pembrokeshire. It appears that Eochaid's descendants, Tryffin, Agricola, and *Gwerthefyr*, *Guotepir*, or Vortipor, were appointed as protectors of this extreme western area, ruling from their court at *Liscastell*, Narberth. Agricola, *c*.475–505, was able to merge his line with descendants of the British protectors further east and out of this union emerged what we call the kingdom of Dyfed. Vortipor or Voteporix, *c*.517–49, Eochaid's great-great-great-grandson, held the title of protector as his ogam and Latin monument proclaims.

MEMORIA
VOTEPORIGIS
PROTICTORIS

At the edge is the Irish ogam inscription translating his British name into Irish, reading *votecorigas*. The stone has been dated to around 550.[33]

If Vortipor did die in this epidemic, then he would have been an old man. Assuming that Gildas was writing in the late 520s, and it is possible to accept this earlier date *and* that Maelgwn died of either the yellow plague or Justinian's plague, then the already greying Vortipor of that decade would in 549 have been white-haired.[34] It is doubtful whether Gildas is saying anything other than that in the late 520s Vortipor was no longer in his youth. That the end of his life was daily approaching was to

33_ Jackson, 1994, p. 139.

34_ The arguments concerning the dating of *De Excidio Britanniae* are well summarized in Vermaat, 1999–2007.

state an obvious fact for anyone at any time, a fact loved by preachers of eternal judgement and hell-fire.

> Thou ... whose head is now growing grey, who art seated on a throne full of deceits ... from the bottom to the top art stained with murder and adulteries ... Vortipore, thou foolish tyrant of the Demetians, why art thou so stiff?[35]

But to include Vortipor in our list of those who succumbed to illness and disease is guesswork. In Maelgwn's case, it is not a guess.

MAELGWN'S LAST DAYS: THE CHRISTMAS FEAST OF 548

In a fourteenth-century manuscript entitled *The Book of Taliesin* is a story, the *History* or *Tale of Taliesin*, which may date to as early as the ninth century.[36] In this, Taliesin, the future court bard of Powys and then of Rheged, is born to someone described as a witch living where Bala Lake now lies in north Wales. Thanks to his mother's cauldron and a brew giving inspiration and knowledge to the person tasting it, Taliesin grew up as a wonder child and a seer. He was fostered by Gwyddno, a king with a court just south of the Dyfi, whose son 'Elphin', Elffin, gave him his name after exclaiming *Dyma dâl iesin*, 'What a beautiful forehead!' to which the three-day-old child replied, *Taliesin bid*, 'Let it be Taliesin!' The name is made up from *tâl*, forehead, and *iesin*, radiant, giving us radiant brow.[37]

Here then we encounter the Gwyddno of the genealogies, son of the murdered Clydno, still apparently ruling over Meirionydd, though undoubtedly now only by favour and courtesy of his great uncle, Maelgwn Gwynedd. Elffin, *Alpinus*, was invited to Maelgwn's Christmas court. In the tale Maelgwn is described as Elffin's uncle, though more accurately he was his great, great uncle. Throughout the story Elffin appears as a

35_ Gildas, *De Excidio Britanniae*, Ch. 31, Giles, 1841, p. 27.

36_ Haycock, 2007, p. 1, cf. Jarman, 1981, pp. 21 and 101–5. The *Tale of Taliesin*, a late version in the *Mabinogion* [Iolo Morgannwg's copy!], in an English translation, Guest, 1877, pp. 471–94.

37_ Haycock, 2007, p. 125.

mere youth, though old enough as we are later shown to be newly married and still very impressed by his new wife. If Gwyddno had Elffin when he was in his late teens, then this allows for Gwyddno to have been about a year old when Maelgwn murdered Clydno his father, which is what we suspected. Now, here was Elffin, at the court of the man whom he knew had killed his grandfather. This man was not only his great, great uncle, but he was also one of the most important and powerful rulers in Britain. Now, Elffin was required to join in the praise of Maelgwn: 'Is there in the whole world a king so great as Maelgwn, or one on whom Heaven has bestowed so many spiritual gifts as upon him? First, form and beauty, and meekness, and strength, besides all the powers of the soul!' It is implied that Elffin refused, and because of Elffin's boasting about his own court, he was thrown into prison.

We are here talking about homage due at a Christmas court, and a refusal to perform this by a youth more than conscious of his family's history. The medieval references are obvious, though this does not automatically undermine what we are being told. In the Middle Ages, kings often sent their sons to do homage for lands they held of other sovereigns, in this way avoiding themselves having to 'bend the knee', and thereby saving their pride. English kings often dealt with the problem of homage due to the French kings for their continental possessions in this way. So, pushing the story to its limits, we can envisage Gwyddno sending his son to the Christmas court of Maelgwn in Degannwy precisely for this purpose. Humiliated in some way, the act already one Elffin found repugnant, when it came to the point he refused and was thrown in prison.

It was now that Taliesin, aged thirteen, arrived in Degannwy, intervening like some guardian angel. Here, Taliesin beat Maelgwn's bards in competition by composing an epic poem in twenty minutes, and managing to frustrate a horse race which he was supposed to lose. As a result, Maelgwn deprived him of the lands given him by *Gwyddnyw*, Gwyddno, whom Iolo places in Arllechwedd west of the Conwy rather than Ceredigion.[38] Taliesin retaliated by cursing the king, or at least he prophesied his death, leaving Degannwy, and moving to the court of Brochwel *Ysgythrog*, Long in the Tooth, king of Powys, arguably Maelgwn's western rival. At one period, he was brother-in-law to Maelgwn because the notorious Sanan was Brochwel's sister. The dating is acceptable as Brochwel probably ruled Powys from the 490s into the 550s. Taliesin also served under his son, Cynan *Garwyn*, Cynan of the White Chariot, who was the subject of what is probably the oldest Welsh poem we have and one which is thought to be genuinely the work of Taliesin.[39]

MAELGWN'S DEATH: THE DATE

Taliesin's curse or prophesy was to have dreadful consequences.

AC: an. (547) *Mortalitas magna, in qua pausat Mailcun rex Guenedotae.*
A great [mortality] pestilence in which dies Maelgwn, King of Gwynedd.[40]

Simply on grounds that the opening phrase is identical to the more reliable AU entry for 548=549, *Mortalitas magna in qua isti pausant*, which then lists several names, it has been suggested that the Welsh copyist had no right or cause to alter it by adding Maelgwn's name, and that because of this the entry is suspect. It *is* suspect, merely on the grounds that it is our *only* source and that, uncorroborated, we cannot use it as *fact*. We are back to the flimsiness of *all* our evidence for this period and the obvious point that if we want to attempt to reconstruct a possible history for these years, every hint or scrap of evidence has to be considered, but *always* with the understanding that we will only end up with constructs, models, for the likely pattern of events. Reading some

38_ Williams, 1848, pp. 466–7; Jarman, 1981, pp. 22–3 and 104–7.

39_ The 'contested "core" of the Book of Taliesin ... requires renewed, detailed comparative work on its language, metrics and diction before a judgement can be passed with any real confidence' – Haycock, 2007, p. 6.

40_ AC, Wade-Evans, 1938, p. 87.

writers dissecting this sort of material, one encounters the unstated, unexamined, inherent belief that there *are* some things that can be absolutely asserted and that, one day, we will have enough to write the history. That day will never come.

As for the date, if the Welsh copyist was simply taking his entry from AU, blindly inserting a name that had to go somewhere, why did he go so far as to change the date from AU's 549 to 547? As all comment, AC's dates are badly out in this early period, but here we may actually have a specific record, a correct date. After the first appearance of the plague in 545, by 549 we have *two* plagues raging, one bubonic and the other the yellow plague or relapsing fever. Both could have been appearing in 547. Indeed, if the 545 date is accepted for the first outbreak in the British Isles, they would almost certainly have been widespread by 547. Maelgwn was one of the most important figures of early Britain, and so the copyist, putting together what we call *Annales Cambriae*, AC, the Welsh Annals, decided to include Maelgwn's death and, almost certainly because of what he knew or believed, claimed that Maelgwn died in the great pestilence. AU, the *Annals of Ulster*, chose to record this outbreak at 549 because of the important people in Ireland who succumbed to disease that year.

MAELGWN'S DEATH: PLAGUE OR FEVER?

Later generations, surprisingly given the sheer drama and scale of Justinian's bubonic outbreak, decided that Maelgwn died of the yellow plague rather than of the bubonic plague. Whichever it was, the weather was still poor. Gregory of Tours in his chronicle for these years describes a particularly bad winter that looks to be that of 547/8.

That year the winter weather was harsh and more bitter than usual. The mountain torrents were frozen solid and people walked across them as if they were dry ground.

The snow lay deep and the birds were numbed with cold and famished with hunger, so that they could be taken by hand without any need for snares.[41]

Iolo Morganwg, basing what he wrote largely on the *Tale of Taliesin*, gives us what has become the traditional and, given that Maelgwn was one of the greatest rulers in Britain in the mid-sixth century, the extraordinary story of his death.

He [Taliesin] pronounced his curse on Maelgwn, and all his possessions: whereupon the Vad Velen [*y fâd felen*, the yellow plague] came to Rhos; and whoever witnessed it, became doomed to certain death.

Maelgwn saw the Vad Velen, through the key-hole in Rhos church, and died in consequence.[42]

Had Iolo, or if he had copied this from another source, had that writer read his Procopius on the bubonic plague and added the description there to the record that Maelgwn died of the yellow plague?

For there ensued with some a deep coma, with others a violent delirium, and in either case they suffered the characteristic symptoms of the disease ... But those who were seized with delirium suffered from insomnia and were victims of a distorted imagination; for they suspected that men were coming upon them to destroy them, and they would become excited and rush off in flight, crying out at the top of their voices. And those who were attending them were in a state of constant exhaustion and had a most difficult time of it throughout ... For when the patients fell from their beds and lay rolling upon the floor, they kept putting them back in place, and when they were struggling to rush headlong out of their houses, they would force them back by shoving and pulling against them. And when water chanced to be near, they wished to fall into it, not so much because of a desire for drink (for the most of them rushed into the sea), but the cause

41_ Gregory of Tours, *The History of the Franks*, Book III, Ch. 37, Thorpe, 1974, p. 193.

42_ Williams, 1848, p. 467.

was to be found chiefly in the diseased state of their minds ... And many ... threw themselves down from a height.[43]

But this is a description of the bubonic plague, not of the yellow fever called the yellow plague. In the late Mabinogion version of *Hanes Taliesin*, the History of Taliesin, what carried off Maelgwn is undoubtedly thought of as the yellow plague.

THE RHIONYDD CURSE

When Taliesin was at Maelgwn's Christmas court in Degannwy he mocked Maelgwn's bards. The sea marsh of *Rhianedd*, or rather, as it should be, *Rhionydd*, is the flat promontory on the Creuddyn peninsula, linking the Great Orme headland which projects into the Irish Sea with the higher land at the peninsula's start. Today it is covered by the seaside resort of Llandudno, but during the Roman period and for centuries after it was a marsh flooded by the sea at high tide. *Rhianedd* is either someone's name or it means the Ladies' or Maidens' Marsh. Given the proximity of the two royal capitals at Degannwy and Rhos, one might guess that the meaning here was the Queens' Marsh. However, it is almost certain that *Rhianedd* is a corruption of *Rhionydd*, earlier *Ryoned*. Just like the original name for Stranraer in Scotland which was, in Latin, *Rerigonium*, coming from the British *ro-rigonio*, it means 'a very royal place'. If the prefix *pen* was added, as was the case when the Welsh referred to *Rerigonium* in the north as *Pen-Ryoned* or *Penrhyn Rhionydd*, it could refer to this very royal place being at the head, top, or end of something. In Stranraer's case this was Loch Ryan. In the case of the sea marsh referred to in the 'Taliesin' poem below, it would refer to the marsh at the end of the Creuddyn peninsula where Llandudno now stands. In both cases, however, *pen* could mean chief, supreme, or even the *very* royal place as in the translation given by Rivet

43_ Procopius, *History of the* [Persian] *Wars*, Book II, Ch. XXII, Dewing, 1914–28, Vol. I, 1914, pp. 459–61.

and Smith for *ro*.[44] We can now listen to 'Taliesin' pronouncing his curse. The passage comes from Iolo Morganwg's copy of the *Mabinogion*.

I am Taliesin,
Chief of the bards of the west ...
Be silent then ye unlucky rhyming bards,
For you cannot judge between truth and falsehood.
    If you be primary bards formed by heaven,
Tell your king what his fate will be.
It is I who am a diviner and a leading bard ...
And will tell your king what will befall him.
    A most strange creature will come
From the sea marsh of Rhianedd [i.e. Rhionydd],
As a punishment of iniquity,
On Maelgwn Gwynedd;
    His hair, his teeth.
And his eyes being as gold;
And this will bring destruction
Upon Maelgwn Gwynedd; ...
    The strong creature from before the flood,
Without flesh, without bone,
Without vein, without feet ...
    It will cause consternation
Wherever God willeth.
On sea and on land,
It neither sees, nor is seen.
Its course is devious ...
    It is not confined,
It is incomparable ...
It is extremely injurious.
It is concealed ...
    It is yonder, it is here
It will discompose,
But it will not repair the injury ...
One Being has prepared it,
Out of all creatures,
By a tremendous blast,
To wreak vengeance
On Maelgwn Gwynedd.[45]

44_ Rivet and Smith, 1979, p. 447.

45_ Transl. Guest, 1877, pp. 483-7, at pp. 485-7.

Top: The Sea Marsh
of Rhionydd seen from
Degannwy.

Bottom: Llandrillo's 'cell',
or protection for a spring
in time of uncertain
climatic conditions?

Inside Llandrillo's cell, the
well under the modern
altar clearly visible.

Many deplore the activities of Iolo Morganwg. It is difficult to avoid the conclusion that, in Maelgwn's case, the person with most to answer for is the cleric Gildas who has been responsible for all the attacks on this Gwynedd king, even down to this prediction where his death is interpreted as divine retribution. Gildas can get away with it, however, because *all* deaths at this time were seen as God's retribution on a disobedient and sinful world.

Another version of AC, used by Mommsen in his 1892 edition, as well as giving the great mortality notice of Maelgwn's death, adds the following.

Thus they say 'The long sleep of Maelgwn in the court of Rhos'. Then was the yellow plague.[46]

There is a late tradition that Maelgwn was buried on *Ynys Lannog*, the later *Ynys Seiriol, Priestholm*, or Puffin Island off Anglesey, probably based on no more than the isolation and beauty of the site. The reality seems to be more prosaic as indicated in this AC reference: that he would have been buried in the church and royal mausoleum in his capital at Degannwy, that is, in Llanrhos.

So what was the cause of death? Maelgwn could have been one of the twenty-five million and more in the western world who died of Justinian's plague, the bubonic plague.[47] Instead, he might have succumbed to the closely-related yellow fever just as the traditions assert. Whichever it was, for Maelgwn as for countless others, it was, indeed, the end of the world.

[46] AC, 547, Morris, 1980, p. 45.

[47] Rosen, 2007, pp. 3, 209–10 and 261.

CHAPTER TEN

ALL MEN SHALL COME AND TAKE COUNSEL

The Gwynedd Confederation after Maelgwn, 547–664

MAELGWN – DYNASTIC INNOVATOR

Could Maelgwn be compared to the emperor Diocletian, or if that seems too extreme, at least to Muirchertach Mac Erca, the northern Uí Néill over-king of the Uí Néill confederation in Ireland, 520–34? Not only to him, but to those kings in Greater Rheged, the Rheged confederation, such as *Marcianus*, Meirchion, in the early years of Maelgwn's rule, and then his son Elidir the Stout and Handsome, his brother Cynfarch, leader of the *Cynferchyn* warband, their second cousins Gwallog, ruler of Elmet, modern Welsh Elfed, Pabo Pillar of Britain, king of the Pennines, and Eliffer of the Great Retinue? In other words, did Maelgwn reveal himself to be a dynastic innovator: someone who had a clear idea of how the dynasty could continue to rule strong and united despite the growing claims of an ever-widening family?

The question has to be asked because, despite Maelgwn apparently butchering and murdering his way to the top, scandalizing the church with his shameless use of ecclesiastical law and monasticism, and involving himself in adultery and trickery, how was it that on his death the throne passed *not* to his son Rhun but to Einion *Frenin*? This king Einion, who had been ruling Llŷn as his apanage, was in all probability *not* the son of Owain of Rhos, as Dr Miller thought possible, but was his grandson, son of the *Cuneglassus*, Cynlas, so reviled by Gildas.[1] Any other possibility does violence to the dating as we can calculate it and to the story as we have seen it emerge. Rhun's strange position, the son of Britain's most powerful king yet not succeeding, no doubt gave rise to later talk that the boy was illegitimate.

[1]_ Miller, *Saints*, 1979, pp. 109–10 and 111, Table III. Not all Dr Miller's suggestions have been followed but in places they have been pushed even further.

As Dr Bromwich remarked, such a consideration would not have been important at the time.[2]

EINION, *c.*547–66: GWYNEDD'S DARK AGE

Einion's reign, *c.*547–66, these dates for the most part a guess, must have been an extraordinarily depressed period in both Ireland and Wales. It is not surprising that for these years religious matters, the founding of monasteries, the lives of their founders, and the deliberations of councils against heresy fill the pages of the annals. Then, in 554, news broke announcing that the world had not been scourged enough.

AU 553=554. A pestilence called *sámthrosc.*

This appears with a gloss written in another hand: 'i.e. leprosy'.[3] Our record for Welsh affairs at this time is so thin that its absence from AC is meaningless. The sickness would have raged on both sides of the Irish Sea. Despite the gloss, this was smallpox, which until the twentieth century when it was for the most part eradicated, was a highly contagious and fatal disease, the main symptoms being, yet again, fever and pustules. If the sufferer survived, the lasting effect was scars on the skin where the pustules had erupted. The Irish word for these is *clamtrusg: sámthrosc*, its supposed Irish name, was probably a copyist's error.[4]

For an exhausted, and in many sections of society, a dispirited people, this epidemic must have seemed like a last straw. But worse was to come for, just as in 545 and especially 549, death on a massive scale disrupted agriculture and the distribution of food so that famine followed, and in the steps of famine came yet more disease. The yellow plague, in all probability never having left, was now raging with a vengeance. Despite its awful impact the line in AU is in an additional hand. The two similar names are given.

2_ Bromwich, 1961, p. 502.

3_ AU, 553=554, Mac Airt and Mac Niocaill, 1983, p. 79.

4_ MacArthur, 1949, pp. 183–4 and 186–7.

555=556. *Mortalitas magna hoc anno, .i. in Chron Chonaill, .i. in Bhuide Chonaill.*[5]

A great mortality this year, [and attempting to translate the words] i.e. the saffron or dark-yellow ?result: the yellow ?result.[6]

For a great number of years, it would have felt to those living through these terrible times that the end had indeed come, and just as it had been prophesied and preached. More monasteries were established: in Ireland in *c.*550 Coemgen or Kevin founded the famous Glendalough; Lasrén, or *Mo-Laisse* as he was known, founded Devenish on Lough Erne; probably in 557 Colman founded Bangor on Belfast Lough, its name once more echoing the expected transitory nature of these moves. In 558 Brendan established Clonfert, and in 565 Colum *Cille* founded Iona. On the night of 1 August 551 in China, small meteors were seen gliding along intersecting paths from all directions. They were 'extremely numerous and beyond reckoning'.[7] This was the time of anchorites and hermits. There was now a *peregrini* movement in which monks set out to sea, sometimes without even oars or sails, in order to seek 'deserts in the ocean', watery equivalents of the desert retreats sought out by early Christian hermits.

And, of course, no one would have been disappointed in their expectations: the end of the world comes to us all. Much later, the record would be gradually adjusted, dates shifted, and some of what was then said conveniently forgotten. However, as Christopher Hitchens has recently reminded us, religion never ceases to proclaim the Apocalypse and the Day of Judgement, and just as in our own day when dates are still being set for this event, afterwards people experience a sense of anti-climax, disappointment, and even betrayal.[8]

5_ AU, 555=556, Mac Airt and Mac Niocaill, 1983, p. 78.

6_ AU, Hennessy, 1887, Vol. I, p. 54, note 5.

7_ Hetherington, 1996, quoting Zhuang Tian-shan, Chinese Astronomy, 1, 1977 pp. 197–220. Also Miller, *Saints*, 1979, pp. 109–10.

8_ Hitchens, 2007, pp. 56–61. His comments on the connection between 'the sinister, spoiled, selfish childhood of our species' and 'the repressed desire to see everything smashed up and ruined and brought to nought' are well worth reading by anyone interested in end of the world scenarios.

It is also interesting to see how in these years of crisis, Pelagianism reared its head once more. This view of Christianity largely rejected Augustine's view of humankind as totally depraved and completely dependent on the grace of God for salvation. Britain turned again, as it had in the years after 410 when it was told it had to shift for itself in government and defence matters, to the views of Pelagius, the Irish radical who emphasized man's responsibility for his life and salvation through his own efforts. This form of moral rearmament had been seen as a direct challenge to both Christianity and the church. It had been savagely opposed when it first appeared and it was again now. Neither should we be surprised that one of its greatest opponents at this time was David who had founded his monastery in south Wales with all its savage austerities at the height of the apocalyptic fervour.

Interestingly, these years see the emergence of Irish and Welsh literature, poetry, chroniclers, people who, in effect, were journalists, and political essayists. In the dark days of repression and intolerance under the Russian Tsars in the late nineteenth century, we see just such a flowering: an expression of creativity denied any other outlet. Here, centuries earlier, the sheer awfulness of the physical and intellectual climate was producing the same results. A thirteenth-century poem expresses this well, its sentiments doubly applicable in the dark days of plague.

Should poetry be suppressed, men;
if there is to be no historic lore, no ancient laws –
save the name of each man's father –
none will be heard of ...

In the words of Edmund Spenser, no one, least of all someone who was a king, wants to 'die in obscure oblivion'.[9]

[9]_ Williams, 1971, pp. 4–5, and p. 4, note 4.

RHUN AND THE EXCLUSION OF THE MEIRIONYDD LINE

At some date, possibly in the mid-560s, quite simply a guess, Einion's reign as over-king of the Gwynedd confederation ended. In the Jesus College MS 20, probably based on a pre-1200 source, *Ewein* appears between Cynlas and the name appearing as Cynlas's son in the other pedigrees, namely Meic or Maig, and this is the position for Einion that has been followed here. However, Maig may have been Einion's *younger* son, who did apparently go on to establish the separate line in Rhos which eventually furnished a king of Gwynedd in the person of Caradog ap Meirchion, 754–98. More controversially, it might be that Einion's *eldest* son was the Beli who eventually became king of Gwynedd in *c.*580, but not until then, making Einion the ancestor of its later kings, Iago, *c.*597–616, Cadfan, 616–25, Cadwallon, 625–35, and Cadwaladr, 656–64.

It appears that Maelgwn's plan for the future dynastic map of Gwynedd was followed up to the time of Beli's death in *c.*597. At least this is true for the descendants of two of the three original usurpers, Owain of Rhos east of the Conwy and Cadwallon of *Arfon* and *Môn* west of the Conwy. This is because it looks as though the over-king following Einion was Maelgwn's son Rhun, and following him Beli son of Einion. But it would seem that there was a determined effort to exclude the descendants of Cadwaladr who kept what in the earlier days was the most powerful part of this north Wales area, Meirionydd, *Gwynedd Maritima*, which seems to have been largely responsible for the naval side of the war against the Irish. The repercussions of this exploded in the reign of Rhun, Maelgwn's son, *c.*566–80. If he had been born in the year when Maelgwn took kingship in 517, presumably as a result of the marriage to Sanan of Powys, rather than a liaison with Gwenllian the daughter of Afallach, then Rhun would still only have been forty-eight years old when he took the throne.

Rhun is supposed to have married Perweur, suspiciously daughter of another Rhun, Rhun *Rhyfeddfawr*, Rhun of Great Wealth, which, if this really is an epithet or nickname, should surely be rendered as Rhun the Loaded! By Perweur, he supposedly had Beli and a daughter Tymyr who was eventually married to Hywel of Brittany. Again, we have to be careful. So much of this material was put together in the ninth century when one of the aims of the compilers in the British renaissance of this century was to establish links between Gwynedd and the heroic north of the past. If, as most believe, the Rhun intended was Rhun son of Urien *Rheged*, who was killed in *c.*592, on dating grounds alone such a marriage is highly unlikely. Suffice it to say, that Rhun's father-in-law was more probably someone from Wales. Beli was certainly his son.

Maelgwn had been a physically big man, certainly he was tall as his nickname *hir* testifies and so, apparently, was his son Rhun. He makes an appearance in the Mabinogion's *Dream of Rhonabwy*.

A big curly-headed auburn man [that is, with reddish-brown hair] ... Rhun son of Maelgwn Gwynedd, a man whose authority is such that all men shall come and take counsel of him.[10]

In one of the triads he is described as one of the Three Fair Princes of the Island of Britain.[11]

In *Hanes Taliesin*, however, the picture is expanded somewhat and not entirely in Rhun's favour.

Now Rhun was the most graceless man in the world, and there was neither wife nor maiden with whom he held converse, but was evil spoken of [him, or both, as a result].[12]

Gildas would no doubt have commented, 'like father, like son!' In this tale, whilst in Degannwy Meirionydd's Elffin had boasted of his wife's virtue, part and parcel of his refusal to bow the knee to Maelgwn. As a result he

10_ The Mabinogion, 'The Dream of Rhonabwy', Jones and Jones, 1973, pp. 150–1.

11_ Trioedd Ynys Prydein, Bromwich, 1961, p. 7, No. 3.

12_ Tale of Taliesin, Guest, 1877, p. 478.

had ended up in Maelgwn's prison. Rhun could not then get to Elffin's court in Ceredigion quickly enough in order to expose the weaknesses of Elffin's wife. When he arrived in Ceredigion, he was 'received with joy, *for all the servants knew him plainly*' – he was, in other words, one of the lads. Here, by getting her drunk he put to sleep Elffin's maid, mistaking her for Elffin's wife, and, when she was out cold, cut off her little finger which had on it Elffin's ring. On the Meirionydd side, the whole masquerade was designed from the outset to fool him. For Rhun, the aim was to expose Elffin's wife, her intemperance, and Elffin's idle boast. When Rhun returned to the court in Degannwy, however, Elffin pointed out that the finger was clearly that of a servant.

Rhun was ruler in a period when restraints on power, though not absent, could be very limited. Where this tale is important, possibly, is in what it tells us about the relations between Maelgwn and Elffin. Late as it is, the story would seem to be based on the political realities of sixth-century Gwynedd. Gwyddno in the *Tale of Taliesin* is clearly the son of Clydno of Meirionydd whom Maelgwn had had murdered in *c.*517 and whose wife, Sanan of Powys, he had then married. The story claims that Taliesin the future bard was brought up or fostered by Gwyddno. It also says that Gwyddno's court was near the shore between the Dyfi and Aberystwyth. Of course, this could come from the confusion between Gwyddno of Meirionydd and the legendary Gwyddno of the Drowned Lands in Cardigan Bay, lord of *Cantref Gwaelod*, the lost or bottom *cantref*.[13] However, at this date there is nothing implausible in Meirionydd's kings exercising lordship over territory to the south of the Dyfi, certainly over the area known as Genau'r Glyn. Here, one site for Gwyddno's court could be Llanfihangel Genau'r Glyn, or Llandre, where today there is a Norman motte and nearby an Iron Age fort. Seven miles to the southeast of Aberystwyth and only just over eight miles to the south of Llandre, as this chapter was in its final stages of composition, an imposing fourth century Roman villa was being unearthed at Aber Magwr. The

13_ Ibid., pp. 397–400, at p. 400.

314

academics involved have stated that the discovery is raising significant new questions about a Roman villa so far north and west. Good indeed, then, to see archaeologists at last beginning to question assumptions that have been based merely on the scanty evidence provided by their own occupation. History, such as is being attempted here, could have raised these questions years ago.

Hanes Taliesin would seem to be saying that when Maelgwn demanded the homage of Meirionydd, Gwyddno sent his son Elffin, who certainly appears as a young man in the tale. As we have seen, in the Middle Ages kings often sent their sons to perform homage due from them for lands held of other rulers, though this is possibly not what Gwyddno intended on this occasion. Elffin hardly makes an appearance in the pedigrees and the Elffin who *is* there is the son or grandson of Urien *Rheged* in the north. The family is also confused with a line in Strathclyde. Here, descending from Dyfnwal *Hen* or Donald I and through his son Garmonion or Germanianus, we have Cawrdaf and then his son Gwyddno, who is the one correctly called *Garanhir*, Tall Heron, often appearing as Long-shanks, or *Goron aur*, Gold-crown. He was of the same family and in the same generation as Rhydderch *Hen*, the person clearly acting as the overlord of the Strathclyde confederation.

In *Hanes Taliesin*, Maelgwn was angry with Elffin 'for so strongly withstanding him'. This was the Christmas feast in Degannwy. It was probably already common for kings to hold three crown-wearing courts a year, at the great religious feasts of Easter, Whit, and Christmas. Here, ambassadors would be received, homage given and taken, and great matters of state dealt with in the company of the leading landholders. As the centuries passed, this business came increasingly under the jurisdiction of the church, making its penalties also available for any breaking of the agreements entered into. So, the tale tells us, 'the bards and the heralds came to cry largess, and to proclaim the power of the king and his strength'. Elffin had been summoned, and had refused to render his father's homage. In other words, Gwyddno, knowing that Maelgwn had had a hand in his father's death, was claiming equality with Maelgwn in contravention of the fundamental agreement that bound the federation together. Talk of a silver chain about his feet might indicate an honourable confinement, but for refusing to bow the knee he was, nevertheless, confined. When he exposes the trickery of Rhun concerning his wife, he is committed again. Taliesin comes or is summoned from Meirionydd and somehow – the story tells of a terrible wind that scared the court near to death – managed to get Elffin released a second time. Nevertheless, in the end, Taliesin fled to Powys. Did Elffin return to prison?

Staying with the guess that Rhun took the overlordship of the Gwynedd confederation in *c.*566, one might expect a challenge to this from Meirionydd. If Maelgwn had established the confederation on the understanding that this would pass between the *three* main branches of the dynasty that had seized power in *c.*485 with the assassination of Anianus the Anvil, it was becoming clear that this was being disregarded and that the descendants of Cadwaladr were being sidelined and humiliated. In *Hanes Taliesin* the Elffin story more than hints that this dispute was there from the earliest days, with Gwyddno showing extreme reluctance to bow the knee and possibly demanding some recompense for Clydno's death.

NINTH-CENTURY COMPLICATIONS/INVENTIONS

The Chirk codex version of the Welsh laws dated to *c.*1200 contains the following strange story.

Elidir Mwynfawr, a man of the North, was slain here (i.e. in Gwynedd), and after this death the Men of the North came here to avenge him. The men who came after their leaders were Clydno Eiddyn and Nudd Hael son of Senyllt, and Mordaf Hael son of Serwa(n), and Rhydderch Hael son of Tudawal Tudglyd. And they came to Arfon, and because Elidir was slain at Aber Meuhedus in Arfon, they burned Arfon as a further revenge.

And then Rhun son of Maelgwn and the men of Gwynedd with him, rose up in arms, and came to the bank of the Gwerydd in the North, and there they were long disputing who should take the lead through the river Gwerydd.

And Rhun dispatched a messenger to Gwynedd to ascertain who were entitled to lead. Some say that Maeldaf the Elder the lord of Penardd adjudged it to the men of Arfon: (I)orwerth son of Madawg on the authority of the story affirms that it was [?instead from or as a result of] Idno Hen [?that it was given] to the [men of Arfon, the] men of the black-headed shafts.

And thereupon the men of Arfon went in the van, and were good there.

And Taliesin sang:
"I heard the clash of their blades,
With Rhun in the rush of armies,
The men of Arfon of red spears".[14]

By the time this version of the Welsh laws of Hywel *Dda* was produced in Gwynedd in about 1200, purely Welsh events had been mixed up with stories from what is called the heroic period of northern history before the states there collapsed in the face of the English advance and the growth of Northumbria. This was the legacy of the ninth-century Welsh renaissance associated particularly with the reign of Rhodri *Mawr*, Rhodri the Great, 844–78. One such erroneous linkage was the alleged marriage of Eurgain, Maelgwn's daughter, into the dynasty of Strathclyde. Her husband was supposedly Elidir *Mwynfawr*, Elidir the Wealthy. He was a son of Gwrwst *Briodor*, the Landholder, who was a son of Dyfnwal *Hen*/Donald I, the real founder of the dynasty of Greater Strathclyde. In terms of the dates, this was plausible enough.

However, the result was an extraordinary saga, which Professor J. E. Lloyd expressed his doubts over in

14_ Bromwich, 1961, pp. 501–2.

1910, but which Dr. John Morris in 1973 accepted in its entirety, making much of it in his history.[15] As the law text shows, this involved an invasion of Rhun's Gwynedd by his brother-in-law Elidir. In other words, Rhun's position as overlord of the Gwynedd confederation was being challenged by his sister and Elidir. The invasion force inevitably came by sea and, if the identification is correct, landed not far from Clynnog Fawr west of Caernarfon at *Aber Wefus*; see the *Meuhedus* or *Meweddus* in the above quotation. Lloyd noted that this brook, the Wefus, 'runs into the Desach from Bron-yr-Erw' so that the landing place was Aberdesach.[16] An alternative identification with the Cadnant, a stream which flows into the Menai near Caernarfon, put forward by Aneurin Owen, seems to be based on nothing more than the fact that there was a place nearby known as Elidir['s] bank, probably derived not from Elidir but from a Welsh version of steep hill.[17]

Dr Bromwich drew attention to a story concerning Elidir in Geoffrey of Monmouth's *History* which may reflect the northern context of Elidir's history. Here, Elidir, *Elidurus Pius*, Elidurus the Dutiful, replaces his deposed elder brother *Arthgallo*, Archgallo in Thorpe's translation, who had been ruling badly. After five years Arthgallo returns and, being found in a pitiful state in *Coed Celyddon*, the Caledonian Forest, by his brother the king, he is taken to *Alcud*, Dumbarton, Strathclyde's most important capital on the Clyde. Here Elidir the Dutiful forces his followers to restore Arthgallo whom he crowns himself, though supposedly in York. On Arthgallo's death after ten years of good rule, Elidurus became king once more, only to be deposed and imprisoned in London by his younger brothers Ingenius and Peredurus. On their death, he becomes king for a third time.[18] Despite Geoffrey's determination to extend the geographical area to fit his story of the kings of Britain, it seems that there is here a traditional tale about divisions within the Strathclyde confederation resulting in depositions and restorations. But in the

15_ Lloyd, 1912, Vol. I, pp. 168–9; Morris, 1973, pp. 216–18 and 192. For the story's rejection, see Miller, *Saints*, 1979, pp. 81, 105–7, and 110, and earlier Williams and Williams, 1968.

16_ Lloyd, 1912, Vol. I, p. 168, note 28.

17_ Bromwich, 1961, p. 344.

18_ Geoffrey of Monmouth, *The History of the Kings of Britain*, III. 17–18, Thorpe, 1966, pp. 103–4; Bromwich, 1961, p. 344.

Gwynedd story, we are told the death of Elidir was not the end of matters.

In response to Elidir's death during his invasion of Gwynedd, Rhydderch king of Strathclyde, who was a relative of Elidir through descent from Donald I, along with other northern allies, sailed south to Gwynedd bent on revenge. Arfon was burnt and, satisfied, the invaders sailed back home. In turn, Rhun marched to the Forth with a vast army and because the men of Arfon in Gwynedd excelled in fighting at a ford on a northern river, the men of this area of Gwynedd had certain privileges dating from the time of Hywel's laws and later. Again, this was a good story for a winter's night, but can we be sure that this is all it was, a story?

The tale owed much to a mix-up, highlighted by Dr Molly Miller in 1979.[19] Because stories were current that Clydno, *or his successors*, had invaded Gwynedd, this Clydno of Meirionydd was deliberately changed into Clydno *Eiddyn* or *Eidin* of Greater Rheged. This is Clydno of Edinburgh, who was the son of Cynwyd, leader of a war-band called the *Cynwydion*. Cynwyd was of the same generation as Urien *Rheged*. With him now thought of as the Clydno from Rheged, Meirionydd's invasion of Gwynedd is turned into one mainly from Strathclyde, which of course is where Elidir the Wealthy, the man they were supposed to be avenging, came from.

Apart from Clydno, the other three named, all Strathclyde men, were Nudd *Hael*, Mordaf *Hael*, and the over-king Rhydderch *Hael*, who appear in some pedigrees as cousins, respectively the sons of Senyllt, Tudwal, and Serwan, who were the sons of Cedig the son of Donald I. Instead, Tudwal seems to have been the son of Clydno, Cedig's brother. They then appear together in the triads as 'Three Generous [Hael] Men of the Island of Britain'.[20]

We can push what Dr Miller wrote a little further. We cannot entirely rule out an invasion of Gwynedd by Clydno, now Clydno of Meirionydd. This would give us another reason why he was murdered on the orders of

19_ Miller, *Saints*, 1979, pp. 107–10.

20_ Bromwich, 1961, p. 5, No. 2.

Maelgwn. If so, this would place these historical events back in *c.*517. However, a more plausible setting is the opening part of Rhun's reign. The supposed marriage of Eurgain, Rhun's sister, to Elidir, possibly represents her opposition to her brother's accession as over-king of the Gwynedd confederation. The story given us in the Welsh laws is clear: Rhun was ruling at the time.

566/7 GWYDDNO OF MEIRIONYDD INVADES GWYNEDD

Gwyddno would have known that if Rhun's accession went unopposed, then Meirionydd would for the foreseeable future and probably for all time be excluded from the high-kingship. If the story in the *Book of Taliesin* can be treated as evidence, then the tension would have been building for some years. Einion of Gwynedd represented the Rhos line, but he died in *c.*560. It should have been the turn of the Meirionydd line at last. Of course, this is guesswork, but it fits the few scraps of evidence we have. Did Gwyddno lead the invasion? Was his son Elffin still alive after his clash with Maelgwn, or could this invasion have been, in part, to avenge his likely fate? Had Meirionydd been pacified by promises from Einion? Was Rhun's accession, in fact, a usurpation, a repudiation of understandings reached earlier, to be compared, say, to the usurpation of Constantine I in York in 306 when Diocletian's system of inheritance was overthrown? Is that why Eurgain opposed her brother? Had Rhun eliminated Elffin as part of his coup?

We know that an invasion of Gwynedd did occur. We will come to that evidence shortly. If it was one from Meirionydd, it would have demonstrated that its naval power, seen in the days of Gwyddno's grandfather Gwrin, was still to be reckoned with. Deciding on such a radical course, the invasion *had* to succeed. If it did not, then Meirionydd's power would be broken for who knew how many generations.

One of the *Trioedd y Meirch*, the Triads of the Horses, a distinct group within the triads, drawn from many sources and showing considerable alteration, adaptation, and confusion, deals with these supposed events. In *Three Horses who carried the Three Horse-Burdens* we have the following:

Black Moro, horse of Elidir Mwynfawr, who carried on his back seven and a half people from Penllech in the North to Penllech [Benllech] in Môn [Anglesey].
  These were the seven people:
Elidir Mwynfawr, and
Eurgain his wife, daughter of Maelgwn Gwynedd, and
Gwyn Good Companion,
and Gwyn Good Distributor,
and Mynach Naomon his counsellor,
and Prydelaw the Cupbearer, his butler,
and Silver Staff his servant, and Gelbeinevin his cook,
who swam with his two hands to the horse's crupper –
and that was the half-person.[21]

We can discard the inclusion of Elidir and Eurgain, but does the rest of this triad show a household on the move? Did the whole of Gwyddno's court as well as his army disembark on the east coast of Anglesey at Benllech or rather just a mile or so to the south where the great sands of Red Wharf Bay afforded an easy landing for both men and horses? A brave, even in places a funny, sight, as they struggled ashore, the troops, their commanders, the king's companions, his chancellor, his counsellors, his cup-bearer the butler, his household staff, even the *gilla*, Benevin, his Irish cook.[22] As for the evidence confirming that an invasion *did* take place, this consists of two lines in a praise-poem, a panegyric, though not to Gwyddno or to Rhun. We will look at this in detail later. *Two lines*, but what they refer to must have been a matter of the world or nothing, life or death, glory or oblivion, for those participating.

21_ Ibid., p. 109, No. 44.

22_ Ibid., p. 355.

Battle in Anglesey – great and fair – renowned the praise:
An expedition beyond Menai – the rest was easy …

Two obstacles, the local opposition in Anglesey itself, and then the Menai Strait, had to be overcome. To have gone immediately into Arfon might possibly have been thought too risky. A 'battle in Anglesey' won, and the island would be theirs. At the right time of the year, in early autumn, there would have been food enough to feed an army. The local lords then pacified and rewarded for abandoning their loyalty to Rhun, Gwyddno would have been in a position to cross the strait. The fleet would have sailed again: 'an expedition beyond Menai'. The landing sites on the mainland suggest that embarkation was now on the west coast of Anglesey – Aberffraw must have fallen under their control – to cross at the western end of the Menai Strait and land at Aberdesach and possibly, though we are not told this, at Pontlyfni or Aberllyfni, just over three-quarters of a mile further up the coast. 'The rest was easy.' But it shouldn't have been. Was Rhun showing himself to be, as our only real evidence says he was, a 'wretched ruler'?

'And they came to Arfon, and … they burned Arfon as a further revenge.' This was the rest described as easy in our invaluable source. What was Rhun doing? Clearly, there was a delay. Were others hostile to Rhun's accession? Had Einion *Frenin* named his successor before his death, possibly Gwyddno, and with the agreement of his landholders? If so, this would have been done with the specific aim of avoiding needless bloodshed and disruption from which none or very few would benefit.[23] If Rhun was disregarding this in his own interests, then he would have been testing to the limit the loyalty of his friends and Gwynedd's landholders.

We are told in the story involving Elidir, although the account may, of course, be so much nonsense, that 'Rhun son of Maelgwn and the men of Gwynedd with him, rose up in arms, and came to the bank of the Gwerydd in the North'. The same source adds that 'there they were long disputing who should take the lead through the

23_ Mac Niocaill, 1972, pp. 55–6.

322

river Gwerydd'. *Gwerydd* means pure or virgin. Almost certainly, the intended river was the Gwyry or, as it is named today, the Gwyrfai, which divides the cantref of Arfon into two: *Is Gwyrfai*, Below the Gwyrfai, in the east and *Uwch Gwyrfai*, Above the Gwyrfai, in the west. This river, which rises at the Snowdon watershed and flows along its western side through Llyn Cwellyn, swings to the west before reaching Caernarfon and emptying into what is now a large bay, the Foryd, at the western end of the Strait. His army gathering in *Is Gwyrfai*, Below the Gwyrfai, no doubt on the coastal plain running alongside the Menai Strait, Rhun supposedly dispatched a messenger or messengers throughout Gwynedd. Later, it was made to read as though this was some heroic dispute over who had the right to lead the army, itself an indication that Rhun's power was limited. The story's conclusion that this right to be in the lead was awarded to the men of Arfon, the men of the black-headed shafts, hardly sounds convincing for a tale supposedly illustrating how precedence in any battle-line was to be accorded. If true, one might guess at protracted negotiation with the confederation's overlord in which concessions were won before agreements were reached: agreements that, in effect, sealed the fate of Meirionydd's expedition.

It is at this point that our sources, if they deserve that description, let us down. We are not told anything about the end. It is almost certain that Rhun survived the challenge. If not, even the thin record we possess would have some note of the fact. Was Gwyddno killed? Was Elffin with him to suffer the same fate or already dead? All we know is that the pedigrees give us a son of Gwyddno ruling in Meirionydd after him. This was Idris, described as Idris *Garw*, the Rough or the Coarse, but possibly *Gawr*, the Giant. He was supposedly killed in *c.*632 on the Severn, but this seems to be an unwarranted inference from the double entry under this year.[24]

24_ AC 632; AU, 632=633.

What happened to Eurgain, whom the sources seem to implicate in this opposition to her brother's accession? According to Baring-Gould and Fisher, there is a tumulus near Rhuddlan in which she is supposed to be buried.[25] She is remembered in the dedication of Llaneurgain in Northop, Flintshire, next to the Dee estuary on what may have been the most easterly border of Gwynedd. Possibly the tradition of hostility to Rhun accounts for the report by Lewis Morris that Eurgain married Aethelfrith, king of Northumbria, *Edelflet Ffleissavc vrenhin Lloegr*, 'Aethelfrith the Twister, king of England', in fact king of Bernicia from *c.*592, king of Northumbria 605–17, and invader of north Wales in 616. The triads have the saying, 'Eurgain, daughter of Maelgwn Gwynedd, who set the candle to the wild birds, in order to show the way to her lover.'[26] These are almost certainly libels meant to more than just hint at disloyalty and treachery against Gwynedd.

OTHER CONFEDERATION STRUGGLES

If it is right to see Rhun as taking the overlordship of the Gwynedd confederation in *c.*566, and having to fight to keep that position, this situation is mirrored throughout the British Isles, here including Ireland. Taking just a narrow time frame, in 563 there was a struggle between Dál Riata, Dál nAraide, and Dál Fiatach for the over-kingship of Ulidia, the area west of the Bann in northern Ireland. In 565, the year Emperor Justinian died on 14 November, the year the plague broke out once more in the Mediterranean, Diarmait mac Cerrbél/Cerbaill, the southern Uí Néill over-king of the Uí Néill confederation, was killed to be replaced by Forgus and Domnall of the northern Uí Néill, who were killed in their turn in 566 in battle against Leinster forces, and replaced by the northern Uí Néill Ainmere. In Britain, the best example of what was happening in

25_ Baring-Gould and Fisher, 1907–13, Vol. II, 1908, p. 474: Bromwich, 1961, pp. 350–1.

26_ Bromwich, 1961, p. 351, No. 44.

Gwynedd is to be found in Greater Rheged, the Rheged confederation. Here, Gwrgi and Peredur, the joint kings of York, fought and killed the over-king of the confederation, Gwenddoleu, who ruled over the heartland Carlisle region. This was the famous battle of *Arthuret* in 573, after which the over-kingship passed to Urien *Rheged* who held it until his death in 590 or 592. Rather like Diocletian's plans for the future government of the empire freed from petty family feuds and the influence of an over-mighty army, the system that had been emerging in Ireland and Britain for orderly succession within these great confederations had shown that it could work, but so often it fell foul of the all too common vices of greed and ambition.

THE THREAT FROM POWYS. WAS IT MERELY WORDS?

Times were changing. It is probable that Gildas, the shadowy figure on whom we are dependent for so much of our knowledge of the sixth-century, died in 570, possibly in Brittany.[27] Of more importance to Rhun and Gwynedd was news the following year that 'Cuthwulf', a British king in the east midlands, had been defeated at *Bredcanford*, uncertainly identified as Bedford.[28] This was something of a breach in the dam, and though its significance was to be appreciated more in retrospect, it did open the way for Saxon expansion westwards. One event of immediate significance was the death at around this time, probably *c.*550–60, of Brochwel or Brochfael *Ysgythrog*, Brochwel Long-in-the-Tooth, king of Powys since *c.*500.

Like Gwynedd, Powys had come a long way since *c.*429 and its inception as a new province in the diocese of Britain. Its first *praeses*, president or governor, was someone of real distinction. Whatever his Roman name, Brictius, Bruttius, or Brutus, for he would have had one, this was Brydw or Britu, son of the dictator of Britain and grandson of an emperor. It seems more

27_ AC, 570; AU, 569=570, 576=570; AT and AI.

28_ ASC, 571.

than probable that the centre of his administration, a combined military and civilian government, was in the great Roman city of Wroxeter. It may be that the later development on the site of the former baths basilica indicating the building of a new timber-framed headquarters or palace, with a verandah, central portico, and towers was merely another phase in the affairs of the developing provincial capital.[29] The names of Britu's immediate successors are somewhat obscure, but Brochwel's father, Cyngen, ruled in the period 475–500, Brochwel *Ysgythrog* from *c*.500 to 560, and Cynan, Brochwel's son, till near the end of the century.

All kingdoms at this time had a number of principal courts, and it was by moving from one to the other that rulers kept control and certainly an eye on their affairs. The medieval division of Powys into north and south, Powys Fadog and Powys Wenwynwyn, reflects Powys's tendency to fragment, which is seen from its very inception when separate appointments for defence and road maintenance were made in the time of Magnus Maximus in the north and the south. When these areas were brought together by Vortigern in *c*.430 and with later expansion, Powys covered a vast area, from Chester and the Clwyds in the north, to Hay and Glasbury on Wye in the south, and even to the estuary of the Dyfi in the west. The choice of Wroxeter as the original capital for the province probably reflected the desire to continue in the Roman tradition. The Midland Gap, with its entrances via the Dee and the Mersey, was a particularly vulnerable area and it was almost certain that it was to defend this that what we call Powys was created. Later, however, the strategic needs of this newly emerging state changed. As well as its position vis-à-vis the area it controlled, the great problem with Wroxeter was its size. With the inevitable shrinkage of the economy compared with the Roman period, the population fell. Wroxeter's two-hundred acre site was simply too large, and the two miles of wall too difficult to defend. Increasingly, smaller and more easily defended sites to the west commended themselves as more suitable capitals.

[29]_ Barker, 1975.

326

Cyngen, king of Powys in the last years of the fifth century, c.475–500, would almost certainly have used other courts in his enormous domain. In the north of Powys, for example, there was Foel Fenlli – although it is doubtful if it was used again after Benlli's fall – Mold, Caergwrle, Overton on Dee and, even by this date, possibly Castell Dinas Brân near Llangollen. During the reign of Brochwel his son, c.500–560, Powys was emerging into a state of considerable power. We have seen how between 530 and 580 there was a considerable building programme in Wroxeter. Clearly there was a determination to hold this former imperial city, even if it was on low land and as a result exposed to attack. And so the new timber-framed headquarters or palace, with a verandah, central portico, and towers was built. The suggestion that this might have been an ecclesiastical initiative seems unlikely. Shortly after, however, the decision was taken to abandon Roman Wroxeter. From then on, the place was systematically and unhurriedly dismantled as its inhabitants moved to the more westerly and more easily defended sites of Shrewsbury, five miles west of Wroxeter on a hill in a bend of the Severn, Baschurch, twelve miles northwest, and back to the conical hill called the Wrekin, just five miles east of Wroxeter, which continued to be important in time of emergency. Not long after 600 Wroxeter was empty apart from the squatters who moved in to take advantage of what was left. The final phase of the moves probably coincided and had something to do with Iago ap Brochwel's short reign, c.600-2, that of his wife, *Haiarnwedd*, Iron Face, c.602-4, and Selyf son of Cynan Garwyn, the Selyf who was to meet his death in the battle of Chester 616. By these dates, these rulers would have been using other courts.

It is clear that by the reign of Cynan *Garwyn* who was Rhun's contemporary, Powys was experiencing something similar to what was happening in Gwynedd, that is, a westward drift of power and focus. As the lowlands to the east looked more and more vulnerable, such a shift was strategically sensible with Saxon armies, however small, on the move. As the kingdom emerged out of the once Roman province, and as other states were also developing, particularly Gwynedd, it became increasingly important to think about the integrity and security of its borders.

So it is possible that in southern Powys, sites in the region of *Castell Coch*, the Red Castle, Welshpool, supposedly founded in 1250, had a much earlier history than the thirteenth century. Nearby there are many similar vantage points. Another court must have been *Llys Fechain*, the palace or court of Mechain, the centre of the cantref named after the nearby river Cain flowing east into the river Vyrnwy. Near Llanfechain is a mound known as Tomen or Domen Gastell, certainly a Norman site. But just a few miles higher up the river Vyrnwy, on the combined rivers Banwy and Einion, its tributaries, is the site of Mathrafal. Set in the midst of the most beautiful countryside, in the Middle Ages Mathrafal came to be regarded as one of the three great royal residences of Wales. The other two were Aberffraw in Anglesey and Dinefwr on the river Tywi in Ystrad Tywi, lying between Dyfed and Morgannwg. Aberffraw was one of the principal seats of northern Gwynedd, Dinefwr was the same for Deheubarth, and between the two, in the Powys of mid-Wales, was Mathrafal. Possession of these sites, just like Tara in Meath, came to be seen as the ultimate test of rule in these areas.

It is worth staying with Powys for a while for here we will find a very important clue as to how Gwynedd fared in this emerging Wales. Too much has been made of what, with a first glance at the map, might seem to be the apparently remote situation of Mathrafal, in a river valley backed by the hills of Caereinion. It was nearer the heart of southern Powys than either Shrewsbury or Baschurch and it had a prominent position on a Roman road, today the A495. The Roman route left Whitchurch and went from Ellesmere to the south of Oswestry and so up the Vyrnwy, eventually reaching Caersws, as did a more southerly route from Wroxeter. The oft-repeated and erroneous view that Mathrafal became the capital,

itself a somewhat misleading concept if used in the
singular, only after Offa of Mercia, 757–96, conquered
between the Wye and the Severn, appears first in David
Powell's 1584 *Historie of Cambria*. Even a refinement
of this view, which places the supposed move after the
fall of Cynddylan's *Pengwern*, possibly in 657, has to
be rejected. Guarded over by lookout points on higher
ground to its east and west, Mathrafal looks down over
the fertile lands that would have supported the court's
life. The name *mathrafal*, triangular plain, refers to
this lowland vista of mowed fields, south up the Banwy,
and to the west and northeast up and down the valley
of the Vyrnwy.

With Tysilio/Siliau his brother enthroned from *c.*566
in Meifod as bishop and abbot, Cynan had achieved
that unity of church and state which both sides saw as
being mutually beneficial. Meifod was now re-founded
as the mausoleum of the kings of Powys, a position it
held until the twelfth century, and so the implication is
that by *c.*566 Cynan *Garwyn* was already beginning to
regard the court of Mathrafal, two miles higher up the
Vyrnwy, as his principal residence.

There might seem to be evidence that Cynan
Garwyn was intent on imposing lordship over his
neighbours. It might seem that there was a possibility
that Gwyddno's invasion of northern Gwynedd was
a joint operation with forces of Cynan *Garwyn* from
Powys. This, some believe, is indicated by the poem
which is the source of the two lines we have already
looked at describing the expedition. In fact, the idea is
extremely doubtful. However, the poem is of real
importance for other reasons. It is one of only twelve
believed by Sir Ifor Williams in 1960 to be the genuine
work of Taliesin even if it was only committed to
manuscript in the form we possess it in about 1275. Its
name is *Trawsganu Cynan Garwyn*, In Praise of Cynan
Garwyn. Taliesin was probably a native of Powys and
had Cynan as his first patron. *In Praise of Cynan Garwyn*
is, Ifor Williams believed, 'the earliest surviving poem in
the Welsh language'.[30]

30_ For the traditional,
conservative view of the
poem, accepting that it
lists Cynan's victories, see
Jarman in Jarman and
Hughes, 1976, pp. 55–6
and 66–7; Clancy, 1970,
pp. 191–2; Jarman, 1981,
pp. 21–6; and Williams,
1971, pp. 26–9.

The panegyric falls into three parts: the first details the gifts made by the king to the poet; the second, making it similar to many 'battle-list' poems, describes the king's victories; and the third tells of the fame the king will have. This fame comes, of course, not simply because of his greatness as a king, but because he had a poet, a great poet, to put this into verse so that it was on record for all time. We are back with Pacatus Drepanius delivering his extraordinary panegyrics in front of the emperor Theodosius I. This was the continuing Roman tradition, now with the extraordinary refinement that these eulogies were increasingly delivered in verse form, and with ever more complex rhyming patterns making them supreme works of art.

Because of this poem, some have believed that Cynan's policy was to bring together the Welsh states into some alliance with Powys that could then more easily withstand moves by Mercia. A conservative, even by now traditional, reading of this poem might seem to imply this, but it raises very many questions. For reasons that will emerge, we can be reasonably sure that Taliesin, and if not him, someone, delivered this panegyric to Cynan *Garwyn*, dated here to *c.*560–600, *after* Rhun had had to confront an invasion of Gwynedd from Meirionydd.

Cynan, battle [*or* army] protector, gave me bounty –
for it is not false to praise – provider of homesteads:
a hundred horses equal in swiftness,
silver on their equipment;
a hundred purple mantles of equal size;
a hundred bracelets and fifty brooches;
a stone-sheathed sword, yellow-hilted, better than any –
from Cynan received – hostility cannot be seen.
The lineage of Cadelling, immoveable in battle
[*or* a steadfast army]:
a war attack on the Wye – innumerable spears –
men of Gwent were killed with bloody blade:
battle in Anglesey – great and fair –
renowned the praise;

an expedition beyond Menai – the rest was easy:
battle in Crug Dyfed – Aergol on the move,
his [Cynan's] cattle were never seen in front of anyone.
The son of Brochfael, boundary-extending,
conquest-seeking,
threatening Cornwall –
not a matter for praise their fate –
he brings it hardship until it begs [for peace].
Cynan my support, the glory of armies,
the light of his flame spreading, raising a mighty fire:
battle in Brychan's land –
their battle-enclosure a mole-hill.
You wretched rulers, tremble before Cynan,
his breastplate in battle like a dragon,
of the same nature as Cyngen,
supporter of a wide dominion.
I have heard men conversing –
everyone acclaiming him:
all around the world under the sun –
they are subject to Cynan.[31]

Can the interpretation of the poem from Sir Ifor Williams down to the present day be challenged? A daring suggestion, but is it really likely that Cynan *Garwyn* did take war from Powys into Dyfed, Gwent, Brycheiniog, *and* Gwynedd, and, on top of all this, threatened Cornwall? Certainly we have to remember the Roman road system. This would still have provided relatively quick and easy access to these areas, especially for a state strategically positioned as was Powys. Nevertheless, to operate on such a scale, taking on all-comers, would have left more than just this poem as a record. For Powys to have attempted this would have caused the kingdom innumerable problems in the years ahead. Is it not just as likely that Taliesin is here comparing his lord, army protector, provider of homesteads, whose cattle were never seen in front of anyone, with the other rulers in Wales in the 560s? Driving away your intended subject's cattle, rather like hostages, was a way of forcing a coming-to-terms and

31_ Taliesin, *Trawsganu Cynan Garwyn*, In Praise of Cynan Garwyn, transl. Foster, in Foster and Daniel, 1965, pp. 229–30, based on the Williams 1960 text.

an acceptance of lordship. The poem is claiming that the lords of Cornwall, Dyfed, Gwent, Brycheiniog, and Gwynedd were, in stark contrast to Cynan of Powys, *wretched rulers*, well acquainted with setbacks and defeats. Because of this, they simply had to acknowledge Cynan's superiority.

You wretched rulers, tremble before Cynan,
his breastplate in battle like a dragon,
of the same nature as Cyngen,
supporter of a wide dominion.

This elder Cyngen had been ruler of Powys from *c.*475 to 500. Here then is one of the key sources for the Meirionydd invasion of Gwynedd, *c.*566 or 567, that we looked at earlier: the reference to Gwynedd concerns Rhun, ruling between 566 and 580. He is being mocked. One battle in Anglesey, an expedition beyond the Menai, and the rest, the burning of Arfon, was easy! Cynan *Garwyn* would never have allowed this to happen to him!

Again, much is made by modern commentators of the lack of any mention of clashes with the real threat, that from the Saxons, but this is wrong for two reasons. Firstly, it misses the point of the whole poem, which was to compare and contrast Cynan with his fellow rulers in western Britain. Secondly, it reveals an imperfect grasp of how far Saxon encroachments had reached by this date. This issue centres on the dating of the poem. A battle at the Wye when the men of Gwent were killed might seem to be the battle of Llantilio Grosseney in 584, but in this Iddon of Gwent *defeated* the Saxons, a victory that no one in Powys could afford to mock. The defeat must have occurred during the reign of Tewdrig king of Gwent who abdicated before 584 only to come out of this retirement in order to join in the battle for the Wye. He was mortally wounded, again not something to mock in the circumstances. It is more likely to have been an incident nearer 577. In this year, as ASC puts it, Cuthwine, probably king of southwest

Cambridgeshire, and Ceawlin king of Winchester and the West Saxons defeated and killed three British kings, Conmail, Condidan, and Farinmail, in the battle of Dyrham just north of Bath, and captured their three Roman cities, Gloucester, Cirencester, and Bath.[32] Conmail was overlord of the province, now kingdom, of Gwrtheyrnion. Whatever the event being referred to, it is compared, as are all the other lapses by western British rulers, with 'the lineage of Cadelling', the rulers of Powys, in particular Cynan, 'immoveable in battle'.

'Aergol on the move' is a phrase mocking events in the history of the southwest Wales dynasty of Dyfed now lost to us. These were probably in the reign of Gwerthefyr or Vortipor, the *bad son* of a good king according to Gildas, who may have ruled in the period 500–50, *or* in that of his son Cyngar or Cyngar's son Peter, which might bring us up to 600 or later. What the phrase did *not* refer to was the reign of the good king, Vortipor's father Aergol/Airgul, who ruled in the period *c.*487–500, if only because of the simple reason that his reign was too early to be derided now. *Crug Dyfed*, the hill or hills of Dyfed, would mean the Prescelly Mountains. The phrase might indicate a descendant of Airgul having to retreat before an enemy, or his cattle being driven off by an attacker: 'Cynan's cattle were never seen in front of anyone.' Mention of the glory days of Airgul simply emphasized the insult.

The reference to Cornwall – 'not a matter for praise their fate, he [the enemy] brings it hardship until it begs for peace' – is in order to make a comparison with 'Cynan my support, the glory of armies, the light of his flame spreading, raising a mighty fire.' The incident referred to is described in too general a way to pin down. Certainly, when it is Brycheiniog's turn, the contempt is obvious. This little Welsh state grew out of appointments made probably as far back as the time of the western usurper Magnentius in 351 in order to protect the fort at Brecon Gaer and its pivotal position in the road system of south Wales. A marriage between Marchell

32_ ASC, Whitelock et al., 1961, p. 14.

daughter of Tewdrig of this kingdom, then known as Garth Matrun, and Anlach son of Cormac of the line of Irish immigrants in Dyfed, which was itself expanding to merge with the native ruling line, seems to have been the catalyst for Garth Matrun's own growth. Their son Brychan, who gave his name to the kingdom, in this way replacing Garth Matrun with Brycheiniog, was acutely aware of the small size of his kingdom. Attempting to remedy this, and punching above his weight, his weapon was the marriages he arranged for his many children. Brychan was the father of the terrible sisters Tudglid, first wife of Maelgwn and mother of his second, Cerddych, and Marchell. One of at least thirteen sons, Clydwyn, actually began a process of conquest, or so it seems, supposedly invading all south Wales.[33] But despite this, Brycheiniog, whilst keeping its independence, remained small. Then, threatened by Dyfed and Seisyllwg, it accepted the overlordship of Wessex under Alfred only to be swallowed up in Deheubarth under Hywel *Dda* in 935. In other words, Brychan's and Clydwyn's efforts achieved nothing and probably brought invasion of Brycheiniog in their wake: 'battle in Brychan's land – their battle enclosure a mole-hill'! Clydwyn's brother Cynog entered the religious life. His other brother Rhain, who probably succeeded Clydwyn, was known as the Red-Eyed!

The references to Gwynedd, Gwent, and Brycheiniog may possibly date the poem to around 577. At this time, Powys was not facing the Saxon threat. According to J. E. Lloyd and A. W. Wade-Evans, Cynan's epithet *Garwyn* made him Cynan of the White Chariot. Perhaps *Garw*, rough, is an alternative. We are *not* looking at evidence showing that Powys was now becoming the most important state in Wales as some have claimed. Rather, because of the difficulties which some of the Welsh states had encountered, even the most powerful like Gwynedd, Cynan's bard felt he could boast on his master's behalf. Here, in the land ruled by the descendants of the first known ruler in northern Powys, Cadell or Cathaíl, 'the lineage of Cadelling, hostility

[33] Bartrum, 1966, p. 15, No. 11 (3). It is difficult to follow Miller, 1977–8, pp. 37–41, in associating this Clydwyn with the Clydwyn of the native line in Dyfed who, it seems, lived much earlier.

cannot be seen'. And peace itself can bring prosperity and fame, especially if there is a bard like Taliesin to proclaim it.

THE POWER OF GWYNEDD

Despite Taliesin's assertions, Gwynedd remained the main power in north Wales. After the battle of Chester in 616, and for a period of sixty-three years, Powys, under consecutively Brochwel, and Elfoddw, Cynan *Garwyn*'s sons, actually became part of the Gwynedd confederation, a situation lasting till 679. Indeed, if we take the 640 years between the inception of Powys as a province in 429 and 1069, the start of the Norman incursions, Powys was independent of Gwynedd for only 60 per cent of the time. In other words, for nearly half of that period, Powys was under Greater Gwynedd. Perhaps we should extend Powys's history back to its more primitive beginnings in 383, when the government of the emperor Maximus made the first appointments for this area, and forward to 1160 when Powys split into two, something that was inherent in Powys's political history from the start. For these 777 years as a single unified state, Powys was independent of Gwynedd for only 508 years, that is, just over 65% of its history, being under Gwynedd's direct control or ruled by members of Gwynedd's dynasty for 269 years, for one third of the time. Of course, we have to be careful. Lordship was a complicated business that commonly crossed boundaries which are more the creation of nationalist historians in much later periods than a reality for people living at the time. Nevertheless, these figures do illustrate the greater power and influence of the dynasty which claimed descent from Paternus of the Red Robe, in other words from the Roman army, and from rulers who had had to fight for their position on the very fringes of the empire. Powys's origins lay in the appointments of Irish navvies as road patrollers and repairers some time in the 380s, even if the area they controlled was later elevated to the rank of province by the dictator Vortigern and was given his son as its first *praeses*. But when this Brutus, grandson of the emperor Magnus Maximus, came to preside over Powys, Gwynedd had been spearheading the campaign against the Irish for nearly fifty years.

In Gwynedd, Aberffraw, the former Roman fort, soon superseded the courts of *Dineirth* and Degannwy. Nearby, the church of Llangadwaladr became the new mausoleum for Gwynedd's kings. Another important royal site was Abergwyngregyn, Estuary of the White Shells, known now, and probably then, simply as Aber, lying just inland between Bangor and Conwy on the Menai Strait. On a coastline already enjoying far more hours of sunshine than its mountainous hinterland, climatologists have found this place to be uniquely blessed with a microclimate giving it even more favourable conditions. In other words, these early rulers, their builders, and engineers knew through observation what we manage to conclude only after years of study and scientific monitoring. As ruling dynasties followed the fashion of even greater courts, with all ultimately keeping a watch on continental developments, these principal residences, Aberffraw, Aber, and Degannwy, would have been used in a way similar to Winchester, Westminster, and Worcester or Gloucester in England. Here were celebrated the major festivals of Easter, Whit, and Christmas, where the crown was worn and the most important business of the state transacted.

There were also a whole series of lesser courts. It became the law that each commote, the local neighbourhood unit for taxation purposes usually comprising a number of townships, should have its own *llys*, court or royal *vill*, at which the inhabitants would pay their dues and present their suits. The principal centre in each cantref, the wider area, was also the place where the royal court, forever on the move, would, from time to time, take up residence. There was Cemais in northern Anglesey to the west of Point Lynas and the *Llys Caswallawn* we have already encountered; to their

At the start of the
valley seen here lies
Abergwyngregyn, the
Estuary of the White
Shells, court of the kings
and princes of Gwynedd.
It has its own very
favourable microclimate.

Pen y Bryn,
Abergwyngregyn, a
sixteenth-century house
built on part of the site
of the early-medieval
court complex.

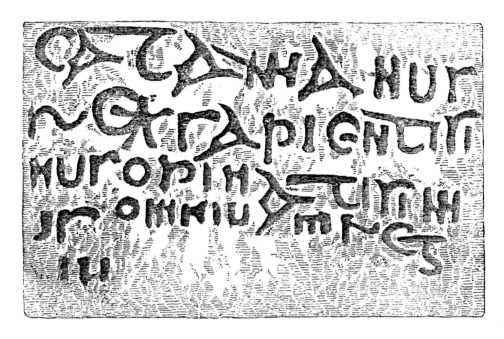

Above: The Cadfan Memorial, Llangadwaladr church, Anglesey. (From *Archaeologia Cambrensis*, Vol. I, 1846, p. 165, by courtesy of the Cambrian Archaeological Association)

Left: The *Draig Goch*, the Red Dragon, ready for a sand castle.

Dragons flying over the
Eagle Tower, Caernarfon
Castle. In the distance, the
Menai Strait and Anglesey. **340**

south Penrhosllugwy, and on the south coast of the island, near the site of Edward's later castle of Beaumaris, Llanfaes. Since 1993 excavations have been carried out at the *llys* or court at Rhosyr in Newborough in southwest Anglesey, and more information, at least concerning the later thirteenth-century period, has been gathered.

THE CONFEDERATION CONTINUES: BELI c.580

Who wore the crown after Rhun died? It seems more than probable that it passed to Beli, not the son of Rhun, a direct descendant of Maelgwn, but the son of Einion who had ruled between *c.*547 and *c.*566. In other words, Maelgwn's system was holding, and the over-kingship of the Gwynedd confederation reverted to the Rhos line.[34] This is exactly what the much-maligned Geoffrey of Monmouth claimed: 'Ennianus begat Belin, Belin begat Iago, Iago begat Cadvan and Cadvan was my [that is, Cadwallon's] father.'[35] However, even this claim can be doubted, because we always have to contend with genealogists transforming what were probably mere king lists into genealogies by the insertion of that little word *ap*, son of. Were some of the kings which the scribes and historians could not satisfactorily place in fact much nearer the lines of descent from the original three who had usurped the throne as far back as 485? For example, was the Cadfael ap Cynfedw who supposedly intruded in 636, sprung, as the triad says, from villeins? The Caradog ap Meirchion who ruled Gwynedd 754–98 *was* from the Rhos line. Merfyn *Frych*, the Freckled, 825–44, was an intruder, though his mother was daughter of a mainline Gwynedd king. Who was Aeddan ap Blegywryd ruling *c.*1003–18? 'Mighty, loth to flee, mighty, resolute … in every assembly, his will was done.' Was he just an Anglesey lord as is often stated or someone of an altogether more illustrious lineage? The list goes on. However, the almost certain truth is that, as centuries passed, families became ever more jealous of their

34_ Miller, *Saints*, 1979, pp. 109–10.

35_ Geoffrey of Monmouth, *The History of the Kings of Britain*, XII. 6, Thorpe, 1966, p. 274.

rights, ever more concerned to keep the possession of the crown firmly within the direct and immediate family.

So emerged the Welsh kingdom of Gwynedd. Born in a welter of war, invasion, defence, ethnic cleansing, disease, the imminent threat of Armageddon, and dynastic division, the resilience of its rulers having to confront all this should not be underestimated. Despite what has been hazarded in these pages, it is a sad fact that the paucity of our evidence still prevents us from seeing the detail of this heroic story: the history of the transformation from Roman province into sovereign state. Some time after Maelgwn, Cadfan, king of Gwynedd *c*.615–25, saviour of the day in the 616 battle of Chester, was laid to rest in the mausoleum of the Gwynedd kings, Eglwys Ael, next to the royal court at Aberffraw. His grandson was Cadwaladr ap Cadwallon, 656–64, known as *Bendigaid*, the Blessed, the word used, not in the religious sense, but instead to link him with the spirits of all who had fought against the Saxons. He rebuilt the royal church, with the result that it came to be known after him, in effect its second founder, as Llangadwaladr. He also was buried here. As part of the restoration, Cadwaladr set up a memorial to his illustrious grandfather, Cadfan. In a script we would hardly recognize, the proud boast is still very much Roman.

CATAMANUS REX SAPIENTIS[S]IMUS
OPINATIS[S]IMUS OMNIUM REGUM

KING CADFAN THE MOST LEARNED AND
RENOWNED OF ALL KINGS

CHAPTER ELEVEN

DRAGON FORTRESS OF THE WELSH
The Dragon and Welsh Independence, 398–1283

COHORTS AND DRAGONS

For anyone travelling along the north Wales coast today, the imagination has to work extremely hard to conjure up the area's history. Despite the obvious geographical features, there is little to speak to us of the extraordinary, dramatic, and at times heroic past that is both Roman and British, or of the birth of a nation, of the country we have usually just rushed through. And yet, as we go through Prestatyn, Rhyl, Abergele, Colwyn Bay, Llandudno, Penmaenmawr, and Llanfairfechan, through places that have to one degree or another been not so much conquered as trashed by the English, from kiosk after kiosk, in newsagents, amusement arcades, and cafés, flutter flags which carry the oldest political and military emblem of the British Isles, the symbol of Rome itself, namely the dragon.

In the late fourth century, Vegetius, a writer on Roman military matters, produced his manual on the army's institutions, *De Re Militari*. In this we find explained the origins of this symbol which has hovered in the background of Welsh history from its very beginnings right down to the present day.

The first emblem of the whole legion is the Eagle which is carried by the *aquilifer*. The dragons, however, are borne into battle by the *draconarii* of the individual cohorts.[1]

Ammianus Marcellinus recorded the arrival in Rome in 357 of the emperor Constantius II, 337–61, dressed in full military attire, in a procession that to all intents and purposes was a Triumph, with Constantius himself, *triumphator*, triumphing general. To a traditionalist like Marcellinus this was outrageous, since

[1] Vegetius, *Epitoma Rei Militaris* or *De Re Militari*, II, 13, Lofmarck, 1995, p. 41. This chapter is heavily indebted to Lofmarck's work: an extraordinarily scholarly book given its small and popular format. At the time Vegetius was writing, the army, originally based on its legions with ten cohorts to a legion, was changing rapidly with the emergence of the field armies that rendered the legionary system redundant.

what was being celebrated was the fall of the usurper Magnentius, a senior army officer who had proclaimed himself emperor in Gaul on 18 January 350.[2] As such, this victory for legitimate authority had involved Roman fighting Roman, hitherto definitely not the subject for such celebrations. Just as bad was the fact that the emperor himself was claiming and receiving the adulation instead of the generals who had actually produced the result. But for our purposes it is what Ammianus Marcellinus says about the procession that is interesting.

His [Constantius's] own appearance might have been designed as a show of strength to overawe the Euphrates or the Rhine; a double line of standards went before him, and he himself was seated on a golden car [or chariot] gleaming with various precious stones, whose mingled radiance seemed to throw a sort of shimmering light.

Behind the motley cavalcade that preceded him, the emperor's person was surrounded by purple banners woven in the form of dragons and attached to the tops of gilded and jewelled spears; the breeze blew through their gaping jaws so that they seemed to be hissing with rage and their voluminous tails streamed behind them on the wind.[3]

Writing on the battle of Strasbourg in the same year, 357, Ammianus describes how the *caesar* Julian, later emperor 360–3, was picked out by his cavalry whom he was attempting to join whilst the battle raged.

He was recognized by the purple dragon attached to the top of a long lance and streaming on the wind like the cast skin of a snake, and the tribune of the squadron [who had been on the verge of flight] stopped and turned back, pale and trembling, to renew the fight.[4]

When Paternus was appointed to a north Wales command in about 398, probably with the rank of *comes*, the forces under him would have been organized

2_ Magnentius was the son of a British father and a Frankish barbarian mother.

3_ Ammianus Marcellinus, *Histories*, Book 16, Ch. 10, Hamilton and Wallace-Hadrill, 1986, p. 100.

4_ Ibid., Ch. 12, p. 111.

into cohorts. The days of the legion in Britain were for the most part over and from now on the dragon was Rome's supreme battle standard. Not surprisingly, therefore, it often appears in contemporary accounts.

On about the third day of January 404, Emperor Honorius, 395–423, moved from his western capital Ravenna in order to celebrate a Triumph in Rome, which was still the symbolic centre of at least the western empire if no longer its seat of government. This was to be in celebration of recent victories over Alaric, king of the Visigoths. Accompanying Honorius was his father-in-law, Stilicho, the real power in the empire. In honour of the event, the Egyptian poet Claudian recited his latest work *On the Sixth Consulship of the Emperor Honorius*. Included in this was a description of the emperor's triumphal entry into Rome in which he imagines a girl asking her nurse about the dragon standards.

"Do they", she would ask, "but wave in the air or is there a veritable hiss, uttered as they are about to seize an enemy in their jaws?" ... Joy and fear fill her mind.[5]

In 458 Sidonius Apollinaris, who lived from about 430 to 488, and who in 469 was to become bishop of *Augustonemetum / Arverna*, Clermont-Ferrand, in the Puy-de-Dôme of France, wrote in praise of the western emperor Majorian, 457–61, and of his armies. Again the dragon pennons received special mention.

Now the broidered dragon speeds hither and thither in both armies, his throat swelling as the zephers [light, balmy winds] clash against it; that pictured form with wide-open jaw counterfeits a wrathful hunger, and the breeze puts a frenzy into the cloth as often as the lithe back is thickened by the blasts and the air is now too abundant for the belly to hold.[6]

The Romans had encountered the dragon standard, and more particularly the inflatable pennon, when fighting the Dacians between the Danube and the

5_ Claudian, *On the Sixth Consulship of the Emperor Honorius*, 404, Platnauer, 1922, Vol. 2, pp. 111–23, at pp. 116–17.

6_ Lofmarck, 1995, p. 41.

Carpathians. Trajan's column, erected in Rome in 113, shows these campaigns and the dragon pennons carried by their opponents. The next fifty years saw the Romans themselves adopting such standards, probably taking the Dacian battle-dragon as their direct model. As the above passages show, because of their particularly dramatic effect even on days of only a slight breeze, the inflatable pennons came to be widely used.

One can only presume that different colours indicated the difference between the persons or groups they were used to symbolize. When the person was the emperor himself or his *caesar*, the colour was purple as the above passages state. Another possible colour for an emperor's use was gold. Owain *Glyndŵr*, after 1400, had a banner with a golden dragon on a white field. For other purposes, and as the dragon was normally associated with fire, when as Vegetius says these pennons came to be the emblem of the cohort, they were almost certainly red or scarlet. Clearly this was the best colour for ready recognition in battle. In Welsh literature, the first reference to a red dragon comes in the early ninth-century *Historia Brittonum* of Nennius.

DRAGONS AND KINGS: RED, WHITE, AND GREEN

The universal appeal of this seemingly terrifying symbol for Rome's military might is seen in its widespread use in later centuries. Cuthred of Wessex reportedly had such a standard in 752. Edmund *Ironside* had one in 1016, and Harold most certainly used them at Hastings in 1066. Later English kings, such as Richard I in 1190 and Henry III, both used inflatable pennons. Henry III's dragon was made of red silk with a tongue resembling fire and with eyes made of precious stones in order to catch the light. He used it in 1257 when between 19 August and 8 September he was invading Gwynedd.

If the sixth-century Maelgwn was beginning to turn away from Gwynedd's Roman past, gradually in the reigns which followed the kings of Gwynedd may have used the standard less often. When we come to later rulers, such as Owain *Gwynedd* in the twelfth century, surprisingly we find that lions are the national symbol. If Matthew Paris, who died in 1259, can be trusted, the arms of Gwynedd consisted of four quarters, each with a lion, a front paw outstretched, its face turned to the onlooker. The top left quarter had a red lion on a gold ground, with this alternating with a gold lion on a red ground. Later references also speak of this same quartering and the same lions.[7]

For the dragon to be used once more in Wales, as a banner, badge, or device of heraldry, we possibly have to wait for it to be resurrected by Owain *Glyndŵr* after 1400, for as we have seen on one of his standards he used a golden dragon on a white field and had a dragon with a lion as supporters for his lion coat of arms. Edmund and Jasper Tudor also used it as a supporter on their modified version of the royal coat of arms granted to them by their half-brother Henry VI of England, 1422–61 and 1470–1. Henry Tudor, Edmund's son, used 'a red fierye dragon on a white and green background' on one of his battle standards at Bosworth in 1485, and when king he adopted the dragon as one of the supporters of the new royal coat of arms which was only changed into a unicorn by James I. Although Gwynedd's colours would seem to have been red and gold, the white and green background used now on these red-dragon flags might also have a long history. Stray lines dealing with Llywelyn the Great refer to his army in green and white. Edward the Black Prince of Wales had his troops dressed in green and white before the battle of Crécy in 1346.[8]

THE DRAGON GUARDING GWYNEDD

Nevertheless, even if we have to wait till the fifteenth century for the dragon's reappearance in heraldry, it remained a potent symbol of authority, power, and history for Welsh writers throughout the centuries. It could be argued that this was in part because it carried

[7]_ Jones, 1969, pp. 158–204, esp. pp. 158–61; Wagner, 1972, p. 42, No. 13, the Matthew Paris shield, and pp. 56–7, No. 45, for *Owain Glyndŵr*.

[8]_ Lofmarck, 1995, pp. 60–1.

echoes of Wales's, and more particularly, Gwynedd's Roman origin and the authority and validation which this conferred. It looks as if the dragon, symbol of Rome and its civilization, became ever more revered as the outside challenge grew, so the Welsh words *draig dragon, dragwn* came over the centuries to be synonyms for *warrior*, or more probably *great warrior*, as Gwynedd and the rest of Wales fought these barbarian invaders.[9] From earliest times and in parts of the world far removed from the mountainous west of Britain, the dragon's function in traditional literature was as a guardian of treasure. In Wales, however, the word came to be used pre-eminently to describe the kings and princes of Wales, and more especially those of the leading Welsh state, Gwynedd. But they also were guarding treasure.

LIONS, EAGLES, BOARS, BEARS, AND BULLS

This is not to say that the word dragon was the only word used in this way. The dragon was the king of serpents, but the lion was the king of animals, and the eagle was the king of birds, so all were considered suitable as emblems of sovereignty and for descriptions of warrior-kings. Strong and ferocious beasts such as the bear and the bull also appear in the literature. Certainly, references to dragons, in the sense of strong and fearless warriors, were not confined to Gwynedd. The heroes of the northern British kingdoms were also described in such terms, but Rheged, Strathclyde, Galloway, and the northern and southern branches of the Votadini also had justification for seeing their origins as lying in a Roman past.

The main literary product of the north in these early centuries is the poem called *The Gododdin* after the northern Votadini, which was produced some time after *c.*599. This has warriors compared not only to dragons, eagles, and lions, but also to boars and bulls, with one reference each to a wolf, an ox, and a bear. Eagles appear most often, in six verses. They describe, in turn, Madog,

9_ The modern word dragoon derives from this same usage.

Buddfan son of Bleiddfan, who was described as a graceful eagle, Gwydyen, Rhys, fierce eagle, Eidef, mighty eagle, and the war-band generally.[10] Yet the next largest number of references is to boars, which appear in five verses, with one verse referring to three bristled boars: Morien, Bradwen, and Gwenabwy son of Gwên.[11] Next come lions, which are mentioned in four verses, and bulls in five, although two of these refer to the same Eithinyn.[12] In other words, dragons come quite low down the list, even if we add the one reference to a serpent, Merin ap Madain. The two other notices are of Llif son of Gan, described as a *savage dragon*, and Gwenabwy son of Gwên, the *mighty dragon*, who has already featured as a bristled boar, and who, in the same dragon verse, is also called *dragon in blood*.[13]

Similarly in Gwynedd, dragon descriptions continued to be used but alongside other animals. Gildas called Maelgwn *insularis draco*, Island Dragon, probably referring to the period when Maelgwn directly ruled over Anglesey as his apanage. It may be that the poem *Moliant Cadwallon*, In Praise of Cadwallon, contains a dragon reference or it was accompanied by a line of the same date linking this symbol directly with Cadwallon ap Cadfan who ruled Gwynedd between 625 and 635. The added significance here is that in 634 Cadwallon allied with Penda of Mercia, and defeated Edwin of Northumbria who between 632 and 633 had managed to win a brief lordship over Gwynedd. In this way, Cadwallon became, albeit very briefly and therefore in name only, high-king over the whole of Britain. This was what the bards in the Welsh courts had sung of often enough, but now it had happened. The barbarians had been conquered.

Draig dinas Cymru Cadwallon.
Cadwallon, dragon fortress of the Welsh.[14]

[10]_ Verses 2, 19, 24, 43, 52, and 86.

[11]_ Verses 43, 30, 42, 87, and 92.

[12]_ Lions, verses 18, 20, 37, and 40; bulls – Eithynin – 38 and 39, with 30, 51, and 74.

[13]_ Dragons, verses 22 and 25; serpent, 63; wolf, 3 with duplicate as 'gold-torqued ox' 42, and in the same verse a bear.

[14]_ Afan *Ferddig, Moliant Cadwallon*, Foster and Daniel, 1965, pp. 230–1; Jarmon and Hughes, 1976, pp. 42 and 98–100; and Bromwich and Jones, 1978, pp. 29–33. The extant text is late seventeenth century but is apparently a fragment of a much older text that may have been nearly contemporary with the victory of Cadwallon and Penda.

The problem is not so much that one is in the hands of translators and poets who have tried to make sense of these lines for an English readership, as that we still cannot know what the poet was thinking when he used the words *draig* or *dragon*. Was it literally a dragon, was it instead a warrior-king, or was it, in a way we will never satisfactorily disentangle, a combination of the two? The line just quoted could mean '*Cadwallon, warrior refuge of the Welsh*'. When Major Francis Jones, Wales Herald Extraordinary, warned in 1969 against 'the tendency to see heraldic significance in bardic references', for the word dragon 'formed only a conventional description, part of the stock-in-trade of a myriad of bards', he was not saying, as Carl Lofmarck did, referring to this passage, that the word dragon 'was commonly no more than a synonym for warrior'.[15] Of course it was used in this way, and for many a warrior, but when used of kings, it was in all probability a metaphor, and one pregnant with meaning. That it was indeed used like this throughout the early and late Middle Ages may be argued from the widespread use of the dragon standard as the supreme symbolic representation of Rome and its military might in the later years of the western empire; from the continued use of the word, and its constant application to the princes of Wales, especially those of Gwynedd; as well as from its reappearance on the banner of Owain *Glyndŵr* after 1400. In this way, it matters not whether modern translators, often and rightly so, themselves poets, use dragon or warrior in their English translations. To the listener in Wales, from the seventh to the thirteenth century, according to the context of its use and the figure being so described, the meaning would have been clear.

Gwalchmai ap Meilyr, who lived during the period 1130–80 and who was for a time the court bard of Owain *Gwynedd*, 1137–70, describes himself as '*a lion in the van*', or '*a lion facing legions*', but in the same

15_ Jones, 1969, p. 172; Lofmarck, 1995, p. 58.

poem Owain was 'Snowdonia's eagle' and a 'dragon in battle'.[16] In *To Owain Gwynedd*, in which the poet was asking to be restored to favour after some rift between the two, Gwalchmai shows his fear of this prince, 'massive in his wrath on a grey and white horse'. Here, as well as being 'champion wolf of the pack', and 'a brave lion', Owain, according to Anthony Conran's translation, was 'Dragon of Ewias'. Ewias is between Brecon and Hereford and was the place where, in the medieval tale *Culhwch and Olwen*, Arthur checked the course of *Twrch Trwyth*, the Wild Boar. In other words, Owain was Arthur.[17]

Cynddelw *Brydydd Mawr*, Cynddelw the Great Poet, who lived in the second half of the twelfth century, was a native of Powys and was court poet at Mathrafal before moving on to Gwynedd. Here, he wrote a series of eulogies of Owain *Gwynedd*, whom he describes in one as 'wolf of warfare, onrushing eagle', and 'swift-winged falcon'. But in this praise poem, the phrase *Cyfarfu dreigiau riau Rufain*, which Clancy translated into English as 'Dragons encountered, rulers of Rome', refers to the English not the Welsh, and Owain's opponent, Henry II, was 'the Dragon of the East'. Owain in distinction was the 'Fair Western Dragon', and, here indulging in no mere poetic hyperbole, 'the best [in battle] was his', that is, Owain's.[18] This usage again seems to imply use of the dragon for anyone wielding supreme power.

Praise poems were by no means confined to the princes of Gwynedd. Madog ap Maredudd, ruler of Powys between 1132 and 1160, had done much to revive the fortunes of this north and mid-Wales state, being described by Cynddelw as 'a firm anchor in a deep sea'. Here Madog is praised as 'a bold lion', the 'eagle of lords', and a 'ferocious war-wolf'.[19] In his elegy on the death of Madog in 1160, Cynddelw described each of Madog's warriors as 'a lion', and Madog himself as 'battle's bull'.[20] In another elegy he described Madog as 'a gold lion', and 'lion of Cadiaith'.[21] Gwalchmai also wrote a eulogy of Madog.

16_ Gwalchmai ap Meilyr, *Celebration*, or *When Chester was Fought for*, Clancy, 1970, pp. 119–23; Conran, 1967, pp. 104–5 for an abbreviated version.

17_ Gwalchmai, *To Owain Gwynedd*, Conran, 1967, pp. 106–7.

18_ Cynddelw, *In Praise of Owain Gwynedd*, Clancy, 1970, pp. 144–6.

19_ Cynddelw, *In Praise of Madog ap Maredudd*, Clancy, 1970, pp. 136–7.

20_ Cynddelw, *Elegy on the Death of Madog ap Maredudd*, or *The Fall of Powys*, Clancy, 1970, pp. 142–4.

21_ Ibid., pp. 141–2: alternative translation in Conran, 1967, pp. 118–19. This is the poem in which Madog is described as 'a firm anchor in a deep sea'.

Na mwy gronni eur nog erwaint flawd
Ni ryd rwysg eryr.

No more do you hoard gold than meadow-sweet
?No longer free is the authority of the eagle.[22]

22_ Gwalchmai ap Meilyr,
Panegyric on Madog
Prince of Powys: Jones
et al., Vol. I, 1801, p. 200;
Morris-Jones and
Parry-Williams, 1971,
pp. 15–16. The 'authority
of the eagle' is apparently
the expansionist power
of England.

23_ Gwalchmai ap Meilyr,
Panegyric on Madog,
pp. 201–2.

24_ Cynddelw, *Ode to*
Owain Cyfeiliog, transl.,
Myrddin Lloyd, in Jarman
and Rees Hughes, 1976,
p. 169.

25_ Owain *Cyfeiliog*,
Owain's Long Blue
Drinking Horn, Clancy,
1970, pp. 124–8: Conran,
1967, pp. 114–16.

26_ Gwalchmai ap Meilyr,
Eulogy of Rhodri ab
Owain, Jones et al., Vol. I,
1801, pp. 199–200:
Lofmarck, 1995, p. 58.
Some would translate this
as 'chief warrior and chief
of warriors'.

27_ Llywarch ap Llywelyn,
Prydydd y Moch, The
Threat of Dafydd ab
Owain, Clancy, 1970,
pp. 153–5.

28_ Llywarch ap Llywelyn,
In Praise of Llywelyn ab
Iorwerth, Clancy, 1970,
pp. 155–6.

However, in his elegy on this great Powys prince, Gwalchmai describes him as *draig dragonwys*, 'dragon of dragons' or 'warrior of warriors', as well as '*dragon of Powys*', in this way, perhaps, paying him the supreme compliment.[23]

When Cynddelw praised Owain *Cyfeiliog*, Owain ap Gruffudd, who ruled southern Powys between 1160 and about 1195, he described him as '*the tall, powerful eagle*'.[24] Owain *Cyfeiliog*, no mean poet himself, praised his own household troops, comparing them to the *Gododdin* war-band, and in part basing his own production on the epic poem. As a result individuals in his corps were '*heroic lion*', '*eagle's heart*', '*armies' eagle*', and others together were '*war-leaders*', '*wolves*', and '*two lions in combat*'.[25] But this was Powys.

Gwalchmai ap Meilyr had a career long enough for him to produce the *Eulogy of Rhodri ab Owain*, a poem to the son of Owain *Gwynedd*, who ruled over north Wales after his father, 1170–4 and 1175–94. Similar to his description of Madog, Gwalchmai hailed Rhodri as *pen draig a phendragon*, 'chief dragon and chief of dragons'.[26] Dafydd, younger brother of this Rhodri, who ousted and imprisoned him to then take the lordship of Gwynedd in his place if only for a year, 1174–5, was praised by Llywarch ap Llywelyn, his bardic name *Prydydd y Moch*, Poet of the Pigs. This poet flourished from about 1173 to around 1220. Here, in *The Threat of Dafydd ab Owain*, Dafydd is '*Eryri's* [Snowdia's] dragon' and the '*soldier's eagle*'.[27] Llywelyn ab Iorwerth, Llywelyn the Great, 1206–40, was '*a Welsh lion*', a '*royal eagle*', and '*dragon's wealth*'.[28]

It is, of course, the dramatic and, as it was to turn out, climactic reign of Llywelyn ap Gruffudd ap Llywelyn *Fawr*, the last great ruler of Gwynedd, reigning 1255–82, which called forth some of the greatest poetry of the early Middle Ages. In fact, Llywelyn began his reign ruling jointly with his brother Owain, an arrangement which lasted from 1246 to 1255: a rare example of divided authority in the later history of Gwynedd, but one that reminds us of the Gwynedd confederation of Maelgwn's days. Llywelyn's period of independent rule began in 1255 with the defeat of his elder brother Owain and younger brother Dafydd in the battle of Bryn Derwin above Clynnog on Thursday, 24 June, and their subsequent imprisonment. Hywel ap Griffri, called the Bald, writing *c.*1240–80, described the imprisoned Owain as dragon, *dilwfyr gwych gweithfuddig,* 'faultless, brilliant, victorious'.[29]

To Llygad *Gûr*, Llygad the Man, possibly the Vassal, writing in the 1270s, Llywelyn ap Gruffudd embodied the Welsh resistance to *estron genedl anghyfiath,* 'a foreign nation of alien speech'. His five odes to Llywelyn are the most nationalist in sentiment of any writing before the days of Owain *Glyndûr*. Llywelyn was '*the gold war-lord who holds three crowns*', those of Gwynedd's Abeffraw, Deheubarth's Dinefwr, and Powys's Mathrafal. He was '*war's bold lion*', '*the Prince of Arllechwedd*', '*the pillar of princes*', '*the prosperous governor of Gwynedd*', '*a heroic wolf from Eryri*' Snowdonia, '*an eagle among his nobles of matchless prowess*', and '*the lion of Gwynedd*'. Supremely, he was the '*dragon of Arfon of resistless fury*'.[30]

Naturally it was Llywelyn's death on Friday, 11 December 1282, near the bridge across the Irfon not far from Builth, seemingly announcing the collapse of Gwynedd, that provided Wales's bards with their greatest challenge, one which, according to every literary critic, they rose to magnificently. But it is not this literary achievement which concerns us here so much as the fact that right at the end of Gwynedd's independent history, which had begun in the last years of the Roman empire, we find the same references not just to the bestiary which was the stock of all royal descriptions, but also to the dragon, the most important badge of late Roman authority. The word may also have meant

29_ Hywel ap Griffri, in Jones et al., Vol. I, 1801, p. 392. In *The Progress of Llywelyn ap Gruffudd*, Dafydd *Benfras*, David Bighead, mentions 'dragon's hostages' – ibid., pp. 317–18.

30_ Translations by Revd Evan Evans in Parry, 1851, pp. 162–4.

warrior, but it was a warrior in that tradition and from that line. In the great elegy on Llywelyn by Gruffudd *ab yr Ynad Coch*, Gruffudd son of the Red Judge, the prince was *'a falcon unblemished'*, *'a lion'*, *'the strong lion of Gwynedd'*, *'a king-hawk'*, and *'a kingly and thrusting wolf'*. But he was more than this.

Pen milwr, pen moliant rhag llaw,
Pen dragon, pen draig oedd arnaw;
Pen Llywelyn deg, dygn o fraw – i'r byd
Bod pawl haearn trwyddaw.

31_ Lofmarck, 1995, p. 59; Conran, 1967, pp. 128–31, at p. 31; Clancy, 1970, pp. 171–3, at p. 173; and Jones et al., Vol. I, 1901, p. 396. There may have been a heraldic dragon on his helmet.

32_ Bleddyn *Fardd, Elegy on the Three Sons of Gruffudd ap Llywelyn*, Clancy, 1970, p. 169 translating *Dreigyeu* as 'Lords'. See also Morris-Jones and Parry-Williams, 1971, pp. 67–8. Llŷr's sons are two of the great mythological characters in *The Mabinogion*. They are associated with Gwynedd. Brân *Vendigeit*, Brân the Blessed, was a giant ruling over Britain who waded across the Irish Sea from his court in Harlech to avenge a family insult, and Manawydan, in Irish Mannanán, was the great 'power behind the throne' and god of the sea. Mannanán's name possibly came from *Manaw*, the Isle of Man, and from *Manaw Gododdin*, the plain of the Gododdin, the family home of Paternus.

Head of a warrior, head of future glory,
Head dragon with a dragon's head upon him;
Head of the fair Llywelyn, a grievous fright for the world
That it is pierced by an iron pole.[31]

Bleddyn *Fardd*, Bleddyn the Bard, who wrote between 1257 and 1285, also produced what many consider to be his greatest poem at this time. In his elegy, more restrained than Gruffudd's, Llywelyn is a *'calm-paced eagle'*, *'a manly lion'*. Yet it is not so much in this as in his lament for the last three princes of Wales – Owain, 1246–55, Llywelyn the Last, 1246–82, and Llywelyn's brother Dafydd, 1282–3 – that Bleddyn seems carried away, and in so doing, intentionally or not, reminds us of Gwynedd's origins. Owain was a *'swift-eagle'*, Llywelyn a *'red-speared hawk'*, and Dafydd, possibly *'hawk's assault'*. Then, in the ninth verse, the three princes are described together.

Dreigyeu rwyc arueu yn ragori
Dragon ddeitil uil uanyeri
Drwc yn gwnaeth hiraeth hir dewi trywyr
Uegyí [uegys] meibyon llyr llwyr glod ynni.

[Dragons] of slashing [or shattering] weapons, excelling,
Powerful thousand-bannered dragon,
Yearning has hurt us; long silent three men,
Like Llŷr's sons, the whole of our glory.[32]

The former Cistercian abbey of St Mary in Conwy, now the parish church. Burial place of Gruffudd ap Cynan, 1094–1137, Llywelyn the Great, 1200–40, and Dafydd ap Llywelyn, 1240–46. After the conquest, Edward I moved the monks to a new site higher up the Conwy river at Maenan.

West front of St Mary's,
Conwy. The stonework of
this west door was probably
first used for the entrance
to the monastery's chapter
house, but the lancet
windows above are in their
original position.

356

Above: Chester castle showing part of the extensively restored curtain wall of the upper or inner ward. Gruffydd ap Cynan was imprisoned in the castle in 1081, only escaping possibly late in 1093, as was Llywelyn the Last in December 1282 on his way to Shrewsbury and execution.

Left: All that remains of the Cistercian abbey of Cwm-hir, Maelienydd, once the largest church in Wales with a nave only exceeded in length by those of Winchester and Durham. Here is the resting place of Llywelyn the Last's headless body.

I love today what the English hate ...
I love its household and its strong buildings
And its lord's wish to go to war.
I love its strand and its mountains,
Its castle near the woods and its fine lands,
Its water meadows and its valleys,
Its white gulls and its lovely women ...
O Son of God, how great a wonder!
... Lovely Gwynedd.

Hywel ab Owain *Gwynedd*, d.1170.

CHAPTER TWELVE

THE NORMAN CONQUEST COMPLETED: THE ROMAN PROVINCE RESTORED

Llywelyn and Dafydd of Gwynedd and Edward I of England, 1282–1301

THE BATTLE OF THE RIVER IRFON 1282

On Friday, 11 December 1282 a battle was raging. On one side was the army of Roger Lestrange which had been moving into Wales from Montgomery. It was part of a three-pronged invasion of Wales by King Edward I this year in what was his second war against Gwynedd. On the other side was an army belonging to Llywelyn ap Gruffudd, prince of Wales, which was defending its position on the slopes of a promontory lying between the Wye and the Irfon. Whilst the battle was being fought, a scouting party from Lestrange's army came across a small group of Welsh soldiers, possibly eighteen in number, who were apparently attempting to rejoin their men. This was at a site not far from the fight, close to the bridge across the Irfon at the village of Cilmeri, two and a half miles to the west of Builth Wells. For some reason or other, they were not with their army when the action started, but neither, indeed, was the scouting party that discovered them. They were set upon by archers, and killed as they fled. One was run through the back by an English soldier. Stephen of Frankton, a Shropshire man, and Sir Robert Body, who was connected with this county having lands there, were both subsequently named as the person who struck the blow.

   After the battle had been won by the English, the suspicion grew that the men killed earlier might have included the prince of Wales himself. A party went back to the scene of the skirmish. One of the Welsh soldiers was still alive when he was found, and, refusing his pleas for a priest, Edward Mortimer beheaded him. Mortimer must have realized that the man at his feet was indeed the object of the whole invasion, none other than Llywelyn ap Gruffudd, lord of Wales, prince of Aberffraw, head dragon with a dragon's head upon him.[1]

So it seemed ended the kingdom of Gwynedd and, with it, the independence of Wales. Gwynedd's line of kings and princes could be traced back for nearly nine centuries. The day of Llywelyn's death was the feast of Pope Damasus I who had ruled from 1 October 366 to 11 December 384. In Britain, his pontificate saw the *barbarica conspiratione*, Count Theodosius's relief expedition, and the rise of Magnus Maximus who was firmly established as western Roman emperor by the time of Damasus's death in 384. As someone who had come to power by organizing the mass murder of his opponents immediately before his consecration, this early Renaissance pope born out of time, who had been 'indefatigable in promoting the Roman primacy', should have well understood, if not actually sympathized, with Maximus.[2] More to the point, it is to the period of Damasus's reign that we can trace the probable elevation of several local leaders in Britain to official positions within the imperial hierarchy in order to carry out patrol, defence, and maintenance duties. As we have seen, one of these appointments was in the area between the Tweed and the Forth, the lands of the northern Votadini where the first prefect or protector may have been Tacitus or Tegid son of Iago. It may even have been Iago himself. It was Paternus son of Tacitus, or Padarn son of Tegid who, as the result of a twist of events reasonably ascribed to 398, came to be the founder of that line of kings and princes which appeared to end somewhere near the present Cilmeri, earlier known as *Cefn-y-bedd*, and its church Llanganten, above the river Irfon in 1282. Damasus's successor on the chair of Peter between 1281 and 1285 was 'a mild, indecisive Frenchman', Martin IV. Devoid of political judgement and totally dependent on the Angevin king Charles of Sicily, Martin had nothing to say on Llywelyn's end. By this date, the Welsh church had long been under the control of Canterbury. To assert political control over

1_ Smith, 1998, pp. 561–7, and Smith, 1982–3, pp. 200–13. Llywelyn's proper title was prince of Wales. The descriptions here are in Gruffudd ab yr Ynad Goch, *Elegy for Llywelyn ap Gruffudd,* Conran, 1967, pp. 127–31.

2_ Kelly, 1986, p. 33.

Gwynedd, Edward had used the whole might of the English state. Powys, in fact, was to continue as a marcher lordship until 1536. It had taken Edward two wars to achieve his ambition: the first between 1276 and 1277, and the second from 1282. Now, he was determined to make the most of his victory.

DISPOSING OF LLYWELYN

Llywelyn's headless corpse was buried in the Cistercian abbey of Cwm-hir in Maelienydd in central Wales. Today, a slate slab marks the spot where some believe his grave to be. His head was sent to Edward, who was in Rhuddlan on the north Wales coast near the mouth of the river Clwyd throughout December 1282 and for the first half of 1283. From there it was sent, via Chester, to London. In the *Chronicle* of the Benedictine abbey of St Werburgh's in Chester, an entry for 1282 acknowledges the power of Llywelyn and the threat to England he supposedly represented. In it two monks, one Welsh, the other English, enter their epitaphs on the late prince.

The Welshman as follows:
"Here lies of Englishmen
The tormentor; the guardian of the Welsh,
The prince of the Welsh,
Llewelin the example of manners,
The jewel of his contemporaries,
The flower of the kings of the past,
The model of those of the future,
The leader, the glory, the law, the light of the people."
  The Englishman thus replied:
"Here lies the prince of deceptions
And the plunderer of men,
The betrayer of the English,
A livid torch, a school of the wicked,
For the Welsh a deity,
A cruel leader, a murderer of the pious,

[Sprung from] the dregs of the Trojans,
From a lying race, a cause of evils."[3]

Just as Aeneas and his descendants, especially Romulus, founded Rome, tradition asserted that Brutus, who also fled from Troy with his grandfather Aeneas, came to Britain and was the first Briton. He has this position in Nennius and Geoffrey of Monmouth gives us the details.

Brutus [who had called the island of Britain from his own name because before it had been called Albion and was uninhabited except for a few giants] had consummated his marriage with his wife Ignoge. By her he had three sons called Locrinus, Kamber [or Camber] and Albanactus, all of whom were to become famous. When their father finally died, in the twenty-third year after his landing, these three sons buried him inside the walls of the town [*Troia Nova*, New Troy, London] which he had founded.

They divided the kingdom of Britain between them ... Locrinus, who was the first-born, inherited the part of the island which was afterwards called Loegria [modern Welsh *Lloegr*, possibly *the lost country*, England] after him.

Kamber received the region which is on the further bank of the River Severn, the part which is now known as Wales but which was for a long time after his death called Kambria [Latinization of *Cymru*] from his name. As a result the people of that country still call themselves Kambri today in the Welsh tongue [*combroges*, modern Welsh *Cymry*, fellow countrymen, the Welsh].

Albanactus, the youngest, took the region which is nowadays called Scotland in our language. He called it Albany [from the British *albio*, the land or country], after his own name.[4]

It is interesting that a monk of Chester should have described the Welsh, or at least the Welsh who supported Llywelyn's stand, as the dregs of the Trojans. In effect,

3_ *Annales Cestrienses* or the *Chronicle of St Werburgh*, 1282, Christie, 1887, p. 111. The extant copy of these annals dates to the late fifteenth or early sixteenth century, with additions made at that time. The principal scribe was a Welshman. Not surprisingly, given Chester's border position, many of the entries concern Wales.

4_ Geoffrey of Monmouth, *The History of the Kings of Britain*, II. 1, Thorpe, 1966, p. 75.

he was saying they were the miserable remains of those who were descended from the Romans.

WESTMINSTER ABBEY RECEIVES THE SPOILS

In all probability, Edward's son Alphonso, still a boy, accompanied the grisly trophy of the prince of Wales's head on its way to London, also taking with him Llywelyn's ring, possibly even his coronet, along with other jewels that had been captured. Llywelyn's head was exhibited on one of the turrets of the Tower at the end of a spear and adorned with either a paper-gilt crown or one of ivy. This last touch was in mockery of the age-old prophecy that the princes of Wales would sweep the Saxons back into the sea with Llywelyn or another Welsh prince then being crowned in London. One writer adds that yet another indignity had befallen the head. 'Then it was placed in the pillory to glut the revenge of a brutish rabble.'[5] His head was still on a turret of the Tower fifteen years later.[6] Alphonso, acting as Edward's heir, offered up Llywelyn's ring and the other jewels that had been taken on the high altar of St Peter's abbey, Westminster.[7] He was destined to survive this ceremony by only a few months.

1283: DAFYDD'S REBELLION

But the history of Gwynedd's princes could not be extinguished so easily. If Edward believed it would all be over with Llywelyn's death, he was to be bitterly disappointed. Dafydd, Llywelyn's brother, had waited too long and schemed too hard to take the place of Llywelyn only to sit back and see this snatched away from him now by an English king who, he believed, had paid him very poorly for all the help he had given. Assuming his brother's place, Dafydd summoned a Welsh parliament and won sufficient support to continue the struggle. Then, on 18 January 1283, Dolwyddelan

[5] Parry, 1851, p. 147. *Chronicle of St Werburgh*, Christie, 1887, p. 113. It is more than probable that some such public mocking at the pillory was allowed before the head appeared on a spike above one of the turrets of the Tower.

[6] Carr, 1995, pp. 355–6.

[7] 'Urien', 1846, pp. 42–3; Parry, 1851, p. 171; and Davies, 1991, pp. 355–6.

castle fell to Edward's troops, to be followed in February by Cricieth. Dafydd moved south to the castle built by his grandfather Llywelyn the Great which lay under Cadair Idris, Castell y Bere in south Meirionydd. However, when Roger Lestrange and William de Valence moved in from Montgomery and Llanbadarn respectively, Dafydd was forced back into Snowdonia. The castle of Bere surrendered on 25 April. On Sunday, 2 May, Dafydd issued two letters from Dolbadarn ordering the recruitment of troops and signing himself *Princeps Wallie et dominus Snaudonie*. But it was no use. Leading Welsh figures, seeing their country exhausted by the struggle, themselves arrested Dafydd on 21 June. Only one of those involved was afterwards named: Einion ab Ifor, in other words, Anian II, bishop of St Asaph 1268–93.

DISPOSING OF LLYWELYN'S FAMILY AND POSSESSIONS

Arrested with Dafydd was his wife Elizabeth, daughter of the earl of Derby and formerly wife of William Marshal, earl of Norfolk. Dafydd had married her in December 1277 after Edward's first successful Welsh war. Also taken were their sons Owain and Llywelyn, and at least one of his daughters, probably Gwladus.[8] It was probably at the same time, in June, that Gwenllian, daughter of Dafydd's brother and predecessor Llywelyn, also fell into Edward's hands. Llywelyn's wife, Eleanor de Montfort, princess of Wales, lady of Snowdon, had died giving birth to Gwenllian in June 1282, so that Dafydd's niece was less than a year old at this point. Eleanor had been buried in the friary of Llanfaes in Anglesey near the later Beaumaris castle. This was the church built by Llywelyn's and Dafydd's grandfather, Llywelyn the Great, in 1237, to cover the burial site of *his* wife Joan, daughter of King John, who had died that year on Monday, 2 February. Gwenllian, Llywelyn's daughter, lived until 1337 in the Gilbertine nunnery of

8_ Dafydd supposedly had seven daughters, but only Gwladus's name is known. Unless there were several twins, *if* these were his daughters they must have been the issue of an earlier relationship or relationships than that with Elizabeth.

Sempringham, Lincolnshire, to which as a tiny infant she was sent, and where, against her will, she was later made a nun. Gwladus, Dafydd's daughter, ended up in the Gilbertine priory of Sixhills, also in Lincolnshire, dying there in 1336, a year before Gwenllian. Edward did his absolute best, short of ordering murders, to ensure that the family line would not continue.

Dafydd and his family were examined at Edward's headquarters at Rhuddlan where the king was in residence from 18 June till at least the 30th. When Dafydd had been arrested it was found that he had in his possession what was reputedly a fragment of the True Cross. This, the *Croesenydd, Croes Naid*, the Cross of Refuge or Protection, was normally kept in a reliquary, gilded and ornamented with precious stones. Hitherto, it had on occasion been carried in procession before the princes of Wales. Also taken, probably now rather than earlier after Llywelyn's death, was the crown or jewel of Arthur. No doubt for their protection rather than as a token of any further surrender, these extraordinarily valuable objects were taken to Rhuddlan by Anian/Einion, the bishop of St Asaph, who was accompanied by others involved in Dafydd's fall, the whole party no doubt protected by soldiers sent from Edward's army. Letters of protection were issued for the safe return of these Welsh envoys.

For Einion the son of Ivor [bishop of St Asaph] and the others who bore to the king [at Rhuddlan] that part of the most precious wooden cross which is called by the Welsh *Croysseneyht*, may they have this liberty, that they may not be held to follow in another army of the king outside the four cantreds [of Rhos, Rhufoniog, Tegeingl, and Dyffryn Clwyd, in northeast Wales, where Edward was then based].[9]

Among 'the others' mentioned in the writ, was Hugh ab Ithel. This was possibly the unnamed secretary of Prince Dafydd, who according to the *Chronicle of William of Rishanger*, was one of those who handed over the Welsh

9_ *Rotulus Walliae*, Welsh Writs, II Ed. I, 20 Nov. 1282–19 Nov. 1283; 'Urien', 1846. That Dafydd was brought to the king at Rhuddlan is shown in the *Chronicle of St Werburgh*, Christie, 1887, p. 133. See also Parry, 1851, pp. 148–9. Cf. Smith, 1998, p. 580, note 244, who, whilst citing the Calendar of Welsh Rolls, the *Rotulus Walliae* quoted above, and saying that the cross relic was handed over in June, states that this took place in Aberconwy: cf. Prestwich, 1990, p. 204, who also says the cross was handed to Edward in Conwy, but who places this event on the 1284 progress! Edward was in Conwy 4–15/16 June, but in Rhuddlan 18–30 June. Dafydd was arrested and handed over to English troops on 21 June and taken immediately to the king who was in Rhuddlan.

royal treasures. He was to receive financial support from Edward to study in Oxford.[10]

CELEBRATIONS IN CHESTER, SATURDAY, 28 AUGUST 1283

Whilst in prison at Rhuddlan, Dafydd pleaded to be allowed to speak directly to the king, but this was refused. At the end of August troops escorted Dafydd and his family to Chester. Possibly he was in Edward's train for part of the journey.[11] Edward and Queen Eleanor were in Hope castle on 26 and 27 August and in Chester from 28 to 30 August. On Saturday, 28 August, with Dafydd probably safely lodged in Chester's castle, King Edward, with or without his queen, heard mass in the Benedictine abbey of St Werburgh on what was the feast day of St Augustine of Hippo. It was to be one of many celebrations for the conquest of Gwynedd and its territories.

1283 ... Our lord the king and the queen came to Chester after the conquest of Wales.
On S. Augustine's day [Saturday, 28 August 1283] the king heard mass in the church of S. Werburgh of Chester, and offered a valuable cloth.
The king himself took to preserve the liberties of S. Werburgh.[12]

Augustine, author of *The City of God* and the autobiographical *Confessions*, had been born in 354 in *Thagaste*, in the province of Africa, which comprised the modern states of Tunisia and eastern Algeria. He died on 28 August 430 as the Vandals were besieging his own cathedral city of Hippo, a north African port second only to Carthage now situated in northeastern Algeria. In *Civitas Dei* he had tried to show that all these happenings were part of God's plan, as indeed was the whole of human history. This plan was for the building of two great cities: the City of God, containing those

10_ Smith, 1998, p. 580, note 244.

11_ From the calendars of close and patent rolls, it is clear that after 30 June 1283, Edward moved from Rhuddlan to Conwy, being there from 4 July. He was in Caernarfon from 12 July, briefly moving over to Anglesey. He was in Dafydd's castle of Hope, known today as Caergwrle castle, on Thursday, 26 August, after visiting Ruthin on 25 August. Eleanor and Edward arrived in Chester on Friday, 27 August.

12_ The *Chronicle of St Werburgh*, Christie, 1887, p. 113. The editor gives a mistaken 26 May date, which is that of Augustine, apostle of England and archbishop of Canterbury. A look at Edward's itinerary shows that the festival was that of Augustine of Hippo.

St Werburgh's abbey,
Chester, now the cathedral,
seen from the northwest.

The former abbey of
St Werburgh viewed here
from the Roman parade
ground outside the city's
in part Roman walls.

The Norman arch in
the north transept of
what was formerly,
St Werburgh's, Chester.
The arcading above is
very probably Roman,
salvaged from some part
of the original fortress.

Right and below: The chapter house of St Werburgh's abbey. Abbot Simon de Whitchurch in his 28 August 1283 Saturday guided tour would have shown Edward I not only the north transept but also this chapter house which Simon had recently had built.

predestined to reign with God for all eternity, and the City of the World, for all those unredeemed and unredeemable who were destined for eternal damnation. Augustine published *Civitas Dei* at intervals between 414 and 426, after the shock and horror caused by the capture and sack of Rome by the Goths in 410 had begun to give way to either sober reflection or vicious recrimination. In part, the book was designed to prove that Christianity was not responsible for such calamities, by either dethroning Rome's ancient deities or undermining the empire's traditional values. All history was part of the Divine Plan even if mere human beings could not fathom the inscrutable mind of God.

The cause of the greatness of the Roman Empire was neither chance nor destiny ... Without the slightest doubt, the kingdoms of men are established by divine providence ...

the one true God, who never leaves the human race unattended by his judgement or his help, granted dominion to the Romans when he willed and in the measure that he willed ... The same God gave power to Marius and to Gaius Caesar, to Augustus and to Nero, the Vespasians, father and son, the most attractive emperors, as well as to Domitian, the most ruthless tyrant; and (we need not run through the whole list) the same God gave the throne to Constantine the Christian, and also to Julian the Apostate ...

It is clear that God, the one true God, rules and guides these events, according to his pleasure. If God's reasons are inscrutable, does that mean that they are unjust?[13]

Possibly, in 1283, Edward did indeed feel that he was an instrument in the accomplishment of at least one part of this unfolding plan. If Paternus was appointed to a north Wales command in 398, then it was only 115 years short of 1,000 years after this, on St Augustine's Day in 1283, that Edward was offering up thanks in Chester's St Werburgh's for the end of a history that began with

13_ Augustine, *Concerning the City of God against the Pagans*, Book V, Chs. 1 and 21, Bettenson and Knowles, 1972, pp. 179 and 215–16.

this count's control over north Wales. No doubt the king had only the vaguest understanding of the Roman beginnings of the story he was now in the process of finishing, but, as we shall see, at the time this Roman background was very much on his mind.

DAFYDD'S EXECUTION IN SHREWSBURY, SATURDAY, 2 OCTOBER 1283

On Thursday, 30 September 1283, Edward held a parliament in Shrewsbury to try Dafydd on a charge of treason. In other words, he was being treated as a mere vassal of the English crown. The result was hardly in doubt. Dafydd was dragged to the gallows in Shrewsbury's market place on Saturday, 2 October.[14] Geoffrey of Shrewsbury, probably a butcher by trade, was paid 20 shillings for carrying out the execution.[15] A later gruesome tradition relates that as Dafydd's heart was being burned in the fire at the gallows the heat caused it to swell and explode, so blinding the courtier who had thrown it in.[16]

1283. In the same year on the day of S. Dionysius [Dionysius the Areopagite, 3 October], in the great Parliament of the king at Shrewsbury, David, son of Griffin, perished by a miserable death. He was first torn in pieces [dragged by horses to the gallows], then after being hanged and his head cut off, he was divided into four quarters.[17]

The four parts of Dafydd's body were sent to English cities; the head was sent to London to join that of his brother on the Tower. This was a common enough occurrence in such circumstances but, as in Llywelyn's case, there was in this gesture a reference to Welsh dreams of recovering their island to rule once more in London: dreams which should have ended with the death of Cadwallon ap Cadfan in 635. Dafydd's daughters, like Llywelyn's Gwenllian, were packed off to Lincolnshire

[14]_ The date is also in Smith, 1998, and Carr, 1982, but 3 October, the Chester date, in Carr, 1999, and Evans, 1974. Commonly this 3 October date features in internet sites. *Brut Y Tywysogion*, The Chronicle of the Princes, Peniarth MS 20, gives no date, and *Brenhinedd Y Saesson*, The Kings of the Saxons, gives Christmas Eve 1283! For the *Chronicle of St Werburgh*'s 3 October to be true we have to accept that the execution took place on a Sunday. The Saturday market day is likelier.

[15]_ Smith, 1998, p. 579, note 235.

[16]_ Parry, 1851, pp. 149–50 and note 5.

[17]_ The Chronicle of St Werburgh, Christie, 1887, p. 118. It is difficult to know what weight to place on the absence of any reference to disembowelling in this account, but a butcher was involved and the heart was pulled out. Possibly this, the most dreadful part of the execution process, was omitted in deference to Dafydd's rank.

and the religious life. Dafydd's sons Owain and Llywelyn both died as prisoners in Bristol castle.[18]

THE BUILDING OF CAERNARFON CASTLE: BEGUN 1283

It is what Edward I created in Caernarfon that shows just how much the Roman past was on his mind in these last months of the conquest of Gwynedd. It was probably in May 1283 that his troops occupied *Segontium* and Caernarfon, the sites of the Roman fortress and, lower down on the shores of the river Seiont as it entered the Menai Straits, the later Norman motte and bailey castle. One of the principal seats of the kings of Gwynedd, the others being Degannwy, Abergwyngregyn, and Aberffraw, the *Segontium-*Caernarfon site had been used particularly by Merfyn *Frych*, ruling between 824 and 844, giving it another name, Merfyn's Town. Llywelyn ap Gruffudd, Llywelyn the Last, also had a special liking for the place. The site had an obvious strategic importance, commanding as it did the western entrance to the Menai Strait, and standing at the northwest corner of Gwynedd's mountainous heart, where deep and awesomely impressive valleys contained other royal strongholds, particularly those of Dolbadarn and Dolwyddelan.

Building work on Edward's new castle in Caernarfon probably began in June 1283. The site chosen was the area surrounding the remains of the motte built by Earl Hugh of Chester some time during the period 1081–93 when the Normans achieved a quick, if short-lived, mastery over north Wales.[19] The site was even more suited to thirteenth-century needs than it had been to the needs of the early Normans, because not only was it bounded on the south by the river Seiont, and on the west by the Menai Strait, to the north there was another smaller stream, the Afon Cadnant. As Edward intended to create an English borough extending north from the castle along the shore of the strait, this stream flowing

[18]_ Llywelyn in 1287, and Owain c.1325.

[19]_ The motte is still visible inside the walls of Edward's castle on a photograph taken about 1870. It was levelled soon after, its debris creating the higher ground of the castle's eastern or King's Ward.

along the town's eastern and northern sides gave it a ready-made defensive ditch and mill-pond.[20]

On 20 June 1283, probably the day before Dafydd was arrested, Edward, in his headquarters in Rhuddlan, ordered that all material prepared for the enclosure of Rhuddlan's borough should instead be forwarded to Caernarfon. This is the first reference to building work on the Seiont and shows that Edward had already abandoned plans for making Rhuddlan his pre-eminent fortress in north Wales in favour of the more westerly site. So a timber stockade began to grow around the Norman motte. Inside this, the first buildings were timber-framed structures to accommodate the king and queen and their needs. Edward and Eleanor duly arrived on 12 July, having travelled from Conwy. Even a lawn was laid for the queen's use. Edward stayed in Caernarfon for most of July, and visited it twice in August before he finally moved from Rhuddlan to Chester with Dafydd at the end of the month. All this time, vast quantities of timber and other materials poured in by sea.

It is difficult to avoid the conclusion that Edward was becoming almost obsessed with the site at Caernarfon and the castle he intended to build there. In the first instance, this fortress was to be the home of Edward's viceroy, who would have the task of imposing the new order upon a conquered Wales. That man was Sir Otto de Grandson who, from his appointment in October 1284, was also to be the constable of the castle. For this reason alone, Caernarfon was to be the largest, strongest, and most imposing of all Edward's castles. The principal architect was the man responsible for all Edward's building projects in north Wales, namely Master James of St George, with, at his side as principal assistant, Master Richard the Engineer of Chester. Another prominent figure was Master Manasser de Vaucouleurs, that is, from Vaucouleurs in Champagne, who was employed as master mason and director of diggers. He ended his days as burgess and bailiff of the new English town of Caernarfon. The first constable during this early planning period was not Sir Otto, but Thomas de Maydenhach.

20_ Today, passing through the now expanded town of Caernarfon, the Cadnant flows mainly underground, emptying into the New Basin, the Victoria Dock, just outside the northern section of the town wall.

Caernarfon castle. The Eagle Tower and the start of the south curtain wall.

Right: The Eagle Tower seen from the Justiciar's ward.

Below: The south curtain wall facing the river Seiont showing, from left to right, the Queen's tower, the Chamberlain's tower, and the Black tower.

NEW ROMES: ON THE BOSPHORUS AND ON THE MENAI

Caernarfon, however, was intended to be more than just the largest or the strongest castle in Wales. It is, in fact, the largest medieval castle in the whole of Europe. More important than this, as one of the leading experts on Edward's wars and castle building has written, Edward intended that this fortress-capital should be the fulfilment of a tradition and the interpretation of a dream.[21] Edward was not only aware of the site's importance in Welsh history. He also saw that it had a significance in England's history, as well as in a past beyond that. There for all to see were the ruins of the great Roman fort at *Segontium*, a mere 700 yards up the hill from Edward's rising fortress.

By the thirteenth century the great Welsh tales together known today as *The Mabinogion* had a considerable circulation and one of these concerned the dream of the western emperor Magnus Maximus, Macsen *Wledig*.

And he [Macsen] saw a great city at the mouth of the river, and in the city a great castle, and he saw many great towers of various colours on the castle. And he saw a fleet at the mouth of the river, and that was the biggest fleet that mortal had ever seen ... a great castle, the fairest that mortal had ever seen, and the gate of the castle he saw open, and he came to the castle.

Inside the castle he saw a fair hall. The roof of the hall he thought to be all of gold; the side of the hall he thought to be of glittering stones, each as costly as its neighbour; the hall doors he thought to be all of gold.[22]

When he awoke from the dream, Macsen knew he had to find this castle and the girl he had seen there with whom he was now in love. His scouts eventually found the place, in Britain, in Snowdonia, between Arfon and Môn. 'And Aber Seint they saw, and the castle at the mouth of the river.' Having made Elen, the girl in the castle, his wife, she chose 'that the most

21_ Taylor, 1963 and 1974.

22_ *The Dream of Macsen Wledig*, in The Mabinogion, Jones and Jones, 1973, pp. 79–88, at pp. 79–80.

exalted stronghold should be made for her in Arfon, and soil from Rome was brought there so that it might be healthier for the emperor to sleep and sit and move about'.[23]

Although the Four Branches, that is, the four tales of Pwyll, Branwen, Manawydan, and Math, in the form we have them, can be reasonably dated to the twelfth century, the other independent Welsh tales and romances now included under the general nineteenth-century title *The Mabinogion* are almost certainly of a later date.[24] It would seem, however, that stories concerning Maximus were current in Wales in the late thirteenth century and that when the story was written down, the description of Macsen's *Segontium* was clearly one based on Edward's Caernarfon. Edward was almost certainly told the tale and it was possibly his interest that led to the story being committed to the page.

To excite even further Edward's growing appreciation of the place where he was beginning to erect his new imperial capital, presumably at some point during his July 1283 stay in Caernarfon, he was shown an inscribed stone, possibly in the burial ground surrounding Llanbeblig church just outside what remained of *Segontium*'s walls. This church had allegedly been founded by Publicius, a son of the emperor Magnus Maximus, 383–8. Edward would also have been told, and no doubt repeatedly, that Magnus's empress, Publicius's mother, was British. The stone would have been badly eroded by the ninth century when it was referred to in the writings of Nennius's *The History of the Britons* and in an even worse state in the thirteenth century when it was shown to Edward.

The memorial apparently carried some form of the words CONSTANTINE, CONSTANTIUS, or CONSTANTINUS; PRINCEPS or perhaps IMPERATUR; and MAGNUS or MAXIMUS. Probably Edward was also shown the passage in the *Historia Brittonum* that listed the emperors of Rome who were alleged to have visited Britain. This begins with the name of Julius Caesar, and was followed by Claudius,

23_ Ibid., p. 85.

24_ The term *mabinogi* originally meant boyhood, then a tale about a hero's boyhood, and then just a tale. Now, it is used as a collective term for the *Four Branches* or the four tales. *Mabinogion* comes from a scribal error at the end of the first tale, taken by Charlotte Guest as the title for her collection of translations, 1838–49, which included, as well as the *Four Branches*, seven other stories including *The Dream of Macsen Wledig*.

Severus, Carausius 'who was a tyrant', and then Constantine son of Constantine the Great.

The fifth [to come to Britain] was Constantine, son of Constantine the Great, and there he died. His tomb is to be seen by the city called Caer Seint, as the letters on its stonework show. He sowed three seeds of gold, of silver, and of bronze, on the pavement of that city, that no man should live there poor ...[25]

This was repeated in the Latin *Life of Gruffudd ap Cynan*, who, briefly ruling in 1081, was king of Gwynedd from 1094 to 1137. This *Vita* or *Historia* was written between Gruffudd's death and the appearance of the earliest extant version, which is a Welsh text datable to the thirteenth century. Here it states that Earl Hugh of Chester built a castle 'in Arfon, in the old fortress of Constantine, emperor, son of Constans the Great'.[26]

If Edward was told of the Nennius text, he was probably given a corrected version making Constantius the *father* of Constantine the Great as Roger of Wendover states.[27] This is indeed correct, but after the death of the western emperor Constantius in York on 25 July 306 and the proclamation of his son Constantine as emperor in his place, Constantius's remains were taken back to the Continent. The stone outside *Segontium* could have been that of Constantine, the son of Magnus Maximus, who may well have returned to Britain in the company of his mother Helena, brother Publicius, and sister Sevira, when their father made his bid for Italy. However, it is more than likely that the Constantine who was a son of Magnus Maximus was the Constantine III who died in Italy.

We are left with the simple fact that this tombstone could have belonged to almost anyone of that name or variation of it. There may or may not have been some official with a personal connection to the imperial family, but it was common for tombstones to record the name of the emperor ruling at the time of death. It is possible that Edward *was* made aware of the conflicting evidence

25_ Nennius, *Historia Brittonum*, Ch. 25, Morris, 1980, p. 24.

26_ *Hanes Gruffudd ap Cynan*, The History of Gruffudd ap Cynan, Jones, 1910, p. 133.

27_ Wade-Evans, 1930, p. 335.

and only enormous condescension towards the past allows us to see the king and his advisers completely falling for some grossly inflated claim. Perhaps he did tend to believe, or more accurately chose to believe, that the tomb *was* that of Emperor Constantius I who ruled from 305 to 306. Whatever he thought of the remains, he now had these exhumed and reburied in Llanbeblig church.

Llanbeblig was now the church of the castle and then, when it began to grow, of the new English borough, a situation that lasted up until 1303. Then the chapel of St Mary was built in the northeast angle of the town walls alongside the Menai Strait, although this may only have been a chantry chapel. Possibly Edward hoped that one day a church worthy of the castle and borough now rising on this north Wales coast would be built, even a cathedral. If so, he was to be disappointed. For the moment, however, the existing church would have to suffice as the resting place of a Roman emperor.

In the region of Kaernervan the body of the great prince, the father of the Emperor, noble Constantine, had been found, and, with the king ordering it, it was placed in a church.[28]

Edward would certainly have had a firmer grasp of more recent English history. His conquest of Gwynedd and with it that of Wales was justified in his eyes, not only by Welsh rejection of clearly established feudal ties, but also by a supposed earlier Saxon lordship over the land. There was also the incontrovertible evidence of Earl Hugh's motte where Edward was now building his castle. In effect, Edward's conquest completed the Norman conquest of Britain south of Hadrian's Wall which had begun in 1066. More than that, it placed Edward in the line of kings such as Alfred, 871–99, Athelstan, 924–39, Edgar, 959–75, William, 1066–87, and Henry II, 1154–89, as one who had expanded the empire of Britain. In the process, Edward was restoring an imperial authority that derived from the Roman

28_ Roger of Wendover, *Flowers of History*, in Wade-Evans, 1930, p. 335.

empire itself. Neither should this impress us as merely one other historical curiosity. The whole of European history since the abdication of the last western Roman emperor, Romulus Augustulus, in 476 can be seen as one long series of attempts to recreate that lost empire, to restore what was seen as a lost unity, order, and peace.[29]

This often under-appreciated theme in European history reveals itself in the most unexpected places. King Henry II of England, 1154–89, who added Ireland to the lands owing obedience to him, was acutely aware of his prerogatives and independence as king. Nevertheless, he could happily write to the Holy Roman Emperor, Frederick I, Frederick *Barbarossa*, in 1157, acknowledging the emperor's *superior authority*. This superiority did not just stem from greater military or political power. It came also from the position of the German empire as the most obvious successor and inheritor of the authority once exercised by the Roman empire.

We place our kingdom and everything subject to our rule anywhere at your disposal and entrust it to your power so that all things shall be arranged at your nod and that the will of your *imperium* shall be done in everything.

Let there be then between us and our peoples an indivisible unity of peace and love and of safe commerce, yet in such a way that the authority to command shall go to you who hold the higher rank and we shall not be found wanting in willingness to obey.[30]

In Edward's company through many weeks of 1283 was Sir William de Cicon, constable of the new royal castle of Rhuddlan, who was shortly to be appointed as the first constable of Conwy. He had returned from the east in 1276 and so was probably one of the very few people in Edward's train who had seen Constantinople. The building of that great city, at this point still the capital of the eastern Roman empire, the Byzantine empire as it was now called, had been formally begun in November 324 and it was solemnly

29_ The paradox involved in this assertion will be obvious, because such attempts by Germany, France, and Spain have produced most of the division, disorder, and war in European history.

30_ Henry II to Emperor Frederick I, 1157, Flanagan, 1989, pp. 215–16: Leyser, 1975, pp. 492–3. As though emphasizing the *theoretical* nature of such lordship, this letter comes as part of Henry II's refusal to hand over to Frederick a relic that had once belonged to the German treasury!

inaugurated as the new centre of the Roman world on 11 May 330. Constantine named it *Nova Roma*, New Rome. Theodosius II, 408–50, extended the capital's defences with a new wall further out than Constantine's line because by this date development had spilled well beyond the original confines of the city. The new wall was built between 408 and 413, like its predecessor running from the *Propontis*, the Sea of Marmara, to the Golden Horn. It was constructed of alternate layers of brick and stone, partly to anchor the exterior to the mortar core and partly to make earthquakes less damaging. The result was a patterning in the walls that immediately captures the eye. Almost certainly, Sir William had taken a keen interest in these defences.

It is, as the great expert on Caernarfon castle A. J. Taylor wrote, too great a coincidence that Constantinople's walls and Caernarfon's castle walls both have polygonal towers and turrets, that both have horizontal bands of different coloured stone or brick along the walls and round the towers, and that both have Golden Gates.[31] This is all strikingly different from the round towers and the white-painted plastering found in all of Edward's other castles. That Caernarfon had a Golden Gate is confirmed by a reference to *the Gildyn yeate* in 1524. However, by then the name had been transferred to the town's Watergate, never properly completed, which lay to the north of the Eagle Tower, and which gave access from the Strait into the moat running along the north side of the castle.

The original Golden Gate was the entrance into the castle directly from the waters of the Strait at the base of the Eagle Tower. This building rears up as the greatest and most imposing of the castle's structures, ten-sided, with a basement and three storeys. It was designed and built to house the king's lieutenant or viceroy in Wales, the justiciar, who was also the castle's constable. No doubt symbolizing the three powers of king, viceroy, and constable, the tower has rising above it three tall hexagonal turrets, each originally surmounted by an eagle. In early documents it is called the Tower of

[31]_ Taylor, 1974, pp. 370–1. Abigail Wheatley's 'Caernarfon Castle and its Mythology' in Williams, Diane, and Kenyon, John, eds., *The Impact of the Edwardian Castles in Wales*, Oxbow, 2009, misses far too much and merely reminds us that Edward had plenty of Roman work in England to further excite his dreams. In all descriptions of the castle it has to be borne in mind that the Menai Strait, generally flowing northeast to southwest, at the site of the castle is briefly flowing from north to south, these directions being reversed with the tides. The castle therefore lies east to west along the river Seiont which here enters the Strait.

Eagles.[32] Here was the supreme symbol of imperial Rome: the badge of the legions that had created that greatness. The dragon, so important in the later empire as well as in the British states considering themselves its heir, would hardly have been appropriate.

Erasmus once observed that the device chosen by wise men to represent kings is the eagle, which is cruel and murderous, not musical or beautiful, and confers no benefit on mankind. He considered the choice appropriate.

Similarly whole nations, since the earliest times, have preferred to take the deadliest of beasts as their emblems: the Vulture and the Cobra were chosen to be the sacred animals of Lower and Upper Egypt (where the crocodile also was worshipped). In north east India and Tibet, the man-eating tiger, as well as the dragon, was venerated. The English chose the lion.[33]

The eighteenth-century traveller and antiquarian Thomas Pennant claimed that at least one of the eagles used by Edward I to adorn the topmost position in his castle was itself Roman.

The Eagle tower is remarkably fine, and has the addition of three slender angular turrets issuing from the top. The Eagle upon the tower (says my antiquary friend) is, with good reason, supposed to be Roman, and that Edward found it at old Segontium.[34]

Apart from the stupendous scale of the whole conception, the plan of Caernarfon appears, superficially, to be very similar to that of Conwy, a castle already well advanced by the time Caernarfon was begun. That is, both consisted of two wards, which in both cases might seem to be outer and inner baileys. In Caernarfon, however, the concept was quite different. Despite the somewhat misleading terms used today, it is clear that the novelty of the original design for Caernarfon lay in giving the two wards equal status, instead of adopting the usual

[32]_ The eagle on the western turret is reasonably complete and recognizable; the eastern turret possibly has the remains of one; the other turret's bird has flown. In Constantinople/Istanbul today, a white marble Byzantine eagle can be seen above the small Yedikule Kapisi gate.

[33]_ Lofmarck, 1995, p. 34.

[34]_ Pennant, Vol. II, Part 2, 1783, pp. 224–5. The fact that the Eagle Tower was not completed until well into the fourteenth century does not exclude the possibility that Edward did indeed have a Roman eagle from Segontium prominently displayed on his castle's walls.

plan of having an outer bailey giving greater security for the real heart of the castle which was the inner bailey, usually with its back to the sea or a river.[35] In Caernarfon the western ward on the Menai Strait side was to be the centre of the vice-regal administration; the eastern ward on the land side provided accommodation for the king himself, or later the prince of Wales, whenever they visited. Consequently the Watergate entrance to the Eagle Tower on the west had its counterpart in the massively tall and imposing Queen's Gate at the eastern end, which was approached from the town by a long stone ramp and then by a turning bridge over a narrow chasm. Because of an apparent determination to raise the curtain walls as quickly as possible, the inner side of the Queen's Gate and its rooms were never finished and the long stone ramp may also have been left incomplete. Perhaps the most surprising fact about Caernarfon is that because it was planned and begun on such a vast scale, most of the design was never built.

Such an organization of the castle's functions led to the final architectural expression of its rôle as the seat of Edward's imperial government in Wales. Between the two wards, instead of a dividing wall running across the castle, in which, in the usual designs of such bastions, a narrow entrance gave access to the inner ward via a ditch and drawbridge as at Conwy, the plan at Caernarfon was for a huge ceremonial entrance hall, entered by way of the King's Gate on the north side of the castle. This gate, with two drawbridges, five huge doors, six portcullises, and a vault containing murder holes, was, and still is, awesomely impressive. The gate was to have led into the entrance hall which would have been rather like the nave of some great cathedral. It was to span the fortress from north to south and from this, on either side, further impressive entrances would have led into the administrative and royal wards of the castle. However, although the outward appearance of the castle as we see it today was reasonably complete by about 1330, this inner development, as with so much else on the site, was never finished.

35_ Today in Caernarfon, one often hears talk of the upper and lower wards. The so-called upper ward looks just this because of the higher level of the ground, but this is entirely due to the nineteenth-century levelling of Earl Hugh's motte, and to the fact that this was the ward reserved for the king's use. A. J. Taylor himself added to this confusion by referring to this ward as the *inner ward*. The more accurate terminology would be *King's Ward* and *Justiciar's Ward*.

Caernarfon castle. Part
of the south curtain wall
viewed from the
battlements and showing
the river Seiont

The massive main
entrance to the castle, the
King's gate in the north
curtain wall. The statue
above, placed here in 1321,
is of Edward II, created
prince of Wales in 1301.

Edward's eldest son, Alphonso, born in 1273, was only to live to his twelfth year: he had probably always been of a weak disposition, and in early 1284 may already have been seriously ill. Two other sons born to Eleanor, John and Henry, had died in infancy, one in 1266, the other, aged six, in 1268. However, when Eleanor was with Edward in Rhuddlan in March 1284, whilst he was laying down his blueprint for the future government of Wales in the *Statute of Rhuddlan*, she was pregnant. If it was to be a boy, the chances were that he would be their only son. With Alphonso's death in August 1284, this was indeed to be the case.[36]

As final proof of Edward's obsession with Caernarfon – its past history, present significance, and future rôle – in March 1284, despite the severe cold of the season, the king had his pregnant wife moved to Caernarfon, riding, as she did, on horseback, just so that his hoped-for son would be born there. On Tuesday, 25 April 1284, Queen Eleanor gave birth to a boy. He was born in Caernarfon's royal apartments, hastily constructed the previous year in wood and plaster. The baby was baptized by Anian, bishop of Bangor 1267–1305, someone who had fallen out badly with his former master Llywelyn ap Gruffudd.[37] The boy was named Edward after his father and was to be the future Edward II. On the verge of manhood, in 1301 he was made the new prince of Wales in a parliament held at Lincoln.[38]

At last, the Norman conquest was complete and what was formerly the Roman province of Britain had, in effect, been restored, not by the British, but by Normans and Saxons. The descendants of Paternus had fought like Romans to resist this for nearly nine centuries, faithfully carrying out the orders of Emperor Honorius in 410:

The Roman government urges that Britain should rather by itself, after accustoming itself to arms, and bravely fighting, defend with all its powers, land, property, wives, and children, and, what is greater than these, liberty and life.

[36] For Edward's fourteen children, see Prestwich, 1990, pp. 126–7: Edward was the last born in April 1284. In the expenses for Edward's second Welsh war and the castle building it entailed, coming to £98,421, is the entry 'Money going to Alphonso, but taken back because he has died ... £2,380' – Morris, 1901, pp. 196–7. In August 1282 whilst in Rhuddlan Eleanor had given birth to her previous child, the princess Elizabeth, who died in 1316.

[37] The story that, to mark the baptism, the king granted Anian the Porthaethwy and Cadnant ferries over the Menai Strait with manors in Caernarvonshire and Anglesey has to be rejected – Davies, 1966, p. 61, note 3. Anian died in 1305 and was buried in his cathedral, but there is no notice of the grave's position.

[38] Technically speaking, Edward I was the first Anglo-Norman prince of Wales, taking that title with its lands by right of conquest from the last native holder, Dafydd, although, in all probability, Edward would have regarded Llywelyn as the last person rightfully to occupy the position.

387

Caernarfon, castle and
borough, seen from the
Menai Strait.

WORKS CITED

Ammianus Marcellinus, *Histories*, see Hamilton, W., 1986.

ANDERSON, Alan Orr, and ANDERSON, M. O., eds. and transl., *Adamnán's Life of St Columba*, Edinburgh, 1961.

ANDERSON, Alan Orr, *Early Sources of Scottish History AD 500 to 1286*, originally published 1922; Edinburgh and London, 1990.

Anglo Saxon Chronicle, ASC, see Whitelock, D., 1961.

Annales Cambriae, AC, see Wade-Evans, A. W., 1938.

Annales Cestrienses, see Christie, R. C., 1887.

Annals of Clonmacnoise, AClon, see Mageoghagan, C., 1627, and Murphy, D., 1896.

Annals of Inisfallen, AI, see Mac Airt, S., 1951.

Annals of the Kingdom of Ireland by the Four Masters, AFM, see O'Donovan, J., 1851.

Annals of Tigernach, AT, see Stokes, W., 1895–7/1993.

Annals of Ulster, AU, see Hennessy, W. M., 1887, and Mac Airt, S., 1983.

ARNOLD, Christopher J., and DAVIES, Jeffrey L., *Roman and Early Medieval Wales*, Stroud, 2000.

ASHE, Geoffrey, ALCOCK, Leslie, RADFORD, C. A. Ralegh, and RAHTZ, Philip, *The Quest for Arthur's Britain*, London, 1968.

Augustine, *City of God*, see Bettenson, H., 1972.

BAILLIE, Mike, *Exodus to Arthur. Catastrophic Encounters with Comets*, originally published 1999; paperback reprint, London, 2000.

BARING-GOULD, S., and FISHER, J., *Lives of the British Saints*, 4 vols., London, 1907–13.

BARTRUM, Peter C., *Early Welsh Genealogical Tracts*, Cardiff, 1966.

BARTRUM, Peter C., *Welsh Genealogies AD 300–1400*, originally published by the Board of Celtic Studies, ND; University of Wales Press, Cardiff, January, 1991.

Bede, *Ecclesiastical History*, see Colgrave, B., and Mynors, R. A. B., 1969.

BETTENSON, Henry, transl., and KNOWLES, David, OSB., ed., *Augustine. Concerning the City of God against the Pagans*, Harmondsworth, 1972.

BOWEN, E. G., *Wales. A Study in Geography and History*, Cardiff, 1943.

BOWEN, E. G., *Saints, Seaways and Settlements in the Celtic Lands*, Cardiff, 1969.

BROMWICH, Rachel, *The Welsh Triads or Trioedd Ynys Prydein*, Cardiff, 1961.

BROMWICH, Rachel, and JONES, R. Brinley, eds., *Astudiaethau ar yr Hengerdd. Studies in Old Welsh Poetry in Honour of Sir Idris Foster*, Cardiff, 1978.

BYRNE, Francis John, *Irish Kings and High Kings*, originally published 1973; paperback reprint London, 1987.

CAMERON, Alan, *Claudian, Poetry and Propaganda at the Court of Honorius*, Oxford, 1970.

CARR, Antony D., *Llywelyn ap Gruffydd*, Cardiff, 1982.

CARR, Antony D., *Mediaeval Wales*, London, 1995.

CARR, Antony D., 'Dafydd ap Gruffudd, the Last Prince of Wales', *The Welsh History Review*, Vol. 19, No. 3, June 1999, pp. 375–99.

CARTWRIGHT, Jane, ed., *Celtic Hagiography and Saints' Cults*, Cardiff, 2003.

CHADWICK, Nora K., *Studies in Early British History*, Cambridge, 1954.

CHADWICK, Nora K., ed., *Studies in the Early British Church*, Cambridge, 1958.

CHALMERS, Muriel J., *The Bible Picture Book*, Thomas Nelson and Sons, Ltd., London, ND.

CHRISTIE, Richard Copley, ed. and transl., *Annales Cestrienses or The Chronicle of S. Werburgh*, The Record Society for the Publication of Original Documents Relating to Lancashire and Cheshire, Vol. XIV, 1887.

CLANCY, J. P., *The Earliest Welsh Poetry*, London, 1970.

Claudian, see Platnauer, Maurice, 1922.

COLGRAVE, Bertram, and MYNORS, R. A. B., eds. and transl., *Bede's Ecclesiastical History of the English People*, Oxford, 1969.

Colvin, H. M., ed., *The Middle Ages*, 2 vols., 1963: see Taylor, A. J., 1974.

CONRAN, Anthony, ed. and transl., in association with CAERWYN WILLIAMS, J. E., *The Penguin Book of Welsh Verse*, Harmondsworth, 1967.

Cybi, Life of, see Wade-Evans, A. W., 1944.

DAVIES, Ellis, *The Prehistoric and Roman Remains of Denbighshire*, Cardiff, 1929.

DAVIES, H. R., *The Conway and the Menai Ferries*, Cardiff, 1966.

DAVIES, R. R., *The Age of Conquest. Wales 1063–1415*, originally published 1987; paperback reprint Oxford, 1991/2.

DAVIES, Wendy, *Wales in the Early Middle Ages*, Leicester, 1982.

DEWING, H. B., transl., *Procopius, History of the Wars*, 5 vols., Loeb Library of the Greek and Roman Classics, Harvard University Press, Cambridge, Mass., 1914–28: part of a seven-volume edition of Procopius's work.

DUMVILLE, David N., 'Sub-Roman Britain: History and Legend', *History*, N.S., Vol. 62, June, 1977, pp. 173–92.

Evagrius Scolasticus, *A History of the Church, 322–427, and 431–594*, see Walford, Edward, 1854.

EVANS, D. Silvan, ed., *Lewis Morris. Celtic Remains*, London, 1878.

EVANS, Gwynfor, *Land of my Fathers. 2000 Years of Welsh History*, Swansea, 1974.

EVANS, Gwynfor, *Magnus Maximus and the Birth of Wales the Nation*, a bilingual pamphlet, Swansea, 1983.

EVANS, Gwynfor, *The Fight for Welsh Freedom*, Talybont, 2000.

Finnian of Clonard, Life of, see Stokes, W., 1890.

FLANAGAN, Marie Therese, *Irish Society, Anglo-Norman Settlers, Angevin Kingship*, Oxford, 1989.

FORBES, Alexander Penrose, ed., *Lives of S. Ninian and S. Kentigern*, The Historians of Scotland, Vol. V, Edinburgh, 1874; also available in a Llanerch facsimile reprint, Felinfach, 1989/2000.

FORBES, Clarence A., ed. and transl., *Julius Firmicus Maternus, De errore profanarum religionum*, Ancient Christian Writers. The Works of the Fathers in Translation, No. 37, gen. eds, Quasten, J., Burghardt, W. J., and Comerford Lawler, T., New York, 1970.

FOSTER, I. Ll., and DANIEL, G., eds., *Prehistoric and Early Wales*, London, 1965.

FRERE, Sheppard S., *Britannia. A History of Roman Britain*, London, 1967.

Geoffrey of Monmouth, *The History of the Kings of Britain*, see Thorpe, Lewis, 1966.

Gerald of Wales, *Expugnatio Hibernica*, see Scott, A. B., 1978.

Gerald of Wales, *Journey through Wales*, see Thorpe, Lewis, 1978.

Gildas, *De Excidio Britanniae*, see Wade-Evans, A. W., 1938; Winterbottom, M., 1978; and Giles, J. A., 1841.

GILES, J. A., *The Works of Gildas and Nennius*, London, 1841.

Gregory of Tours, *History of the Franks*, see Thorpe, Lewis, 1974.

Gruffudd ap Cynan, Life of, see Jones, Arthur, 1910.

GUEST, Lady Charlotte, *The Mabinogion from the Welsh of the Llyfer Coch O Hergest (The Red Book of Hergest) in the Library of Jesus College, Oxford, Translated* [into English], *with Notes*, London, 1877.

HAMILTON, Walter, transl., with introduction by WALLACE-HADRILL, Andrew, *Ammianus Marcellinus. The Later Roman Empire (AD354–378)*, Harmondsworth, 1986.

HAYCOCK, Marged, *Legendary Poems from the Book of Taliesin*, Cambrian Medieval Celtic Studies, Aberystwyth, 2007.

HENNESSY, W. M., *The Annals of Ulster*, Vol. I, Dublin, 1887.

HESS, Hamilton, *The Canons of the Council of Serdica AD 343*, Oxford, 1958.

HETHERINGTON, Barry, *A Chronicle of Pre-Telescopic Astronomy*, Chichester, 1996.

HIGHAM, Nicholas J., 'Gildas and 'Agitius': A comment on De Excidio XX, 1', *Bulletin of the Board of Celtic Studies*, Vol. XL, Cardiff, 1993, pp. 123–34.

HITCHENS, Christopher, *God is not Great*, London, 2007.

JACKSON, Kenneth H., *Language and History in Early Britain. A Chronological Survey of the Brittonic Languages, First to Twelfth Centuries AD*, originally published Edinburgh, 1953; reprinted Dublin, 1994.

JACKSON, Kenneth H., 'The Sources for the Life of St Kentigern', in Chadwick, Nora K., ed., *Studies in the Early British Church*, Cambridge, 1958, pp. 272–357.

JANKULAK, Karen, 'Alba Longa in the Celtic Regions? Swine, Saints and Celtic Hagiography', in Cartwright, Jane, ed., *Celtic Hagiography and Saints' Cults*, Cardiff, 2003.

JARMAN, A. O. H., and REES HUGHES, G., *A Guide to Welsh Literature*, Vol. I, Swansea, 1976.

JARMAN, A. O. H., *The Cynfeirdd. Early Welsh Poets and Poetry*, Cardiff, 1981.

JONES, Arthur, ed. and transl., *The History of Gruffudd ap Cynan. The Welsh Text with Translation, Introduction and Notes*, Manchester, 1910.

JONES, Francis, 'Wales Herald Extraordinary', *The Princes and Principality of Wales*, Cardiff, 1969.

JONES, G., and JONES, T., eds. and transl., *The Mabinogion*, originally published 1949; reprinted London, 1973.

JONES, Owen, (Myfyr), WILLIAMS, Edward, (Iolo Morganwg), and PUGHE, W. O., (Idrison), eds., *The Myvyrian Archaiology of Wales*, 3 vols., London; Vols. I and II, 1801; Vol. III, 1807; Vol. I, poetry.

KELLY, J. N. D., *The Oxford Dictionary of Popes*, Oxford, 1986.

KENNEY, James F., *Sources for the Early History of Ireland: Ecclesiastical*, originally published, New York, 1929; reprinted Dublin, 1968.

Kentigern, Life of, see Forbes, A. P., 1874.

KOCH, John T., in collaboration with CAREY, John, *The Celtic Heroic Age. Literary Sources for Ancient Celtic Europe & Early Ireland & Wales*, Celtic Studies Publications, Andover, Mass. and Aberyswyth, 1994; 3rd edn, 2000.

LANE FOX, Robin, *Pagans and Christians in the Mediterranean World from the Second Century AD to the Conversion of Constantine*, originally published 1986; paperback reprint Harmondsworth, 1988.

LEYSER, K., 'Frederick Barbarossa, Henry II and the Hand of St James', *English Historical Review*, 356, 1975, pp. 481–506.

LLOYD, John Edward, *A History of Wales from the Earliest Times to the Edwardian Conquest*, 2 vols., 2nd edn, London, 1912.

LOFMARCK, Carl, *A History of the Red Dragon*, Llanrwst, 1995.

Mabinogion, see Jones, G., 1949.

MAC AIRT, Seán, ed. and transl., *The Annals of Inisfallen*, originally published 1951; Dublin, 1977.

MAC AIRT, Seán, and MAC NIOCAILL, Gearóid, eds. and transl., *The Annals of Ulster (to AD 1131)*, Dublin, 1983.

MACALISTER, R. A. S., 'Eliseg's Pillar', *Archaeologia Cambrensis*, Vol. XC, 1935, pp. 330–3.

MACARTHUR, Sir William, 'The Identification of Pestilences Recorded in the Irish Annals', *Irish Historical Studies*, Vol. VI, No. 23, 1949, pp. 169–88.

McGRATH, F., S. J., *Education in Ancient and Medieval Ireland*, Dublin, 1979.

MAC NIOCAILL, Gearóid, *Ireland before the Vikings*, Dublin, 1972.

MAGEOGHAGAN, Conell, i.e., Conall Mag Eochagáin of Lismore in County Westmeath, transl., 1627, and

MURPHY, Denis, ed., *The Annals of Clonmacnoise*, Dublin, 1896; Llanerch facsimile reprint, Felinfach, 1993.

MANN, J. C., *The Northern Frontier in Britain from Hadrian to Honorius*, Newcastle upon Tyne Museum of Antiquities, 1969.

MAUND, Kari, *The Welsh Kings. The Medieval Rulers of Wales*, Stroud, 2000.

MEYER, Kuno, ed. and transl., 'The Expulsion of the Déisi', *Y Cymmrodor*, Vol. XIV, 1901, pp. 101–35.

MILLER, Molly, 'Date Guessing and Pedigrees', *Studia Celtica*, Vol. 10/11, 1975/6, pp. 96–109.

MILLER, Molly, 'The Foundation Legend of Gwynedd', *Bulletin of the Board of Celtic Studies*, Vol. 27, 1976/8, pp. 515–32.

MILLER, Molly, 'Date Guessing and Dyfed', *Studia Celtica*, 1977–8, pp. 33–61.

MILLER, Molly 'The Disputed Historical Horizon of the Pictish King Lists', *Scottish Historical Review*, Vol. 58, 1979, pp. 1–34.

MILLER, Molly, *The Saints of Gwynedd*, London, 1979.

MOKYR, Joel, and Ó GRÁDA, Cormac, 'Famine Disease and Famine Mortality: Lessons from Ireland, 1845–1850', University College Dublin, Dept. of Political Economy, *Papers*, 1999, No. 99/12 [http://faculty.wcas.northwestern.edu/~jmokyr/mogbeag.pdf].

MORRICE, J. C., *Detholiad O Waith Gruffudd ab Ieuan ab Llewelyn Vychan*, The Bangor Welsh Manuscripts Society, Bangor, 1910.

MORRIS, John, *The Age of Arthur. A History of the British Isles from 350 to 650*, London, 1973.

MORRIS, John, ed. and transl., *Nennius, British History and the Welsh Annals*, London and Chichester, 1980.

MORRIS, John E., *The Welsh Wars of Edward I. A Contribution to Mediaeval Military History, based on original documents*, Oxford, 1901.

MORRIS, Lewis, [article on the Sanctinus Stone] *Archaeologia Cambrensis*, 1896, pp. 138–9, and 1897, pp. 140–2.

MORRIS-JONES, J., and PARRY-WILLIAMS, T. H., eds., copied by MORRIS-JONES, Rhiannon, *Llawysgrif Hendregadredd*, originally published 1933; reprinted, Cardiff, 1971.

MURPHY, Denis, ed., *The Annals of Clonmacnoise being annals of Ireland from the Earliest Period to AD 1408 Translated into English AD 1627 by Conell Mageoghagan*, Dublin, 1896; facsimile reprint by Llanerch Press, Felinfach, 1993.

NASH-WILLIAMS, V. E., *Early Christian Monuments in Wales*, Cardiff, 1950.

Nennius, see Morris, J., 1980, and Wade-Evans, A. W., 1938.

NEWTON, Robert R., *Medieval Chronicles and the Rotation of the Earth*, Baltimore, 1972.

Ó CATHASAIGH, Tomás, *The Heroic Biography of Cormac Mac Airt*, Dublin, 1977.

Ó CORRÁIN, Donnchadh, and MAGUIRE, Fidelma, *Irish Names*, originally published 1981; 2nd edn, Dublin, 1990.

O'DONOVAN, John, ed. and transl., *The Four Masters. Annals of the Kingdom of Ireland from the Earliest Times to the Year 1616*, 7 vols., Dublin, 1851; 1856 3rd edn. Also in a facsimile reprint with an introduction by Kenneth Nichols, Blackrock, 1998.

O'GRADY, Standish H., *Silva Gadelica*, 2 vols., London, 1892.

OWEN, Aneurin, ed., *Ancient Laws and Institutes of Wales*, Record Commission, 2 vols., London, 1841.

OWEN, Hywel Wyn, and MORGAN, Richard, *Dictionary of the Place-Names of Wales*, Llandysul, 2007, reprinted with corrections 2008.

OWEN, Nicholas, *History of Anglesey*, London, 1775.

PARRY, Edward, *Royal Visits and Progresses to Wales*, 2nd edn, London, 1851.

PENNANT, Thomas, *A Tour in Wales*, 2 vols., London, 1784; Vol. I, *A Tour in Wales, MDCCLXXIII*, London, 1778; Vol. II, Part 1, *A Journey to Snowdon*, London, 1781, Part 2, *From Downing to Montgomery and Shrewsbury*, London, 1783, entitled in the 1784 complete edition *Continuation of the Journey*.

PLATNAUER, Maurice, *Claudian with an English Translation*, 2 vols., London, 1922.

PLUMMER, Charles, *Lives of Irish Saints*, 2 vols.; Vol. 1, Texts, Vol. 2, Translations; Oxford, 1922.

PRESTWICH, Michael, *Edward I*, originally published London, 1988; paperback 1990; reprint Yale University Press Paperback, 1997.

Procopius, see Dewing, H. B., 1914–28.

RICHMOND, Ian A., *Roman Britain*, originally published 1955; Harmondsworth, 1963.

RIVET, A. L. F., and SMITH, C., *The Place-Names of Roman Britain*, London, 1979.

ROSEN, William, *Justinian's Flea. Plague, Empire and the Birth of Europe*, London, 2007.

SALWAY, Peter, *Roman Britain*, originally published 1981; rev. imp. 1982; paperback reprint Oxford, 1984.

SCOTT, A. B., and MARTIN, F. X., eds. and transl., *Expugnatio Hibernica. The Conquest of Ireland by Giraldus Cambrensis*, Dublin, 1978.

SMITH, J. Beverley, *Llywelyn ap Gruffudd Prince of Wales*, Cardiff, 1998.

SMITH, Lacey Baldwin, *Tudor Prelates and Politics, 1536–1558*, Princeton Studies in History, Vol. VIII, Princeton, 1953.

SMITH, Llinos B., 'The Death of Llywelyn ap Gruffudd: the Narratives Reconsidered', *Welsh History Review*, 2, 1982–3, pp. 200–13.

SMYTH, A. P., 'The Earliest Irish Annals: Their First Contemporary Entries, and the Earliest Centres of Recording', *Proceedings of the Royal Irish Academy*, Vol. 72 C, 1972, pp. 1–48.

STEVENS, C. E., 'Marcus, Gratian, Constantine', *Athenaeum* [Pavia], Vol. 35, 1957, pp. 316–47.

STEWART, A. T. Q., *The Shape of Irish History*, Belfast, 2001.

STOKES, Whitley, *Lives of the Saints from the Book of Lismore*, Oxford, 1890.

STOKES, Whitley, ed. and transl., 'Annals of Tigernach', Fragments 1–4, with 'Continuation AD1088–1178' and 'The Dublin Fragment', *Revue Celtique*, 16–18, 1895–7; repr. in a two-volume facsimile edition by Llanerch Publishers, Felinfach, 1993.

Taliesin, The Story of, see Guest, C., 1877.

TAYLOR, A. J., 'The King's Works in Wales 1277–1300', Chapter 6 of Volume 1 of COLVIN, H. M., ed., *The Middle Ages*, 2 vols., 1963, published separately as a paperback by HMSO, London, 1974.

THORPE, Lewis, ed. and transl., *Geoffrey of Monmouth. The History of the Kings of Britain*, Harmondsworth, 1966.

THORPE, Lewis, ed. and transl., *Gregory of Tours. The History of the Franks*, Harmondsworth, 1974.

THORPE, Lewis, ed. and transl., *Gerald of Wales. Journey through Wales*, Harmondsworth, 1978.

TUCKER, Norman, *Colwyn Bay and its Growth*, Colwyn Bay, 1953.

TURCAN, Robert, *The Cults of the Roman Empire*, transl. NEVILL, Antonia, Oxford, 1996.

'URIEN', 'The Regalia of Wales', *Archaeologia Cambrensis*, Vol. I, 1846, pp. 42–32.

VERMAAT, Robert, 'When did Gildas Write?', *Vortigern Studies*, 1999–2007. [http://www.vortigernstudies.org.uk /artsou/ gildwhen.htm]

Virgil, *Aeneid*, see West, David, 1990.

WADE-EVANS, A. W., ed. and transl., 'Buched Beuno', *Archaeologia Cambrensis*, Vol. 85, 1930, pp. 315–41.

WADE-EVANS, A. W., ed. and transl., *Nennius's History of the Britons together with the The Annals of the Britons and The Court Pedigrees of Hywel the Good and also* [Gildas *De Excidio Britanniae*] *The Story of the Loss of Britain*, London, 1938.

WADE-EVANS, A. W., ed. and transl., *Vitae Sanctorum Britanniae et Genealogiae*, Cardiff, 1944.

WAGNER, Sir Anthony, Garter Principal King of Arms, *Historic Heraldry of Britain*, Oxford, 1939 and 1948, Chichester, 1972.

WALFORD, Edward, transl., *EVAGRIUS: A History of the Church from AD322 to the Death of Theodore of Mopsuestia, AD427, by THEODORET Bishop of Cyrus and from AD431 to AD594, by EVAGRIUS*, Bohn's Ecclesiastical Library, London, 1854.

WEBSTER, Graham, 'Chester in the Dark Ages', *Journal of the Chester Archaeological Society*, Vol. 38, 1951.

WEST, David, *The Aeneid. A New Prose Translation*, London, 1990; paperback reprint Harmondsworth, 1991.

WHITE, Roger, and BARKER, Philip, *Wroxeter. Life and Death of a Roman City*, originally published 1998, revised edition 2002; Stroud, 2006.

WHITELOCK, Dorothy, DOUGLAS, David, and TUCKER, Sophie, eds., *The Anglo-Saxon Chronicle*, London, 1961.

WILLIAMS, Ifor, *Canu Taliesin*, Cardiff, 1960.

WILLIAMS, J. E. Caerwyn, 'The Court Poet in Medieval Ireland', Sir John Rhŷs Memorial Lecture, British Academy, 1971: *Proceedings of the British Academy*, Vol. LVII, London and Oxford, 1971.

WILLIAMS, J. E. Caerwyn, and WILLIAMS, Ifor, *The Poems of Taliesin*, Dublin, 1968.

WILLIAMS, Taliesin, *Iolo Manuscripts*, Llandovery, 1848.

WINTERBOTTOM, Michael, ed. and transl., *Gildas. The Ruin of Britain and Other Works*, London and Chichester, 1978.

WRIGHT, R. P., and JACKSON, K. H., 'A Late Inscription from Wroxeter', *The Antiquaries Journal*, 48, Part 2, 1968, pp. 296–300.

THE BITTER SEA

THE BITTER SEA is a series of books covering British history during the period of the Roman empire. The last book continues the story for the Welsh state of Gwynedd down to its conquest by England in 1283. Having fought to resist barbarians for nearly a thousand years, Gwynedd finally succumbed to a king, bent not only on completing the Norman conquest of Britain, but also on restoring the Roman province.

These books give a long-overdue account of how Rome established its power in the British Isles, how it fought to maintain that power, and how the various component parts of these islands emerged from the collapse of imperial control in the west. The studies are based on contemporary and near contemporary accounts, make extensive use of quotations, and once more confront the issue of employing what purport to be sources composed at a much later date.

Here history is interpreted in the traditional sense of trying to understand how change happened. As such, people take centre stage, many of them emerging far more vividly than one might have thought possible. With this emphasis on narrative, the series provides accessible and polemical texts for all who are concerned to understand Britain's past.

AVAILABLE AT PENRHYNBOOKS.COM:

Penrhyn Books,
83 Five Ashes Road,
Westminster Park,
Chester CH4 7QS

email: info@penrhynbooks.com
www.penrhynbooks.com